D1632185

Rethinking Federalism

Federalism is at once a set of institutions – the division of public authority between two or more constitutionally defined orders of government – and a set of ideas which underpin such institutions. As an idea, federalism points us to issues such as shared and divided sovereignty, multiple loyalties and identities, and governance through multi-level institutions.

Seen in this more complex way, federalism is deeply relevant to a wide range of issues facing contemporary societies. Global forces – economic and social – are forcing a rethinking of the role of the central state, with power and authority diffusing both downwards to local and state institutions and upwards to supranational bodies. Economic restructuring is altering relationships within countries, as well as the relationships of countries with each other. At a societal level, the recent growth of ethnic and regional nationalisms – most dramatically in Eastern Europe and the former Soviet Union, but also in many other countries in Western Europe and North America – is forcing a rethinking of the relationship between state and nation, and of the meaning and content of 'citizenship.'

Rethinking Federalism explores the power and relevance of federalism in the contemporary world and provides a wide-ranging assessment of its strengths, weaknesses, and potential in a variety of contexts. Interdisciplinary in its approach, this book brings together leading scholars from law, economics, sociology, and political science, many of whom draw on their own extensive involvement in the public policy process. Among the contributors are such leading analysts as Tommasso Padoa-Schioppa and Jacques Pelkmans on the European Union, Paul Chartrand on Aboriginal rights, Samuel Beer on North American federalism, Alan Cairns on identity, and Vsevolod Vasiliev on citizenship after the breakup of the Soviet Union.

The themes refracted through these different disciplines and political perspectives include nationalism, minority protection, representation, and economic integration. The message throughout this volume is that federalism is not enough – rights protection and representation are also of fundamental importance in designing multi-level governments.

Karen Knop is an Assistant Professor in the Faculty of Law at the University of Toronto. *Sylvia Ostry* is Chair of the Centre for International Studies, University of Toronto, and Chancellor of the University of Waterloo. *Richard Simeon* is a Professor of Political Science and Law at the University of Toronto, and Vice-Chair of the Ontario Law Reform Commission. *Katherine Swinton* is a Professor in the Faculty of Law, cross-appointed to the Department of Political Science, at the University of Toronto.

Edited by Karen Knop, Sylvia Ostry,
Richard Simeon, and Katherine Swinton

Rethinking Federalism:
Citizens, Markets, and Governments
in a Changing World

UBCPress / Vancouver

Printed in Canada on acid-free paper ∞

ISBN 0-7748-0500-5

Canadian Cataloguing in Publication Data

Main entry under title:
Rethinking Federalism

  Revised papers from the conference Federalism and the nation state, held in
Toronto.
  Includes bibliographical references and index.
  ISBN 0-7748-0500-5

1. Federal government. I. Knop, Karen, 1960-

JC355.R47 1994   321.02   C94-910656-9

UBC Press gratefully acknowledges the ongoing support to its publishing program
from the Canada Council, the Province of British Columbia Cultural Services
Branch, and the Department of Communications of the Government of Canada.

Set in Stone by Vancouver Desktop Publishing Centre
Printed and bound in Canada by D.W. Friesen & Sons Ltd.
Copy-editor: Peter Colenbrander
Proofreader: Judith Parker
Indexer: Annette Lorek

UBC Press
University of British Columbia
6344 Memorial Road
Vancouver, BC V6T 1Z2
(604) 822-3259
Fax: (604) 822-6083

Contents

Preface

This volume grew out of a multi-disciplinary conference on 'Federalism and the Nation State' held at the University of Toronto with the financial support of the Federal-Provincial Relations Office of the Government of Canada, the Ministry of Intergovernmental Affairs of the Government of Ontario, the Henry N.R. Jackman Foundation, and the CRB Foundation.

Selected papers presented at that conference have been revised, edited, and organized to illustrate some of the most important challenges to federalism in various settings throughout the world today. Support for their publication in this form has been generously provided by the University of Toronto's International Business and Trade Law Programme and the Centre for International Studies. The editors are also grateful to the Faculty of Law at the University of Toronto for secretarial and administrative support during the editorial process.

Part One:
Introduction

1

Introduction: Rethinking Federalism in a Changing World

Richard Simeon and Katherine Swinton

Federalism is at once a set of institutions – the division of public authority between two or more constitutionally defined orders of government – and a set of ideas which underpin such institutions. As an idea, federalism points us to issues such as shared and divided sovereignty, multiple loyalties and identities, and governance through multi-level institutions. Increasingly, the latter are not only central and state governments, but also local and supranational entities.

Seen in this way, federalism is deeply relevant to a wide range of issues facing contemporary societies. Global forces – economic and social – are necessitating a rethinking of the role of the central state, with power and authority diffusing both downwards to local and state institutions and upwards to supranational bodies. Economic restructuring is altering relationships within countries, as well as the relationships between countries. At a societal level, the recent growth of ethnic and regional nationalisms – most dramatically in Eastern Europe and the former Soviet Union, but also in many other countries in Western Europe and North America – is necessitating a rethinking of the relationship between state and nation, and of the meaning and content of 'citizenship.'

As societies and economies encounter these dramatic changes, traditional political forms come under enormous stress. Centralized or unitary national states seem less able to manage their economic relationships or to contain their social diversity. Federal systems are challenged – and sometimes, as in Czechoslovakia, defeated – by separatist movements. Once unitary countries like Italy, Spain, and Belgium move towards federalism, or something close to it. And in the European Union, formerly sovereign nations are constructing institutions deeply inspired by the federal idea.

We are rethinking concepts like sovereignty, autonomy, and independence, for economic and social flux has produced institutional change and an enormous need for new institutional designs. Given the simultaneous pressures of global interdependence and the desire for local control, the fundamental question is, as Mihailo Markovic asks later in this volume, whether federalism can 'reconcile the autonomy of the parts with the coordination of the system as a whole.'

This volume explores these issues – of citizens, markets, and governance – through the lens of federal ideas and experiences. It asks: what is the relevance of federalism, and its associated concepts and practices, as we address contemporary pressures and challenges? Does federalism, with its layered identities and institutions, offer opportunities for flexibility and innovation not possible in the more rigid unitary nation state? What opportunities does federalism present; what are its limits? What accounts for federalist success; what explains its failure?

We bring together an international group of scholars – political scientists, economists, lawyers, and sociologists – to focus attention on federalism and federalist debates in several different historical and geographic contexts: Eastern Europe and the former Soviet Union, where old regimes have broken apart and divisions within and between countries have produced a witches' brew of ethnic tensions; Western Europe, where we simultaneously see the building of a quasi-federal Europe and decentralization within many of its member states; and North America, where Canadian federalism wrestles with linguistic and regional diversity, where the United States sometimes looks to federalism to overcome sclerosis at the centre, and where North American Free Trade raises the question whether economic integration also has a political dimension. Many of the contributions are borne of a combination of theory and practice, which sometimes generates strong views. While we do not associate ourselves with all the positions taken in this volume, we consider each an important addition to the federal idea.

Drawing together the lessons of these diverse national experiences is not an easy task. We have chosen to organize the chapters thematically rather than geographically in order to facilitate comparison. Accordingly, the volume is arranged in three parts: citizenship, identity, and the federal idea; the economic dimensions of federalism; and the legal and political dimensions of federalism. Several of the papers cut across these broad categories. In each section, there is a combination of specific case studies and broader comparative chapters.

One of the clearest lessons of this book is that there is no single model of federalism; rather, federalism takes many forms. Indeed, in some respects, every federal system seems to be sui generis, both in the circumstances which gave it birth and in the forms that it takes. Victor Knapp reminds us that the political ideas underpinning socialist or Leninist federalism are very different from those on which US federalism is based. Therefore, the term 'federalism' almost always occurs alongside a qualifying adjective: 'new federalisms' in bewildering variety, classical federalism, quasi-federalism, centralized and decentralized federalism, picket-fence federalism, marble-cake federalism, interstate and intrastate federalism, symmetrical and asymmetrical federalism.

Federal systems vary in many of their dimensions: in the powers assigned to the different levels of government; in the mechanisms for conducting relations among governments; in the degree to which state or provincial units are represented within central institutions, and so on. Federalism also interacts in different ways with other elements of national institutional structures. Canada, for example, combines federalism with British-style parliamentary government; the United States combines it with a presidential, congressional system. Thus, if we are to talk about the effects of federalism, we have an almost infinite array of institutional variants from which to choose.

Federalism also overlaps with other political forms, such as confederalism and yet looser associations on the one hand, and non-territorially constituted consociational models on the other. Moreover, federalism is not so much a fixed state, but a fluid and dynamic *process*. On the one hand, it may be a building process, bringing together previously separate units whether for security or economic reasons. Here the dynamic is one of nation building – as we saw in the US experience or in Canada in 1867, or as we have been seeing recently in Western Europe. Federalism may be a way station on the path towards a single unitary state, or it may result in a stable equilibrium of shared powers and responsibilities between central and constituent governments.

In contrast, there is the dynamic of 'dis-building.' Here, areas or groups within a single country are seeking greater autonomy or freedom from the dominance of the majority or of another ethnic or social group. This is the perspective of some Québécois in Canada today and in much of Eastern Europe. Here federalism seeks the middle way between retaining some semblance of a national community, economy, and government and full independence for some or all of the constituent units. Again, the important question is what is the logical terminus?

The dynamics of these two processes are likely to be very different and similar sets of federal institutions can have quite different meanings in different contexts. To take just one example: there are many similarities between the Canadian federation and the quasi-federalism of the European Union, but comparison is difficult, because the trains seem to be moving in opposite directions.

These competing dynamics also raise the question of what we are comparing federalism to. In some settings, we think of it as an alternative to a centralized unitary state; in others, it is an alternative to a collection of smaller individual nation states. At its core, federalism is about the desirability or possibility of bridging these two alternatives; about finding some antidote to the pathologies of centralization and to the risks faced by small, perhaps vulnerable, individual nations. Within the federal idea, then, there are yet other debates about the relative balance between these two extremes.

These observations – and many chapters in this book – demonstrate that discourse about federalism and the practices it engenders are intimately related to the historical context of each country. Federalism is at the heart of both the constitutions and the political culture of the US and Canada, as Beer and Simeon show, although the divergent historical experiences of these two countries have led to quite different models – of 'national federalism' in the US and more province-centred federalism in Canada.

In strong contrast to these experiences, most of the papers from Eastern Europe show that federalism can resonate very differently. Here we see rejection and distrust of federalism. Victor Knapp, for example, explains that the failure of the Soviet, Yugoslav, and Czechoslovak federations cannot be understood without some knowledge of the theory and practice of 'socialist federalism.' Bakhtior Islamov describes the regional inequalities and exploitation that were built into the Soviet system, especially in its economic and financial arrangements. Volodymyr Vassylenko tells a similar story for Ukraine, where the federal facade masked a centralized totalitarian state. Little wonder that federalism as a solution to current problems is regarded with scepticism, or that the calculus about its advantages and disadvantages compared with alternative arrangements varies.

Such a history suggests that federalism cannot be imposed from above. Markovic argues persuasively that a rich concept of federalism requires the prior development of a modern civil society, democratic institutions, and a democratic political culture. He also suggests, in light of East European experience, that a multi-level federalism can succeed only if the constituent units have already experienced independence and democracy and have thus gained the self-confidence and security which allows them to come together on equal terms.

This need to relate federalism to its historical context reinforces the argument that abstract generalizations about federal institutions are difficult. It is at best risky, and at worst foolhardy, to believe that federal institutions that are successful in one context will be appropriate or successful if transplanted to another. Thus, whatever the lessons of the North American, German, or Swiss experience, they will only be tentative, suggestive, and indirect. But this variety is also a strength: it suggests the adaptability of federalism to many circumstances, and underlines the variety and experimentation embedded in federal forms and ideas.

Like other institutions, federalism is not a value in itself. It can be defended, justified, or attacked only in terms of the political values it is believed to serve. Three sets of concerns underlie many of the chapters in this volume. Each provides a different vantage point for evaluating the strengths and weaknesses of federalism.

The first perspective explores the relationship between federalism and the character of political communities. One of the primary justifications for federalism is that it is able to balance the preservation of the autonomy, the self-consciousness, and the influence of territorially concentrated social groups, on the one hand, with desires for a strong country-wide community on the other. It is both a device for nation building (or preservation) and a device for the preservation (or expansion) of subnational political communities. It facilitates – and indeed requires – multiple loyalties and identities, and a blend of interests and preferences expressed on both a country-wide basis and on a regional, provincial, or state basis.

A number of the chapters underline the complexities and ambiguities of federalism in this context, and the increasing tensions between the territorial distribution of federally institutionalized power and alternative conceptions of dividing authority and providing representation. First, while federalism does indeed foster and facilitate the maintenance of multiple identities – local, regional, national, and increasingly supranational – it also requires a willingness to tolerate, indeed welcome, such multiple identities if it is to survive. Where the term 'federalism' itself has been devalued by its association with a discredited regime, as in the former Czechoslovakia, Yugoslavia, or the Soviet Union, the underlying *vouloir vivre ensemble* has eroded, and the institutional glue of federalism alone cannot keep the different groups together.

Second, the institutions of federalism are designed to manage situations in which various ethnocultural groups are territorially concentrated, so that each can exercise authority to pursue its particular concerns within its own geographic space. Federalism is much less effective when the various groups are intermingled. Devolving power to one minority often creates another minority embedded within it. At the extreme, we see the brutal attempts to force populations into a territorial mould by creating ethnically homogeneous units through 'ethnic cleansing.' It is this problem of 'cascading minorities' or minorities within minorities which leads Alan Cairns to argue forcefully that 'federalism is not enough.' At a minimum, it must be accompanied by country-wide guarantees of rights for all minorities, as embodied in a national charter of rights. Another approach to this problem is to develop institutions which empower distinct cultural groups whose members are scattered throughout the national territory. Federalism, in this sense, has much in common with Lijphart's model of consociational democracy.[1]

In addition, the federal regime may ignore the presence of important communities within the country. Paul Chartrand describes the experience of the Aboriginal peoples in Canada and their claim for a third order of Aboriginal governments in Canada, standing alongside federal and provincial governments. In this case, the Aboriginal peoples can be seen as the victims of the design and practice of Canadian federalism – while at the same time, the federal idea opens the way to self-government within the federation. There would be much less room for such a model within the logic of a unitary state.

Third, Jane Jenson and others emphasize the recent growth of conceptions of identity and community – such as gender – which owe nothing to territory and, indeed, cut across or transcend it. If federalism institutionalizes the territorial distribution of power, predicating representation and citizenship on location, then does it necessarily frustrate or undermine the representation of other groups? Does federalism afford privileges to some while disempowering others? As Jane Jenson, Thomas Hueglin, and Raymond Breton demonstrate, the relations between federal institutions and the multiple bases of interest and identity in modern societies are enormously complex. Issues of citizenship and representation are highly contested matters – especially, as Vsevolod Vasiliev shows, when systems are being reordered as dramatically as they are in what was once the Soviet Union. While these issues are an important part of political life, balancing these competing interests is also, as Katherine Swinton shows, a central task of courts, especially in countries with constitutional bills of rights.

Finally, there is an important question of the 'fit' between societal characteristics and political institutions. Guy Kirsch, examining regionalism, ethnicity, and language in Western Europe, argues that as West European countries have devolved part of their statehood to the European Union, part of their nationhood has also devolved to the regions. The result is a twofold disequilibrium: the Union, as an economic and political unit, lacks necessary social cohesion, while the regions are social units whose political institutions remain underdeveloped.

Closely related to the theme of identity, citizenship, and community is the second theme running through much of the book, the relationship between federalism and democracy. Here again there are tensions and contradictions. Federalism, especially in the US context, has been frequently justified as a basis for democracy – on the grounds that dispersed authority checks and limits the power of majorities, that multiple levels of government provide more opportunity for participation by citizens, and that it permits a closer fit between citizens' preferences and the public goods that governments provide.

But federalism in practice has also been criticized from the democratic perspective. The concern is that it may frustrate majority opinion, and that the complexities of intergovernmental decision-making arising from the interdependence and overlapping responsibilities between multiple orders of government contribute to excessive executive and bureaucratic control, diminish government accountability to the electorates, and the like. Thus both Canadians and West Europeans talk of a 'democratic deficit' in their respective institutions, a major concern for Thomas Hueglin and Jane Jenson in this volume. Issues of democratic participation will be especially important as supranational organizations challenge the sovereignty of nation states, where democratic and citizenship rights are currently inscribed.

The third perspective addressed in the volume is the link between federalism, with its division of responsibilities among governments, and governmental performance and effectiveness. Some of the arguments here tend not to support federalism, suggesting that the complexities of shared and divided authority complicate and delay decision-making, thereby contributing to paralysis and immobility in policy-making, especially in federations that are characterized by considerable overlap and duplication. In addition, a large body of argument suggests that the policy needs associated with modernization inexorably lead to centralization. The extension of this argument in the contemporary era is that federalism may be incompatible with effective responses to the demands and pressures of globalization. This view is strongly espoused by Robert Howse.

Another line of argument, however, suggests that federalism provides opportunities for innovation and experiment, for diverse responses to different needs, and for service delivery linked more closely to citizen consumers. As Kenneth Norrie argues, one reason for decentralist pressures is the perceived incompetence at the centre; decentralization can then be seen as an effective response to the sclerosis of overburdened central governments. This view is also articulated by Alice Rivlin for the US and Richard Simeon for Canada.

It is also argued that globalization is a greater threat to central governments than to state and provincial governments, and, hence, that authority in the present era is being stretched like a concertina, with influence flowing both upwards to public and private supranational institutions and downwards to smaller units. The dilemma for central governments today is that they are both too small to encompass the social and economic forces which affect them, and too large to respond effectively to the variety of domestic needs and interests. The trick is to match the scale and scope of the problems with the scale and scope of the authorities needed to regulate them. In the West European case, both Jacques Pelkmans and Tommaso Padoa-Schioppa argue that the European Union, despite recent stumbles, has made major progress towards the single market, harmonization of policies, and the development of some common policy, although the level of integration still falls well short of full federalism. There remain, however, important tensions between centralization and decentralization which are not fully resolved by the principle of 'subsidiarity,' which asserts that competencies should be assigned to the smallest possible political level.

This tension is even more evident in the countries of the former Soviet Union. Bakhtior Islamov emphasizes the requirement of political and economic sovereignty for each state, while at the same time stressing the need for states to form an economic community with a common market, common credit and financial policies, and effective coordinating institutions. It is difficult to reconcile political autonomy and independence with the overwhelming degree of economic interdependence.

As Jacques Pelkmans and Guy Kirsch note, the same dilemma faces Western Europeans as they seek to reconcile Union-wide economic integration with the loss of sovereignty by individual member states. Domestic political pressures and international economic forces often seem to compete, as do the desires for economic efficiency and for democracy and independence. Norrie also notes a tension between decentralized authority and a continuing commitment to sharing and redistribution across regions.

Thus, all federations face the continuing need to rethink the division of responsibilities: how to draw the line between those matters which should be central, those which should be regional, and those that, by their very nature, need to be shared between the two orders of government.

These observations underline the importance of institutional design. There are several concerns here. First is the division of responsibilities – or competences – between different orders of government. Increasingly, this must be thought of not only in terms of two orders of government, central and state, but also in terms of local, municipal, and regional authorities, and in terms of the powers to be devolved to supranational bodies. This greatly increases the complexity of the task, placing ever greater weight on the mechanisms for achieving harmonization and coordination among the different levels and units. Often the logic of economic integration pushes against the logic of democratic participation and accountability.

Other issues of institutional design explored in this volume include the role of the courts in managing the relationships among units, as well as in ensuring the rights of citizens and groups (Katherine Swinton); the relative merits of representing regional diversity within central institutions (intrastate federalism) and of doing so in state or provincial governments (interstate federalism) (Richard Simeon); and the relative merits of asymmetry, with all subnational units exercising identical powers as against a more varied pattern in which the powers of subnational units are tailored to the characteristics and aspirations of each constituent unit.

This introduction began with the suggestion that federalism, or more precisely the ideas associated with it, might provide one possible solution to the dilemmas faced by modern states, in which increasing interdependence on a global scale is matched by a renewed search for community and identity at the local level. As this introduction demonstrates, federalism poses many of its own dilemmas; it is no magic solution. But at the same time, the volume demonstrates the very high cost of both excessive centralization and of the fragmentation of the political world into a multiplicity of separate, ethnically homogeneous nation states. Woodrow Wilson's image of 'one nation, one state' is neither desirable nor practicable. If federalism creates dilemmas for the representation of non-territorial interests, or of minorities within minorities, this is even truer of countries that fragment entirely. Federalism constitutes the variety of political arrangements in the middle ground, balancing unity and diversity, majority rule and minority rights, common purpose and local need, interdependence and autonomy.

The volume proceeds as follows. In Part One, we explore the issues of citizenship and identity in federal societies, both as broad general themes and in different settings (Canada, Western Europe, the former Yugoslavia, and the former USSR). In Part Two, we explore the economic dimensions of federalism in several national and regional contexts. In Part Three, the focus is on the legal and political dimensions of federal institutions and practice, with Thomas Hueglin's overview followed by chapters on the United States, Canada, Ukraine, and the former Soviet Union. The volume ends with John Meisel's reflections on the issues raised in the book.

Notes
1 Arend Lijphart, *Democracy in Plural Societies: A Comparative Exploration* (New Haven, CT: Yale University Press 1977).

Part Two:
Citizenship, Identity, and Federal Societies

2

Constitutional Government and the Two Faces of Ethnicity: Federalism Is Not Enough

Alan C. Cairns

Given the complexity of the task assigned to me in this chapter, the interaction of ethnicity and forms of government in Canada, the European Union, East and Central Europe, and the successor states of the former Soviet Union, I have no alternative but to simplify. Further, I have interpreted my mandate in the manner of a creative judiciary keeping an ancient written constitution up to date. I have adhered to the wise maxim that too great fidelity to a written instruction from the past impedes creative judicial statecraft.

The chapter proceeds as follows: the first section analyzes the contemporary Canadian experience with multiple nationalisms. There is no suggestion that the Canadian case is typical. However, even the rather bland Canadian situation reveals many of the major centrifugal trends in the contemporary world that are buffeting constitutional orders. The paper then discusses five key themes or issues that are common to the countries and political areas discussed: how the breakup of old orders unleashes hitherto suppressed ethnic forces; whether centres can hold; the problem of minorities within minorities; the chronic instability of ethnic forces; and immigration and the diffuse ethnicity of the modern state. These analyses suggest the need to develop constitutional models that can respond simultaneously to the dual face of contemporary ethnicity, to the territorialization of language and ethnic groups *and* to the dispersed cultural and racial minorities that will characterize the democratic capitalist welfare states of the future, both federal and unitary. Throughout, I have drawn my examples from North America, the Soviet Union and its successors, Western Europe, and Central and Eastern Europe.

Competing Nationalisms in Canada

A brief analysis of contemporary constitutional tensions in Canada will set the stage for the more general survey that follows. Canada, with one of the oldest uninterrupted constitutional regimes in the world, is not a pure type, the understanding of which will generate insights readily transferable to other lands and climes where constitutional forms and ethnic forces interact. In fact, a perusal of the literature on ethnicity, nationalism, and the shape of possible constitutions in the European Union (EU), the former USSR, and Central and Eastern Europe casts doubt on the possibility of constructing any pure type. The seeker of comprehensive contemporary generalizations of state-society interactions is easily defeated by the plethora of particulars. However, several common themes, tendencies, and developments can be found.

Many of the trends buffeting governments and peoples elsewhere are also evident in Canada – a reflection of the globalization of social forces, intellectual fashions, and normative assumptions. Further, the possibility that a country, whose blessings would attract millions in the absence of immigration barriers, might come apart testifies to the powerful centrifugal forces of disintegration that challenge the contemporary nation state system.

Four political nationalisms confront each other in contemporary Canada:

(1) *The historic pan-Canadian nationalism* that sustains the federal government and is the political expression of a pan-Canadian community of citizens. It is on the defensive. Its supporters fight a rearguard action to salvage a minimal definition of Canada based on an undifferentiated citizenship and equal status for the ten provincial governments. It is challenged by the nationalisms of (2), (3), and (4) below.

(2) *Québécois nationalism* drawing on the perception of francophone Québécois that their society is distinct based on history, the Civil Code, language, and culture. It is an expansive nationalism that seeks to weaken the hold of pan-Canadian nationalism on its people. It is resistant to Aboriginal claims that could erode the Quebec government's authority over Aboriginal peoples and lands within Quebec territory. The quest to accommodate it has been on the Canadian constitutional agenda for three decades. Both Québécois and pan-Canadian nationalism have governments to speak for them. In that sense they are official nationalisms.

(3) *Rest of Canada (ROC) nationalism.* A Quebec nationalism capable of breaking up Canada automatically elicits a counter-nationalism in the Rest of Canada as a necessary psychological preparation for a potential Canada without Quebec. This residual ROC nationalism is ill formed, largely because it lacks institutional expression. In terms of official governmental spokespersons, it is effectively headless and voiceless. No single government speaks for it as such. The federal government speaks for all of Canada, and the nine provincial and two territorial governments speak only for Canadians as an aggregation of provincial and territorial jurisdictions embracing eleven

different peoples in ROC. The latency of ROC nationalism categorizes it as a social cleavage that is kept weak by inhibiting structures, but which could find vigorous expression in a different setting.

(4) *Aboriginal nationalisms*. A newly emergent cluster of Aboriginal nationalisms based on the indigenous Indian, Inuit, and Métis peoples of Canada challenges the preceding three nationalisms with assertive claims based on distinctive histories, on historical priority before the European arrival (except for the Métis), and on historic cultures and identities whose contemporary flourishing requires separate Aboriginal jurisdictions based on an inherent right of self-government.[1] Aboriginal governments, prospectively defined as a third order of sovereign governments, will give Canada a unique three-layer federalism. When implemented, given the unavoidably marked variations in governing powers the Aboriginal peoples will possess, Canadian governing arrangements will be paralyzingly complex. Formerly, Aboriginal nationalisms, like contemporary ROC nationalism, were latent. Their vigorous birth and aggressive expression reflect an unusual conjuncture of domestic and international developments, crucially including the opening up of the constitution in response to non-Aboriginal pressures. Four major Aboriginal political organizations, heavily funded by the federal government, are the recognized public voices of the Aboriginal peoples. Their hegemony, however, is challenged by the Native Women's Association of Canada which disputes their credentials to speak for Aboriginal women.

This brief ethnic/nationalist/indigenous tour of Canada readily elicits several sociopolitical observations:

(1) Internal nationalism has acquired new clients among the Aboriginal peoples and ROC. Twenty-five years ago the revocation of tenure would have been visited on any academic who predicted that Aboriginal peoples would imbibe the language of nationalism so fully in only a few decades. Indeed, in 1969 the federal government assumed, incorrectly, that the time was ripe to abolish separate Indian status and integrate the Aboriginal peoples, then subject to the *Indian Act*, fully into the Canadian population. Further, thirty years ago Rest of Canada as a potential national people would have been literally inconceivable, for ROC nationalism is a reactive response to the reluctantly admitted, and unwelcome, possible exit of Quebec from the whole Canada that ROC would prefer to retain.

Nationalism, accordingly, should always be thought of as expanding or contracting. When a nationalism of the centre is contracting, this can mean either that its hold over the citizenry is weakening, or that it is retreating to a more compact population base, following the actual or anticipated defection of one of its components.

(2) There is a contagion at work. The invigorated political expression of

nationalism by one key actor, such as Quebec, changes the models available for others to follow. By changing the definition of available self-labelling within what had hitherto been a stable constitutional order, and given the status-enhancing capacity of nationalism, it was almost ordained that the awakening Aboriginal peoples would find nationalist terminology attractive. In partial contrast, while the nationalism of ROC is also partly imitative, it is not status-enhancing when compared to the pan-Canadian nationalism it might replace. It is, in the first instance, a contingent nationalism, a nationalism of necessity arising from a reluctant recognition of potential loss.

Put differently, when multiple nationalisms coexist within a single polity, transformations in the position of any particular nationalism change the environment for all the other nationalisms. This is especially the case when a political country-wide nationalism is attacked by a domestic ethnic nationalism seeking to increase its hold over its members by weakening the hold of its rival. In the Canadian case, the attacking nationalisms are the Québécois and the Aboriginal; that which is attacked is Canadian nationalism which simultaneously fights back and adapts. Pan-Canadian nationalism, devoid of linkage to a homogeneous ethnic base, has difficulty competing with the emotional force of its Quebec and Aboriginal sub-state rivals, which are driven by a more cohesive sense of national selfhood. The residual contemporary nationalism of ROC is potentially the ultimate adaptation of Canadian nationalism, the anticipatory recognition of possible future defeat.

The coexistence of pan-Canadian and ROC nationalisms underlines the obvious point that, in situations of uncertainty, individuals may juggle two coexisting national identities, one inherited from the past that is weakened but still powerful, and a second prospective national identity that, in the Canadian case, can be quickly assumed should Quebec nationalism triumph over Canadian nationalism on Quebec territory. ROC nationalism can be thought of as an 'insurance nationalism.' I suspect that insurance nationalism is a widespread phenomenon, and simultaneously an underexamined category of nationalism, for the indicators of its existence tend to be fragmentary and elusive.

(3) The contagion is strengthened when the constitution is opened up for examination. Latent nationalist political ambitions kept dormant by the existence of a stable constitutional order burst forth when the mould of constitutional custom is shattered and nationalist goals are no longer out of reach. Yesterday's stability, now seen to be precarious, is jettisoned in favour of competitive mobilization driven by nationalist visions of escape to a purer future.

(4) The internal nationalist assault on an inherited constitutional order is

not the only ethnic challenge confronting Canada. Canada, as one of Hartz's fragment immigrant societies, has always been dependent on new arrivals for the rapid population growth deemed politically and economically necessary.[2] English Canada, as Breton notes,[3] has successfully shifted its sense of self from one grounded in ethnic Britishness bent on assimilating newcomers to Anglo-conformity, to a more open society sensitive to its own heterogeneity and united by the English language. Québécois nationalism is impelled by the equality of citizens to move in the same direction, thus divorcing language from ethnicity as diverse immigrants become French speakers, and accepting the presence of an anglophone minority and Aboriginal nations on its own territory as full citizens – a transformative process that is still under way.

The shift in source countries for immigrants from the English-speaking world and continental Europe to non-European regions challenges the ethnic assumptions on which the constitutional order formerly rested. Fifty per cent of Canada's immigrants now come from Asia. This change in ethnic demography, supplementing the older communities of multicultural Canadians unable to claim British and French founding people status, has clearly destabilized the traditional constitutionally hegemonic position of British and French founding peoples, already challenged by Aboriginal peoples who claim a superior priority as the 'First Nations.'

Here, too, a contagion is at work among ethnic communities whose spatial diffusion precludes any possibility of having a government of their own. Thus the attempt to sensitize the Canadian constitution to linguistic dualism and biculturalism in the late 1960s, in addition to stimulating Aboriginal nationalism, unexpectedly led to an official policy of multiculturalism, subsequently given constitutional status, and elicited a proliferation of ethnic organizations demanding a place in the constitutional sun for their clientele. When the official message is given that ethnicity is a status-giving political identity, citizens will regroup themselves under its banners.

Non-territorial ethnicity, including the waves of new immigrants, many of whom fall into the Canadian category of 'visible minorities,' cannot be handled by federalism. In fact, diffuse populations of visibly different immigrants and their descendants challenge federalism on three grounds: a territorial solution to their concerns about majoritarianism is not available – they cannot opt out; they tend to be more sympathetic to the centre than to provincial governments because they see a national definition of citizenship as a protection; and the *Charter of Rights*, an inherently anti-federal instrument, attracts them with its capacity to reduce the significance otherwise attached to priority of arrival.

(5) The Canadian *Charter of Rights*, conceived as an instrument of pan-Canadian integration, has obviously not met the political ambitions of its

sponsors. It has not been an effective suppressant of either Québécois or Aboriginal nationalism. On the other hand, it has clearly taken root in Rest of Canada. In recent constitutional misadventures, identification with the Charter in English Canada seriously impeded accommodation of Quebec's demands that the constitution, including the Charter, be interpreted to recognize Quebec's status as a distinct society. Charter supporters in English Canada, especially in the women's movement, feared that the distinct society interpretive clause would lead to lesser availability of Charter rights in Quebec, thus negating the principle of uniform rights the pan-Canadian Charter regime was supposed to embody.[4]

The Charter has destabilizing consequences for both Québécois and Aboriginal nationalism. Within Quebec, allegiance to and identification with the Charter are strongest among the minority anglophone and 'allophone' communities. The Charter has generated tensions among the Aboriginal peoples, especially the status Indian community, represented by the Assembly of First Nations. The male-dominated Assembly has opposed the application of the Charter to self-governing Aboriginal nations, whereas the Native Women's Association, fearing the abuse of power by male-dominated governments, has adamantly insisted on its application.

The cleavages within the Québécois and Aboriginal communities revealed by the different responses to the Charter have immense significance for those who seek constitutional instruments to manage ethnic tensions. Whatever the claims of nationalist leaders, there are always marginalized individuals and groups within any ethnonational community that fear and seek protection even from prospective political majorities of their own people. If the political unit on whose behalf nationalists are seeking enhanced power contains minorities of different ethnic background, religion, or caste, the desire for protection from majoritarianism will be redoubled. Dispersed ethnic minorities lacking the geographic base to gain majority political power in their own unit of government are the natural defenders of individual rights and citizens' equality. Even where self-government within federalism is possible for concentrated ethnic minorities, the message of other ethnic minorities scattered in their midst is that federalism is not enough.

I turn now to the parallels and differences between the Canadian and comparative experiences.

The Breakup of Old Orders and the Stimulation of Ethnicity

When long established patterns of governance are broken, previously suppressed or concealed ethnic/national cleavages emerge. This is evident in Canada, in the demise of the USSR, in the former Czechoslovakia, and in the bitter conflicts in what used to be Yugoslavia. In each of the preceding cases, a former constricting order is either gone or seriously challenged. In the Canadian case, it is not coercive force that has vanished, but the milder constraints of habit, routine, tradition, and accepted normality. In Eastern and Central Europe, force, a repressive ideology, and alien rule kept nationalist passions in check, but did not tame them. Writing in 1975, the great historian of Eastern Europe, Hugh Seton-Watson, stated: 'Today about eighty million Europeans are subjected to national humiliation, and this makes Europe one of the most explosive parts of the world.'[5]

For nearly four and a half decades after the Second World War, rigid Soviet control of the East Central European satellite states, supplemented by the bipolarities of the Cold War, kept 'national identities ... [and] ... latent national conflicts ... frozen and suppressed during communist rule.' Its ending by glasnost and perestroika and the East Central European revolutions of 1989 led to an explosion of ethnicity.[6] In Spain, the centralizing authoritarianism of Franco, 'with the ruthless crushing of all expressions of regionalist opinion including the use of languages other than Spanish, ... [inevitably] provoked a violent reaction and ensured that any successor regime would be decentralist.'[7]

The same pattern of explosive ethnicity, this time in the guise of tribalism, occurred in many African colonies as the imperial bureaucratic pattern of government was displaced by an African political class. The latter elites found to their chagrin that they had not inherited a people, or a national community, but an aggregation of historic tribal communities brought together by the happenstance of arbitrary boundaries drawn by imperial powers. The colonial powers in Africa and Asia, notes Anthony Smith, created no 'unifying memories and myths, symbols and values for the inhabitants of the territories' they vacated when empire ended. Rather, the new nationalist elites encountered a 'multiplicity of smaller nodes of "myth symbol" complexes among the several *ethnie*' that were impediments to territorial nationhood.[8]

The explosive assertiveness of hitherto suppressed ethnic nationalism is likely to be the greater if the decaying or deceased former regime ruled by force, as in the Soviet Union. This is partly because the coercive regime from which an ethnic/national group is escaping has given its former citizens lessons in the use of force as a policy instrument. In addition, the resentments that build up in coercive totalitarian regimes are likely to be much greater than in democratic regimes where ethnic tensions are modulated by democratic politics and majoritarian insensitivity is likely to be softer. Frye notes the tendency to 'settle accounts' in the transition process from authoritarian rule to democracy, partly because the ethnic groups that have experienced persecution from coercive governments undergo an ethnic resurgence fuelled by 'pent-up historical grievances.'[9] When the retreat of empire in the Soviet case leaves about twenty-five million Russian and Russian speakers behind in newly independent states, where they are generally viewed with suspicion, serious ethnic tensions are inevitable.[10]

The deformation of human character and the erosion of the values of civil society characteristic of totalitarian regimes is a legacy conducive to violence. The Communist party apparatus in the Soviet Union, especially in the Brezhnev era, was, according to recent analysis, 'the most gigantic mafia the world has ever seen,' with the party elite a corrupt, privileged, exploiting caste.[11] In Romania, 'repression ... was so severe under Ceausescu that a civil society had no opportunity to develop ... no human rights movement, no samizdat press. No groundwork had been laid for the development of democratic institutions.'[12] Even in former Czechoslovakia, one of the more fortunate successor states of the Soviet empire, there has been 'an enormous and blindingly visible explosion of every imaginable human vice,' according to Václav Havel.[13] East Germany was probably 'the most intensively spied upon society in history,' with 100,000 full-time spies, and several times that number of informers reporting on friends and fellow citizens, to the communist secret police (Stasi). The legacy of this Orwellian past is a post-communist society of suspicion, guilt, and remorse that will not find reconciliation quickly or easily.[14] Not surprisingly, there is much more violence against foreigners in the less stable social environment of former East Germany than in the more prosperous, stable former West Germany.

The evidence from the Soviet Union, Yugoslavia, the black South African community, and more ambiguously Spain, contrasted with Canada and Belgium, is consistent with, without confirming, the previous hypothesis that interethnic violence is greater in post-totalitarian situations than in democratic polities searching for terms of coexistence between ethnic/linguistic communities. The major contemporary Canadian exception is also consistent. The alienation and relative willingness to resort to violence in Canada appears to be greatest among status Indians who were, in effect, placed outside the Canadian community by being defined as wards, subjected to a separate administrative and policy regime, and deprived of the right to vote until 1960.

Can the Centre Hold?

According to Gellner, writing in 1983, there are five potential states for each actual state in the world 'in terms of the number of ethnic and linguistic enclaves within existing states that originally had just as good a claim to separate statehood as those which did achieve it.'[15]

Canada, with more than twelve decades of uninterrupted constitutional evolution, confronts the question – can the centre hold? The theory and practice of a common Canadian citizenship is challenged by two internal nationalisms, that of the Quebec majority and of the Aboriginal peoples. In each case, the emotional power behind these nationalist forces derives from a sense of distinctiveness from the larger society, supplemented by a perceived lack of recognition by the majority. In each case, history is a storehouse of defeats, injustices, and insensitive majoritarianism. That is especially true, of course, for the Aboriginal peoples, particularly status Indians, whose culture was stigmatized, who were subjected to a version of colonial administration, and who were treated as minors.

In both Yugoslavia and the USSR, now prefaced by the adjective 'former,' the traditional centre, with its ideological union of party and state, could not hold, as its coercive capacities were undermined by democratizing tendencies and an enfeeblement of governing will. In both cases, their 'national projects were a monumental historical failure ... the melting pot simply did not work.'[16] The historic judgment will likely be that these two former countries, especially the Soviet Union, were empires, coercive unitary states behind federal façades, not truly federal polities. Their breakup is more analogous to the end of empire than to the struggle between national minorities and the centre in democratic federal systems.[17] According to Lukic, the memories of the 'captive nations' of their recent 'federal' treatment in the Soviet Union and Yugoslavia are too unpleasant to allow 'any possibility for future federal coexistence.'[18] Their disillusionment flows directly from the 'anti-national legitimating ideology [of both states], Marxism-Leninism in the Soviet Union and neo-Leninist Titoism in Yugoslavia.'[19]

When former Czechoslovakia is added to the list of federal polities where the centre's ability to hold has been questioned by Czechs and Slovaks, and negatively answered, that question's centrality is confirmed. Slovakia itself is ethnically diverse, with extensive Gypsy and Hungarian minorities, the latter close to the Hungarian border, as well as Ruthenians and Ukrainians.

The question of the centre's capacity to hold is not confined to formally federal states. It is appropriately asked throughout Eastern and Central Europe, where ethnic minorities are ubiquitous. Formerly, Bulgaria and Romania, with 'intractable national minority problems,' eschewed federalism in their Stalinist phase and opted for 'policies of repressive centralism.'[20] Now the Romanian majority confronts its minority Hungarian community in Transylvania; Bulgaria confronts its Turkish minority, savagely persecuted in the closing years of the Zhivkov regime; and majorities throughout East and Central Europe confront minority Gypsy populations, historically maltreated and despised. Accordingly, in these states 'it is almost superfluous to emphasize the lack of congruence between political and national units,'[21] so that the issue of civic coexistence between majorities and minorities cannot be evaded. As Marcin Krol argues rather pessimistically, with the Balkans particularly in mind, the future of Europe depends primarily on whether European states can accept the presence of part of their people outside their states and the existence of different national minorities within their boundaries.[22] Precisely the same situation prevails in the former Soviet Union, where ethnic and political boundaries of the successor states are frequently highly discrepant.[23]

In the European Union, the question needs to be phrased differently – not can the centre hold, but can the European centre take hold? In general, the powerful emotional realities of citizen identities continue to derive from the historic European state system. The individual states, of course, still control the instruments of civic socialization. Countries such as Germany, France, and Italy are sustained by historic identities and the continuing naturalness of the state form as the vessel for political community. The principle of subsidiarity is vigorously wielded to retain control of governing powers within the historic national states. Thus one would expect what appears to be the case, that a sense of European citizenship is weak and shallow compared to the robust sense of national citizenship. The issue, as Smith notes, 'has always been whether a European political identity could develop to underpin political unification.' The answer, thus far, is clearly no. Each state in the Union places its own interests ahead of a European policy and 'a single presumed European interest ... ' There are no popular European myths or symbols, no European counterparts to Bastille or Armistice Day.[24] Sharpe agrees, noting that in spite of the significant enhancement of 'integrative institutions' there has been negligible weakening of the 'resilience of the [Western European] nation states from which those institutions have been formed.' He also notes that in the long perspective, the post-Second World War integration movement has to be set against the counter-trend of the last century, with the twenty-one states in 1875 growing to the contemporary thirty-nine states.[25]

This does not mean that the idea of a European civilization and of a certain commonality of values and implicit assumptions does not exist, especially when contrasted with what is not Europe, but only that they contribute to a secondary identity of citizenship and community. Or, put differently, the idea of Europe includes the political units we know as the historic states. Centuries of conditioning and mental map-making would have to be obliterated before Europe, even the Europe of the twelve, emerged as a single people unfragmented by historic state divisions. Further, although the European Union was built as a reaction to the nationalist rivalries behind two world wars, and hence from a desire to contain destructive nationalist xenophobes, those very same nationalist backgrounds and memories limit the degree of erosion of national identity that is acceptable.[26] Individual states are still in the saddle and are capable of mobilizing citizen resources in a way that the European Union is not.

Further, as the Union broadens to include more member states – conceivably moving from twelve to more than twenty – its internal diversity will increase dramatically. This diversity is not only ethnic/national/linguistic, but applies also to living standards, social rights, democratic background, state capacity, and government-market relations.

The most important factor, however, that sustains the nation state in the midst of the European Union is the fragmented structure of citizen memories. These memories are national. They derive from the state-nation, or they are national in being linked to minority ethnies and regional identities within states. In fact, as the member states give up some of their jurisdiction on the altar of European integration, the latter more ancient identities are resurrected within the state system. In either case, new information is filtered, interpreted, and given meaning by the inherited moral and intellectual national capital in the citizens' minds. It is not that human beings use history, but that they have been made by history. They are history, and that history, in political terms, is overwhelmingly that of the political state or smaller ethnic nation to which they belong.

By contrast, the emotional reality of Europe is thin. It is not sustained by tradition embedded in living memories. It is perhaps not as shallow and devoid of historical memories as is global culture, contrasted with national culture by Anthony Smith as follows:

> The revival of ethnic myths, memories and traditions, both within and outside a globalizing but eclectic culture, reminds us of the fundamentally memory-less nature of any cosmopolitan culture created today. Such a culture must be consciously, even artificially constructed out of the elements of existing national cultures. But existing cultures are time-bound, particular and expressive. They are tied to specific peoples, places and periods. They are bound up with definite historical identities. These features are essentially antithetical to the very nature of a truly cosmopolitan culture.[27]

The European Union and culture share many of the weaknesses of that global culture when contrasted with memory-filled and tradition-sustained national cultures and national identities.[28] Accordingly, while the centre may hold in the EU, and even be strengthened, it will not be sustained by a vibrant Union-wide allegiant citizenship in the immediate or medium-term future. This probability is supported by the universally admitted 'democratic deficit' which attends the Union's decision-making powers. For the foreseeable future, the Union is more appropriately thought of as a confederation in which real power resides with the constituent state units than as a federal system with a central authority sustained by its own citizenship and pan-European Union base.

Two powerful messages emerge from the preceding survey. First, the creation of an encompassing community sense and a vibrant pan-citizenship transcending historic nation states, geographically concentrated linguistic communities, ethnic/cultural communities, and tribal peoples is a perilous enterprise, probably more prone to fail than to succeed. The attempted state-fashioning of new Soviet – or Yugoslav – man and woman are instructive failures. The new Europe-identifying citizen has shallow supports compared to the robust German, French, and Italian civic identities. The idea of a single pan-Canadian citizenship is threatened by powerful internal Québécois and Aboriginal nationalisms. Accordingly, the fundamental political task for federal polities that contain concentrated ethnic, national, or indigenous minorities is the nourishing of a country-wide sense of identification and belonging.

Second, as the subsequent sections note, the mixing of peoples produces minorities within minorities virtually everywhere. These minorities, either because of their small numbers or their geographic dispersal, find federalism of limited use in ensuring their security and respect for their particularity. Hence, many of the sub-units of existing or prospective federal states are themselves internally heterogeneous. They share, therefore, with most unitary states the virtually ubiquitous problem of accommodating ethnic, racial, or indigenous diversities within their jurisdiction.

Federalism Is Not Enough: Minorities Within

An almost universal problem of ethnically based territorial federalism is the existence of minorities within minorities. If the Wilsonian vision of a world of nation states with coterminous nation and state boundaries is chimerical, even more so is the vision of a federal system with coinciding ethnic and 'provincial' boundaries. In the former Soviet Union, according to Gorbachev, over seventy million Soviet citizens lived outside, or lacked, national territories of their own.[29] The federal structure of the former Socialist Federal Republic of Yugoslavia responded to 'traditional historical territories' and 'vague historical boundaries' that did not coincide with actual patterns of ethnic settlement, resulting in frustrated national minorities.[30] Thus the breakup of Yugoslavia has produced unstable successor states with internal minorities, and has led to savage warfare and genocide in the service of 'ethnic cleansing.'

In democratic federalisms the extensive movement of citizens across internal 'borders' is difficult to control without violating norms of equal citizenship. As a result, an ethnically pure political unit will be a rarity. Consequently, the devolution of power to an ethnically based political unit nearly always means the devolution of power to a particular ethnic majority, which then raises the problem of the status and treatment of those who do not belong to the empowered regional majority.

Even in the best circumstances, therefore, federalism is only a partial solution to the political management of ethnicity. There is nearly always another layer of minority ethnicity that, even if it is relatively concentrated, cannot be managed by federalism. As Watts notes, the multiplication of provinces/cantons in response to internal demands for separate government is not out of the question, as Swiss practice shows,[31] but it is highly unlikely to become constitutional routine. In Canada a proposed third order of sovereign Aboriginal governments that will remove their peoples from some of the jurisdiction of both federal and provincial governments is a federal-type response to a particular minority problem. However, it is a limited solution, for most Aboriginal peoples do not live on discrete land bases.

If, therefore, the political constitutional issue is how peoples of varying cultures and races can harmoniously coexist in the same polity, federalism is not enough; even where ethnic/national geographic concentration is extensive, smaller minorities within larger minorities will continually ree-merge, for they are by-products of human freedom.

Change, the Only Certainty
Political and constitutional strategies for the management of ethnicity cannot stand still. The relative population size of coexisting ethnic commu-nities is not stable. Birth rates change; intermarriage takes place; and slow assimilation transforms identities. When these occur the relative political power of groups changes, majority/minority relationships may need read-justment, and some forms of historic accommodation may become obso-lete.

The self-consciousness of ethnic groups is enhanced as new messages that stimulate ethnic introspection surface from the global environment. For example, the explosion of small states on the world stage supports the ambitions of small internal nations for independence, a previously uni-maginable goal in the era of empires and vast national consolidations. Or, as is clearly the case at present, a form of cultural relativism, influenced by post-modernism and post-colonialism, weakens the 'standards of civilization' argument formerly employed to deprive indigenous peoples of the right to self-government. In the Canadian case, the once ubiquitous rationale for withholding self-government from Aboriginal peoples – their attributed cultural backwardness – has been effectively banished from public discourse.

Further, even if immigration is excluded from the calculation, the geog-raphy of ethnicity is unstable, as internal migration responds to economic opportunities, to security considerations, or simply to malaise in the home community. Thus the contemporary geography of status Indians in Canada, with more than one-third now living off reserves, differs markedly from that of forty years ago. In the former Soviet Union a vast reshuffling of the population is now under way as many Russians leave republics where they are in a minority, where local legislation discriminates in favour of local residents, and where they no longer feel secure. In the United States, of course, the vast movement of blacks from the southern to the northern states transformed the politics of race relations. As Schopflin states, with not extreme exaggeration, 'on the whole, in dynamic societies, members of different segments will tend to be dispersed throughout the entire area of the state.'[32]

Constitutional and policy responses to ethnicity, therefore, should always be susceptible to ongoing experimental modification. Even where a federal response is initially appropriate, future changes in ethnic circumstances within each unit will require recurrent policy adjustments by governments.

Immigration and Diffuse Ethnicity

Prevailing patterns of ethnic demography and geography are constantly upset by the flow of peoples across state borders. Although borders matter, they are also porous. No country, especially a democratic one, can long be insulated from global population pressures, the global movement of peoples, and changes in the intellectual climate that influence how the various peoples of the world judge each other. There is a direct link between the end of colonialism in the Third World, and of the racial assumptions that sustained it, and the emergence of significant Asian and African populations in the western democracies.

According to Hobsbawm, the new internationalism reflects technological advances in communications and transportation and the remarkable international mobility of the factors of production since the Second World War. It 'has also led,' he continues,

> to the massive wave of international and inter-continental migration, the largest since the decades before 1914, which has, incidentally, both aggravated inter-communal frictions, notably in the form of racism, and made a world of national territories 'belonging' exclusively to the natives who keep strangers in their place, even less of a realistic option for the twenty-first century than it was for the twentieth.[33]

The quantitative impact of immigration on population growth can be striking. Since the Second World War, immigration has given Australia 38 per cent more people than it would have had, Canada 19 per cent, Germany

15 per cent, and France and Belgium 5-10 per cent more.[34] A Canadian demographer has estimated that 46 per cent of Canada's population growth in the twenty-first century will be due to immigration.[35]

Immigration changes the ethnic mix. As the source countries for immigrants are increasingly those in Africa and Asia, the cultural, religious, and linguistic heterogeneity in the host societies may increase dramatically. In Canada, for example, the visible minority population is projected at nearly 18 per cent by 2001, heavily concentrated in large urban areas, and comprising nearly 45 per cent and 40 per cent of the projected populations of Metropolitan Toronto and Vancouver, respectively.[36]

Growth of the immigrant population in the West is driven by multiple factors. The aging population of many Western countries, coupled with low birth rates, generates pressure for enhanced flows of immigrants. The ethnic and racial diversification already produced by the immigration of recent decades acts as a magnet attracting more kin. Further, the world is awash with refugees, 17 million by recent estimate, disproportionately concentrated (87 per cent) in developing countries.[37] Their future numbers will be greatly supplemented by environmental refugees fleeing ecological deterioration, including deforestation and desertification. The combination of international pressure, humanitarian motivation, and zealous goodwill lobbyists ensures that some of the alleviation of this distress will come from developed Western countries. In addition, the correlation of North and South with wealth and poverty generates powerful incentives for resourceful residents of the disadvantaged South to enter the promised northern lands by legal means if possible, and by illegal means if necessary. 'Tens of millions of would-be immigrants from Eastern Europe and the Soviet Union enter into competition with hundreds of millions from Africa and Latin America for access to the prosperous and democratic West.'[38] The consequences are most evident in wealthy northern countries with extensive borders with much less affluent neighbours, the United States and Mexico for example, or within striking distance of much poorer peoples, as with France and North Africa. In 1985, more than five million illegal immigrants were conservatively estimated to be in the United States.[39] There is a general consensus that the industrialized world has experienced a 'marked increase' in illegal migrants in recent decades. It seems, according to Widgren, 'as though practically any border is penetrable, apart from those of a handful of remaining terror-states.'[40] The consequence is not only an underground economy, but an underground society of illegals, outside the community of citizenship of recognized rights and responsibilities.

There is also a worst-case scenario for Western Europe. Widespread economic and social distress in the former Soviet Union and the countries of Eastern, Central, and southern Europe could produce massive pressure for admission from the disillusioned inheritors of the legacy of economic backwardness, ecological devastation, and social fragmentation left behind by socialist central planning.

In sum, the direction of demographic change within the wealthy developed West, whether unitary or federal, is towards increased racial and cultural diversity fed by new arrivals. In the European Union the declining significance of national frontiers will accelerate an intra-European movement of citizens of member states. Further, it appears that in the Union 'the foreign population originating outside Europe is growing faster than that of European origin.'[41]

The resultant tensions are difficult enough in those New World countries that were built on immigration and have long been familiar with the task of making Canadians, Australians, or Americans out of newcomers. They are more serious in historic nation states which assume that identity derives from history and a natural intergenerational transmission of heritage. The difference is seen in the European practice of guest workers, who, along with dependents and resident aliens, numbered about fifteen million in the mid-eighties,[42] and who in some cases were in the second and third generation as outsiders.[43]

Immigration exacerbates the tension between equality and historically derived superior status and privilege. Immigrants preparing for, or who have already achieved, citizen status wield the language of rights and equality. They seek protection from discrimination and may request affirmative action if they feel they suffer systemic discrimination. Although there is a tendency especially for first generation immigrants to cluster, immigrant communities almost never become a geographically compact majority of the sort for which federalism represents an escape from country-wide majoritarianism.

In a federal society such as Canada's, or the quasi-federalism of the European Union, immigration changes the terms of civic and constitutional discourse about citizenship and community. It supplements the debate on the terms of coexistence for geographically compact ethnic groups or nation states, normally with deep historical roots, with a non-territorial, non-historical discourse of citizen equality that is more congenial to dispersed newcomers.

In federal states, immigrants are likely to look to the centre because their demands derive more from citizenship than from cultural particularism. At the same time, the territorial communities that federalism protects may see immigrants as Trojan horses. Not only is their allegiance problematic, but their claims are likely to deny the primacy of the territorially-based cultural, ethnic, or national community in whose midst they reside. In Breton's terms, the political communities in which they reside are challenged by the newcomers to move from an ethnic to a civic nationalism – that is, from one in which historical ethnicity is equated with the nation, and those who are not of it even if they live in its territory, are, in some fundamental sense, outsiders, to one in which citizen status is independent of ancestry in law and policy.[44] Thus in the Canadian case, as well as in the Quebec case, there has been a running tension between conceptions of status based on time of arrival and more neutral assessments that do not discriminate on the basis of time.

To summarize: immigration is driven by forces only partly amenable to control by individual states. Contemporary immigration, in particular, is likely to challenge existing ethnic demography. The political significance of that transformation will be greatly influenced by the ease or difficulty of obtaining full citizenship. Here, practices vary even among historic European nation states such as France and Germany. In the former, the citizenry is defined in territorial terms; in the latter as 'a community of descent.' These different conceptions are reflected in the fact that the naturalization rate of foreign residents in France is four times higher than that in Germany. (The Canadian rate of naturalization is more than twenty times higher than the German.)[45]

New immigrants, especially if culturally and racially dissimilar to the host population, challenge a federal constitutional order in two ways. If, as is usual, they are geographically dispersed minorities, they challenge the federal practice of privileging territorial diversity. As equality-seeking newcomers, they also challenge federalism's tendency to accord constitutional priority to historic communities that were there at the creation. Immigrants, by their very nature, are hostile to Mayflower conceptions of citizen worth. Thus new, culturally and racially distinct immigrants challenge the assumptions of both space and time on which a historic federal constitutional order is based.

Responses to the Dual Face of Contemporary Ethnicity[46]
The preceding analysis has major consequences for how we think of constitutional arrangements. We need to juxtapose two sets of facts too often kept separate. On the one hand, there is the widespread ethnic revival manifested in sub-state nationalism – the Basques, Scots, Bretons, Flemish, Slovenians, Walloons, Québécois, Armenians, Tamils, Palestinians, indigenous peoples around the world – the list is virtually endless. Since the preceding tend to be geographically concentrated, their futures can be visualized in terms of more or less self-government. The choice reduces to federalism, independence, or some half-way house that involves economic and other linkages with contiguous states, and some de facto loss of sovereignty. This perspective leads the missionaries of federalism to see their

preferred constitutional instrument as the wave of the future, as its system of shared rule allows both local autonomy and the economic, social, and citizen benefits of belonging to a larger political unit. Clearly, however, federalism can respond to only one of the two faces of ethnicity – when it is territorially concentrated, and thus amenable to devolution of powers as a positive constitutional response.

The second set of facts is the dramatic increase in internal ethnic and racial diversity in countries that are both open to and attractive to immigrants. These are mostly the liberal, capitalist, welfare democracies of the West, both unitary and federal.

Linking these two sets of ethnic facts – the dual nature of contemporary ethnicity – also requires linking two bodies of constitutional literature that tend to be parcelled out to different practitioners – the students of federalism and the students of rights. In fact, I would further argue that scholars of polities with territorially divided ethnic/national communities need to think of composite constitutional packages that respond both to ethnic/national concentrations of peoples and to the geographically fragmented ethnicities often scattered throughout major metropolitan agglomerations. In the real world, this is not a hybrid constitutional category, since Canada, the United States, Germany, and nominally the former USSR have all wedded federalism to a regime of rights sustained by charters or bills of rights.

The minorities that are too small or territorially fragmented to control a government need protection from both orders of government, from both country-wide and regional majorities. The classic instrument for that protection is a charter. The resultant wedding of rights and ethnically based federalism should be seen as a difficult but productive balancing act, an attempt to respond to the two faces of modern ethnicity with constitutional instruments directed at very different ethnic situations. The balancing act is difficult because the tension is real. Diffused minorities possessed of rights are prone to see power-wielding regional ethnic majorities, intent on cultural continuity, as potentially hostile to whatever cultural or other difference the minority individual possesses. Conversely, the nationalism of a power-wielding regional majority may see the smaller ethnic fragments in its midst as practical or symbolic challenges to its cultural integrity. The latter may be viewed as the 'enemy within,' reviving the threat of cultural contamination, escape from which is a primary reason for opting out of country-wide majoritarianism by the federal vehicle of provincial or state power.

Although a charter or bill of rights is only one of the instruments available to the modern state charged with governing a heterogeneous, densely intermixed assemblage of peoples, it is perhaps the most practicable. Its lustre is enhanced by the pervasive rights rhetoric of the modern world and the tendency to see a highly visible charter as an appropriate, even necessary, emblem of contemporary statehood. Further, the symbolic impact of a well publicized charter on a society's consciousness is probably much greater than that of more instrumental commissions dealing with fairness in employment and housing.

Tentatively, this new composite constitutional category might be called 'charter federalism' in honour of the two constitutional instruments most appropriate to the task of managing the dual face of ethnicity of the future. The suggested label is admittedly both tentative and too cryptic. Also, it may falsely suggest a functional equivalence for the beneficiaries of these two different constitutional instruments. Clearly, however, the control of a government by a territorial majority, and the availability of individual and minority rights for those lacking the requisite territorial concentration does not create an ethnically level playing field. The local majority wields government power to shape the local society, while the rights of dispersed minorities are, with exceptions, negative rights that protect against discrimination. Nevertheless, overall such a complex constitutional package represents a commendable attempt at fairness in circumstances where a purely federal response would be captive to ethnic partiality.

Conclusion

Constitution-making is not a task for the faint hearted. There are no quick fixes. There are, however, useful constitutional instruments available to every constitution-maker who confronts an ethnically/nationally diverse population that seeks both togetherness and the recognition and protection of difference. If the ethnic, national diversities are territorially concentrated, federalism has much to offer with its capacity to support local self-rule at the provincial/state/canton level and shared rule at the centre.

There is general agreement among scholars of federalism that certain attitudinal prerequisites are necessary if such a system is to survive. Klaus von Beyme describes *'a political culture of mutual trust and bargaining'*[47] as a necessary condition. Samuel LaSelva recently identified fraternity as the basis for 'Federalism as a Way of Life.' Fraternity assumes 'that peoples with distinctive ways of life ... [can] ... possess good will towards each other, participate in common endeavours, develop and sustain common allegiances and common sentiments, and operate political institutions for the welfare of all.'[48] In the late seventies, Ivo Duchacek assembled an impressive list of attributes and beliefs identified by various authors as necessary to enable an ethnically diversified people to act 'federally.' They included 'federal creed,' 'federal feeling,' 'federal qualities of the society,' 'sense of independent interdependence,' and 'federal political culture.'[49]

This federal political culture needs to sustain two separate sets of behaviours and attitudes that are not always distinguished. On the one hand, it must support the peaceful coexistence of Serbs and Croats, Welsh and English, and Catalans and Basques. Simultaneously, it imposes on each citizen the more difficult task of balancing two sets of loyalties, that is, loyalty to a rooted ethnonational identity – Corsican and French, Scots and British, Québécois and Canadian – and allegiance to the larger polity of which it is only a part. In a stable federal system, the division of jurisdiction between the two orders of government is duplicated by dual identities and loyalties in the psyche of each citizen.

The coexistence over long periods of 'two historic identities, one within the other like concentric circles of allegiance, both of which ... [are] ... deeply value[d],' by the citizenry is not easily sustained, especially in what Smith calls 'an age of possessive nationalism.' Particularly when the going is difficult, or rival ethnic claims resist compromise, such coexistence is 'on trial.'[50] For the apostles of ethnic nationalism the divided allegiances and identities that federalism requires and fosters are experienced as a mutilation, as a psychic fracturing of a sense of wholeness that a healthy people needs. Thus Québécois within federalism are described by nationalist advocates of independence as an incomplete people with a crippled existence 'without an arm or a leg – or perhaps a heart.'[51]

As Wheare noted long ago, the predispositions necessary to support a federal system – which imposes an ambiguous double identity on each citizen and also requires the sharing of a common citizenship with culturally or linguistically different fellow citizens – depend on a fundamental commitment to democracy.[52] Federalism and democracy both require self-restraint, and acceptance of tension and contradiction for which totalitarian and authoritarian governments have little sympathy. Hence, in much of the former Soviet Union and East and Central Europe, where a culture of suspicion is common, conditions are unpropitious. In the latter, according to a Hungarian writer, 'all peoples tend to feel unrecognized, unrewarded, and unloved.'[53] Particularly in Bulgaria, Romania, Albania, several of the emergent successor regimes in the former Yugoslavia, and in much of the former Soviet Union, the possibility of democracy and, therefore, federalism is undermined by the relative absence of a supportive civic culture.

The demands that constitutional democracy imposes on leaders and citizens in ethnically complex societies, however, are even more challenging than suggested above, for federalism responds only to the territorial face of ethnicity. In most circumstances, the geography of ethnicity arising from immigration and internal mobility insistently indicates that federalism is not enough. The composite constitutional package, therefore, capable of responding to the dual presence of ethnicity is charter federalism. This

institutional blend requires an even more complex, demanding, and nuanced balancing of contradictory tendencies than federalism itself. To
federalism's requirement of dual identities and loyalties to both the provincial *ethnie* and the country-wide community is added an additional constraint on the use of majority power by either provincial or country-wide
majorities. As the Canadian case illustrates, the tension here is real. Some
Québécois and Aboriginal nationalists view the Canadian Charter as an
instrument for their assimilation, or, in the case of Aboriginals, as an alien
instrument of a foreign culture. Territorially based majorities who have used
federalism to limit the reach of country-wide majorities, and who often have
a siege mentality, may oppose restraints on their own use of majority power
in order to protect the rights of the smaller, fragmented minorities in their
midst. The country-wide community has to accept a double constraint on
its majoritarianism – the exclusion from its jurisdiction of the subject
matters handled at the canton/state/provincial level *and* the Charter's
court-enforced rights that limit policy flexibility. These constraints are
particularly frustrating to an ethnic/linguistic majority that views the central government as its rightful possession.

A charter is not the only instrument available to the modern state to
facilitate peaceful coexistence among its intermixed diversities. It is a limited
instrument whose essential virtue is its capacity to protect minorities against
majoritarian abuse. Unlike federalism, however, it does not put power in
the hands of minorities. Hence its supplementation by more positive
measures may be appropriate, such as constitutionally guaranteed minority
language education rights, affirmative action, and customary or guaranteed
representation on courts, appointed boards and agencies, and in legislatures.
The use of electoral systems that facilitate minority representation can
enhance the state's image of fairness among otherwise under-or unrepre-
sented minorities. Such representation provides minority communities with
platforms from which they can address the majority.

In general, the ethnically heterogeneous state should publicize an ethic
of racial and cultural pluralism. Such a state should transmit a positive
symbolic message that constantly reminds citizens of their heterogeneous
nationhood. The state's identity should explicitly include citizens who are
not part of the natural ethnic/linguistic majority. The state not only exists
at the centre of a constitutional order, and must fine-tune the economic
order; it also presides over and manipulates a symbolic order. By means of
the latter, the well-functioning state incessantly reminds its people of the
evolving nature of the political nation by providing a comprehensive answer
to the incessant question – 'Who are we as a people now?'

A state capable of democratically governing a heterogeneous populace by
means of federalism, a charter, and additional, ethnically sensitive consti-

tutional and policy instruments is a noble achievement. If it simultaneously builds an overarching, widely accepted common citizenship with which its diverse peoples identify, it is not only noble but is probably durable as well.

Acknowledgments
I wish to thank Stephen Phillips for providing me with excellent research assistance.

Notes
1 For further discussion, see Paul Chartrand, 'The Aboriginal Peoples in Canada and Renewal of the Federation,' Chapter 8.
2 Louis Hartz, with contributions by Kenneth D. McRae, Richard M. Morse, Richard N. Rosecrance, Leonard M. Thompson, *The Founding of New Societies* (New York: Harcourt, Brace and World 1964).
3 Raymond Breton, 'From Ethnic to Civic Nationalism: English Canada and Quebec,' *Ethnic and Racial Studies* 11, No. 1 (January 1988):85-102.
4 For further discussion, see Katherine Swinton, 'Federalism, the Charter, and the Courts: Rethinking Constitutional Dialogue in Canada,' Chapter 18.
5 Hugh Seton-Watson, *The 'Sick Heart' of Modern Europe: The Problem of the Danubian Lands* (Seattle and London: University of Washington Press 1975), 74.
6 Reneo Lukic, 'Twilight of the Federations in East Central Europe and the Soviet Union,' *Journal of International Affairs* 45, No. 2 (Winter 1992):575-6. Hugh Poulton concurs: 'The whole area of post-communist Eastern Europe is experiencing an explosion of nationalist forces which are filling the power vacuum vacated by the mostly discredited former official ideology of Marxist-Leninism' (Hugh Poulton, *The Balkans: Minorities and States in Conflict* (London: Minority Rights Group 1991), 208).
   Earlier, the 'golden age of national statehood in the Balkans (from the Congress of Berlin to the First World War) was also a period of extreme national tensions and attempts to correct history not just by pen, but by state policy. Expulsions and exoduses of whole populations, culminating in the Balkan wars of 1912-1913, were the sad epitaph to the lifting of the Turkish yoke' (Ivo Banac, 'Political Change and National Diversity,' *Daedalus* 119, No. 1 (Winter 1990):144).
7 Alistair Hennessy, 'The Renaissance of Federal Ideas in Contemporary Spain,' in Murray Forsyth, ed., *Federalism and Nationalism* (New York: St. Martin's Press 1989), 18.
8 Anthony D. Smith, 'The Myth of the "Modern Nation" and the Myths of Nations,' *Ethnic and Racial Studies* 11, No. 1 (January 1988):11.
9 Timothy M. Frye, 'Ethnicity, Sovereignty and Transitions from Non-Democratic Rule,' *Journal of International Affairs* 45, No. 2 (Winter 1992):607.
10 John Lloyd, 'Painful Legacy of an Empire,' *Financial Post*, 13 July 1992. See also Vsevolod I. Vasiliev, 'Questions of Citizenship after the Breakup of the USSR,' Chapter 6.
11 David Remnick, 'Dons of the Don,' review of *The Soviet Mafia*, by Arkady

Vaksberg, *New York Review of Books*, 16 July 1992, 45.

12 Helsinki Watch/Human Rights Watch, *Since the Revolution: Human Rights in Romania* (New York: Helsinki Watch 1991), cited by István Deák, 'Survivors,' *New York Review of Books*, 5 March 1992, 51.

13 Václav Havel, 'Paradise Lost,' *New York Review of Books*, 9 April 1992, 6.

14 See Amos Elon, 'East Germany: Crime and Punishment,' *New York Review of Books*, 14 May 1992, 6.

15 As cited in L.J. Sharpe, 'Fragmentation and Territoriality in the European State System,' *International Political Science Review* 10, No. 3 (July 1989):228.

16 Lukic, 'Twilight of the Federations,' 580.

17 According to Lukic, the claimed federal character of the USSR and Yugoslavia was 'nothing more than a fig leaf, designed to hide a highly centralized state. [They] ... were able to hold together in the past only because of the nature of their political systems, as the totalitarian control of the party-state over the mosaic of nations created an appearance of false unity' ('Twilight of the Federations,' 597). Christopher Binns offers a somewhat more positive assessment of the federalist nature of government in Yugoslavia after the late sixties in 'Federalism, Nationalism and Socialism in Yugoslavia,' in Forsyth, ed., *Federalism and Nationalism*, 115-45.

18 Lukic, 'Twilight of the Federations,' 597.

19 George Schopflin, 'Nationalism and National Minorities in East and Central Europe,' *Journal of International Affairs* 45, No. 1 (Summer 1991):57. Further discussion is found in Mihailo Markovic, 'The Federal Experience in Yugoslavia,' Chapter 5; Viktor Knapp, 'Central and Eastern European Federations: Communist Theory and Practice,' Chapter 19; Volodymyr Vassylenko, 'Disintegration of the Soviet "Federation" and the "Federalization" of Ukraine,' Chapter 20.

20 Binns, 'Federalism, Nationalism and Socialism in Yugoslavia,' 116.

21 Koen Koch, 'Back to Sarajevo or Beyond Trianon? Some Thoughts on the Problem of Nationalism in Eastern Europe,' *Netherlands Journal of Social Science* 27, No. 1 (April 1991):31-2.

22 Marcin Krol, 'A Europe of Nations or a Universalistic Europe?' *International Affairs* 66, No. 2 (1990):286.

23 Ann Sheehy, 'The Ethnographic Dimension,' in Alistair McAuley, ed., *Soviet Federalism, Nationalism and Economic Decentralisation* (Leicester and London: Leicester University Press 1991), 58-60.

24 Anthony D. Smith, 'National Identity and the Idea of European Unity,' *International Affairs* 68, No. 1 (January 1992):55, 56, 73. In this volume, see, as well, Guy Kirsch, 'The New Pluralism: Regionalism, Ethnicity, and Language in Western Europe,' Chapter 4; Tommaso Padoa-Schioppa, 'Economic Federalism and the European Union,' Chapter 10; Jacques Pelkmans, 'Governing European Union: From Pre-Federal to Federal Economic Integration?,' Chapter 11.

25 Sharpe, 'Fragmentation and Territoriality,' 225, 227.

26 'Experiences, traditions and collective memories of the events that took place in the first half of this century are still very much alive. That is why Europeans are less than eager to transfer one of the central duties of the state, namely the defence of its territory, to supranational organizations' (Jochen Thies, 'Europe – Just a Daydream?' *European Affairs: The European Magazine* 5, No. 6 (December 1991):27).

27 Smith, 'National Identity and the Idea of European Unity,' 66-7.
28 See Anthony D. Smith, 'The Supersession of Nationalism?' *International Journal of Comparative Sociology* 30, nos. 1-2 (January-April 1990):8.
29 Sheehy, 'The Ethnographic Dimension,' 85.
30 Binns, 'Federalism, Nationalism and Socialism in Yugoslavia,' 123, 142.
31 Ronald Watts, 'The Soviet Federal System and the Nationality Question in Comparative Perspective,' in McAuley, ed., *Soviet Federalism*, 200.
32 Schopflin, 'Nationalism and National Minorities,' 64.
33 E.J. Hobsbawm, *Nations and Nationalism since 1780* (Cambridge: Cambridge University Press 1990), 174.
34 Daniel Blot, 'The Demographics of Migration,' *OECD Observer* 163 (April-May 1990):22.
35 Ibid., 24.
36 T. John Samuel, 'Visible Minorities in Canada: A Projection,' pp. 17, 35 (mimeo distributed as part of a news release: Canadian Advertising Foundation 'Race Relations Advisory Council on Advertising,' 30 May 1992. Visible minorities were defined as non-white, non-Caucasian, and non-Aboriginal (p. 1)).
37 Department of International Economic and Social Affairs, *Concise Report on the World Population Situation in 1991* (New York: United Nations 1991), 28.
38 Pierre Hassner, 'Europe Beyond Partition and Unity: Disintegration and Reconstitution?' *International Affairs* 66, No. 3 (July 1990):469.
39 Barbara Schmitter Heisler and Martin O. Heisler, 'Transnational Migration and the Modern Democratic State: Familiar Problems in a New Form or a New Problem?' *Annals, AAPSS* 485 (May 1986):14.
40 Jonas Widgren, 'International Migration and Regional Stability,' *International Affairs* 66, No. 4 (October 1990):754-5.
41 Department of International Economic and Social Affairs, *Concise Report on the World Population*, 27.
42 The estimate is from Heisler and Heisler, 'Transnational Migration and the Modern Democratic State,' 13-14.
43 See Rosemarie Rogers, 'The Trans-National Nexus of Migration,' *Annals, AAPSS* 485 (May 1986):34-50, for an incisive discussion of the ambiguous status of these migrants.
44 Breton, 'From Ethnic to Civic Nationalism,' 85-102.
45 William R. Brubaker, 'Immigration, Citizenship and the Nation-State in France and Germany: A Comparative Historical Analysis,' *International Sociology* 5, No. 4 (December 1990):379, 384.
46 Raymond Breton in 'Stratification and Conflict between Ethnolinguistic Communities with Different Social Structures,' *Canadian Review of Sociology and Anthropology* 15, No. 2 (1978), presents an insightful analysis of two ideal-type ethnic situations – one in which an ethnic community has its own institutions, and hence a high degree of institutional completeness, the most developed version of which involves ethnic control of a government wielding extensive jurisdiction. In the other, when there is limited institutional completeness, 'the more the issues of inequality will tend to have to do with the status of individuals in the society at large and in its institutions and with the conditions for individual participation and advancement in the institutional systems.' Here,

'the issues that arise between ethnic communities tend to have to do with individual civil rights and with the set of opportunities available to individuals of different ethnic origins and with the constraints they have to overcome in the pursuit of their life goals. In short, the issues have to do with the conditions necessary for full citizenship; for full participation of individuals in the institutional system of the society'(pp. 150, 154).

47 Klaus von Beyme, 'Social and Economic Conditions of Ethnic Strife in the Soviet Union,' in McAuley, ed., *Soviet Federalism*, 108 (italics in original).
48 Samuel LaSelva, 'Federalism as a Way of Life: Reflections on the Canadian Experiment,' *Canadian Journal of Political Science* 26, No. 2 (June 1993):219, 229.
49 Ivo D. Duchacek, 'Antagonistic Cooperation: Territorial and Ethnic Communities,' *Publius* 7, No. 4 (Fall 1977):28.
50 Anthony D. Smith, 'State-Making and Nation-Building,' in John A. Hall, ed., *States in History* (Oxford: Basil Blackwell 1986), 260.
51 Richard Handler, *Nationalism and the Politics of Culture in Quebec* (Madison: University of Wisconsin Press 1988), 31, citing René Lévesque.
52 K.C. Wheare, *Federal Government*, 4th ed. (London: Oxford University Press 1963), 47.
53 István Deák, 'Survivors,' *New York Review of Books*, 5 March 1992, 51.

3

Identification in Transnational Political Communities

Raymond Breton

There are many ways in which social structures are becoming more complex in contemporary societies: urban agglomerations, large-scale bureaucratic organization, elaborate communication systems, interorganizational networks, and the multiplication of organized groups and associations in all areas of activity. The progressive formation of 'transnational' structures constitutes another dimension of complexity. Increasingly, economic, political, and cultural life takes place in organizations and social networks that cut across local, regional, and national collectivities.

Although transnational organizations are not a new phenomenon, they could be considered as such, given their considerable expansion in recent decades. This growth takes place in virtually all domains of activity and involves a larger and more diversified set of players.[1] The expanding scope and diversity of players is accompanied by increased institutionalization.

The construction of a social system at any level has several dimensions. One involves the formation of organizational and interorganizational structures and of networks of communication in different spheres of activity. This can be a long, complex process, as it involves the distribution of control, costs, and benefits among a range of actors. This is certainly the case at the transnational level, but it was also the case in the earlier formation of national societies that incorporated local and regional communities.

Another dimension is socio-psychological: the shaping of institutional structures as meaningful objects of identification. As with organizational formation, this process does not occur automatically. The creation of European or North American structures does not mean that being European or North American will automatically become an important component of people's self-conception. Transnational identities may be adopted only by certain segments of the population. For instance, some regional, ethnic, and linguistic groups may identify with such identities, while others remain uninterested, or even perceive them as detrimental to their own national or subnational identity. The transnational identity may not extend to the middle and working classes, but may remain restricted to the political, economic, and technocratic elites who construct and manage transnational organizations.

In the process of being incorporated into a larger, more encompassing system, national identities may change. It should be remembered in this connection that national identities have not always existed; there was no historical or sociological necessity for their formation. They can, accordingly, change, weaken, and even cease to exist. Similarly, transformations may occur at the subnational level. Smaller territorial units may find it advantageous to relate directly to the transnational system in pursuit of their interests, rather than through intermediate nation state organizations. The more distinctive their situation (as a result of ecological, economic, cultural, and historical circumstances), the more this could occur. For example, Scottish nationalists see in the development of their ties with the European Union ways in which to increase their autonomy vis-à-vis the central British state. Similarly, one reason why Quebec nationalists strongly favoured the Canada-United States Free Trade Agreement was that stronger linkages with the United States would diminish those with the rest of Canada, and would even make cutting them less threatening and disruptive.

Such issues can be addressed from two perspectives: that of the transnational entity itself and that of the individuals who are joining it. The first perspective requires investigation of the conditions conducive or detrimental to the moulding of an overarching, transnational system into a meaningful object of identification for individuals in different national and subnational units. The second requires examination of the conditions under which individuals are likely to define their own identities in relation to the larger, more encompassing collectivity and of the factors that can affect the nature of the emerging identification. Before proceeding with this analysis, the notions of identity and identification will be examined briefly.

Identity and Identification

There are at least three ways in which a particular system of collective organization[2] can shape individual and social identities – that is, people's conceptions of themselves and of the groups to which they belong. First, it can provide a network of opportunities and constraints that impinge on people's interests and that partly determine their life chances. This constitutes the pragmatic or instrumental linkage of individuals to a collectivity.

Among the main organizational systems involved in this type of linkage are those that pertain to exchange, technology, communication, and training. They structure the social and organizational networks through which individuals transact affairs with each other and acquire the information and other resources required to exploit opportunities and to cope with constraints. The central legitimating ideology focuses on the form of economic organization, such as capitalism or socialism. The key symbols refer to major economic or technological achievements, such as the size of the national product, megaprojects, and various indicators of affluence, and to territory as an economic resource (for purposes of industry, commerce, or tourism).

Utilitarian identities tend to emerge from this type of linkage. People conceive of themselves and the groups to which they belong as beneficiaries or losers in relation to the collective organization. Identification with the system tends to be calculative and contingent on circumstance. Based on a means-ends rationality and a calculus of gains and losses, this type of identification tends to be relatively unstable. It is fairly easily swayed by changing perceptions of the available opportunities and constraints. It would also be correlated with the individual's position in the social structure as defined by class, occupation, and industry (e.g., finance, agriculture, manufacturing sector, or public administration).

The second way in which a system of collective organization can shape identities and identification is by structuring interdependencies among individuals and groups. Individuals become more conscious of their dependence on others and of the advantages of cooperating in the pursuit of common objectives. The more the interdependence is perceived as permanent (due, for example, to geographic circumstance, dependence on the same energy sources, linked transportation networks, and past or present enemies in common), the greater its impact on social identities.

The critical institutions here are those established for collective decision-making, mobilization and allocation of resources, circulation of information, coordination of activities, and control of free riders. The corresponding ideologies are those that legitimate particular institutional arrangements (e.g., policy-making structures and processes, division of powers between levels of governments, and criteria and mechanisms for pooling resources). The key symbols evoke the values of collaboration, resource sharing, and joint achievements.

The experience of interdependence tends to generate a 'community of fate' identity, a pragmatic solidarity. People perceive their well-being, and even their survival, as being tied to that of other collectivities. Members of individual countries may perceive their security and economic welfare as being linked in significant ways to that of other countries. Identification with the system of organized interdependence is based on reciprocity, on joint investments and participation in collective achievements, and on the perceived fairness of the distribution of costs and benefits. 'Community of fate' identities and identifications tend to be more stable than those with only a utilitarian basis.

Third, a system of collective organization can affect identities and identification through its distinctive character based on factors such as historical experience, cultural heritage, religion, and language. What counts at this level is the commonality or the presumed commonality of these elements.

The principal organizations are those through which common traits are expressed and transmitted from generation to generation. These include institutions in the fields of art (literature, music, and theatre, whether popular or elite), the family, schools, universities, churches, and the press. But the common traditions and practices can pervade all institutional spheres. Democratic structures can vary from one society to another (as they do, for instance, between Britain, Canada, and the United States), each embracing somewhat different practices and traditions. Similarly, a capitalistic economy can take different forms from one sociocultural context to another.

A 'sense of peoplehood' identity emerges from the awareness of a collective experience and heritage.[3] Identification is primarily socioemotional. The attachment is to a particular collectivity and to the organizational systems that are seen as embodying its cultural distinctiveness.[4] The key symbols are those that evoke the collective experience over time (heroes, historical events), collective accomplishments that evoke sentiments of common pride, and grievances and historical memories of conflict and oppression. The symbols are also those that variously express the cultural distinctiveness (elements of life-style and language) and the land as an element of the collective heritage – that is, as the homeland.[5]

A 'sense of peoplehood' can develop at all levels of social organization, whether subnational, national, or transnational. Also, it should be emphasized that these levels are not necessarily mutually exclusive (although, as will be discussed later, they can be defined as such to suit the sociopolitical interests of particular groups, such as those seeking to gain power or political independence). Individuals can feel that as Europeans they are, as a people, different from North Americans, even though there are distinct cultural identities within Europe and North America.

Finally, it should be noted that individuals may simultaneously have different types of linkages with particular collectivities. Accordingly, their identification with them can have more than one basis. In addition, the more the utilitarian, 'community of fate,' and 'sense of peoplehood' bases of identification with a particular collectivity accumulate, the more stable and intense that identification is likely to be.

Several factors and processes can affect the construction of political entities as objects of identification and the corresponding shaping of individual identities. We will consider six: 'bottom up' processes, 'top down' processes, isolationist versus collaborative systems of beliefs, competition for the identification of citizens, inequalities among constituent units, and the exercise of citizenship.

'Bottom Up' Processes
'Bottom up' processes pertain to people's daily experiences in their roles as parent, citizen, worker, farmer, professional, technician, and so on. In order for a particular structure to become meaningful, it has to be experienced in some way by individuals or groups.[6] It has to make a difference to the organization and conduct of their lives. Otherwise, people may only know of its existence without developing a sense of membership in it, let alone identification with or loyalty to it. Needless to say, particular structures may have an impact on individuals without their being aware of that fact. However, it is conscious experience that shapes identities and identification.

The new economic, political, or social structures may be beneficial or detrimental to the well-being of a collectivity; beneficial to or destructive of the system of opportunities that its members had previously taken for granted; reinforcing or threatening their identity, their values, and way of life. Accordingly, identities and identification can be either positive, negative, or mixed. People's identity and self-esteem may be enhanced when they think of themselves as members of a particular collectivity; or the system may become an object of 'negative identification,' a point of negative reference in the definition of one's own identity ('I am not such and such'; 'I resent being referred to as an ... ').

It is important to note that it is the perceptions that matter. Such perceptions may arise directly from individual or group experience, or they can be influenced by elites and opinionmakers who accumulate and disseminate information and interpret its significance for the collectivity or for some parts of it.

In addition, two dimensions of an individual's experience of a particular institutional system should be distinguished. The first relates to the utilitarian basis of identification described above, and arises from the resultant benefits and disadvantages to one's material well-being, power, status, identity, values, or life-style. The second relates to the 'community of fate' type of identification and derives from what one invests in the collective organization rather than what one gains from it. Individuals identify with a collectivity and its organizations to the extent that they participate in them. When people invest of themselves in a collective enterprise, they experience that enterprise as something that 'belongs' to them; they feel that they are an integral part of it. Failing this, they will tend to see the entity as 'belonging' to someone else, whether their relationship to it is beneficial or detrimental.

Such 'bottom up' processes suggest that identities and identifications at the transnational level will tend to be utilitarian. Membership in such systems will often be evaluated in terms of costs and benefits. A sense of peoplehood is not likely to emerge, except perhaps in the very long run – assuming that the experience is positive. Even a sense of 'community of fate' is likely to take time to become part of a people's consciousness.

'Top Down' Processes

Community building may also entail processes of symbolic definition, that is, of construction of the community as an object of identification. This usually involves a fairly deliberate articulation of a system of ideas that define and justify the distinctive features of the community and its institutions. The objective is to create an entity with which individuals can identify – an entity they feel is *their* own and that commands their loyalty.[7]

This entails the formulation of arguments and images demonstrating that the institutions embody the character of the people (the national character, the spirit of our civilization, the group's distinctiveness, etc.) and that demands on citizens to ensure institutional survival and growth are justifiable. Such an interpretive and legitimating scheme is usually accompanied by a set of symbols and rituals that, in a condensed way, represent the community to its members and to outsiders. This process of symbolic construction involves the active intervention of people such as artists, political leaders, cultural functionaries in government, and mass media managers.

The importance of such 'top down' processes is underscored by the fact that the incorporation of sociopolitical units into larger, more encompassing systems has usually been carried out from the top down. Nation states, for instance, were not spontaneous creations of grassroots social movements. In fact, their formation was often, if not usually, accompanied by the repression of such movements.

Nor are transnational systems the result of grassroots forces: they are created by elites of large-scale organizations primarily in the pursuit of economic and/or political power.[8] However, if they are to be successful in the long run, they need to be legitimated – that is, defined in such a way that people perceive a positive relationship between them and their own lives, well-being, and identity. If elites succeed in this task of legitimation, it will be easier for them to mobilize support for their transnational project and to control those whose objectives and projects run counter to it.

The theories to explain and justify a particular system of transnational organization may emphasize the material benefits that it brings or promises. They may stress interdependence between regions or nation states in the face of common dangers, opportunities, and competition, or with regard to particular objectives. Or they may highlight the commonalities between national and subnational societies while minimizing the differences.

The particular elements that will be underscored, however, depend in part on the resources available to those who define reality and who construct interpretive schemes at each level of the collective organization. These may be more or less limited. For instance, cultural entrepreneurs may emphasize utilitarian benefits, because they can only conceive of human motivation and of individual and collective action in terms of material self-interest; they have trouble seeing the collective organization other than as a machine for producing and distributing goods and services.

However, emphasis on utilitarian benefits may also stem from the fact that little exists in the collective experience and character of the peoples involved to allow for meaningful definition of the collectivity beyond its utilitarian merits. For instance, the discourse of federalists in Canada who seek the support of francophone Quebec tends to emphasize economic benefits. This is partly due to the relative lack of symbolic resources to evoke a common sense of peoplehood in both francophone Quebec and English-speaking Canada. In short, symbolic constructs are like any other: they cannot be erected without tools or with unsound materials.[9]

Isolation versus Collaboration as Systems of Belief

The prevailing system of beliefs in particular localities, regions, and nation states may emphasize autonomy rather than collaboration. The sociopolitical culture may be 'isolationist,' preferring autonomous development rather than collaboration with others. The group will engage in joint ventures only if necessary, and on an ad hoc basis.

Thus a new, permanent collective organization may be viewed with suspicion, if not as an outright threat. Either because of their relatively small numbers, or their cultural, economic, or political insecurity, members of a collectivity may fear that they will be swamped and lose their identity, become dependent, or be subject to exploitation by the larger system. The emphasis on group self-reliance may also stem from historical tensions with potential collaborators.[10] Finally, the premium on autonomy may be based on a desire to sustain or bolster nationalistic pride. This appears to be the case, for instance, among the British, who 'consistently favour independent action by sovereign governments to concerted European action.'[11]

Where such suspicions exist, overarching structures are unlikely to become objects of identification. At best, participation will be based on a utilitarian calculus of costs and benefits, and even these may be ignored, rejected, or misperceived if the suspicion and insecurity are sufficiently great.

Members of the group may see participation in the larger collectivity either as a threat to the vitality of their own community, or as reinforcement of or support for it. This ambivalence may exist within individuals. But it may also be articulated by different sociopolitical groups, as in the disagreement between Quebec independentists, who see the Canadian union as a threat, and federalists, who see it as a way to ensure Quebec's vitality. The advantages and disadvantages of integration into larger systems need to be continuously balanced. On the one hand, buttressing the local/regional at the expense of the national system, or the national to the detriment of the transnational level (the self-reliant, isolationist stance) could mean foregoing the benefits of integration into the larger system. This realization could encourage people to invest in national or transnational structures. On the other hand, strengthening these structures could be perceived as a loss of economic independence, political autonomy, and cultural distinctiveness at the national or local/regional level, leading to reluctance to enter into – or inciting departure from – overarching structures. Thus, people are likely to be ambivalent about integration into a larger system, and different groups may well confront each other over the merits of autonomy and self reliance as against integration into a larger system.

Competition for Citizen Support

The interests of some groups and social classes are based primarily on local or regional organizations; others depend mostly on national or transnational structures. The result is that competition among interest-groups and social classes is transmuted into inter-level competition. Thus political and economic actors at the transnational level may come into competition with those at the nation state level. In order to increase their chances of winning in this competition, the former may establish direct linkages with subnational units – a phenomenon that is already apparent, for example, in the European Union. Brussels has initiated a number of assistance programs to regions in order to bypass reluctant national states concerned with the erosion of their sovereignty.[12] As a result, the national state could progressively weaken as its structuring and regulating role in various spheres of activity becomes less and less effective.[13]

Such competition is particularly intense in periods of social, political, and economic change.[14] Even if it results in overall growth, change generates winners and losers.[15] Thus, the changes may pit locality against locality, region against region, ethnocultural[16] group against ethnocultural group, and nation state against nation state.

Such confrontations usually involve the mobilization of individual identities and loyalties (regionalism, nationalism, ethnonationalism) for 'the struggle to capture the core of personal identity mirrors more or less the struggle to control resources.'[17] The political discourse of the opponents of integration into a larger system will tend to define the issue as a stark choice between two options: the possibility of multiple identities and identifications will be rejected, fudged, or not even considered. The discourse will tend to focus on the discordance between the levels of collective organization and to dramatize the negative impact of the encompassing system. It will also tend to ignore or play down any positive impact. The discourse of the advocates of integration will tend to be in the opposite direction. For example, Goybet mentions that at one time, the sums contributed by the EC for regional and social assistance represented 17 per cent of its budget, but that some countries refused to publicize that fact (e.g., the EC name was not allowed to appear on the billboards associated with the projects).[18]

There is, however, an important difference between the two sides regarding the possibilities for mobilization. As indicated earlier, citizens experience some levels of collective organization more directly than others and most organizations in which people carry on their daily lives are local or regional. Only certain social classes and occupational groups operate primarily through national and transnational organizations. Thus local and regional groups and elites may be better placed than those at the national, and especially transnational, levels in their attempts to mobilize support by evoking common identifications. Their advantage stems from the ability of their appeals to combine the utilitarian, community of fate, and peoplehood components of identity and identification. On the other hand, support for transnational organizations will tend to be mobilized on the basis of utilitarian benefit, since there is as yet no experienced and symbolically constructed transnational community of fate or sense of peoplehood.

A similar difference in the potential for the formation of identities and identifications may exist between national and subnational collectivities. National elites may be disadvantaged in fostering identification with the national collectivity and institutions as compared to regional elites, especially those that can appeal to ethnonationalistic or regional sentiments by repeated reference to historical grievances.

There is, however, a significant difference in degree between the two situations. The cultural-symbolic resources available to national elites far exceed those available to transnational elites, but the comparable differences between the symbolic resources of national and subnational elites is much less pronounced. There are also important variations across countries. In Canada, for example, the Québécois identity is in serious competition with a Canadian identity. To a significant extent, the identification of many Québécois with Canada is utilitarian and there is some sense of being part of a community of fate (for historical and geographic reasons), but little sense of common peoplehood. This is not the case in France, for instance, where the Breton and Occitan identities do not threaten French identity in any significant way.

Inequalities among Constituent Units

The units that are integrated into an overarching system, be it a single state or a transnational system, may vary in population, natural resources, military might, political organization, or economic and technological development. Such pronounced inequalities may make it more difficult to create an encompassing system, or, once established, to ensure its stability and legitimacy.

The transnational economic and political order is likely to have a significant impact on the distribution of resources across countries and national regions. Thus, the operation of the system may increase utilitarian and 'community of fate' identifications among certain people and simultaneously have the opposite effect on others. In other words, those who can extract greater benefits from the system will tend to look favourably on it, while those who gain less, and especially those who lose, will tend to see it negatively. This is likely to generate conflict not only among groups and organizations at different levels, but also among groups and regions within particular societies.[19]

It is difficult to gauge when the inequalities become too great to manage. However, a transnational system that included one unit much larger than the others would be unlikely to generate positive identities and identifications. Indeed, such a large entity could swamp the others economically and politically, either by the very fact of its size and power, or because it uses these characteristics to the disadvantage of the other units. The anxieties arising from this possibility would lead the threatened groups to mobilize opposition to the transnational project (or to the national one, as the case may be). For example, there has been speculation that a certain fear of Germany, especially since reunification, may dampen support for the European Union.

Inequalities may also be experienced as cultural-symbolic threats. These are frequently the most important perceptions, since they pertain to individual and collective identities. Decisions about official languages and patterns of language-use can be critical in this regard. This concern underlies the adoption of all national languages as official languages of the European Union. Another concern is the day-to-day use of languages in Union institutions. At the moment, French and English are the main languages of the functionaries, a situation not wholly acceptable to German speakers who constitute the largest linguistic group in the Union.[20] The question of common, official language(s) will become even more serious with the accession of other countries to the Union. A linguistic debate may under-score the sense of national peoplehood and lead to emphasis being placed on the larger community in terms of utilitarianism and interdependence.

The North American situation is one of cultural-symbolic inequality, given the dominance of the United States in culture and mass communications. Consequently, a North American entity would be largely American in character, making it difficult for people of other countries to identify with it and easier for nationalist groups to oppose membership in it.

The Exercise of Citizenship

Three aspects of citizenship will be considered here: input in political decisions, social security, and contributions to the collectivity.

Citizen Input in Decisions: Civic and Political Rights

In a transnational community, the distance between individuals and orga-nizations (and their elites) is considerable, even more than in national societies with large-scale organizations. Hence, there is the danger of 'ad-ministrative despotism' warned of by Tocqueville in his analysis of Ameri-can society.[21]

The presence of formal democratic institutions, such as the European Parliament, does not eliminate this danger – and in any case, such institu-tions are rare. Indeed, the proliferation of large-scale organizations creates complexity which, in turn, distances citizens from the centres of decision-making. The distance is both cognitive – individuals may have 'real difficulty piecing together a picture of the whole society and how they relate to it'[22] – and experiential – citizens lose control over the structures and decisions that affect them. Thus, the emergence of a transnational system raises, in a particularly acute way, the question of political rights and the distribution of control over decisions and their implementation.

The exercise of political rights requires institutions such as political parties, the secret ballot, and parliaments.[23] A critical issue here is how citizens' political rights are to be expressed in relation to transnational institutions: will they be voiced directly or mediated through national governments? Identification with the transnational political community and its institutions, however, is more likely to ensue if representation is direct. Representation through national governments tends to reinforce identification with that level of government. The same could be hypothe-sized about identification in federal regimes where regional or provincial governments play a critical role in articulating the interests of their constit-uencies vis-à-vis the central government: the more the former articulate interests vis-à-vis the central government, the more citizens tend to identify with them.

There are also different modalities of direct representation. Holland notes that

> the distribution of Members of the European Parliament according to nation is incompatible with the idea of a supranational federal Community. Once a common system is in place the logic of national quotas disappears. Party lists would become trans-European in the truest sense: voters in Spain, for example, would not be limited to selecting Spanish candidates but would choose from party lists that were multinational in composition.[24]

The system proposed by Holland would be more propitious to the formation of a transnational political identity than one based on national quotas.

Another important issue concerns the interests of political elites in national societies. In negotiating transnational structures and arrangements, will they respond primarily to transnational economic and political actors, or will they advocate the interests of their own citizens? Will they be influenced primarily by the economic interest-groups based in their own country, but largely integrated into transnational interorganizational networks? It cannot be assumed that these elites necessarily understand and take account of, let alone defend, the interests of their national constituencies in relation to the transnational system unless citizens have the institutionalized means to articulate these interests and impress them upon decisionmakers. This is especially important because policy-making at the transnational level is quite remote from most citizens, as are the means by which they can exert political influence.

Citizenship, however, goes beyond political and legal institutions. 'The issue of who can practice citizenship and on what terms is not only a matter of the legal scope of citizenship and the formal nature of the rights entailed in it. It is also a matter of the non-political capacities of citizens which derive from the social resources they command and to which they have access.'[25] At the moment, citizenship rights are exercised in institutions of national and subnational governments. The exercise of citizenship at the transnational level will require institutional innovation.

Tocqueville pointed out that the exercise of citizenship depends on the social and economic conditions of civil society.[26] This supposes that civil society must become organized at the transnational as well as the national and subnational levels. And the more the powers vested in transnational political institutions, the more pressing the question of citizen rights and civil society becomes.

Citizens will need to organize at the transnational level in order to secure political rights in the first place. Rights have rarely been granted without sociopolitical struggle,[27] because they impose constraints on those in positions of power and authority. In the struggle for such rights at the transnational level, governments of national and perhaps subnational societies will experience intense conflicting pressures. The pressures will come, on the one hand, from transnational actors – financial and business corporations, for example, – seeking the support of national governments in pursuit of their interests at that level and, on the other, from organized citizens' groups defending their class, professional, territorial, or cultural interests.

A transnational civil society is already beginning to emerge. Interorganizational networks extending across state borders already exist in various policy areas: the environment, economic development, human rights, and indigenous peoples.[28] As this civil society becomes more visible to individual citizens, the formation of a 'community of fate' identification with a transnational community is likely to be fostered.

Social Security: The Issue of Social Rights
In most Western democracies, citizenship also includes social rights: entitlement to some protection against adversity such as sickness, unemployment, or disability. Such entitlements have been institutionalized at the local, regional, and national levels.

One issue regarding institutionalized social rights (i.e., social programs) is whether or not integration into a transnational system will erode the financial capacity needed to sustain them. There is considerable fear that international competitiveness is the ideological justification for the curtailment of publicly provided social support systems.[29] If so, then the question arises whether this pressure can be countered by the development of transnational institutions which can regulate international business behaviour, and whether transnational institutional partners can develop common standards for social programs such as the European Social Charter.

Perhaps a more fundamental concern is the nature of the implicit social bargain between transnational economic actors and national societies. That is to say, what can transnational actors legitimately expect from a society, and what can a society, in turn, legitimately expect from them? It can be argued that, within nation states, an implicit understanding between economic corporate actors and society has been worked out over time. In a general way, the bargain allows considerable discretionary decision-making and freedom of action to economic actors. It provides that taxpayers will pay for much of the economic infrastructure (e.g., education systems, job training, and roads). In exchange, economic actors are supposed to 'deliver the goods' – namely, an adequate standard of living and contributions to infrastructure and the social security system.

This issue is especially significant in view of the increasing loss by global players of their national identity and interest 'both in terms of employees and their willingness to cooperate with the initiatives of their "home" country governments,'[30] including the important area of social security matters.

Will emerging transnational communities include such an implicit social bargain, or are they likely to be used by corporate actors to free themselves from the obligations that had been imposed on them at the national or subnational levels? To secure their long-term legitimacy (and the continued legitimacy of national systems), it would seem rational for transnational actors to ensure that the system they are creating has significant and visible benefits for the groups that it will directly or indirectly affect. It would also seem to be in their long-term interest to back measures that maintain the social support infrastructure generated by national or subnational states. In other words, if the system is perceived as of use only to certain classes and regions – classes and regions that may already be regarded as privileged – and especially if it is perceived as destructive of existing advantages, such as employment and career opportunities or social programs, its formation and expansion will generate social unrest and socially destructive results.[31]

The EU Social Charter is an important step in establishing common rights across member states.[32] Measures adopted to reduce the large economic disparities (the ten wealthiest regions have an average per capita income 160 per cent larger than the ten poorest ones) can also be viewed as an implementation of social rights: in 1991, 27 per cent of the budget of the Union was allocated to the poorest countries to help them catch up.[33] In North America, on the other hand, similar programs barely exist, except for the propaganda campaigns to negate the arguments that transnational organization is a tool of the business/financial class to reduce or remove social programs and that the ideology of competitiveness is simply a way of justifying this course of action.

Contribution to the Collectivity
Citizenship, which defines the nature of membership in a collectivity, involves not just rights but also the willingness to and possibility of helping with the construction, maintenance, and improvement of the collectivity. In national societies, this contribution can take many forms, such as the obligation to pay taxes, participation in voluntary associations, and military service.[34] The forms of contributory participation in a transnational community may be partly the same as in national societies. However, the scope of transnational social systems will probably require the creation of new ways by which citizens can invest themselves and their resources in the evolving new order.

Conclusion

Multiple identities and loyalties are required for the existence and effective functioning of a multi-level system of collective organization.[35] If social identities and identifications operate entirely at one level, the overall structure is likely to be unstable.

Multiple identities and loyalties require that *all* levels of collective organization are meaningfully and positively related to the experience and life conditions of individuals and the groups to which they belong. It was suggested that different types of linkages can exist between individuals and the collectivities of which they are members. One is based primarily on calculations of costs and benefits and results in a utilitarian identification with the collectivity. Another is based on considerations of joint accomplishment based on perceived interdependencies, leading to a 'community of fate' identification with the collectivity. A third is based on a perceived commonality of cultural traits and history leading to a peoplehood identification.

The experience of individuals at the local, regional, national, and transnational levels is likely to differ in significant ways and, as a result, the character of their identification with each level is also likely to vary. For instance, most people do not operate directly at the transnational level, even though that level has important impacts on their lives.

Thus, even if multiple identities occur, they are unlikely to be of the same strength, or of the same nature, at all levels. At the transnational level, they are most likely to be utilitarian initially. The organization of cooperative ventures could eventually foster a 'community of fate' identification. It will take considerable time and symbolic creativity for a sense of peoplehood to be formed at the transnational level. Such identification is more likely to exist only at the national and, in some societies, subnational level.

Generally, the more encompassing the level of organization, the more remote it is from the activities of individuals and the less amenable it is to their social participation. Consequently, the relationships that individuals establish with its structures and managers are generally more indirect. It can then be expected, other things being equal, that a more encompassing level of organization is more likely to involve identities and identifications that rest primarily on calculations of benefits and costs and on the sense of interdependence. The cultural, socioemotional element of commonness will tend to be weak, if not entirely absent.

The growth and maintenance of multiple identities and loyalties also supposes that existing levels of social organization are not perceived to be under economic, political, or cultural threat from another level. If such threat is perceived, opposition to it will tend to rise. Threats can be real: they arise from inequalities between constituent units, from more or less explicit opposition to social programs by certain transnational actors, and from loss of control over critical decisions. They can also arise from the perception that one's subnational or national government (or elites, generally) are not defending one's interests within transnational institutions. The perception of threats can also result from competition between groups and organizations at different levels of the system. In order to gain support, elites may invent threats or exaggerate existing ones and thus foment opposition to groups and organizations at other levels.[36]

A federal structure is probably the most consistent with multiple identities and identifications, because it is designed to embrace entities that retain a certain degree of autonomy. Federalism allows for a mixture of autonomy and integration into a larger system conducive to optimal conditions for the protection and enhancement of each level of collective organization. It is a system that can mitigate existing inequalities (at least if they are not extreme). It is also a regime that permits different types of identities and identifications to exist simultaneously, but at different levels in the overall system.

However, federalism will work only if it is structured in such a way as to deal with issues like power inequalities, conditions for the exercise of citizenship, and conflict-resolution among those with interests rooted in different levels of organizational systems. Because the potential for building identity and identification is different at each level of the collective organization, federalism also implies that different types of identities and identification may possibly emerge at each level. For instance, identification with the federal collectivity and institutions may be primarily utilitarian, while identification at the regional level (provinces, cantons, states) may entail a greater sense of peoplehood. Federalism is also more likely to work and be accepted as legitimate if a sense of peoplehood is not necessarily expected at all of its levels. This would be especially the case for transnational federations, but it may also apply to national federations in highly regionalized or ethnically segmented societies.

Notes

1 Elliott R. Morss, 'The New Global Players: How They Compete and Collaborate,' *World Development* 19 (1991):55-64.
2 The expression 'collective organization' refers to the political, economic, and sociocultural organization of a particular collectivity.
3 Some authors have made the distinction between 'utilitarian' and 'affective' support for a collectivity (L.N. Lindberg and S.A. Scheingold, *Europe's Would-be Polity* (Englewood Cliffs, NJ: Prentice Hall 1970); Miles Hewstone, *Understanding Attitudes to the European Community: A Social-Psychological Study of Four Member States* (London: Cambridge University Press 1986). There is an important prob-

lem with this distinction – namely, it implicitly assumes that people do not become emotional about their utilitarian interests and the organizations to which these are linked. The typology presented here pertains to the content or bases of identification. Each basis of identification – utilitarian, interdependence, and peoplehood – can be laden with emotions, positive or negative. Thus, the utilitarian-affective distinction confounds two dimensions of identification.

4 It should be noted that the cultural distinctiveness in question is that which is perceived by members of the community, not necessarily that which can be 'objectively' described.

5 Similar distinctions have been made by Daniel Katz, 'Nationalism and Strategies of International Conflict Resolution,' in C.G. Smith, ed., *Conflict Resolution: Contributions of the Behavioral Sciences* (Notre Dame: University of Notre Dame Press 1971), 416-44; Harold Guetzkow, *Multiple Loyalties: Theoretical Approach to a Problem in International Organization* (Princeton: Princeton University Center for Research on World Political Institutions 1955); and Bernard Mennis and Karl P. Sauvant, *Emerging Forms of Transnational Community* (Lexington, MA: Lexington Books 1976).

6 William Bloom, *Personal Identity, National Identity, and International Relations* (Cambridge: Cambridge University Press 1990), 61.

7 Peter du Preez, *Social Psychology of Politics* (Oxford: Basil Blackwell 1980); Bloom, *Personal Identity*.

8 Temporary military alliances constitute a different type of organization. The concern, here, is with what could be called societal systems.

9 On this question, see Raymond Breton, 'Collective Dimensions of the Cultural Transformation of Ethnic Communities and the Larger Society,' in Jean Burne et al., eds., *Migration and the Transformation of Cultures* (Toronto: Multi-Cultural History Society of Ontario 1992).

10 Harold Guetzkow, 'Isolation and Collaboration: A Partial Theory of Inter-Nation Relations,' in Smith, *Conflict Resolution*, 401.

11 Euro-barometer data reported by Hewstone, *Understanding Attitudes*, 30.

12 Examples of such programs are those pertaining to regional economic development (INTERREG), research and development capabilities (STRIDE), advanced telecommunication services for less favoured regions (STAR), and the development of the energy potential of regions (Jean-Pierre Husson and Yves Pérez, 'L'Europe industrielle naîtra-t-elle dans les régions,' *Le Monde Diplomatique* (mars 1992):11).

13 Martin Kolinsky, 'The Nation-State in Western Europe: Erosion from "Above" and "Below"?' in Leonard Tivey, ed., *The Nation-State: The Formation of Modern Politics* (Oxford: Martin Robertson 1981), 82-103; Anthony Richmond, 'Ethnic Nationalism and Post-Industrialism,' *Ethnic and Racial Studies* 7 (1992):4-18.

14 One of the changes relevant in the present context involves powerful forces deployed to build or expand national or transnational organizations. Such change involves 'global players shedding their national identities,' and borders losing importance as a result of trade and movements of population, capital, pollution, information, and technology (Morss, 'New Global Players,' 57).

15 Mancur Olson, Jr., 'Rapid Growth as a Destabilizing Force,' *Journal of Economic History* 23 (1963):529-52.

16 The terms ethnocultural and ethnic groups include groups whose distinguishing traits are cultural, linguistic, or racial, and sometimes, religious.

17 Kenneth Westhues, 'Foreign Goods and Nation-States in the Americas,' *Canadian Review for Studies in Nationalism* VII (1980):351-71. On the competition between elites and groups whose interests are rooted in different levels of collective organization for the allegiance and support of citizens, see Raymond Breton and Daiva Stasiulis, 'Linguistic Boundaries and the Cohesion of Canada,' in Raymond Breton, Jeffrey G. Reitz, and Victor Valentine, eds., *Cultural Boundaries and the Cohesion of Canada* (Montreal: Institute for Research on Public Policy 1980), Chapter 3.5; and Bloom, *Personal Identity*, 66-71.

18 Catherine Goybet, 'La Cohésion en Europe: Mythe ou Réalité?' *Revue du Marché commun et de l'Union européenne*, No. 357 (1992).

19 On the impact of international inequalities, see Robert W. Tucker, *The Inequality of Nations* (New York: Basic Books 1977).

20 Bernard Cassen, 'La Casse-tête des langues,' *Le Monde Diplomatique* (février 1993):32.

21 Alexis de Tocqueville, *Democracy in America* (New York: Vintage Books 1954; originally published in Paris 1835).

22 Robert N. Bellah et al., *Habits of the Heart: Individualism and Commitment in American Life* (New York: Harper & Row 1985), 207.

23 T.H. Marshall, *Class, Citizenship and Social Development* (Westport, CT: Greenwood Press 1964); Bryan S. Turner, 'Outline of a Theory of Citizenship,' *Sociology* 24 (1990): 189-217; J.M. Barbalet, *Citizenship: Rights, Struggle and Class Inequality* (Milton Keynes England: Open University Press 1988).

24 Martin Holland, *European Community Integration* (London: Pinter Publishers 1993).

25 Barbalet, *Citizenship*, 1.

26 Tocqueville, *Democracy in America*, vol.1, esp. chapter XVII.

27 Marshall, *Class, Citizenship and Social Development*; Barbalet, *Citizenship*; Turner, 'Theory of Citizenship.'

28 Ronnie D. Lipschutz, 'Reconstructing World Politics: The Emergence of Global Civil Society,' *Millennium: Journal of International Studies* 21 (1992):389-420.

29 In Canada, for example, the demand by some groups that the Constitution explicitly recognize social rights has probably been triggered by the promotion of competitiveness by other groups.

30 Morss, 'New Global Players,' 57.

31 Ibid., 60.

32 Holland notes that 'the great disappointment at Maastricht was the refusal of the UK to accept the idea of a Community Social Charter that was designed to create a uniform basis for the protection of individual and collective rights within the Community.' It was a disappointment, he notes, in relation to social rights in the Community, but also because it was the occasion at which the opting-out principle was introduced into the structure of Community institutions (Holland, *European Community Integration*, 154).

33 Goybet, 'La Cohésion en Europe,' 285.

34 Morris Janowitz, 'Observations on the Sociology of Citizenship: Obligations and Rights,' *Social Forces* 59 (1980):1-24.

35 Harold Guetzkow, *Multiple Loyalties.*
36 Explicit conflicts and external threats, however, are not necessarily required for the construction or reinforcement of a particular level of collective organization, such as a nation state or an ethnocultural group: 'This is because the modern international system provides ever-present images of competition and threat' (Bloom, *Personal Identity*, 74).

4

The New Pluralism: Regionalism, Ethnicity, and Language in Western Europe
Guy Kirsch

Introduction: From Nation States towards One Community and Many Regions

Western Europe is evolving in two opposite directions. On the one hand, the traditional nation states are losing at least part of their sovereignty and competency to the European Union. On the other hand, we are witnessing the renaissance of regional sentiment and loyalty. At a time when Western Europe strives to impose its new-found supranational identity on future history, it is rediscovering its own plurality, as infranational identities from past history are reborn.

The situation is confusing, and one may be tempted to see in it the result of mere chance, the fortuitous outcome of the interplay of unrelated forces. At most, one may see reviving regionalism as a rearguard action against the irresistible progress towards future unification. However, we should resist the temptation to accept so simply obvious and so obviously simple a diagnosis: European unification and regional plurification are not unrelated phenomena which, by chance, exist simultaneously. They coexist simultaneously, because the one cannot exist without the other; they coexist because regional plurification is caused, in part, by European unification, and because regional plurification is a necessary condition for unification. Just as we cannot have one side of a coin without the other, the unity of Western Europe will not be found unless its plurality is actively sought.

It is the contention of this chapter that Western Europe now faces two possibilities: either it considers the renaissance of regional feelings as a nuisance to be ignored and, if necessary, to be crushed, or it regards the new pluralism; as an opportunity to be seized. If it opts for the latter, there is at least some probability that renascent regionalism can be a constructive element in the further integration of Europe. If it opts for the first possibility, there is a very high probability that the emerging new pluralism will turn into a destructive force that will disturb – perhaps disrupt – European unity.

In order not to be hindered by the renascent infranational regionalism, the emerging supranationalism of the European Union must not just tolerate the new pluralism; it must further pluralism.

In order to understand developments in Europe, it is necessary to have a point of reference. For psychological and political reasons, the natural standpoint is the nation state as we have known it for nearly two centuries, for our minds are still used to regarding the nation state as the political prism through which any development, whether in an infranational or supranational direction, is to be seen and judged. For analytical reasons, too, the nation state is a sound reference: the components and relations identified as its cohesive elements by political theory are useful to an analysis of the simultaneous emergence of a supranational entity and infranational collectivities.

A State + A Nation = A Nation State

Although it may sound trivial, it is important to note that it takes two to make a nation state – a nation and a state. If a state and nation do not match, there will be a state without a nation or a nation without a state. We tend to forget that most states in history were not nation states, just as we tend to overlook the fact that in the past and in the present many (most?) nations were, and are, without states. Now, if the nation and the state are the constituent parts of the nation state, it is necessary to examine these elements closely.

The State

The state can be defined as an institution that, on a given territory, claims the monopoly of legitimate power in foreign and domestic affairs and has the potential and the means to enforce its decisions. An organization which has the power to enforce its decisions but which can not legitimately claim the monopoly of authority, is not a state, but a criminal organization. The Mafia is an example. An institution that claims the monopoly of authority, but does not have the power to enforce its decisions, is no state either; it is a would-be-state, like the Soviet Union in the last moments of its existence.

Given that a claim to authority may be more or less far-reaching and that its legitimacy may be more or less (un)questioned, the possibility of enforcing the institution's decisions may correspondingly be more or less complete. We do not simply have a state or not, but a range of possibilities. At the end of the eighteenth century, the Mafia was less of a criminal organization and more of a state than at present, as there was at least some legitimacy to its claim to power. Noriega's Panama, on the contrary, was less of a state and more of a criminal organization.

The value of the power which underlies any state is strictly instrumental, for any state is, as Thoreau puts it, 'the child of expediency and the offspring of calculus.' If the state is not instrumental in achieving certain objectives, it is of no value whatsoever. The core of the state is reason, not emotion. By definition, relations between individuals are pragmatic, with citizens interacting in order to achieve certain desired objectives. They do not interact on the basis of shared sentiment.

The Nation

A nation state requires not only a state, but also a nation. What is a nation? While a great number of definitions have been advanced and discarded, there is one which may be more helpful in discussing the unification and the plurification of Europe: a nation is a group of people who share the feeling they belong together without knowing – in fact without even asking – why and who want to have their own state. This definition implies that:

- A nation can only exist in relation to the concept of the state. There may be and there were states in a world without nations; but there cannot be, and there never have been, nations in a world without states. A group of people who share the feeling that they belong together without knowing why and without asking why, is and remains an *ethnie* as long as the concept of and the desire for a state do not enter their minds.
- The nation is a child not of reason, but of emotion; not of calculus, but of sentiment. In contrast to the state, the nation is by definition irrational. It does not need any articulate reasons to explain the feeling of belonging together. A group of people who know that they belong together because they share the same religious convictions constitute a religious movement or a sect, but they are neither an *ethnie* nor a nation. While a common religion, a common history, or common ancestors may contribute to the feeling of belonging, this is not of importance in the minds of the group members. At most, these elements may express the feeling of belonging together: we share a common history, because we feel that we belong together; we do not feel that we belong together, because we have a common history.
- The nation, in contrast to the state, is not founded on expediency. The nation does not serve any purpose; it is its own objective. We may recall Montaigne's answer to the question why he was a friend of La Boétie: 'Parce que c'est lui, parce que c'est moi.' We are not part of a nation because it gives us healthcare, old age pensions, highways, etc.; we are part of a nation because we are 'we.'
- In the eyes of a member of the group all other members are interchangeable. A member of the group is one's 'compatriot,' whoever he or she may be and whatever individual traits he or she may have.
- The feeling of belonging to a group of people requires that there be other

people whom one regards as 'them.' A tribe living in the rain forest without any contact with 'others' is together, but it does not feel together – that is, its members do not feel that their mutual relationship is something special. How could they, as there is no other relationship? The mutual feeling of belonging together because 'we' are 'we' is stronger the more frequent the encounters are with 'them,' the closer the contact is with 'them,' and the more frustrating are the relations with 'them,' although this does not imply that 'we' necessarily have hostile feelings towards 'them.'

- A nation as a nation can do without a very articulate language. As so much is implicitly understood by the members of the national group, the informational exchange between them can rely on a language which is intensive, but which is not extensive; that is, a nation as a nation will have a language that allows people to say much while talking little. The closer the national group, the stronger will be the mutual feeling of belonging together, and the tighter the relationship, the more intensive will be the language of the group. This language will allow the exchange of very subtle emotional information on a limited number of factual topics between a restricted number of people; it will do justice to the specific details of the present situation, but it will be less able to cope with abstract reasoning. However, the more a language allows the members of an *ethnie* or a nation to say much while talking little to one another, the less it permits an emotional exchange with non-members; the less, also, it permits the exchange of information on factual topics that are not specific to the group and to the circumstances in which they live. People who do not share the feeling that they belong together without knowing and without asking why will have an extensive language. In relation to what they say they will talk a lot, for their language will hardly be able to convey the subtle richness of emotions, and their factual communication will tend to be abstract and to neglect the specific characteristics of the concrete circumstances. Thus, dialects are more intensive than literary languages.

From Nation to State and from State to Nation

If a nation state is to exist, a state and a nation must combine. History gives examples of states creating the accompanying nations; it also gives examples of nations creating the matching states. France is an example of a state which, by introducing, among other things, compulsory military service and compulsory school attendance and by abolishing all feudal ties and loyalties, created 'la nation française.' The aim and, to a lesser extent, the result was that a French baron felt closer to a French grocer than to a German baron, a situation that had been reversed prior to the French Revolution.

The nation did not exist and Louis XIV quite realistically limited his claim to be 'l'Etat.'

Another example of a state that gave birth to a nation is Luxembourg. In 1839, the inhabitants of the territory of the present Grand Duchy of Luxembourg were either hostile or indifferent to the idea of an independent state, but independence was forced upon them by the great European powers. Obliged to accept their own state in an international context characterized by nation states, the citizens had to become a nation, and that is exactly what they did.

Examples of nations giving birth to states can be identified, although contrary to widespread opinion, they do not seem to be very numerous. National legends and myths are no counter-evidence.

Whether a nation gives birth to a state or a state engenders a nation, the nation and the state must combine if there is to be a nation state; the collectivity in which an individual interacts as a citizen with other citizens must be coextensive with the group in which he or she is a compatriot among compatriots. In other words, the rational calculus which underlies the state must not contradict the emotional sentiment that is the essence of the nation, and vice versa. The group of people who share the feeling that they belong together without knowing or even asking why, and who want their own state, must be able to achieve in that state the objectives they want to realize; otherwise the state is not viable. On the other hand, if the citizens of a state do not develop the feeling that they belong together and that they should have a common state, the state is not viable either, at least not as a nation state.

One may wonder if all the nations emerging from the ruins of the USSR will be able to have viable nation *states*; it is highly probable that at least some of them will not meet the rational calculus. The USSR, while a state, was never a *nation* state: her citizens were supposed to interact politically, yet never felt compelled to do so, nor did they ever share a feeling of belonging together without knowing and without asking why. Terror bound them together, and communist phraseology told them why they had to feel that they belonged together. As terror disappeared and as the phraseology withered away, the emotional and physical bonds between citizens vanished. As the citizens did not feel implicitly and unquestioningly that they belonged together, they quite naturally began to separate.

In the nineteenth century, conditions in Western Europe enabled nations to give birth to matching states and enabled states to engender matching nations. The conditions were such that states could no longer exist except as nation states, and at least some national groups were able to attain their own nation states. These nation states largely met both the demands of expediency and the demands of emotional cohesion. Individuals were able to be citizens amongst citizens without neglecting themselves as compatriots, and they were able to be compatriots amongst compatriots without betraying themselves and others as citizens. Although there were numerous and important exceptions, this was undoubtedly the general rule.

The European Union: A Suprastate, No Supranation

In the 1950s, matters changed. Expediency, or the rational calculus, demanded larger political units in the form of suprastate structures and institutions. European integration was initially essentially a child of reason, not of emotion, and to a large extent, still is. Consequently, the European Union is still less a supranational institution and more a supranation-*state* organization. Europeans seek supranation-*state* policy, because it suits their objectives better than a nation state policy; lacking the feeling that from Dublin to Dresden, from Copenhagen to Cagliari they belong together, they do not want a supra*nation* state. One should not be misled by the political rhetoric about European patriotism; if it exists, it certainly does not match the transfer of political competencies from the national to the European level. The European Union to this day is a form of a suprastate, but it is definitely not a supranation.

Individual Europeans (while still being citizens of nation states) are, to a large extent, already citizens of the Union. They are still compatriots in nation states while being hardly, if at all, compatriots in Europe. So it comes as no surprise that it is ever more difficult to have Union policy accepted by those who will be negatively affected by its consequences: as there is hardly any feeling that 'we' belong together, why should a German readily accept obligations to pay for a Greek? For the individual, being a good European citizen means neglecting oneself and others as compatriots. Although rational calculus may justify Union policy in the eyes of individuals (if ever they think about it), the emotional impetus is lacking. Europeans may know why they should act collectively, but they do not feel that they belong together.

This is not only frustrating for individuals, it is also problematic for the European Union. If the thesis is right – that a state organization can achieve cohesion only if people feel that they belong together without knowing why – then the present European Union suprastate will encounter trouble, unless a matching supranation is created. At most, further integration will either become increasingly difficult or, if pushed through, will be ever more perilous for society and ever more frustrating for individuals.

European integration has thus far engendered a limited, but nonetheless very real, suprastate, so that existing nation states have lost at least part of their sovereignty. Although European Union policy is the result of haggling between governments of the different nation states, these states increasingly tend to serve as executive agents of the European Union in their own countries. Once Union decisions have been taken, the authorities and institutions of the different nation states have to implement them, even if they run counter to the interests and preferences of the national citizens. This being so, these citizens inevitably realize that, although they still feel that they belong together without knowing why (that is, although they still have national feelings and still want to manage their own political affairs), they are, to a certain extent, no longer able to do so.

Just as they realize that in the European Union they are already citizens without being compatriots, they sense that they are compatriots in their nation states without still being full citizens. A simple, and simple-minded solution to this twofold disequilibrium would be to increase the emotional involvement of individuals on the European level so as to create a European supranation that might attain the necessary social cohesion. Some propaganda has been made to this end, but the results seem rather modest. Another solution would be to curtail the political competencies of the European Union so as to align them with European feelings. There are some tendencies that strengthen the sovereignty of the nation states, or at least slow down the further transfer of competencies from them to the Union.

Most interestingly, these tendencies do not have the same impetus in all countries. This is no surprise: for small countries such as the Luxembourg, a return to the narrow limits of the former nation state would evidently be a disaster. Therefore, for Luxembourgers the rational and expedient choice is the larger political unit of the European Union, whether they feel European or not. The French have begun to realize that a strictly national – as opposed to a suprastate – policy is too expensive a dream, whereas the British cherish the illusion that a perfectly sovereign nation state is still attainable. Accordingly, the French cautiously favour proceeding with European integration, whereas most British are against it. Not surprisingly, the Germans have the fewest problems with European integration: rational calculus tells them that a transfer of some competencies from the national to the European level is both expedient and less risky to them because of their greater importance in Union decision-making. The Luxembourgers and, to some extent, the French know that they must become, to a certain degree, European citizens, although they are not yet European patriots; the British are convinced that they can afford not to be European citizens, because they are not European patriots; the Germans feel that European citizenship will not seriously conflict with their German sentiments. But even the Germans understand that their state has in part become an executive agent of the European Union; consequently, even they have had to realize that their nation state is something less than a nation *state*.

The Regions: Infranations, No Infrastates

One might argue that, although diminished in their statehood, the European nation states need not necessarily be affected in their nationhood. One might also argue that a nation state may be less of a nation *state* without becoming less of a *nation* state. In the short run, this may be the case and, in recent years, there has been a louder intonation of national(istic) rhetoric and an upsurge in patriotism. Chancellor Kohl's frequent reference to 'unser deutsches Vaterland' is just one example. It is also true that in Europe at present one may hear the piercing cry of chauvinism. But chauvinism is, in most cases, a national feeling that has lost faith in itself, and the most blatant and outrageous chauvinist is, in all likelihood, the most convinced that there exists no group whose members share the feeling of togetherness. It is plausible to assume that the partial dismantlement of the nation *states* impairs the *nation* states.

The Regions: A Rediscovery

It is commonly held that the European nation states were created in the nineteenth century by unified nations wanting their own states: the German 'Volk' striving to have one 'Reich,' the Italian 'popolo' realizing Dante's dream of establishing the 'Republica,' the French 'nation' willing and establishing the 'République une et indivisible.' Unfortunately, history mostly unmasks this view as legend. More often than not the European nation states were created not because one nation wanted its own state, but because one state welded together several groups of people who shared the feeling of togetherness and wanted to manage their own political affairs. This was partly done by blackmail, corruption, and sheer force, as in the case of Bismarck's 'Deutsches Reich'; partly by more subtle and sophisticated means, as in France; partly by terrorism and war, as in Italy. But whatever the means, the creation of different states entailed the violation and suppression of distinct smaller nations: in order to become Germans in a 'Deutsches Reich,' the Bavarians were prevented from being full Bavarians; in order to become 'Français,' the Bretons had to partially renounce being Bretons; in order to become 'Italians,' the Lombards had to partly forget that they were Lombards.

At least superficially, they were able to consent to this sacrifice, and could endure it, as long as they could believe that it was expedient and in their self-interest to join with others in one state. Realizing that the 'République Française' conferred advantages, they did not oppose too violently and too overtly the idea that they were not just French citizens, but had to be French patriots as well. The evident utility of the 'République,' of the 'Reich,' made possible the acceptance, at least superficially, of the reality of the 'nation,' of the 'Volk.' The 'Republica' has never been very convincing as a state, so that Italy has never been unquestionably one nation.

Because, and as far as the nation states have been credible as nation *states*, they have been acceptable as *nation* states. This equation held as long as the nation states had the sovereignty, competence, and the potential to live up to individuals' expectations. As a consequence of European integration, they have lost some of these attributes, and thus one of the main reasons for accepting these states as *nation* states has been weakened. As a result, the old, apparently long forgotten, regional feelings of belonging and together-ness have reappeared. Why must one be a French, or a German patriot, when it is no longer so vital to be a French or a German citizen? It is very plausible to assume that the transfer of political sovereignties and competencies to the European Union has led to the reawakening of old group ties and loyalties. It might be even more correct to say that European integration, by partly dismantling the nation *states*, encourages individuals to cease believing that they live in *nation* states, and accepting that they are Bretons, Lombards, or Bavarians. Alsace rediscovers herself as a nation in her own right, as France loses her importance as a state. Those accepting the disap-pointing fact that their nation has never been really cohesive, may redis-cover the ancient regions. However, for those who cannot accept the disappointment or for whom there is no return to the old regions, chauvin-ism will be tempting. Generally, chauvinism is found among the uprooted individuals of the great cities, rather than among their more deeply rooted country cousins.

Of course, it is an exaggeration to say that this is the whole truth, but this thesis is equally unlikely to be completely wrong. Indeed, looking at the renaissance of the different regions in Europe, one cannot help noticing that these regions tend to coincide with entities that existed in the past, before nation states existed geographically and in the mind. Even where nation state borders cut across old regions, these regions are now trying to renew their identity and their unity in transnational associations. Opponents of Switzerland's joining the European Union argue that Switzerland, in losing (part of) her statehood, will jeopardize her national cohesion since the German-speaking Swiss will turn to the nearby southern Germany, the French-speaking Swiss will draw closer to the neighbouring parts of France, and the Italian-speaking Swiss will feel drawn to Lombardy.

One might argue that the coincidence between the regions of today and the regions of the past is mere chance, and that expediency, calculus, and reason are its progenitors. This opinion is belied by the fact that cooperation today seldom reaches beyond sociosentimental rhetoric. More often than not, people in these regions apparently feel that they belong together and that they should act together politically, but they seldom have either the financial or institutional means to do so, or a clear operational view of the objectives they should jointly realize. Although exceptions may exist, regionalism in Europe is essentially a phenomenon centred on emotion, not reason.

The reality of regionalism supports our theoretical argument: regions are the social space where people feel together without knowing and without asking why, and where they want to manage their own affairs. Unfortunately, until now most of these regions have lacked concrete objectives and the necessary institutional and economic means. According to the foregoing definitions, the regions are oscillating between being *ethnie* and being nations: in other words, the nation states of the past two centuries are losing not only some of their statehood to the supranation *state* of the European Union but also some of their nationhood to the infra*nation* states of the regions. As the European Union is becoming a suprastate without evolving into a supranation, the regions (re)discover themselves as infranations without becoming infrastates.

Xenophobia

There is a further reason why individuals turn away from nation states towards infranation-state regions. As noted above, a nation comprises a group of people who share the feeling that they belong together, and this implicitly means that others are seen as non-members of the group. As a result of European integration, contacts with non-nationals have increased in number, closeness, and intensity. The alien-ness of strangers has become more real to most individuals; consequently, the feeling that 'they' do not belong to 'our' group has become stronger, and so has the feeling that 'we' belong together.

One might have cherished the hope that closer contact between Europeans of different nationalities would contribute to a European feeling of togetherness. While in the long run this may be true, we must realistically acknowledge that, so far, the increase in pan-European sentiment has been offset – most probably more than offset – by an increase in the feeling that 'they' do not belong with 'us.' This is no surprise. Abstract feelings of solidarity towards humankind are easy, but acceptance and tolerance of neighbouring 'others' is much more difficult. A German in Hamburg may be enthusiastic about Mediterranean spontaneity and liveliness and feel that, as a European, he shares the classical Greek heritage – but he may not like the smell of garlic and the stamping rhythm of his Greek neighbours dancing the sirtaki next door. Resurgent xenophobia in Europe is the concomitant of the renascent regional feeling of togetherness, both having the same progenitor, the more frequent and closer interactions with 'them.'

Both are essentially irrational, emotional developments and they tend to run parallel to each other: the more strongly 'we' feel that we belong together, the more 'they' are strangers to our group; the more 'they' are strangers, the more we feel that 'we' belong together.

Extensive Languages and Intensive Dialects
This is not to say that 'we' no longer want to do business with them, or to have practical relations with those towards whom we feel no group solidarity. With the dangerous exception of a relatively small number of chauvinistic hotheads, everybody agrees that expediency requires that we not cut relations with those with whom we have no emotional ties. But those who do business with 'them' do so on a pragmatic level, based on calculus and reason, not emotional involvement. The mode of communication, language in a wider sense, is an extensive one based on computer or business language in which even if you talk a lot, you say little, even if you speak a lot, you hardly convey a rich and subtle content. The consequence is that even those who, for reasons of expediency, welcome relations with 'them' and do not limit their contacts to 'us,' and who have frequent exchanges with many different nationals on different topics, have only superficial exchanges with them that exclude considerations too subtle and too rich to be articulated in the extensive language of business. Although this language may be very useful for doing business, and although individuals may be very proficient in it, they will hardly be able to articulate and convey the richness of their feelings or the subtlety of their emotions by using it. Thus, the social space in which individuals from different groups interact is somewhat stark: they may talk about quantities and prices of goods and labour, but will say hardly anything about the value that the items and the labour have in their minds and hearts. The Germans may be very successful in selling to or buying roses from the French, but Peter will hardly be able to convey to Pierre the existential adventure represented by the sight of a rose.

This shorthand metaphor supports the contention that the international exchanges and encounters facilitated by European integration, while useful and expedient, tend to be emotionally frustrating for those involved. Insofar as one is not only interested in doing useful things in cooperation with others, but also in having emotional interactions, the current international exchanges will generally be at least partly unsatisfactory. Even he or she who has many business acquaintances sometimes needs a friend.

If this is the case, it is to be expected that individuals frustrated by their experience of the chilly world of expediency will look for a land of emotional warmth. It is to be expected that individuals who have talked a lot and said little will look for an interchange where they are understood by others without talking, and where they understand others without listening. It is to be expected that individuals who have had to explain themselves in great detail will search for social intercourse where hardly anything has to be explained, because almost everything that matters is self-evident. The regions, with their ancient infranation-state *ethnie*, are the familiar environments which they seek. Either they completely withdraw from political affairs, turning their backs on the greater European society and confining themselves to the cosy group of people who belong together without asking questions and without knowing answers, or they live in both worlds, being businesslike and impassively expedient in the political spheres of the nation state and the European suprastate, and experiencing emotional exchanges with those in their regions with whom they feel they belong.

This is a somewhat simplified portrayal; however, the logic of developments in Europe should be apparent by now. The suprastate of the European Union has operational, although sometimes unrealistic, objectives and operational, although sometimes dysfunctional, institutions. However, it lacks a group consciousness. In contrast, regions tend to be infranations where people have an affinity with one another but where they rarely have clear political objectives and where, if they do, there are in many cases no institutions to pursue them.

Types of Regions
In keeping with our findings, regionalism in Europe today has a wide variety of manifestations. There are regions where people feel they belong together but where they have no intention of managing their own affairs and of becoming a kind of a state. These are highly emotional *ethnie* which, at best, organize folk festivals and readings in dialect poetry. This kind of region, not being very clamorous, is easily overlooked and plays a negligible role for many Europeans.

Second, there are regions where people want to manage at least some of their political affairs. Many of these regions have rather ill-defined objectives, hardly any institutions, and scant financial means. Consequently, they are obliged to limit their political activities to a manageable sphere, most typically the domain of culture where the fact that people understand one another without talking much very often offsets the deficient institutions and finances. These constraints may even stimulate and facilitate cultural exchange. It is generally only when political activity assumes more ambitious cultural goals that these constraints make themselves felt and political activity is hampered.

Third, there are regions where people feel that they belong together and want to manage all, or at least an important part of their political affairs, striving for a more or less far-reaching autonomy, but where there are neither operational objectives nor functional institutions. These are regions where people want to have their own state of sorts, but where there is no possibility of having one. This is a most dangerous situation: untrammelled by the realities of political action, people in this position tend to lose themselves in increasingly unrealistic visions of what should be done. The emotional temperature within the group tends to rise, making the formulation of operational objectives ever more difficult, and any institution that is established is increasingly inadequate to the grandeur of the vision. This, in turn, spurs on the group members to seek still more luminous and unrealistic phantasms. In Sigmund Freud's words, the 'Lustprinzip,' not being controlled by reality, tends to overshadow the 'Realitätsprinzip.'

This seems to be as good an explanation as any for the degeneration of nationalism into terrorism. For example, MLC (Mouvement pour la libération de la Corse) and ETA (Euzkadi Ta Azkatuta) are characterized by the fact they act illegally, since both are unable to act within the limits of the law. In addition, if they have objectives beyond the short-sighted goals of terrorist action, these goals are vague and unrealistic. Although the case of Northern Ireland is much more complicated, the impression exists that the objectives of the IRA (Irish Republican Army) are not precise or very realistic. This is also due to the fact that, denied the possibility of pursuing any political goals, the Ulster Catholics have no means of developing realistic ones; having unrealistically extreme goals, they are denied the possibility of acting and interacting politically.

Of course, frustrated regional sentiment does not necessarily lead to extremism and terrorism. However, it may at least lead to phenomena such as the 'Leghe' in Italy. This entity has certain objectives and acts within the law, but experience shows that these objectives are at best unbalanced, narrow-minded, and short-sighted, midway between somewhat absurd folklore and rather alarming fanaticism.

This analysis is corroborated by the fact that these distorted regional movements are noticeable only in those countries where centralized nation states deny the regions the means to pursue their objectives, at least in part. Britain and, despite timorous efforts towards decentralization, France and Italy are highly centralized nation states, and naturally regionalism in these countries oscillates between terrorism and absurdity. This is also the situation in Spain as a result of the centralized Franco regime.

Fourth, there are regions where feelings of togetherness are matched by operational objectives and by functional institutions. As a consequence, these feelings tend neither to lose themselves in unrealistic visions, nor to degenerate into destructive aggressiveness. Were it not for the danger of being misunderstood, one might say that in these regions there exist regional states: people feel they belong together without knowing, without even asking why; they want to manage their own political affairs; and they have the opportunity to do so. Federal states such as Germany, Austria, and Switzerland seem immune to the aforementioned distortions. These strong and heterogeneous regional feelings are not fanatical, the objectives pursued are realistic, and the means to pursue them are legal. The emotional temperature that exists between members is moderate and, despite the feeling that 'we' belong together and that 'they' do not, the general result is benign indifference rather than virulent hostility.

The Complementarity of European Unification and Regional Plurification

The importance of the regions has increased, and people active within regions of the second category feel more and more constrained. If these regions are to pass not from the second to the third, but to the fourth category, it is essential to equip them with an institutional infrastructure and so to give them the opportunity to formulate their own operational objectives. This means that at least part of the sovereignty and competencies which have belonged to nation states, or which have already been transferred to the European Union, must be transferred to the regions.

Unfortunately, politics in Europe has almost exclusively focused on the question of what competencies should be transferred to the supranation-state level and what competencies should be left with the nation states. Although there is much discussion in Brussels about what should be done for the regions, hardly anybody ever discusses the question of what should be done by them. So far the institutionalization of the supranation state has hardly been matched by the creation of infranation-state institutions. European policy has been characterized by the creation of suprastate institutions and by almost fruitless attempts to stimulate supranational sentiment. Infranational sentiments have either been neglected or tolerated as harmless niceties to be smiled at, or viewed as harmful nuisances to be repressed. Attempts to give regions an institutional infrastructure in the European context and to assign them a meaningful role are rare and half-hearted.

Despite two world wars, there can be no doubt about the success of the nation state: in all those countries where it has been possible to combine state sovereignty and national sentiment, economic prosperity and social stability have been achieved to an extent that did not exist before and that has not been attained elsewhere. In those countries where state sovereignty has been decentralized in accordance with infrastate sentiments, economic prosperity and social stability tend to be greater than elsewhere. The challenge in Europe today is to make use of the teachings of its own history: what made the nation state a success in the nineteenth century and in the first half of the twentieth century should make European integration a

success, combining, if necessary on different levels, the emotional warmth
of group sentiment with the rational calculus of expediency.

One may wonder why so evidently efficient a solution has not been
implemented. A plausible explanation is that although the European Union
is a supranational organization, the important decisionmakers in the EU are
the governments of member nation states. While some competencies have
been transferred from the national to the supranational level, those in power
in the different nation states share the power of the supranation state.
Consequently, it has been easy for them to accept the idea and reality of
the EU, especially as the EU provides a gorgeous stage on which to display
the 'grandeur' of one's own nation and to demonstrate to one's national
electorate the supranational stature of national politicians, particularly at
'European Summits' with all their pomp and circumstance. At times, it may
even be convenient for national decisionmakers to shelter behind Union
policy so as to avoid being called to account by their national electorates.
Owing to the limited competencies of the European Parliament, the transfer
of political sovereignties to the European Union has allowed national
decisionmakers to evade part of their political responsibility without re-
nouncing their power.

This would not be the case if there were a transfer of political competencies
from nation states to the regions. If regions were given the institutions and
the means to define and pursue their own objectives, national
decisionmakers would shed some of their responsibilities but also lose some
of their power. It is not surprising that they view this as a but modestly
attractive proposition, especially as the loss of power would be twofold: on
the one hand, nation state authorities would have to cede some of their
competencies to infranation-state regions; on the other hand, their position
in relation to other nation states in the European Union would be weakened,
in that they would no longer represent all the interests of their national
societies, only those not taken care of and directly represented by the
regions.

Accordingly, the strongest resistance to further European unification and
regional plurification exists in those countries which are most centralized:
Great Britain, France and, to a lesser extent, Italy and Spain. The self-definition and self-perception of these states is such that a European supranation state and regional infranation states are likewise perceived as mortal
threats. Small homogeneous countries and large heterogeneous, but decentralized countries tend to be much less hostile to unification and plurification.

If ever the regions do achieve greater autonomy in Europe, it will mainly
be due to the initiatives of the regions in decentralized nation states. These
regions have at least some institutions to enable them to define political

objectives; they have at least some means to pursue these objectives; and they encounter fewer obstacles in their respective nation states. As their goals are usually neither maximalist nor unrealistic, the nation states do not perceive them as dangerous threats.

As it is probable that new members will join the EU in the future, including countries that are decentralized, regionalism will have a better chance to develop in the Union. When this opportunity is seized, the Union will have a better chance of prospering. However, the possibility exists that centralized nation states, threatened by the outrageously unrealistic demands of their regions, will try to prevent further transfers of political competencies to the regions. The time may come when European nation states will no longer disagree about only the extent and pace of supranation-state integration, but also about the extent and pace of infranation-state plurification.

5

The Federal Experience in Yugoslavia
Mihailo Markovic

This chapter analyzes the experience of federalism in Yugoslavia: why did the Yugoslav federation fail? The first part reviews the historical experience of federalism and democracy in Central and Eastern Europe. The second part serves to clarify the concept of federalism by distinguishing between federations and centralized states, on the one hand, and federations and confederations, on the other. In the process, this part outlines the major disadvantages of centralized states and confederations. In the context of Yugoslavia, the third part analyses which of the chief difficulties encountered by federalism could be and were overcome, and which difficulties were insurmountable. The final part discusses how the idea of federalism might be rehabilitated by replacing the narrow Eastern European idea of federalism as relevant only to the accommodation of many nations in a single state with a broader idea of federalism.

Historical Experience of Federalism in Central and Eastern Europe

Historically, the countries in Central and Eastern Europe that belonged to the Soviet camp, realized militarily in the Warsaw Pact and economically in Comecon, had almost no experience of federalism. The only exception is Yugoslavia, which did not belong to the Soviet camp after 1948.

This statement is true of federalism in both the broad and narrow senses of the term. Federalism in the broad sense refers to any pluralist political structure that reconciles the autonomy of the parts with the coordination of the system as a whole. In the narrow sense, federalism is seen as a possible solution to the 'national question.' Most of these countries (Poland, Hungary, Romania, and Poland) did not need federalism in the narrow sense as they were more or less homogeneous countries, if national minorities are disregarded. Had they been more democratic, they might have incorporated various aspects of federalism in the broad sense since democracy presupposes not only the autonomy of the individual, but also some degree of autonomy for the various subsystems. However, most of these countries, with the exception of Czechoslovakia, were undemocratic and centralized even prior to the imposition of the one-party political system and rigid state planning.

After its reemergence as a state in 1918, Poland was ruled by military leaders. Marshal Pilsudski seized power in a coup d'état in 1926, abolished the parliamentary system, and ruled as a dictator until his death in 1935. He was succeeded by General (later Marshal) Rydz-Smigly.

In Hungary, the communist revolution led by Béla Kun took place in 1918-19. After it was put down, Admiral Miklós Horthy de Nagybanya, the Commander-in-Chief of the Hungarian 'White Army,' became the head of state and unchallenged leader in 1920. Hungary was declared the monarchy 'with the vacant throne.' After 1933 Horthy and the prime minister Gyula Gömbös approached Hitler's Germany, and in 1937 a Hungarian National Socialist party was formed. This was followed by strict anti-Jewish legislation in 1939 and by Hungary's joining the tripartite pact with Nazi Germany and Fascist Italy.

Both Romania and Bulgaria faced peasant unrest after the First World War. In Romania, an attempt at peasant democracy had failed by 1928, and in Bulgaria, the cooperative movement led by Stamboliiski ended in bloodshed in 1923. The 'Iron Guard,' an extreme right wing, nationalist, and anti-se-mitic movement founded by Corneliu Codreanu, eventually came to power in Romania. More or less dictatorial governments supported by the army and the king, Boris III, ruled Bulgaria from 1923 on. All three countries – Hungary, Romania, and Bulgaria – sided with Hitler during the Second World War.

The cases of Czechoslovakia and Yugoslavia are different. Both were multinational states that had had some experience of federalism and a democratic tradition. As a consequence of their anti-fascist stance, both were invaded by Nazi Germany, in 1939 and 1941 respectively .

Czechoslovakia was formed in 1918 after the Czech leader Tómaš Masaryk guaranteed political autonomy to the Slovaks (13 per cent of the total population). Full parliamentary democracy was introduced. Relations be-tween the Czechs and Slovaks were strained, however, when in 1929 the Slovak leader Vojtech Tuka was accused of conspiring against the republic and sentenced to fifteen years imprisonment. After the German occupation of Czechoslovakia in March 1939, Slovakia formed a pro-German 'independent' state.

Yugoslavia was also formed in 1918, on 1 December, as the Kingdom of the Serbs, Croats, and Slovenes. As regions of the Habsburg Empire, Croatia and Slovenia had been dominated by Hungary and Austria for centuries, whereas Serbia had existed as an independent state since the nineteenth century. Serbia introduced a multiparty system in the 1880s and developed full parliamentary democracy in 1903. In the interwar period, Yugoslavia was organized along unitary, centralized lines, which proved incompatible with the initial democratic institutions of a multiparty system, free elections, and a federal parliament. King Alexander abolished the democratic constitution and introduced a royal dictatorship in January 1929. The Croats, who had fought for federalism not as an end, but as a means to form their own nation state, took advantage of the German invasion of Yugoslavia on 6 April 1941 to establish their own pro-fascist 'independent' state.

The conclusion to be drawn from this brief historical overview is that throughout Central and Eastern Europe, the nations that were liberated from centuries of domination within the Turkish, Ottoman Empire and the Austro-Hungarian Empire felt the urgent need to form their own nation states. A strong leadership able to fight for vital national interests took priority for them over democratic demands. For this reason, they invariably passed through periods of more or less rigid authoritarian rule. Where multinational societies were generated, as in Yugoslavia and Czechoslovakia, they were unable to produce a true federal structure before the Second World War for two reasons. First, the ruling elites of both states took the notoriously centralized French and British democracies as the paradigm. Second, the smaller and weaker nations – the Slovaks, the Croats, and the Slovenes – only pretended to struggle for federalism; for them, federalism was only a way station on the road to their own independent nation state. If this aspiration appears anachronistic in a Europe which is well on the road towards a supranational community, it must be remembered that historical time is not the same for all nations. The Romantic nationalism that has long been obsolete in Western Europe is a reality for those nations in Central and Eastern Europe for which historical time stood still for centuries, their development having been blocked by the powerful foreign elites of premodern empires. The indisputable fact seems to be that federalism is only possible for multinational societies where the constituent nations have already passed through the stage of nation statehood and where a plurality of spheres, organizations, and levels has already been clearly differentiated.

Advantages of Federalism as Compared to Centralism and Extreme Decentralization (Confederalism)

The concept of federalism requires clarification not only because it is often reduced to the narrow context of national relations and not properly distinguished from confederalism, but also because the essential advantages of federalism, as compared to centralism and extreme decentralization (confederalism), are not always sufficiently clear. An examination of these advantages is particularly pertinent since some advocates of federalism for

Central and Eastern European countries themselves happen to live in rather centralized Western European countries such as France and Great Britain.

The four limitations of a centralized system seem to be the following. First, too much power is concentrated in the centre of the system and only partially transferred towards the periphery. Such a *hierarchy* entails a considerable degree of domination. While social contract theory postulates a fictitious delegation of power from the individual citizen to a central political authority, citizens are denied the right to take their power back, a right which would have been permanently assured had they ever really delegated power voluntarily.

Second, one consequence of this hierarchy is a high degree of *heteronomy*. Many issues that do not require a high level of coordination and could, therefore, be regulated by local and regional communities are decided at the federal level. People's representatives are no longer responsible to the electorate in their communities; they are more dependent on the centres of state, party, or corporate power.

Third, the more centralized a system, the more mediation is needed between the centre of power and the citizen. A special social group is needed to play this mediating role – *bureaucracy*. There are, of course, considerable differences between a liberal Weberian and a totalitarian bureaucracy. Yet both overemphasize the value of *order*, thereby frustrating all initiative and spontaneity save that which comes from the centre. The particular interest of bureaucracy and the centre it serves is to maintain the existing order by any means against any 'pathological' deviation, disturbance, or unrest. This particular interest is invariably construed ideologically as the general interest of society. The truth is, however, that creative, innovative decision-making requires wisdom and understanding far beyond mere technological expertise and that to the extent that special technical skills are indispensable, they need not be accompanied by excessive centralization.

Finally, while laying claim to rationality and efficiency, all centralized systems suffer from a particular form of *inefficiency and waste*. Since decisions are taken at a considerable distance from the spot where they are needed, there is all too often a harmful delay. Whatever the apparent gains from uniformity and interrelatedness within a large system, the losses may be overwhelming. The distant centre operates on the basis of scanty abstract information, missing too many psychological factors and lacking an understanding of the specific situation. The centre invariably tends to impose simple, uniform solutions on the entire system. Complex, irregular-looking solutions, however, may better do justice to the diversity of the various parts of the system. Worst of all, waiting for orders from the centre reduces the responsibility of individual citizens and groups; they become passive and alienated, and stop caring about the public good. In that sense, all centralized systems become barriers to citizen initiatives and creative innovation from below.

The rational alternative to centralism, with all the above-mentioned limitations, is not excessive decentralization. The excessive decentralization advocated by some traditional anarchists[1] and some contemporary ecologists[2] proceeds from the assumption that all large systems are intrinsically bad and that all those spheres of modern social life that require them, such as heavy industry, big cities, large sources of energy, and jet transport, ought to be abandoned. Giving up a part of power over nature, they allege, would be a reasonable price to pay for a reduction of authoritarian social power. On the contrary, that price in fact would be unbearably high. Without large technological systems, many legitimate present-day human needs could not be met: the need for adequate information, universal culture, easy travel, direct acquaintance with other civilizations, etc. A lower level of production within small systems would require more labour and would result in greater poverty. The absence of necessary coordination, which characterizes excessive decentralization, leads to disorder, inefficiency, and the waste of natural resources. Social organization on a small scale makes many exceptional human skills redundant. Specialized scientific research, the fine arts, and high-level competitive sports cannot be supported by small, self-reliant communities. Such communities produce narrow parochial forms of life and thought, and offer little protection from domination. Far from small being beautiful, masters in small systems may often be more inconsiderate, irresponsible, arbitrary, and sadistic in face-to-face relationships than those in large systems, where some kind of legal order, no matter how formal, offers a minimum of protection for individual citizens.

Federalism offers a real alternative to both centralism and the excessive decentralization of confederation. Federalism is used here in the most general sense of a complex system (composed of various communities structurally situated at different levels of the system) that meets two conditions: (1) the parts are relatively autonomous, and (2) there is a satisfactory level of coordination within the system as a whole. The stability of each federal system depends on the balance of two opposing forces. One force works towards greater identity and uniformity, while the other maintains diversity and preserves a particular communal tradition and specific cultural values. In the same way that an individual experiences a community as an indispensable social environment within which he or she acts and develops freely, a community willingly accepts a larger social framework as its natural surroundings when it can resolve its specific problems autonomously and participate equally in the solution of problems common to the entire society, and when it can collaborate with other parts on equal terms without being abused or exploited by them.

The foregoing analysis of federalism justifies the view of those political forces in Central and Eastern Europe that see in federalism the only reasonable alternative to, on the one hand, the former authoritarian systems and, on the other hand, the rise of aggressive nationalist movements that threaten the continued existence of multinational states in that region.

The only country in Central and Eastern Europe that opted for federalism after the Second World War and was committed to its preservation and development was Yugoslavia. The Yugoslav experience shows, however, how difficult it is to create the conditions necessary for federalism to function properly and survive over longer periods of time.

The Case of Yugoslav Federalism

In 1945 Yugoslavia was reconstituted as a federal state consisting of six federal units: the republics of Serbia, Croatia, Slovenia, Macedonia, Bosnia-Hercegovina, and Montenegro. Each republic had its own national assembly and government, passed its own laws, and developed its own cultural institutions (universities, academies of arts and science, etc.). In the beginning, 1945 to 1953, too much power was concentrated in the hands of the federal government (federalism with strong centralizing elements). During the period from 1953 to 1971, the autonomy of the units of the federation developed sufficiently to offset the regulatory power of the federal institutions (federalism proper). The 1971 constitutional amendments and especially the new 1974 Constitution gave almost complete sovereignty to the units of the federation; introduced the principle of unanimous decision in the federal assembly, with the delegation from each republic having a veto; and established the principle that in case of conflict between a federal law and a republic law, the republic law would take precedence. The balance between the autonomy of the parts and the regulatory power of the whole was clearly lost; Yugoslavia had taken a fatal step towards the rather unstable confederation that paved the way for the secession of four of the six constituent republics.

The case of Yugoslavia illustrates clearly the main difficulties for any federal system and how they might be resolved. One such difficulty is federal units that vary in size and population. If ordinary democratic rules were applied, a bigger and more populous federal unit would have more representatives and hence more power. This result can be avoided if all federal units, regardless of size and population, send an equal number of representatives to one chamber of the federal assembly. Conflicts between vital interests would then have to be resolved by negotiation and consensus, rather than a simple majority vote. While this may not be the most efficient method of decision-making, it is more rational in the long run since it avoids the build-up of unresolved tensions which later might result in irreparable cleavages.

Another key difficulty for federalism is the gap between the levels of economic and cultural development of the various federal units. Normally the absence of regulation would permit this gap to widen. A federal mechanism must, therefore, be put in place that provides federal aid to less developed federal units in order to close the gap gradually. The point is that this kind of solidarity is not just an expression of humanitarian values but also an expression of justice: a return to the less developed regions of what a market economy takes from them in terms of cheaper raw materials and labour. Furthermore, closer scrutiny shows this form of justice to be a matter of mutual interest. Growing social inequalities among the parts of a federation intensify conflicts and make the federation increasingly unstable and vulnerable. The policy of investing in self-development is much more reasonable and less costly than larger welfare programs with their accompanying waste, bureaucracy, and incentives to remain passive. Parts of a federation that overcome material poverty become better partners in the exchange of goods and services. The environmental policies of more developed federal units would not make much sense if less developed units could not afford to participate.

Yugoslavia managed to solve these two problems by giving equal decision-making power to all six federal units, regardless of size, and by instituting a federal fund for aid to less developed regions. It was unable, however, to solve another formidable problem: when Yugoslavia was formed in 1918, two of its constituent republics (Serbia and Montenegro) had existed as independent nation states for nearly a century. They were ripe for a supranational community. More specifically, they were ready to exchange their ethnic identity for a new, common Yugoslav identity. They were ready to call their language Serbo-Croatian, and they accepted the partial incorporation of their original national symbols (national anthem, flag, coat of arms) into the new symbols of the Yugoslav nation.

The situation was completely different in the other four federal units, especially in Croatia. The Croatian nation, with nearly five million people, was the second largest in Yugoslavia. It had spent more than eight centuries as part of Austro-Hungary, dominated first by Hungarians (1102-1526) and then by Austrians and Hungarians (1526-1918). It preserved a vivid memory of a glorious medieval state which in the 10th and 11th centuries was among the most powerful in the Balkans. During the period of Romantic national awakening in the second half of the 19th century, the Croats developed two alternative national ideologies. One was Yugoslavism advocated by Bishop Strossmayer of Diakovo: the idea of uniting the southern Slav people to form an autonomous southern Slav state within the Habsburg Empire. The other national ideology was the extreme Croatian nationalism advocated by Ante Starcevic, which rejecting Austro-Hungarian domination, aimed instead to assimilate the numerous Serbs who since the fifteenth century had lived in the areas bordering on the Turkish, Ottoman Empire and to constitute an independent Croatian nation state.

In 1918, few Croats were truly willing to join a sovereign Yugoslav state dominated by the larger Serbian nation. However, a sovereign Yugoslav state was the only way to get rid of Austro-Hungary, to avoid the payment of heavy reparations as a part of the Central Powers defeated in the First World War, and to retain the Dalmatian coast which the victorious Entente Powers in the 1915 secret Treaty of London had promised to Italy in exchange for her entry into the war on the side of the Entente. In addition, Croatia by itself was defenceless in the face of the social revolution that was approaching from Hungary and Bavaria in 1918. A victorious Serbian army was the only effective defence.

Yugoslavia was formed in 1918 as a unitary centralized state. The Croatian demand for a federal structure was unsuccessful. The truth was, however, that for the strong nationalist forces that had developed in Croatia, federalism was only a first step towards the desired disintegration of Yugoslavia and the formation of a sovereign Croatian nation state, the goal for which Croatian politicians and intellectuals would work throughout the entire seven decades of Yugoslav history. Croatian nationalist forces were temporarily successful during the Second World War with the Nazi-supported independent State of Croatia. They subsequently developed a powerful separatist movement which Tito suppressed in 1971, and eventually managed to secede in 1991 when Yugoslavia found itself in a deep political and economic crisis.

Like the Croats, the Slovenes had been without a nation state for centuries. The most developed federal unit of Yugoslavia, Slovenia also gave rise to a powerful separatist movement and seceded in June 1991.

The Macedonians lived under Ottoman rule until 1912, when the four allied Balkan states of Serbia, Montenegro, Bulgaria, and Greece defeated Turkey and expelled it from the peninsula. Only after the Second World War were the Macedonians recognized as a separate nation with the right to an autonomous existence as one of the six federal units in Tito's Yugoslavia. Macedonia was ready to remain in the federation, but once Croatia and Slovenia seceded in 1991, it decided to follow suit.

Bosnian Muslims, the south Slavs who accepted Islam during the period of Ottoman rule in Bosnia and Hercegovina, were recognized as a nation only in the late sixties. They are the largest ethnic group in Bosnia and Hercegovina (other major ethnic groups are the Serbs and Croats), yet they make up only 39 per cent of the total population and occupy less than a quarter of the territory. Like the Macedonians, the Bosnian Muslims initially preferred to remain part of the Yugoslav federation, but once the disintegration of Yugoslavia had begun, they also opted to secede and form a sovereign, predominantly Muslim state.

The Yugoslav experience supports the thesis formulated in the first part of this chapter that one basic condition for a viable federal state is that all of its constituent parts must have passed through the historical stage of nation statehood. A federal community comprised of some units that are ready for a supranational association and other units that crave nation statehood will not be stable in the long run. During a state of general economic crisis, the forces of disintegration will tend to become overwhelmingly strong.

Citizenship and Democracy in Federalism

A major unresolved conceptual – therefore, also practical – problem with Eastern European federalism is that federalism is most often understood in the narrow sense of a political system applicable to *multinational* societies such as Yugoslavia, Czechoslovakia, or the former Soviet Union.

Thus understood, federalism tends to make national identity and national interest the focus of all social considerations. The subtle and necessary balance between the individual and the ethnic, on the one hand, and the ethnic and the supranational, the universally human, on the other, tends to be dangerously disturbed: priority is inevitably given to ethnicity.

The imbalance begins with the very legitimate demand that all nations regardless of size must be equally represented in one of the chambers of the federal assembly. This demand is legitimate so long as it is only a corrective to the democratic principle of 'one citizen, one vote.' Otherwise the representatives of larger nations could regularly outvote those of the smaller nations in the house of representatives. If, as a result of this demand, the smaller nations are over-represented in the other house, some form of senate, they can use the veto power or some similar device to defend their vital interests. (Which national interests would be considered vital would have to be specified by law, if not by the constitution.)

Up to that point, the balance between individual citizen's identity and ethnic identity would be preserved. However, civil society and liberal democracy came late to Central and Eastern Europe with its big premodern empires – the Habsburgs, Ottomans, and Romanovs – and did not have time to put down strong roots. At the time when nationalism became obsolete in the West, it grew stronger in this part of Europe, especially since the narrow Eastern European conception of federalism was fertile ground for nationalism.

The principle of national self-determination increased in importance and eventually came to take priority over all other political principles. The cultural and political autonomy of federal units tended to be accompanied by an increasing emphasis on economic self-sufficiency. On the one hand, the development of a strong, integrative, unifying force within each federal unit tends to downgrade, subordinate, and eventually resolve subnational identities. On the other hand, the same nationalist movement, struggling for a closed, self-reliant national economy, would increasingly assume a disintegrative economic role with respect to the federal state and the federal economic system.

A major step in a dangerous political direction is the demand to eliminate altogether the role of citizenship and the electoral principle of 'one citizen, one vote.' The usual justification for this undemocratic demand is that the representation of individual citizens coupled with the majority vote rule permits the larger nation to dominate the smaller ones. In fact, once the entire political system is based only on the representation of nations, the way is open for a coalition of smaller nations to control and dominate the larger one.

The irreparable damage done to the entire system consists of the fact that once federalism gets rid of institutions based on the representation of individual citizens and the majority vote rule, it parts company with democracy and becomes irrational and inefficient. A citizen who gives up his civil rights for the sake of a particular national interest is no longer a democratic being. Civil rights and universal principles of ethics are sacrificed to the idea of national unity. Any individual act that disrupts this unity, no matter how morally justified, is treated as a betrayal of the people. With this homogenization within federal units, rational and efficient decision-making within the federal state as a whole becomes impossible.

A good example of this is Yugoslavia's failure to come up with a federal stabilization program in the early eighties, when the economic crisis had just started and when, to an outsider, Yugoslavia still seemed in reasonably good shape. Some of the top Yugoslav experts prepared a program that could have saved the economy and the country. The program in its general form was accepted unanimously. When the program was made operational and various specific bills were proposed to the federal assembly, the various bills were all killed by the veto of one or other of the federal units. At that moment in 1988, it became clear that the federation was doomed.

The idea of federalism can be rehabilitated if we reinterpret it. If it is narrowly conceived as merely a structure of national relations, abstracted from any demands of individual civil rights and democratic leadership, federalism can degenerate, as we have seen, into an unstable and pathological multinational society.

Federalism in a richer, more complex sense presupposes the prior development of a modern civil society and the existence of democratic institutions as well as a democratic political culture. The generic meaning of the term is still 'autonomy of the parts and a rational coordination within the whole,' but the parts are understood not as nationally homogeneous federal units but as any specific sphere of activity and any segment or level of social organization. A large corporation, a university, a radio and television network, a trade union, and a political party all may have a federal rather than a centralized or a loose decentralized structure. That means that individual factories of a corporation, university departments, individual radio and television stations, particular locals of a trade union, or regional and local organizations of a political party each would have a reasonable degree of autonomy and self-sufficiency, while the centre would retain the role of general regulation and coordination, rather than that of directing all operations of the entire system right down to the last detail.

The important point in this conception of federalism is the existence of autonomy at every level. We saw that where the conception of federalism was reduced to national relations, the autonomy of a federal unit was jealously guarded from the incursions of federal institutions, while autonomy was often not permitted to the regions and local communities within these same federal units. The need for inner unity and cohesion was overemphasized in order to achieve a more competitive position with respect to other federal units. National identity was given absolute, irrefutable priority over any other kind of identity.

In contrast, federalism in a broad and democratic sense permits and tolerates different kinds of identities: the identity of a local community, of a particular school within a university, of a particular trade union local, or of a particular local party organization. Here democracy goes hand in hand with federalism since none of these identities is suppressed, and the individual citizen knows that he has the right to act in all those different ways and to belong to all those different organizations. Now we begin to realize that federalism in this broader and richer sense permits a greater degree of democracy than any centralized arrangement.

Centralism is compatible only with *negative* freedom and *representative* democracy. An individual is *free from* any external impediments (except the law) to the realization of his individual desires and aspirations. Democracy exists in the sense that the individual is invited to consent to the election of one of a number of competing elites. In Robert Dahl's view,[3] this is a *polyarchy* – the rule of one among several elites – rather than a *democracy* in the true sense of government by the people.

Federalism with its multi-level autonomies opens the space for participatory democracy. Since the centre does not impose an explicit, detailed order, but produces instead a general regulatory framework to be filled by the autonomous activity of subsystems, individuals who act within the system have a chance to participate in decision-making and in the actual running of the subsystem to which they belong. This participation helps to reduce the level of alienation experienced by individual producers and members of organizations, which is inevitably present in all large systems. The freedom of the individual tends to become *positive*: an individual citizen and producer is not only protected from tyranny and abuse, he also becomes free to take part in public decision-making and to realize his own projects.

In that sense, federalism has a future. The further development of democracy will bring about increased possibilities for individual participation. By providing a reasonable degree of autonomy in its various levels and subsystems, federalism will offer the necessary conditions for an increasingly free and creative play of human powers.

Notes

1 For example, William Godwin, *Enquiry Concerning Political Justice and Its Influence on Morals and Happiness*, 1st ed. 1793, ed. F.E.L. Priestley (Toronto: University of Toronto Press 1946).
2 See, for example, the work of Rudolph Bahro, such as *The Alternative in Eastern Europe* (London: NLB 1978).
3 Robert Dahl, *Polyarchy: Participation and Opposition* (New Haven CT: Yale University Press 1971).

6

Questions of Citizenship after the Breakup of the USSR
Vsevolod Ivanovich Vasiliev

This chapter evaluates the potential of various legal arrangements to realize the individual's right of identity by providing a free choice of citizenship and guaranteeing the fundamental rights of those who are citizens of a state other than the state in which they live. While these arrangements are discussed in the context of the breakup of the Soviet Union and the future of the Russian Federation, they may apply more generally to confederal structures and to those federal states that contemplate the citizenship of a constituent part in addition to the citizenship of the federation as a whole. The Soviet Union and now Russia, both multinational federations, also offer two concrete instances of the more abstract problems of inclusion and exclusion created by the intersection of borders – both internal and external – and national consciousness.

The first two parts deal with the acquisition of citizenship and the rights of non-citizens respectively in a post-federal structure, that is, the three Baltic states and the Commonwealth of Independent States. The third part examines these issues in the context of the Russian Federation.

Introduction
With the breakup of the USSR, the processes by which the inhabitants of the former republics establish their identity, the extent and means of exercising their civil rights, and the possibilities for reconciling various interests have become extraordinarily complicated. Questions of citizenship, that is, the mechanism for developing a reliable legal link between the individual and the state, have come to the fore.

Who am I? Of what state am I a citizen? Where, in what state, in which of the former Soviet republics, do I want to live? For millions of individuals, these questions are becoming ever more pressing, and finding answers to them is no simple matter. Some want to live where they have always lived, but at the same time to be a citizen of another state, that is, of another former republic of the USSR. Others hope to acquire new status on the basis of their permanent residence. Still others emigrate in the hope that the host country will grant them citizenship. And everyone, naturally, expects to enjoy the full complement of social, economic, and political rights. This problem is particularly acute for the more than twenty-five million Russian-speaking people who now reside outside Russia's borders.

The solution to the problem depends, of course, on many things – political realities, economic conditions, and moral imperatives. Nevertheless, it is the legal guarantee, the timely passage of the necessary laws and their strict implementation, that is most essential.

Citizenship

Dual Citizenship
By now, almost all the states, that is, the former republics of the USSR, have adopted new laws on citizenship. The current political situation is taken into account; the new laws treat many issues differently from the old laws of the Union and its republics. In this connection, it is notable that the laws of some states recognize dual citizenship. The institution of dual citizenship is most clearly regulated by the Russian act.[1] The Russian Federation seeks to use this law to defend the numerous Russians that find themselves 'abroad' due to circumstances beyond their control.

It is probably unwise, however, to place much hope in the institution of dual citizenship. After all, dual citizenship results from the cooperation of two states. It is possible only on two conditions: first, both states must permit it in principle and second, they must agree on the actual content of the rights and duties of dual citizens. Dual citizenship thus does not arise automatically. Both conditions are difficult to satisfy, particularly if one takes into account the current relations between the states that formerly comprised a united Soviet state. The appeal of the Fifth Extraordinary Congress of Peoples' Deputies of the Russian Soviet Federative Socialist Republic (RSFSR) to the parliaments of the 'nearby foreign' states to legislate the right to dual citizenship 'such that representatives of national minorities, being citizens of the republics in which they reside, would have the right also to acquire RSFSR citizenship'[2] met with a mixed response. If, for example, the Law on Citizenship of Turkmenistan,[3] adopted after the RSFSR Congress of Peoples' Deputies, recognizes dual citizenship, the analogous law of Uzbekistan[4] rejects the notion.

Obviously the discernible, if still weak, tendency towards closer relations between a number of these sovereign states cannot overcome their striving to strengthen their sovereignty, whose principal attribute is a distinct citizenship. After all, it can hardly be expected that all the former republics will agree to a situation in which hundreds of thousands, perhaps even millions, of their citizens will simultaneously enjoy the citizenship of another state with the concomitant right to be defended by that state.

Clearly dual citizenship must be the exception, rather than the rule. Moreover, as centuries-old international practice has shown, dual citizenship results in legal problems because the civil rights protected by law differ from state to state. The legal defence of dual citizens gives rise to complicated collisions. Since the last century, a number of international treaties aimed at preventing such collisions have been concluded; they tend generally to minimize the possibilities for acquiring dual citizenship.

Facilitating Acquisition of Citizenship for Citizens of the Former USSR

Another way of guaranteeing citizens' freedom of identification after the breakup of the USSR is to make it easier for citizens of one state that was formerly a Soviet republic to acquire the citizenship of another such state. Such an approach is taken in the Russian Federation Law on Citizenship of 28 November 1991.[5] In Russia today, having been a citizen of the former USSR is one of the conditions that facilitates the acquisition of Russian citizenship.[6] This is one way to ensure the rights of an individual who wants to return to her homeland, but finds herself, due to circumstances beyond her control, on the territory of another state that was formerly part of the USSR. This norm is undoubtedly a humane one that corresponds to the moral imperatives of the world community.

However, the laws on citizenship passed in a number of member states of the Commonwealth of Independent States (CIS) and especially those passed in the Baltic countries take a different approach. In an attempt to strengthen their independence, these states read their own meaning into the notion of citizenship, stressing the break of their new state institutions with the continuity of citizenship of the former USSR, which naturally weakens the previous links between the republics of the former Union. In some cases, the severe limitations on the recognition of citizens and the acquisition of citizenship have been received negatively not only by a majority of Russians, but also by the world community, as represented in particular by international human rights organizations.[7]

A letter of 4 November 1991 from the executive director of Helsinki Watch, Jeri Laber, to the chair of the Latvian Supreme Council, Anatolis Gorbunovs,[8] strongly recommended to the Latvian Supreme Council that it not pass the draft law on citizenship, which, in Laber's words, 'denies citizenship to people who, until August 21, 1991, were considered citizens in Latvia and enjoyed the full rights and privileges that citizenship confers.' The letter appealed to the Latvian parliament not to abridge the rights of people who settled in Latvia before the declaration of independence, were good citizens, and could not have foreseen the circumstances that would alter their legal status. Laber's letter underlined the draft law's violation of a number of provisions of the Document of the Copenhagen Meeting of the Conference on Security and Cooperation in Europe (CSCE) and the International Covenant on Civil and Political Rights. Disagreeing with the conclusions of Helsinki Watch, however, the deputies of the Latvian Supreme Council were publicly critical of the letter and are now preparing to issue a newly act that has the potential to exacerbate relations between nationalities still further.

The situation in Estonia is analogous. There too, what is being implemented is essentially a systematic policy of forcing out the Russian population on a 'legal' basis. 'We have the right, as sovereign states, to establish the conditions for acquiring citizenship,' say some Latvian and Estonian politicians. Indeed, universally applicable international law documents, such as the 1928 Bustamente Code and the 1930 Hague Convention Concerning Certain Questions relating to the Conflict of Nationality Laws, provide that it is for each state under its own laws to determine who its citizens are. Arguments about the uniqueness of the situation created by the breakup of the Soviet Union or the dramatic situation faced by hundreds of thousands of completely innocent people have no effect on Estonian and Latvian state officials. Such arguments have no meaning for politicians who defend the 'national idea' and take into account the interests of social groups depending on their ethnicity. Nationalism, which has become a reality in the Baltic states as well as in a number of other former republics of the USSR, continues to play a decisive role in determining the fate of a significant part of the local population, limiting or completely eliminating their opportunity to choose their citizenship freely.

Bilateral Agreements with the Baltic States
What is the solution? For the Baltic states, it lies in bilateral agreements with the former republics of the USSR, above all with Russia which accounts for more emigrants to the Baltic than any other republic. An example of the form that such a treaty might take is the treaty on the fundamentals of interstate relations between the RSFSR and the Lithuanian republic ratified by the Russian parliament in January 1992.[9] This treaty facilitates the acquisition of Lithuanian citizenship, in particular, for persons with the right to RSFSR citizenship who prior to 3 November 1989 resided permanently on Lithuanian territory and have a permanent place of employment or other legal source of support in Lithuania.[10] For these persons, the requirements of a residency period, knowledge of Lithuanian, and several other conditions for the acquisition of Lithuanian citizenship have been removed.

It is true that in comparison with Estonia and Latvia, Lithuania is a special case. The demographic situation in Lithuania does not threaten the predominance of the 'titular' nation; 80 per cent of the population is ethnic Lithuanian. In Estonia and Latvia, the 'native' population is smaller. There is, therefore, less hope that these states will adopt the Lithuanian approach in their treaties. All the same, the Russian government is seeking to defend the rights of the local population regardless of its nationality. To be sure, the former USSR engaged in imperialist politics and disregarded the vital interests of the republics, long populated by their own nationalities, but millions of ordinary people should not be made to pay.

What is being suggested here is the refinement of the treaties concluded by Russia with Estonia and Latvia, and perhaps even their reexamination. In all cases, what is called for is the expeditious conclusion of supplementary agreements that guarantee the just resolution of issues relating to citizenship and the freedom to choose one's citizenship. Additionally – and possibly most importantly – mechanisms must be developed that would guarantee the fulfilment of treaty obligations. These might include the creation of bilateral structures, either temporary or permanent, to supervise the implementation of these obligations, and political and economic measures available to either side in the event of breach.

Joint Action by the CIS Member States
Insofar as the Baltic states are not part of the CIS, it would seem unrealistic to plan on their participation in the collective agreements concluded by the member states of this organization. As regards the participants in the Commonwealth, joint action on the resolution of citizenship questions is also a possibility. Of course, a common CIS citizenship is a long way off, if indeed it will ever come to pass. At present, the issue is rather whether member states of the CIS can reach a solution that will enable all those who were formerly Soviet citizens to opt for citizenship in any of the CIS member states. The issue, in other words, is whether the principle contained in the RSFSR Law on Citizenship can be made universal.

Rights of Foreigners and Stateless Persons

Current Situation
In creating the Commonwealth of Independent States from the debris of the USSR, political leaders gave little thought to what would happen to the citizenship of the former Union. Although by then the problem was already readily apparent, they skirted it, limiting themselves to general statements about human rights. What was not resolved then falls to be resolved now, with the difference that any initiative taken now must overcome the inertia

that has harmed millions of people. At the same time, this initiative does not relate only to the limitation of the rights of inhabitants of former Soviet republics to choose citizenship in one of the newly independent states. Even allowing for the positive effect of the interstate agreements that have been or will be concluded, in the near future numerous groups in the newly independent states will remain either without citizenship or with the citizenship of another state. What are their rights? How do these relate to the rights of citizens of a given state? The answers to these questions paint a far from rosy picture. What follows are some examples.

In the republic of Moldova, to be entitled to a pension, a citizen must have been permanently resident in Moldova on the day of that republic's declaration of independence. Foreigners or stateless persons receive a pension only if two-thirds of the required length of service consisted of work in that republic.[11] Such practice contrasts sharply with, say, that established in Kazakhstan whose law[12] gives foreigners and stateless persons the right to choose between the pension regime under the law of the Kazakh SSR or the old USSR law On Pension Security for Citizens in the USSR.

The laws of some CIS member states define rights such as property rights (for example, land rights) and rights in the area of entrepreneurial activity only with respect to their own citizens.

Proposal for a Multilateral Agreement
between CIS Member States
In order to ensure the equal application to all inhabitants of the CIS member states of the right to work, the right to housing, and other socioeconomic rights – not to mention the right to life which, for many people, is threatened in Nagorno-Karabakh, Georgia, Tadjikistan, North Ossetia, Ingushetia, and a number of other hot spots in the former Soviet Union – consideration should be given to concluding an appropriate multilateral agreement between these states. (As regards states that are not part of the CIS, here again, the only realistic option is bilateral treaties.) The protection of the rights of foreigners under this agreement will achieve essentially the same goals as the protection of the right to acquire citizenship.

True, the question of political rights (the right to take part in elections, to occupy public office, and to engage in other forms of political activity) arises. Ordinarily foreigners and stateless persons do not enjoy such rights. The post-Soviet situation, however, is unusual and must be taken into account: until recently, we were all citizens of a single state and we cannot immediately rid ourselves of the mind-set of full equality within that state. Nevertheless, progress would be made even if the agreement provided only for socioeconomic rights. The right to life, a dignified existence, is after all the most fundamental for the individual.

The moral arguments in favour of such an agreement are obvious. The Declaration on the Human Rights of Individuals who are not Nationals of the Country in which they Live,[13] adopted by the UN General Assembly in December 1985, may serve as the legal basis for this agreement. Drawing on this Declaration, the agreement might include, for example, the following basic propositions:[14]

- reference to the Universal Declaration of Human Rights and the International Covenants on Human Rights, which establish the principles of nondiscrimination, as well as the right of each individual to recognition as a person before the law
- a definition of the term 'alien' as any person who is not a national of the given state
- the sovereign right of each state to promulgate laws and regulations concerning the entry of aliens, the terms and conditions of their stay, and the differences between nationals and aliens; at the same time, such laws and regulations must correspond to the fundamental principles and norms of international law, in particular those in the field of human rights
- the establishment of the principle that the only condition for conferring on aliens resident in the country the rights and freedoms provided for in the agreement are the legality of their presence on the territory of the state and the observance by them of the laws and other regulations of the given state
- complete equality of aliens and nationals of the state in which they are present in relation to:
  - the right to life and security of person
  - the right to protection against arbitrary or unlawful interference with privacy, family, home, and correspondence
  - the right to be equal before the courts and other organs administering justice
  - the right to choose a spouse, to marry, and to found a family
  - the right to freedom of thought, opinion, conscience, and religion
  - the right to retain their own language, culture, and traditions
  - the right to transfer abroad earnings, savings, or other personal monetary assets, subject to domestic currency regulations
  - the right to leave the country
  - the right to freedom of expression
  - the right to peaceful assembly
  - the right to own property alone as well as in association with others, subject to domestic law
  - the right to liberty of movement and freedom to choose their residence within the borders of the state
- an alien cannot be deprived of his or her lawfully acquired assets

- an alien lawfully in the territory of a state may be expelled therefrom only in pursuance of a decision reached in accordance with law
- individual or collective expulsion of such aliens on grounds of race, colour, religion, culture, or national or ethnic origin is prohibited
- aliens lawfully residing in the territory of a state shall also enjoy, in accordance with the national laws:
  (a) the right to safe and healthy working conditions, fair wages, and equal remuneration for work of equal value without distinction of any kind
  (b) the right to join trade unions and other organizations or associations of their choice and to participate in their activities
  (c) the right to health protection, medical care, social security, social services, education, rest, and leisure, provided that they fulfil the requirements
- any alien shall be free at any time to communicate with the consulate or diplomatic mission of the state of which he or she is a national.

Other Means of Protection

Of course, the conclusion of such an agreement requires considerable preparation and, in any event, may be impeded by political obstacles. Consideration should, therefore, be given to less radical organizational and legal means of protecting the rights of the population on the territory of states that are former republics of the USSR, first and foremost the CIS member states (such options being more realistic for them than for the separate Baltic states).

The Declaration on the Social Welfare of Citizens of the Member States of the Interparliamentary Assembly, adopted by the Assembly on 16 September 1992[15] in Bishkek, is a first step in this direction. Further progress might consist of joint decisions taken not on the entire range of socioeconomic rights, but on groups of rights or even on individual institutions. At present, for example, it is extremely important to reach firm agreement on the level of pension security guaranteed to citizens of CIS member states. It is the most vulnerable part of the population of the former USSR that suffers from the absence of such an agreement. Another obvious possibility would be to recognize the operation of the old USSR legislative acts governing the socioeconomic rights of citizens on the territory of the CIS member states for a specified period of time.

Furthermore, it is extremely important to secure the implementation of the treaties already concluded. This objective would be served, in particular, by the creation within the CIS framework of adjudicatory bodies with the power to take measures to redress violations of citizens' rights guaranteed in the agreements concluded.

Citizenship in the Russian Federation

Different Approaches
Particularly significant are the problems of citizenship within the Russian Federation itself. They are part of a series of problems on which the fate of Russia as a single entity depends.

The old RSFSR Constitution, frequently amended but still in force, and now the constitutions of the former autonomous republics provided and continue to provide for citizenship in these republics together with RSFSR citizenship. For a long time, this institution had purely formal, decorative significance as was the case with many other attributes of the Russian Federation, whose subjects were considered national-state formations of the 'highest level.' Once the transformation of autonomous republics into sovereign states had begun, however, the institution of citizenship acquired real political and legal content.

Some experts term Russian Federation citizenship 'joint,' as opposed to dual, in order to underline the fact that such citizenship combines two citizenships within the framework of a single federal state, whereas dual citizenship involves citizenship in two states that are not joined by federal ties.

Joint citizenship, it is suggested, is a construct entirely appropriate to the republics within the Russian Federation. Admittedly, it can be understood otherwise, as it is by some former autonomous formations. Their view of joint citizenship depends on how they see their place in the new Russian state.

The recently adopted Constitution of Sakha (Yakutia)[16] fully resolved the problem of citizenship. 'The Republic of Sakha (Yakutia),' it reads, 'has its own citizenship. A citizen of Yakutia is a citizen of the Russian Federation.' This is the position of a republic that is content with its new economic and political opportunities and that preserves its traditional close ties with all of Russia. Judging from their draft constitutions, several other republics intend to resolve the problem of citizenship in the same way.

But this is not the only possible solution. The Constitution of Tatarstan[17] provides for its own citizenship along with not only Russian Federation citizenship, but the citizenship of any other state; that is, the constitution contemplates both joint citizenship and dual citizenship in the proper sense of the term. This arrangement evidences, in addition to an intent to acquire the trappings of state sovereignty, a tendency to claim special status within the Russian Federation, one with greater independence than other sub-state units.

Finally, yet another variant of citizenship is found in the Constitution of

Chechnia,[18] which mentions neither RF citizenship nor dual citizenship. One may surmise that in this case the institution of citizenship is intended to solve the problem of secession from Russia.

From the perspective of citizens' rights (which is the most important perspective), it is reasonably certain that under current political conditions in Russia as a whole and in its constituent republics, none of these approaches would, by itself, guarantee the observance of international standards. The official policy and legal doctrine of a number of the constituent republics of the Russian Federation (as well as some of the CIS member states) manifest a nationalist bias and recognize the priority of the 'root nation.' Consequently, the observance of the rights of the person and the citizen without regard to nationality and other characteristics, as enunciated in the Universal Declaration of Human Rights, is threatened, and opportunities arise to discriminate against such groups as non-native speakers, recent immigrants, and persons of other religious beliefs.

It is entirely possible that despite the Federal Treaty,[19] other republics may pass laws on citizenship that contradict the all-Russian legislation by restricting the ability to become a citizen by persons who do not belong to the root nationality. Alternatively, while formally observing the Russian Federation law on citizenship, the republics may undermine the law, for example, by their interpretation of its formula that citizens of the republic are persons that are permanently resident there. What does 'permanently resident' mean? The republic may lengthen the period of permanent residence for the majority of immigrants and shorten it for those belonging to the root nation.

Nor may the socioeconomic rights of citizens and those who do not acquire citizenship be identical. Similarly, the subjects of political rights may be determined by citizenship so as to ensure the superiority of persons who belong to the titular nation; an example might be conferring citizenship on persons of the root nationality living outside the republic and giving them the right to vote by mail.

Policy Considerations

Of course, Russian leaders have at their disposal a number of means for legally resolving the problem of citizenship in the republics, including those involving the use of force. Realistically, however, it must be recognized that the procedure for conferring citizenship in the republics and the content of the institution itself must be optimal not as such, but in the context of the national and social policy of the federal powers, and optimal in observing the rights of the person and in securing that person's interests. The most important task, therefore, is to realize the potential of the Federal Treaty. It is entirely possible that the renewal of the Russian Federation will play a positive role in solving many problems of the identification of individuals, including those problems relating to choice of citizenship.

It must also be remembered that along with the rights and freedoms of the individual and the citizen, which determine the general political regime in the Russian Federation, the rights of citizens belonging to national minorities and the rights of these very national minorities themselves may be distinguished. Ethnic groups in Russia are extremely closely interwoven, and this determines, to a significant extent, the general tension in relations between nations, the acuteness of the problems of citizenship and citizens' rights inside the federation, and a number of other social and economic problems.

The relative number of Tatars in the Sverdlovsk (now Ekaterinburg) region exceeds that of the Karelians in the Karelian republic, yet the Tatars are on equal footing with the Russians while the Karelians have their own government. The fact that the interests of the Karelians are formulated by their own government and those of the Ural Tatars are not is largely a historical accident. There are a great number of such cases in Russia. As a result, federal policies can only be considered truly democratic if they take this reality into account and reflect a concern not only for peoples with their own statehood (republics, regions, areas) but also for those without. The (more or less significant) hallmarks of statehood and the status of a subject of the federation are far from imperative for every small national community. These attributes are not essential if – most important – equal political and socioeconomic rights for all are guaranteed. If these rights are guaranteed, then state policy will have taken into account the most important interests of peoples.

Notes

The chapter has been translated by Todd Foglesong and Karen Knop.

1 RSFSR Zakon o grazhdanstve RSFSR, *Vedomosti S'ezda narodnykh deputatov RF i Verkhovnogo Soveta RF*, 1992, No. 6, st. 243, art. 3.
2 Obrashchenie, *Vedomosti S'ezda narodnykh deputatov RF i Verkhovnogo Soveta RF*, 1991, No. 46, st. 1561, para. 2(v).
3 Zakon Turkmenistana o grazhdanstve Turkmenistana (30 September 1992) [copy on file with editors] art. 9.
4 Zakon respubliki Uzbekistan o grazhdanstve respubliki Uzbekistan, *Pravda Vostoka*, 28 July 1992, art. 10.
5 See note 1 above.
6 Ibid., art. 13.
7 See generally *Human Rights Watch World Report 1993* (New York: Human Rights Watch 1992), 215-19; 'New Citizenship Laws in the Republics of the USSR,' *News*

From Helsinki Watch 4 (15 April 1992):7.
8　'New Citizenship Laws,' 9-11.
9　Dogovor ob osnovakh mezhgosudarstvennykh otnoshenii mezhdu RSFSR i Litovskoi Respublikoi (29 July 1991) [copy on file with editors].
10　Ibid., art. 4, second para.
11　Zakon SSR Moldova o gosudarstvennom pensionnom obespechenii v SSR Moldova, *Sovetskaia Moldova*, 13 February 1991, 1, art. 1(b).
12　Zakon Kazakhskoi SSR o pensionnom obespechenii grazhdan v Kazakhskoi SSR (17 June 1991) [copy on file with editors] art. 1.
13　United Nations General Assembly Resolution 40/144 (13 December 1985) reprinted in Centre for Human Rights, *Human Rights: A Compilation of International Instruments* (New York: United Nations 1988), 322.
14　[Trans.] Although the terms 'citizen' and 'foreigner' are used throughout this chapter in order to avoid confusion between the legal and ethnic senses of the term 'national,' the following proposal uses the international law terms 'national' and 'alien' as found in the relevant UN Declaration.
15　Zaiavlenie Mezhparlamentskoi Assamblei Gosudarstv-Uchastnikov Sodruzhestva Nezavisimykh Gosudarstv [hereinafter MA G-U SNG] o sotsial'noi zashchite grazhdan, MA G-U SNG, 1 Informatsionnyi Biulleten' (Dokumenty pervogo plenarnogo zasedaniia MA G-U SNG, 15-16 September 1992) (Moscow: Izvestiia 1992).
16　Konstitutsiia (Osnovnoi Zakon) Respubliki Sakha (Iakutia), *Iakutskie vedomosti*, No. 7 (19), 26 April 1992, at p. 1, art. 12.
17　Konstitutsiia Respubliki Tatartstan [copy on file with editors] art. 19.
18　Konstitutsiia (Osnovnoi Zakon) Nokhchi Respubliki, *Golos Chechno-Ingushetii*, 8 February 1992.
19　Dogovor o razgranichenii predmetov vedeniia i polnomochii mezhdu federal'nymi organami gosudarstvennoi vlasti RF i organami vlasti suverennykh respublik v sostave RF (31 March 1992) [copy on file with editors].

7

Citizenship Claims: Routes to Representation in a Federal System
Jane Jenson

Introduction: Citizenship and Federalism

Citizenship involves much more than the recognition provided by a passport. It has come to mean the attribution to citizens of a range of rights, including civil rights that protect individuals and groups from state interference; political rights of democratic participation; and substantive social and economic rights which recognize society's responsibility for all its members. The call for 'liberty, equality, and fraternity' (or better, 'solidarity'), may have been heard first in the French Revolution of 1789 – which produced the first modern, revolutionary discourse on citizenship – but it continues to resonate more than two centuries later.[1]

The concept of citizenship rights is, nonetheless, ambiguous; it has been used to mean many things. Citizenship has been a revolutionary idea, challenging existing relations of power and generating demands to be *included*, in the name of liberty, equality, and solidarity. At the same time, the modern state's capability of recognizing citizens enables it to *exclude*.[2] This exercise of sovereignty grants immense power to the state, which thereby gains the capacity to order social relations, to recognize some identities while rendering others invisible, and to empower some while putting others at a disadvantage.

Representation: Identities and Interests

One way to address the issue of who, how, and where citizenship claims are mobilized is to use the concept of *representation*. This chapter defines politics as a dual process of representation: the representation of interests via state institutions as well as those of civil society, *and* the constitution of the identities of the represented, through political mobilization and policy innovation.[3] The formation of identities defining the who of politics, therefore, occurs as part of – and central to – the definition of interests.

The meanings created by actors constitute a critical aspect of representation. By translating meanings into practice – often within institutions – actors create, sustain, or change representational arrangements. The creation of meaning, then, is profoundly political, if politics are considered to include actors' struggles to create themselves and their protagonists by generating support for the formulation of their own preferred collective identity, as well as by enunciating their interests.[4] Thus political conflict over who is being represented is as important as the distributional politics of competing interests over where, what, when, and how.[5]

Yet everything is not possible. If gaining representation involves the exercise of power by actors in civil society, it also involves the exercise of power by the state. As the Royal Commission on Electoral Reform and Party Financing wrote:

> In one sense, representation in governance identifies those represented, designates representatives, and legitimizes institutional processes for securing agreements and resolving conflicts. In another more fundamental sense, representative governance incorporates society's definition of itself as a political community ... In the process, a society pronounces whether it is open or closed to the claims of its citizens ... In this respect, a society is explicitly representing itself.[6]

It is state institutions, through their power to provide representation, which thereby identify the terms of inclusion and exclusion from citizenship and its rights. This poses a double challenge for movements for change. On the one hand, they must restructure institutions in order to reflect and represent their alternative conceptions of citizenship and identity. On the other hand, in seeking change, they must work within the existing institutions and the forums which they provide.

Given this understanding of representation, this chapter argues that constitution-making has been one important route through which new citizenship claims have been made and contested recently in Canada.[7] An obvious alternative to using the constitutional forum to make claims is to route them through the party system. In many liberal democracies, including those with federal arrangements, the party system provides the primary route to representation. It is, then, the 'crisis of the party system' and the challenge coming from alternative modes of representation, especially social movements and new parties, which represents the response to the current moment of political and economic restructuring.[8] Representational debates in Canada have indeed taken place through the party system. However, in recent years, the constitutional debate has become the most important forum for discourse on citizenship and representation.

Initially, constitutional argument focused on the classic issues of federalism – the relations between governments, between national and regional communities, and territorially defined language. But, as Canada lurched from constitutional crisis to constitutional crisis in the postwar period, it became more and more difficult to represent the issue as being only 'about' federalism.[9] While numerous actors continue to constitute their identity in 'federalist' terms, this representation of what is centrally important to Canadian politics is now seriously contested.[10] In the 1980s and 1990s, groups mobilizing identities anchored in regions or provinces ceded ground to alternative identities and interests whose proponents located them otherwise and elsewhere.

This is not the first time that regionally based identities and a focus on federal institutions as the preferred route for making claims have been challenged. This chapter documents three periods of Canadian history in which different identities have been mobilized, different interests defined, and different routes utilized for making citizenship claims. Such processes are not simply the consequence of the existence of certain institutions, whether those of federalism or the *Charter of Rights and Freedoms*. Nor are they directly the result of Canadian social cleavages. Rather, variability results from the political strategies of state and non-state actors as they seek to deploy their limited resources under familiar and unfamiliar circumstances.

The Rights of Citizens

The literature on citizenship has tended to treat the concept in too narrow and deterministic a fashion. This section reclaims the concept by arguing that citizenship rights, and the claims thereto, go far beyond a narrow definition of the political equality of individuals.

In much political theory, especially American, citizenship is equated simply with access to civil and political rights. Thus citizenship is reduced to protection from state interference, and the ability to be self-governing. For example, Iris Young, in critiquing the 'ideal of universal citizenship,' defines it this way:

> During this angry, sometimes bloody, political struggle in the nineteenth and twentieth centuries, many among the excluded and disadvantaged thought that winning full citizenship status, *that is, equal political and civil rights*, would lead to their freedom and equality.[11]

This conceptualization of citizenship is unnecessarily limited. The identity privileged is that of the individual, indeed often the 'individual as voter.'[12]

Defining citizenship only in terms of liberalism's political and civil rights then paves the way for the critique that 'universal' citizenship is incapable of recognizing difference and achieving equity.[13]

Yet history demonstrates that citizenship rights can also – and have very often in the past – been claimed for collectivities. This was possible because the idea of collective solidarity was embedded at the heart of citizenship, at least in the European tradition. It expressed the notion of 'fraternity,' which was the expression of the solidarity due within the group to other members of the collectivity.[14] This conceptualization of citizenship again involves exclusion as well as inclusion, but it opens the way to definitions of the included in terms other than simply as individuals. The notion that citizenship may also recognize collectivities in turn provides a platform for claims for citizenship rights made in the name of equity.

The tension between *limits on the state* and *need for the state* in definitions of citizenship first gave life to the concept of equity. From the beginning, there has been a recognition that the principle of liberty, which creates limits to state interference, may itself generate inequality. Moreover, equality rights formally guaranteed in law may not actually operate in a fashion which generates fairness. Thus, definitions of citizenship must be modified by considerations of equity.

Such equity principles involve recourse to principles of justice to correct or supplement some of the effects of liberty itself, as well as of formal guarantees of equality. Recourse to principles of fairness permits the application of those principles to the needs of specific cases. By stressing rectification of injustice for specific citizens or categories of citizens, the concept of equity evokes the need for state action and regulation in order to achieve fairness. Therefore, while some basic concepts of citizenship necessitate limits on state intervention as well as state guarantees, concerns about equity directly lead to claims for the state to recognize new citizenship rights, because neither complete liberty nor formally defined equality rights can alone actually achieve the goals embedded in definitions of citizenship.

A return to the first modern discourse on citizenship reveals that the 1789 Declaration of the Rights of Man and the Citizen was indeed a statement about inclusion and equality. But that ringing revolutionary document also identified community as the goal of citizenship.[15] As such, it provided grounds for making claims which were, at times, contradictory. A tension between the rights of individuals and collectivities emerged once the idea of solidarity and equity entered the discourse of citizenship, and many societies have struggled since 1789 to reconcile the competing principles of the revolutionaries.

Given the potential gap between formal rights and actual outcomes, societies whose notions of citizenship rested on the principles of liberty,

equality, and solidarity drew boundaries which designated the responsibility of the state for guaranteeing equitable access to representation and rights,
as well as differentiating the state from civil society. If concerns for equity
allowed for the conceptual possibility of the mobilization of collective
claims, they never finally resolved the fundamental issue – that is, the
definition of *who* belongs and *who* has access to and will benefit from full
citizenship rights.[16]

Analyzing citizenship in this way makes it possible, then, to ask how rights
were achieved at specific times and places. It looks for variation rather than
similarity in the representations which societies construct of their citizens
and their identities. It recognizes and asks about the power of groups to
disseminate their preferred patterns of inclusion and exclusion. It thereby
sees all identities, but especially the identity of 'citizen,' as contingent results
of political practice. At the same time it recognizes the power of the
meanings and practices of state and societal institutions to organize the
strategy of those contesting the boundaries of their political community and
their rights. Finally, it expects variation in the strategies used by actors to
route their claims for rights through institutions. Neither identities, nor
routes to representation, nor definitions of citizens and the patterns of
inclusion and exclusion are ever uniquely determined by social cleavages or
institutional forms.

Citizenship in Canada: Contesting the National

The boundaries of politics, the representation of the included and excluded,
and the role of the state – all the basic elements of citizenship – have been
frequently contested in Canada. Indeed, any history of this country must
recognize that disputed claims about citizenship rights have characterized
the last 127 years. The boundaries of the nation, practices of inclusion, and
definitions of rights have been front and centre in politics. Moreover, the
content of the claims, as well as the preferred routes for redress, have
changed over time. In Canada, three sets of collective identities have
contended: individuals in a pan-Canadian community; regional and linguistic communities defined by territory; and a variety of other collectivities
defined on bases other than territory – class, gender, ethnicity, and so on.
In addition, given these collectivities, a second debate has been about where
and how they will be represented: in the institutions of the federal government and party system, in provincial institutions, or in the institutions of
federalism itself – the Senate, Supreme Court, and the machinery of intergovernmental relations.

In the early years of this century, region and culture (especially language
and religion) were the primary political cleavages. Actors who focused on
regional identity demanded a more solidaristic sharing of the economic

benefits of citizenship.[17] Others demanded recognition of and equality for cultural duality. Regionally identified actors sometimes turned to provincial governments for redress (for example, Social Credit in Alberta and the Cooperative Commonwealth Federation (CCF) in Saskatchewan), but the Ottawa government was the primary target of groups demanding regional equity, and they used the party system to mobilize their claims.[18] Despite the existence of federalism since 1867, it was only after 1945 that intergovernmental relations were deeply involved in the struggles of those making citizenship claims in the name of a 'national' identity. This pattern has again altered in recent decades. Now groups seeking new citizenship rights mobilize identities which are less particular to regions, provinces, or even the country as a whole. Moreover, in contrast to the two earlier periods, these groups often bypass *both* the party system and intergovernmental institutions. They identify themselves in part via their preference for alternative forms of democratic politics, either autonomously or in coalition.[19]

In the decades following Confederation a system of representation was taking form, based upon an emerging, if fragile, 'national' identity. The dominant identity recognized collectivities within the new nation; it was not individualistic. From the beginning many people insisted that any 'Canadian' identity must be differentiated because of the diversity of religions and 'races' present in the new country.[20] While the goal was to create a new 'nation,' with a common citizenship, the authors of the *British North America Act* (*Constitution Act, 1867*) had a particular concept of Canada as 'a community based on political and juridical unity, but also on cultural and religious duality.'[21] Canadian citizenship was not intended to extinguish the collectivist and collectively defined claims of the diverse communities which it encompassed, nor could it have done so.

A second characteristic of Canadian politics in these years was that claims for citizen rights – recognizing and guaranteeing linguistic duality, for example – were originally made almost exclusively to Ottawa; the provinces were weaker and frequently overridden by federal action. In much of the West, moreover, provincial governments were lacking or were newly created. The *BNA Act* provided little presence for the provinces at the centre; intrastate federalism was notably attenuated.[22] Only as the balance of political forces shifted, as a result of the strategic initiatives of the Liberal party, did provincial action in the realm of cultural politics became feasible.

A third crucial aspect of the national identity generated after 1867 was its *place sensitivity*. Canada was represented as a collection of 'island communities,' distributed unevenly across regions. Groups' claims for access to citizenship, as well as efforts to achieve equality and solidarity, were most frequently represented in terms of such communities. Language and religious groups were particularly concerned to gain recognition of their citizenship rights. Economic actors also defined their interests in place-sensitive ways. Farmers and workers divided along regional lines while business groups turned to municipal 'boosterism' which stressed the importance of urban spaces.[23] One result of such place sensitivity was that politics were most frequently defined in terms of region, even when the 'real' underlying issue was class, language, or religion. Actors developed strategies which allowed them to take advantage of the uneven regional distribution of communities, thereby inserting a place-sensitive emphasis into the universe of political discourse.

These island communities initially identified the federal party system as the primary route for achieving their ends. The severe ethnic conflicts experienced before the First World War clearly exemplify this strategy. Supporters of Louis Riel, as well as of French language rights in Manitoba and Ontario, pressured Ottawa to overrule decisions of provincial governments which denied Métis and francophones rights of citizenship which they had come to expect. In particular, they exerted pressure within the Conservative party.[24] While the federal government was initially willing and able to respond to calls that it disallow provincial legislation on linguistic and religious matters, it became much more difficult to do so once the Liberal party, led by Wilfrid Laurier, constructed its highly successful political organization around a compromise position which recognized greater space for provincial rights.[25]

This solution to the longstanding difficulties of the Liberal party was implemented over the objections of the Catholic church and other advocates of a strong federal presence to protect the citizenship rights of Catholics. By the 1896 election, the Liberals were trying to divert the controversy over religious identities to the provincial level, but the problem would not go away. Nor could Laurier revert to his preferred position, shared with Henri Bourassa, of a *Canadien* nationalism, supported by an active central government.[26] Nevertheless, the strategic solution of 1896 significantly enlarged the legitimacy of provincial rights discourse, at the same time as many groups continued to press the federal government to act.[27]

For the rest of the country, as well, the benefits of citizenship, especially political power, were unequally distributed. Calls for equal and equitable treatment of citizens of all regions were frequently addressed to Ottawa directly, through the party and cabinet system. Armed with a regionalist discourse and their political rights, social movement organizations generated new political parties to fight elections in the name of regional protection. They demanded the creation of institutional arrangements guaranteeing equity for regions, which would recognize the right of regions to be represented at the centre.

The farmers' movement engendered the Progressive party to represent its regional claims against the power of the centre and a nation building strategy which, they claimed, forced the West to pay the costs of industrial growth focused on the centre.[28] The Progressives sought allies among western workers and business groups.[29] The Progressives, like the populists who followed them, consistently used a regional label for the inequities they faced. The Maritime Rights movement also objected to practices of 'nation building' which resulted in the de-industrialization of the Atlantic region. It followed a similar strategy of seeking broadly based regional electoral support, although that support went to an existing party, the Conservatives, rather than a new one.[30]

One result was a pattern of national politics based on the representation of regional interests and their accommodation within the federal cabinet. Whitaker describes this brokerage system, constituted most successfully by Prime Minister Mackenzie King, as one which 'places a premium on the regional representativeness of the executive and encourages the emergence of regional power brokers as key cabinet ministers, who thus play a double role as administrators and as political leaders of regions.'[31] Thus, in the politics of regional accommodation taking shape in the first decades of the century, the party system itself adopted a 'federal' form.[32]

This cabinet and party system were designed to represent the demands for equitable treatment of regions and fair representation. Each place could see 'its' representatives in the federal cabinet. Each place could hope that its sectional needs – whether those of class, language, or religion – would be well represented by the ministers from that place. And this party system thereby contributed to a representation of Canadian society to itself as being first and foremost a country where 'region mattered' and where politics was about the fair treatment of diverse places. This representation reinforced, thereby, a citizenship which stressed collectivities over individuals, which emphasized difference more than equality, and which defined fairness in regional terms.

In the years leading up to the Depression of the 1930s, a complicated, even contradictory, representational system of politics emerged. On the one hand, claims made by citizens against the costs of nation building, as well as for their own rights to collective recognition, continued to be addressed primarily to Ottawa, through the party system and cabinet. They were the primary sites for presenting and righting regional as well as ethnic claims. Whether the goal was to have the central government disallow provincial legislation or to use parliament and the cabinet as a forum for the politics of region, strategic calculations led both claimants and the central government to respect Ottawa's representational capacity. Intergovernmental politics, in particular, were of little concern.[33]

Yet, at the same time, other strategic calculations were making a shift in focus likely, as were the conditions of economic and social crisis in the 1930s. If the Liberals had first discovered the advantages of a 'provincial rights' position for dealing with religious controversy, federal governments led by both Conservatives and Liberals also recognized the benefits, as well as the limits, of 'watertight' federalism.[34] Nevertheless, as popular mobilization for expanded rights of social citizenship began, the central government made some attempts to displace provincial responsibilities for meeting such demands. However, both 'provincial rights' advocates and supporters of limited government hindered any serious move in that direction.

The experience of the economic crisis of the Depression, and of the Second World War, began to alter the character of the national identity, substituting one sense of place for another. A definition of a 'pan-Canadian' identity for individuals began to replace the regionally defined collective identities of prewar years. The beginnings of a commitment to social citizenship in the welfare state had deep implications for *both* the federal and provincial governments, and the provision of such programs came to depend on the institutions of executive federalism since, given the distribution of powers and revenue raising capacities, the new agenda could only be achieved through cooperative federalism.

Pan-Canadian Citizenship: Representation in Intergovernmental Institutions

Economic and political regulation during and after the Second World War came to involve a new concept of space. Political discourse began to represent Canada less as a conglomeration of regions and more as a single space north of the 49th parallel, having one labour market, universal standards for social programs, and a central government responsible for assuring the well-being of the whole.[35] A centralized system for income security was created, rationalized as a means of eliminating interregional disparities and providing benefits to individual citizens.[36] This country-wide system of income security permitted worker mobility in the postwar national labour market as well as a system of national standards.[37] According to Banting, Ottawa could gain access to the field of income security because of 'the special nature of income security as a direct exchange between citizen and state, which bypasses other social institutions.'[38] Ottawa thereby became the guarantor of the 'national,' although it obviously continued to share responsibility for specific programs with the provinces.

With these moves towards a welfare state, a recomposition of national identity had begun, centred around a basic policy consensus. This recomposition redefined the identity of 'citizen,' addressing individuals who had access to country-wide, or pan-Canadian, institutions and protections. Policies stressing redistribution via transfer payments – for instance, unemployment insurance, pensions, and family allowances – addressed Canadians as individuals more than as members of regional collectivities. This consensus was sponsored by the Liberals, supported by the Tories, and claimed as a victory by the CCF. Social spending was represented as part of the state's proposals for reconstructing the nation after the travails of wartime mobilization. It also reflected the growing influence of the labour movement and an, albeit partial, shift in collective identities from region to class.

The shift was not only in the meanings and practices attached to citizens as economic actors. By the 1950s, the federal government also established country-wide cultural, scientific, and educational institutions, stressing Canadian autonomy and downplaying the colonial past. Canada's role in founding postwar international institutions, such as the United Nations and the GATT, was accompanied by an attenuation of post-colonial symbols like 'dominion' and 'royal.' The *Citizenship Act* of 1946 pointed in this direction, as did the establishment of the Royal Commission on the Arts, Letters and Science (Massey Commission), and the reach of CBC television over almost the whole country.

Thus, the extension of social programs, constituting Canada's commitment to social citizenship, was based on the recognition of individuals. This was a national identity based on the common situation of all residents of a large and dispersed territory. It reflected the idea that economic and social modernization went hand in hand with the erosion of regional, cultural, and linguistic particularism, and that the new roles of government embodied in the Keynesian welfare state could only be achieved by a central government endowed with a national reach and major financial resources.[39]

One of the consequences of the focus on a single national – or what has come to be labelled pan-Canadian – identity was that the party system had increasing difficulty coping with regionally specific social or economic needs. Structural variations in the economy meant that all regions did not respond evenly to Keynesian counter-cyclical interventions. Claims for regional policy, satisfaction for farmers, and recognition for resource producers began to resonate through political institutions.[40] At the same time, Ottawa's arrangements for accommodating regional interests, so well tended by Mackenzie King and then Louis St. Laurent, fell into disrepair. They were replaced by new partisan institutions, under the leadership of prime ministers Diefenbaker, Pearson, and Trudeau, all of whom sought to create and/or maintain parties capable of brokering the new and seemingly pan-Canadian system of interests which mirrored their own preferred vision of the national identity.[41]

The pan-Canadian brokerage party system was unwilling – or unable – to respond well to regionally differentiated claims. The system of regional brokering in cabinet gave way to an institutionalized and relatively unmediated relationship between the centre, especially the leader, and the voters. The brokerage politics of these years was based less on the regional organization of power-handlers than on a system of interest representation which stressed the leader and his ability to represent, through creative cross-cleavage brokering, the immediate concerns of the people.[42] Thus, the 'national parties' created out of such postwar politics were leader-focused and had little staying power in their handling of the great issues of the day. Representational capacity began to shift to provincial governments who could speak for 'their' regional economies. In addition, provinces used their constitutional powers to block a wholesale centralization after the Second World War. Thus, despite new federal programs such as old age security and unemployment insurance, much of the responsibility for enacting the new agenda fell to provincial governments, which grew more rapidly than the federal government. This meant that the new national policy would, in fact, be an intergovernmental affair, developed and operated through the mechanisms of executive federalism. At this time the conflation of region with province entered the political discourse.

If this process really took off in the 1970s, the shift was not due simply to the inability to represent 'regions' in Ottawa. Accommodation of the new Québécois identity being mobilized by neo-nationalists after 1960, and with greater intensity in the 1970s, could only challenge the representational capacity of the federal party system. The demand for a stronger Québécois state, centred in Quebec City, also implied the substitution of executive federalism as a route to representation within federal institutions. One result of that challenge and accommodation was that the politics of federalism, and the constitution, became the site of conflicts over competing definitions of Canada.[43]

This shift in representational focus intensified as neo-nationalists in Quebec developed a more elaborate set of demands for a redefinition of Canadian citizenship that would incorporate Québécois specificity. By the 1970s, neo-nationalists in Quebec were not only using social programs as the basis for constructing a new conception of citizenship in Canada – clearly differentiated by province – they were also demanding recognition of Quebec's 'national' identity in the constitution, with a 'distinct' citizenship status for the Québécois, which could only be achieved by powers for the government of Quebec. The neo-nationalist strategy involved using intergovernmental institutions to gain new rights for the collectivity, that of the Quebec 'nation.' For those neo-nationalists who did not consider independence necessary for achieving the rights of nationhood, a shift in the arrangements of federalism was clearly required.

The definition of the nation promoted by Quebec within the institutions of intergovernmental relations was directly at odds with the definition of citizenship and its rights promoted by the Liberal party under the leadership of Pearson and Trudeau. The latter had succeeded in reorganizing the Liberal party around a version of pan-Canadianism which involved protection of language and cultural differences within a 'federal society.' The central government would provide protection for francophones, thereby making a stronger provincial state unnecessary. Trudeau's understanding of citizenship was clearly based on liberal individualism. *The Charter of Rights and Freedoms* included in the patriated constitution of 1982, recognized basic liberal rights. At the same time it protected the rights of linguistic and other minorities, and this too was a classic expression of liberalism. The package was a clear enunciation of a nationalist vision of Canada.[44] Therefore, it became much more difficult to achieve the accommodation of demands for collective recognition embedded in the Québécois neo-nationalist project or in province-building strategies coming from the regions.

At this moment, then, there were clearly two competing definitions of the nation, and of the grounds upon which citizenship claims could be made. The institutions of intergovernmental relations became the major terrain for this conflict over whether citizenship was fundamentally individual or collective. The long saga of federal-provincial conflict was destined to continue after 1982.

But Quebec and the provinces were not alone in contesting the pan-Canadian definition of citizenship. Because it took the individual as the fundamental social unit and sought to maximize individual equality and liberty, the definition of formal equality rights encoded in the original Charter proposals of 1981 was as unable to recognize systemic inequities as it was to cope with the claims for national and provincial rights that were emanating from Quebec.

Constitutional politics in the 1980s were also transformed, then, by the strategic actions of groups concerned to insert their demands for collective recognition and collective rights into the political agenda. Because of the force of these demands through the 1970s and the 1980s, current political debate is no longer confined to the issues of federalism. These demands broadened constitutional conflict to incorporate claims for new citizenship rights beyond those which can be effectively accommodated by rearrangement of the division of powers.[45] The representative capacity of intergovernmental institutions has declined as a result. New political forums are now used to express new claims.

Including the Excluded

The single pan-Canadian 'national' identity was a product of the economic and political conditions of post-1945 Canada. Reflecting as this identity did the elaboration of country-wide, individually based institutions with little capacity for recognizing regional or other differences, it is not surprising that opposition arose to it. This resistance coincided with the period of economic restructuring which has so profoundly shaped the last two decades. Political and economic restructuring have gone hand in hand.[46]

The postwar consensus about space, about identities, about interests and equity has been undone. As a result, a search for the proper balance among the three elements of liberty, equality, and solidarity is again under way. Groups are making claims in the name of collective rights and solidarities, seeking state-guaranteed mechanisms to achieve equity. Demands for alteration to the original proposal in 1981-2, for example, were mounted by those who sought to embed in the *Charter of Rights* a recognition of the limits to formal equality. Sometimes defined in terms of affirmative action, equity claims resonated through the constitutional debate before and after 1982. From Aboriginal peoples, too, came a call for the constitutional recognition of collective differences among citizens. They viewed the 1982 constitution as continuing to exclude them, despite s.35's recognition of three Aboriginal peoples (Indians, Inuit, and Métis). The reason was that the specification of treaty rights, of historic rights, and of the right to self-government – all collective rights – was deferred to the future; the constitution provided only a procedure for addressing the unresolved issues, in s.37, but no resolution.

It is, nonetheless, clear that social movement organizations representing those long disadvantaged both by the 'universal' standards of pan-Canadian citizenship and by territorial definitions of identity are not simply claiming the right to be included. They are also attempting to expand the political spaces and to generate more democratic politics. The movements' demands for 'categorial equity' involve extending democratic practices, and they often take the institutions of intergovernmental relations as the opponent, arguing that the workings of these institutions have generated a serious democratic deficit.[47]

Many of these collective actors present two basic challenges. On the one hand, they dispute the definition of constitutional politics as being 'about' federalism. On the other hand, they reject the liberal democratic notion that politics occurs primarily in elections and the parliamentary process or in bargaining among governments. The social movements of the 1970s and 1980s abandoned the longstanding notion that the preeminent political spaces were parliament, workplace, and nation. They have frequently by-passed federal and intergovernmental institutions, as well as the brokerage party system.[48] As these movements now struggle to elaborate their own identities and to legitimate them in political discourse, the spaces for and of politics proliferate, often being more 'local' and 'global' than 'national.'[49] Behind all of this is more than constitutional jockeying; a renegotiation of citizenship is occurring. In particular, there is an insistence that more actors 'belong' in the political process than can be recognized by a single, country-wide, undifferentiated definition of the citizen, and that these actors will exercise their rights well beyond electoral politics and intergovernmental institutions.

Feminists, for example, have sought not only the right to strive for equality with men, but also the recognition that achievement of that goal could involve, at times, acknowledgment that women are a collectivity distinct in many ways from men. This was the motive for lobbying to entrench not only liberal equality rights, but also affirmative action guarantees in the *Charter of Rights* in 1982.[50] Other equality seeking groups (representing the poor, people of colour, and the disabled, for example) have not confined themselves to using the courts to redress the disadvantages they face as a result of systemic discrimination. They, too, joined the call for a statement of social and economic rights in the next constitution, in recognition of the importance of social solidarity.[51] For these equality seekers, only fair social programs can provide real equity.

Aboriginal peoples are, of course, another obvious example of a collectivity making claims for rights and for a redefinition of citizenship. Mobilization for recognition of their rights as 'peoples' calls for recognition of collective distinctiveness.[52] This strategy explicitly rejects the 1969 proposal to recognize the rights of individual Indians and Inuit – an equality-based strategy – and seeks instead a recognition of collective rights. Land claims and the demand for entrenchment of an inherent right to self-government in the last constitutional round are clear expressions of this strategy. At the same time, the conflict between organizations representing Aboriginal women and men over the importance of Charter guarantees to gender equality reflects community divisions over the mix between individual and collective rights and the balance between alternative conceptions of these rights.[53]

The failure of the 1982 Constitution to resolve basic questions of Aboriginal rights and self-government, as well as the recent acknowledgement of the legitimacy of Aboriginal claims, reflects the continuing difficulty of merging competing definitions of national identity. Whether Canada consists of two founding nations or many is a fundamental conflict which has more than symbolic implications. The choice of answer leads to quite particular solutions to disputes over the division of powers and the existence and responsibilities of governmental bodies.[54]

In this context, definitions of equity have clearly begun to change. Armed with arguments about fairness, various movements have called on the state since the 1960s to guarantee effective justice, since formal equality of rights – supposedly guaranteed by a pan-Canadian citizenship blind to gender, race, or history – has not engendered institutions attuned to widespread current representations of Canadian social categories.

These claims antedate the *Charter of Rights*. Indeed, the Charter, as a *compromise* document, reflects the power of groups mobilized around collective identities as opposed to liberal individualism to mount successful claims for collective rights in 1981-82.[55] Although that document is an important new tool for some, Aboriginal groups fear its impact on the definition of their rights and their identity and seek political guarantees of their historic differences.[56] Feminists, particularly those concerned with reproductive rights, are cautious about the Charter.[57] Increasingly, too, women's groups have shifted away from their Meech Lake strategy of wielding Charter protections as a weapon to beat back that constitutional initiative.[58] In the 1991-2 constitutional negotiations, by contrast, the National Action Committee on the Status of Women (NAC), for example, argued instead for asymmetrical federalism, a social charter constitutionalizing much of the welfare state, protection of equality rights, and Senate reform to guarantee seats to women.[59]

In all these cases we can see the importance of decisions by social movements to pursue particular strategies within particular institutions. The longstanding search for equity by women and minorities has led them to participate in constitutional debate, to approach the courts, and to engage in coalition politics on specific matters such as free trade, the constitution, and policies like childcare. In doing so, they have effectively shifted the locus of political action away from both party politics and intergovernmental institutions. Consequently, their citizenship claims far surpass anything which implies only a rearrangement of federalism. Similarly, Aboriginal peoples' decades-long efforts to create an autonomous space for themselves have culminated in their current insistence on widening the constitutional debate beyond the division of powers, governmental institutions, and European definitions of citizenship.

In this way, criticisms of intergovernmental relations and traditional party politics have generated calls for expanded democracy and political access as the right of all citizens. Critiques of the democratic deficit in the Meech Lake negotiations led many groups to press, individually and through the Action Canada network, for the opening up of the constitutional negotiations.[60] In 1991-2, 'intergovernmental' meetings did involve more types of actors, including territorial governments which do not yet have provincial status and Aboriginal leaders who do not yet have self-government. That negotiation process itself lost some legitimacy as a result of calls for other decision-making procedures, including referenda and a constituent assembly. Such changes were prefigured by the constitutional conferences held during the winter of 1992, which provided categorial representation – via group identity, including that of 'ordinary Canadians' – and legitimated the notion that citizenship in the twenty-first century will continue to recognize difference.

For the moment, neither the party system nor intergovernmental institutions can frame the debate alone. Whether they will ever again be able to do so, depends upon the response to this outburst of demands for greater democracy as well as for guarantees of categorial equity.

Notes

1 Jacques Zylberberg, 'La Citoyenneté dans tous ses états,' in D. Colas et al., *Citoyenneté et nationalité: Perpectives en France et au Québec* (Paris: PUF 1991).
2 This definition of citizenship obviously owes much to T.H. Marshall's classic description of citizenship as involving three kinds of rights: civil, political, and social (T.H. Marshall, 'Citizenship and Social Class,' in *Class, Citizenship and Social Development* (Garden City, NY: Anchor 1965 [1949]). The European Union, in turn, in defining its project for community citizenship, also describes the social and economic rights of 'Europe,' making explicit reference to 1789 and using solidarity in place of fraternity (European Documentation, *A Human Face for Europe* (Brussels: European Community 1990).
3 Jane Jenson, 'Representations in Crisis: The Roots of Canada's Permeable Fordism,' *Canadian Journal of Political Science* XXIII, No. 4 (1990):662-4.
4 As Raymond Breton says: 'Those who are part of a society share its cultural assumptions and meaning, partake in the collective identity, and respond to common symbols. Relationships with institutions involve a symbolic/cultural exchange as well as an instrumental/material one' ('Multiculturalism and Canadian Nation-Building,' in A. Cairns and C. Williams, eds., *The Politics of Gender, Ethnicity and Language in Canada* (Toronto: University of Toronto Press 1985), 27). The insight that relationships with institutions involve both symbolic and material interests is also the basis for the definition of politics given here, which derives from Jane Jenson, 'Paradigms and Political Discourse: Protective Legislation in France and the United States Before 1914,' *Canadian Journal of Political Science* XXII, No. 2 (1989):237-8, inter alia. My formulation differs from Breton's, however, because it does not separate the two types of interests as sharply. Following the quotation given here he goes on to say, 'In other words, people have symbolic as well as material interests.' (at p. 27). I would argue, by contrast, that all interests *simultaneously* involve the symbolic and the 'real,' whether material or not (Jane Jenson, 'All the World's a Stage: Ideas, Spaces and Time in Canadian Political Economy,' *Studies in Political Economy* 36 (1991):51). The important point of commonality in these analyses is, however, the attribution of symbolic as well as material outputs to institutional arrangements.
5 Jenson, 'Paradigms and Political Discourse,' 237-8. Breton puts this another way, arguing that the failure to provide fitting representation has costs. 'Individuals expect to recognize themselves in public institutions. ... Otherwise, individuals feel that they are strangers in society, that the society is not *their* society' ('Multiculturalism,' 31).

6 Canada, Royal Commission on Electoral Reform and Party Financing, *Reforming Electoral Democracy*, vol. 1 (Ottawa: Supply and Services 1992), 8.
7 Of course, Canada is not alone in debating its future in a rapidly changing global environment by reconsidering and representing its constitutional arrangements, including the division of powers and other aspects of federalism. The European Union is currently debating the reassignment of sovereignty; citizens of ex-Yugoslavia and most of the ex-USSR contest the right to national independence; and Belgium again faces constitutional crisis over regional rights. Therefore, the point to be made here is not one of 'Canadian exceptionalism.'
8 Jane Jenson, '"Different" but not "exceptional": Canada's Permeable Fordism,' *Canadian Review of Sociology and Anthropology* 26, No. 1 (1989).
9 Gilles Breton and Jane Jenson, 'La Nouvelle dualité canadienne: L'Entente de libre-échange et l'après-Meech,' in L. Balthazar et al., eds., *Le Québec et la restructuration du Canada* (Sillery, PQ: Eds du Septention 1991).
10 See Richard Simeon, 'Canada and the United States: Lessons from the North American Experience,' Chapter 16 in this volume.
11 Iris Young, 'Policy and Group Difference: A Critique of the Ideal of Universal Citizenship,' in Cass R. Sunstein, ed., *Feminism and Political Theory* (Chicago: University of Chicago Press 1990), 117 (emphasis added). Pierre Rosanvallon, *Le Sacre du citoyen: Histoire du suffrage universel en France* (Paris: Gallimard 1992) similarly collapses citizenship into simple political equality.
12 Recent work on citizenship also describes the achievement of citizenship rights as a reflection of the process of 'individuation.' According to this argument, claims for collective rights supposedly disappear and actors, including social movements, can only make claims to expand the definition of 'person.' The notion that there is a limit on the form of claims derives from a theoretical stance which links the discourse of the individual to citizenship, via the proposition that 'individuals are embodied social agents whose separate identity hinges on their possession of a unique body' (Nicolas Abercombie et al., *The Sovereign Individuals of Capitalism* (London: Allen and Unwin 1986), 33) or that rationalization liberates the individual from the thrall of collectivist connections (ibid., 18; Bryan S. Turner, *Citizenship and Capitalism: The Debate over Reformism* (London: Allen and Unwin 1986), 66). To the extent that modernity is for these authors, by definition, an intersection of the discourse of individualism, rationalization, and equality of treatment, claims to citizenship rights can be voiced only in terms of individuals. Citizenship thereby extinguishes collectivist, or collectively defined, claims.
13 This conflation of liberalism and citizenship is part of Young's – and some other feminists' – political stance of rejecting modernity and its political goals. Modernity is accused of being dominated by a masculine bias (Iris Young, 'Impartiality and the Civic Public: Some Implications of Feminist Critiques of Moral and Political Theory,' in S. Benhabib and D. Cornell, eds., *Feminism as Critique* (Minneapolis, MN: University of Minnesota Press 1987), 57-8). This feminist perspective stands in stark contrast to the efforts of many women, especially those in Latin America and now in Canada, to bend the discourse of citizenship rights to their own emancipatory ends (Elizabeth Jelin, 'Citizenship and Identity: Final Reflections,' in E. Jelin, ed., *Women and Social Change in Latin America*

(London: Zed 1990); Alexandra Dobrowolsky, 'Women's Equality and the Constitutional Proposals,' in Duncan Cameron and Miriam Smith, eds., *Constitutional Politics* (Toronto: Lorimer 1992).

14 For the revolutionaries of 1789, the collectivity was the 'nation' (François Borella, 'Nationalité et citoyenneté,' in Colas, *Citoyenneté et nationalité*, 213). This definition, at the time that the modern nation state was taking form, meant that the state became an important, although not the only, guarantor of collective solidarity. For recent efforts to reclaim and rework definitions of citizenship to meet new needs, see European Documentation, *Human Face.*

15 The French Revolution 'allied citizenship with the notion of community in the principle of social fraternity' (Turner, *Citizenship and Capitalism*, 19).

16 Nineteenth-century attention to 'education for citizenship' and to the right to collective action were followed in the twentieth century by extended attention to the impact on representation of wealth and the inequitable distribution of resources. Then, by the end of the twentieth century, equity concerns also often implied state efforts to include groups – like women and minorities – systematically excluded by societal mechanisms of discrimination or by the actions of political actors.

17 I share Brodie's critique of those institutionalists who conflate 'region' with province (Janine Brodie, 'The Concept of Region in Canadian Politics,' in D. Shugarman and R. Whitaker, eds., *Federalism and Political Community* (Toronto: Broadview 1989), 38-9). If, as she argues, regions are themselves social constructions (p. 41), then their representational practices will certainly differ according to the strategic efforts of actors to give meaning to regional claims and successfully seek equity for regions. Of course, recent efforts at province-building have created – in everyday politics – this conflation (Carl Hodge, 'The Provincialization of Regional Politics,' in A-G. Gagnon and J. Bickerton, eds., *Canadian Politics: An Introduction to Analysis* (Peterborough: Broadview 1990), 193ff.). Nevertheless, present political tendencies to define one in terms of the other should not blind analysis to the 'politics' of such definitions.

18 Of course business groups, concerned less with regional equality than with the strength of their particular region, made use of their access to provincial governments (Garth Stevenson, *Unfulfilled Union: Canadian Federalism and National Unity* (Toronto: Gage 1989), 77ff.).

19 Harold Clarke, Jane Jenson, Lawrence LeDuc and Jon Pammett, *Absent Mandate: The Politics of Discontent in Canada* (Toronto: Gage 1991), Chapter 1; Louis Maheu, 'Les Nouveaux mouvements sociaux entre les voies de l'identité et les enjeux du politique,' in L. Maheu and A. Sales, eds., *La Recomposition du politique* (Montréal: PUM 1991), 174-6.

20 Richard Simeon and Ian Robinson, *State, Society and the Development of Canadian Federalism* (Toronto: University of Toronto Press 1990), 22ff.

21 Ramsay Cook as quoted in Simeon and Robinson, *State, Society*, 23.

22 Simeon and Robinson, *State, Society*, 25-7.

23 For a detailed discussion of the social origins of 'place sensitivity' and 'island communities,' see Jenson, 'Representations in Crisis,' 672-4.

24 Simeon and Robinson, *State, Society*, 37-8.

25 Janine Brodie and Jane Jenson, *Crisis, Challenge and Change: Party and Class in*

Canada Revisited (Ottawa: Carleton University Press 1988), 45-6.

26 Michael Oliver, *The Passionate Debate: The Social and Political Ideas of Quebec Nationalism 1920-1945* (Montreal: Véhicule Press 1991), Chapter 1.

27 Simeon and Robinson, *State, Society*, 38-9.

28 An effective alliance between eastern craft workers and manufacturers left western resource sector workers isolated from their union 'brothers,' at the same time as the economic costs of the National Policy's tariffs encouraged them to make common cause with western farmers for more equitable regional treatment (Jenson, 'Representations in Crisis,' 670-1).

29 Ibid., 670-2.

30 Brodie and Jenson, *Crisis, Challenge and Change*, 142-4.

31 Reg Whitaker, 'Party and State in the Liberal Era,' in H.G. Thorburn, ed., *Party Politics in Canada*, 5th ed. (Scarborough, ON: Prentice-Hall 1985), 146.

32 As Reid wrote in 1932, 'In caucus the party is sectional. In public it is homogeneous. In reality it is federal ... Out of the alliances of sectional parties are created the federations of sectional groups – the national Conservative and the national Liberal parties' (Escott Reid, 'The Rise of National Parties in Canada,' in Thorburn, *Party Politics*, 17). See also Miriam Smith, 'Canadian Political Parties and National Integration,' in Alain Gagnon and Brian Tanguay, eds., *Canadian Parties in Transition* (Toronto: Nelson 1988), 131-4.

33 While retrieving the early history of 'cooperative federalism' immediately after 1867 (thereby demonstrating the availability of alternative routes for mobilizing claims) Stevenson actually testifies to the very limited extent to which intergovernmental institutions organized representation (Garth Stevenson, 'The Origins of Co-operative Federalism,' in Shugarman and Whitaker, *Federalism and Political Community*, 28-9).

34 Simeon and Robinson, *State, Society*, 74ff.

35 Ibid., Chapter 7.

36 Keith Banting, *The Welfare State and Canadian Federalism* (Montreal: McGill-Queen's 1987) describes the concession of jurisdiction by the provinces to Ottawa, by an amendment to the *BNA Act*, which allowed the latter to set up a country-wide Old Age Security Program in 1951. It became the Canada Pension Plan in 1965.

37 Jenson, 'Representations in Crisis,' 681-2. These new arrangements did not arrive overnight. For example, the Unemployment Insurance program became possible with a constitutional amendment in 1940. The original program was quite restrictive throughout the 1950s, but by the 1960s had been revised to make it comprehensive (Leslie Pal, *State, Class, and Bureaucracy: Canadian Unemployment Insurance and Public Policy* (Montreal: McGill-Queen's 1988), Chapter 3).

38 Banting, *The Welfare State*, 51.

39 See Simeon and Robinson, *State, Society*, Chapter 7.

40 Clarke et al., *Absent Mandate*, Chapter 1.

41 Smith, 'Canadian Political Parties,' 138ff. While Diefenbaker's national identity was modelled on multicultural identities, first Pearson and then Trudeau defined the national identity in terms of biculturalism and bilingualism. This definition would in the next two decades 'transform Canada's definition of itself' (ibid., 141).

42 Clarke et al., *Absent Mandate*, Chapter 1.
43 Alan Cairns with Doug Williams, eds., *Constitutional Government and Society in Canada: Selected Essays by Alan Cairns* (Toronto: McClelland and Stewart 1988), 240; Jenson, '"Different" but not "exceptional."'
44 Simeon and Robinson, *State, Society,* 281.
45 Ibid., 323.
46 Breton and Jenson, 'La Nouvelle dualité canadienne,' 200-1.
47 The notion of 'categorial equity' is developed in Jane Jenson, 'Citizenship and Equity: Variations Across Time and In Space,' in J. Hiebert, ed., *Political Ethics: A Canadian Perspective*, Research Studies of the Royal Commission on Electoral Reform and Party Financing, vol. 12 (Toronto: Dundurn Press 1992) to refer to contemporary politics, in which the search for equity by new collective actors has fragmented the post-1945 definition of Canadian identity described above.
48 Breton and Jenson, 'La Nouvelle dualité canadienne,' 210ff.
49 In effect, such movements reflect a shift in the locale of politics, from the national to both the global and the local. Feminists, anti-racists, ecologists, and gays insist on creating new space for new politics in the family, the city, the environment, and the community. Geographical space contracts, as such movements develop ties around the globe (Jenson, 'All the World's A Stage,' 47-8).
50 Simeon and Robinson, *State, Society,* 298, 323.
51 David Shugarman, 'The Social Charter,' in Duncan Cameron and Miriam Smith, eds., *Constitutional Politics* (Toronto: Lorimer 1992), 175-6.
52 Paul Chartrand, 'Aboriginal Self-Government: The Two Sides of Legitimacy,' in Susan Phillips, ed., *How Ottawa Spends 1993-94: A More Democratic Canada ...?* (Ottawa: Carleton University Press 1993).
53 Susan D. Phillips and Marcia Devine, 'The Movement of Aboriginal Peoples in Canada,' unpublished paper, Carleton University School of Public Administration 1992.
54 Jane Jenson, 'Naming Nations: Competing Nationalist Claims in Public Discourse,' *Canadian Review of Sociology and Anthropology* 30 (1993).
55 As noted above, 1982 also reflected the relative weakness of Aboriginal groups, who did not succeed either then or through the process of constitutional reform designed at that time, the latter failing just prior to the Meech Lake Accord in 1987. In that document, too, their claims were ignored, thereby heralding the collapse of that agreement.
56 Paul Chartrand, 'The Aboriginal Peoples in Canada and Renewal of the Federation,' Chapter 8 of this volume.
57 Shelley Gavigan, 'Beyond *Morgentaler*: The Legal Regulation of Abortion,' in J. Brodie, S. Gavigan, and J. Jenson, *The Politics of Abortion* (Toronto: Oxford 1992).
58 Breton and Jenson, 'La Nouvelle dualité canadienne,' 212-13.
59 Dobrowolsky, 'Women's Equality,' in Cameron and Smith, *Constitutional Politics,* 152-6.
60 Breton and Jenson, 'La Nouvelle dualité canadienne,' 201-2.

8

The Aboriginal Peoples in Canada and Renewal of the Federation
Paul L.A.H. Chartrand

The object of this chapter is to provide a general introductory overview of the circumstances of the Aboriginal peoples in Canada in the context of the ongoing dialogue about renewal of the Canadian federation. The discussion includes consideration of the judicial development of Aboriginal rights, as well as some thoughts on the future of the aspirations of Aboriginal peoples to self-government within Canada.

The Canadian federation was established substantially[1] without the participation of Aboriginal peoples. In recent years, however, Aboriginal peoples have formed a strong political movement to obtain for themselves a proper place within the Canadian polity. They have taken advantage of the constitutional renewal process to assert and to try to obtain agreement on the implementation of a right of self-government. At the same time, court decisions in the last two decades have begun to describe the existence of certain Aboriginal rights. Aboriginal peoples have had little power historically, and it is too early to tell what particular means will be preferred by them to assert their place within Canada. It is suggested that Aboriginal peoples' relative lack of political power in Canada makes it difficult to envisage the reordering of federal structures to accommodate Aboriginal participation in Canadian statecraft. Rather, it is easier to assume that local arrangements will be instituted to implement emerging notions of Aboriginal rights, including the right of self-government.

In Canada the Aboriginal[2] peoples comprise approximately 4 per cent of the population, and live in small communities in isolated and rural areas, as well as in towns and cities. They comprise about eleven linguistic groups[3] and are descended from a number of historically and culturally distinct societies. It has been suggested that there are now roughly thirty-five to fifty distinct 'peoples' in the Aboriginal population.

The federal government of Canada has constitutional jurisdiction respecting 'Indians' and the lands set aside for them. Historically, the federal policy has been to adopt a narrow definition of 'Indian' based on its recognition of 'bands' existing in the 1870s. These 'status Indians' today comprise the bulk of the Aboriginal population for whom federal lands have been set aside.[4] In respect of these people, precise statistics are available, because the federal government keeps a register of 'status Indians' and also maintains various records pertaining to the circumstances of the people under its charge. In 1990, registered Indians comprised 1.8 per cent of the total Canadian population. They were generally affiliated to one of the 601 'bands' in the country, and three-fifths of the population resided on reserve and Crown (public) land.[5]

Generally no lands have been set aside for the use of other Aboriginal peoples. They live in various circumstances, from small communities comprised almost entirely of Aboriginal people with an historically and culturally discrete identity, to scattered populations living in towns and cities without any significant Aboriginal community institutions.

The circumstances of the Aboriginal peoples, who find themselves caught as colonized enclaves within the political boundaries of a powerful state, have been likened to those of Third World peoples living in the First World, and called the 'Fourth World.'[6] All the usual indicators show the inferior living conditions of Aboriginal peoples in Canada in comparison with the general population, which enjoys one of the highest standards of living in the world.[7] The present circumstances of the Aboriginal peoples in Canada are the legacy of the enduring injury inflicted by historical policies and actions of dispossession. Contemporary governmental activities, such as massive flooding for hydroelectric power developments, have continued to transform small communities which have subsisted by traditional methods and have retained a relatively independent livelihood into disillusioned groups dependent upon state welfare and subjected to the daily indignity of administration by government officials who are strangers and who, in the eyes of their clients, often despise them.[8]

One of the important factors that has projected Aboriginal interests onto the national political scene has been the judicial development of Aboriginal rights. Decisions of the Supreme Court of Canada over the past two decades have forced certain changes in the policy and practices of the federal government.[9]

In their struggle for a share in the division of social, economic, and political power, the Aboriginal peoples must use the scarce power resources available to them. These have included participation in the dialogue of 'rights,' regardless of the significance of such dialogue within their own societies.[10] One advantage derived from this process has been symbolic: reliance upon notions of Aboriginal rights has assisted in creating solidarity and unity, making it possible to proclaim that all Aboriginal peoples whose rights are now recognized in the Constitution have Aboriginal rights.[11] Throughout the 1980s and 1990s, representatives of the Aboriginal peoples participated in a common forum with government representatives to define the rights of the Aboriginal peoples to be entrenched in the Constitution. This has been a very unusual process, bringing together the representatives of various peoples who have been historically scattered across Canada, and who have no history of acting in concert to promote common interests.

The political significance of this should not be overlooked: diverse, long-colonized peoples are now able to seize the power that derives from large-scale organization in their struggles for their cultural survival, in circumstances where resort to the development of legal principles promises greater success than resort to non-lawful techniques of opposition.[12] Notions of rights are particularly important. The aspirations of Aboriginal peoples have to be translated into proposals for permanent institutions within Canada. Regardless of their own intrinsic morality or logic, these proposals will be implemented only to the extent that they can gain general acceptance within the non-Aboriginal communities which wield political power in Canada.

The acceptance of particular notions of 'rights' is also important for Aboriginal peoples because rights, once entrenched in the Constitution, provide a lever to be used in the broader political context to promote their interests. This is particularly important in Canada where, as one commentator has expressed it, 'law has replaced war, [and] constitutional rules represent the ultimate power.'[13]

The adoption of the discourse of Aboriginal rights and reliance on the courts of Canada to define these rights is, nevertheless, a gamble for Aboriginal peoples. There is much uncertainty not only about the nature of the relevant rights, but also about the process of defining them and about their general acceptability as a basis for crafting new political structures to accommodate Aboriginal aspirations within the public institutions of Canada. The doctrinal basis for Aboriginal rights is not yet firmly established in Canadian jurisprudence, with the judicial analysis to date focused almost exclusively upon 'Aboriginal title' – that is, the rights in respect of land that Aboriginal people are recognized as possessing in law. It has been variously suggested by analysts that the basis of Aboriginal rights lies in fundamental notions of property relations[14], in international and human rights law[15], and in the fact of occupation of the land for a very long time. The latter seems to be the preferred judicial approach.[16]

A number of problems arise if the courts have a significant role in determining the ambit of Aboriginal decision-making in future 'self-government' within Canada. Governmental 'rights' to legislate have usually been expressed in terms of 'powers,' not 'rights.' Judicial creativity will be required to establish, both in the Courts and within the traditional framework, that Aboriginal governments have now entered constitutional lawmaking space. Given the judicially established constitutional doctrine in Canada that all legislative powers are vested in the federal parliament and the provincial legislatures, any notion of Aboriginal legislative powers with respect to their constituents (who are also, in current law, Canadian citizens) will mean a profound shift in constitutional theory.

Past judicial decisions which have permitted the legal abrogation of Aboriginal interests have been influenced by the doctrine of parliamentary supremacy. Under this doctrine, the federal parliament and the provincial legislatures together can do anything legislatively; they can, for example, eliminate the binding treaty promises to which Aboriginal peoples cling in the absence of an original federation compact in the Constitution. The justice inherent in the principle that promises ought to be kept, a principle which has been the foundation of the common law of contract and of the international law of treaty-making, has been forsaken in the case of Aboriginal interests in favour of notions of political theory derived from the absolutist rule of long-dead English monarchs. One commentator has stated that 'the courts have become the caretakers of the racism of times gone by.'[17]

It has been suggested that the courts are not a particularly good forum for the development of a principled approach to Aboriginal rights, because they have adopted a liberal approach of seeking accommodation at the level of practical solutions.[18] Another difficulty in defining Aboriginal rights in the courts is the nature of the judicial process itself. Aboriginal people seek, in their articulation of Aboriginal rights, fairness, justice, and equity. The adversarial nature of court proceedings, however, requires government lawyers to put up arguments and other procedural obstacles against Aboriginal rights irrespective of those lawyers' personal notions of fairness, justice, and equity. From the positivist perspective, law has the essential function of resolving problems, and its use in promoting fairness and justice is problematic.[19]

Aboriginal rights dialogue requires the assertion of the existence of group rights. Aboriginal rights are by their nature group rights, in the sense that they inhere in the individual not as a result of his or her personal existence, but as a result of his or her membership in the group. The widespread failure to appreciate this point is evidenced by the common reference in Canada to 'persons of Aboriginal ancestry.' This terminology fails to acknowledge that it is not personal antecedents per se which determine the present identity of any particular individual. While antecedents are undoubtedly significant, and perhaps necessary components of personal identity, particular ancestry can never be a sufficient component of identity if personal identity is derived from membership of a group.[20]

One of the most pervasive notions in Canada is that Aboriginal peoples comprise a racial minority, and that they are not distinct peoples entitled to political liberty and equality with other peoples.[21] This is a significant obstacle to the acceptance of Aboriginal self-government, because it is easy to argue against the spectre of 'race-based' government with all its negative connotations. Upon examination, the idea makes no sense. Aboriginal peoples are not arguing in favour of maintaining biological purity, but in favour of maintaining cultures. They argue for the maintenance and promotion of their distinct ways of life and thought, wishing to survive as distinct societies. That survival requires self-direction and self-government. Individuals are identified, for these collective purposes, not in a determinative fashion by their biological baggage, but by their membership in, and their political commitment to, a particular culture and a political society that wishes to promote that culture.

Because Aboriginal rights are group rights, they face all the obstacles to the development of group rights present in the Canadian context. 'One of the most pervasive forces underlying the federal government's resistance to aboriginal rights demands is its steadfast commitment to liberal-democratic ideology,' according to a leading academic observer of events in Canada.[22] Liberal democracy stresses equality, individualism, and freedom from discrimination on the basis of such factors as race, religion, and nationality. For many Canadians, if all individuals are treated alike under the law, then self-determination is inapplicable.

For those committed to the ideals of liberal individualism, 'it is better to view Canada as a political community of equal individuals, rather than as an agglomeration of historical communities.'[23] In this view, accommodation with Aboriginal peoples should be sought at a practical level, avoiding confrontation at the level of first principles. But where liberalism has to be sacrificed, accommodation ends. Determining the boundary where liberalism ends in this context has led to a reexamination of traditional liberal values, and Kymlicka has suggested that a liberal account of Aboriginal group rights can be grounded in the unequal circumstances faced by Aboriginal peoples in relation to the rest of the Canadian community.[24] In this view, 'a system of equal rights and common citizenship within an integrated political community is no more prima facie just than a system of plural citizenships and special rights within a federation of distinct national communities.'[25]

If Aboriginal peoples become involved in litigating a division of powers between groups in Canada, the future does not appear particularly harmonious. A leading commentator has stated, 'Collective rights litigation is adversarial. Litigation invites smart lawyers and subtle stratagems. Community is pitted against community, majority against minority, often in a battle for survival. The history of collective rights litigation in the Canadian courts is a history of deep and lasting bitterness.'[26]

The constitutional entrenchment of the *Charter of Rights and Freedoms* in 1982 may be regarded as a boost to the ideals of liberal individualism, and in this sense may be an added obstacle to the general theoretical acceptance of the collective rights asserted by Aboriginal peoples. On the other hand, the Charter itself has assisted in the creation of groups, by recognizing, inter alia, group language rights and other rights of individuals, such as sex equality rights, which are being promoted by groups. It is difficult to assess whether the introduction of such group considerations into Canadian public life will assist or hinder the promotion of Aboriginal group rights.[27] A concern of Aboriginal rights proponents has been to distinguish between the group rights of Aboriginal peoples and other potential group rights, especially those that might be feared by governments in Canada. For the most part, it appears that resistance to group rights in Canada has focused on their potential application to ethnic minorities. This explains why it is important for Aboriginal peoples to assert their distinctness from Canadians generally and from 'minorities' within Canada as well. Any legitimate government fears that the logic of Aboriginal claims can be extended to immigrant and other minorities must be allayed.[28]

Provincial governments have always relied on the notion that they represent the interests of the majority within provincial political boundaries and that majority interests must prevail over the minority interests of Aboriginal peoples. Implicit in this utilitarian explanation is the assumption that Aboriginal peoples are merely individuals whose interests must be measured against those of all other individuals within provincial boundaries. It is instructive to note, however, that the provincial arguments against Aboriginal rights themselves contain elements of group rights. The usual provincial argument – that the greater interests of the majority must prevail over the minority interests of the Aboriginal peoples – must also rely on the existence of a definable group of provincial residents who happen to reside within the province's artificial political boundaries. Furthermore, there is no natural logic upon which the precise location of these provincial boundaries can be defended. This situation permits room for arguments in favour of political boundaries to be erected around natural communities, rather than around artificial provincial enclaves.

It is convenient to review the significance of Aboriginal rights development in Canada as a component of the movement towards greater political autonomy. Traditionally, the judicial dialogue has considered 'rights' as legal boundaries beyond which the individual is shielded from legislative intrusion by the state. An example of this idea is found in the following extract from the reasons of Wilson J. in the Supreme Court decision in

Morgentaler. 'The rights ... erect around each individual, metaphorically speaking, an invisible fence over which the state will not be allowed to trespass. The role of the courts is to map out, piece by piece, the parameters of the fence.'[29] The limitations presented by the piecemeal approach of the judicial arm of government in crafting a large institutional vision of Aboriginal peoples' preferred future are obvious. In the particular context of Aboriginal rights, the narrow scope of the Court's vision is illustrated by the following extract from the leading case of *Kruger* v. *R.* in the Supreme Court:[30] 'Claims to aboriginal title are woven with history, legend, politics and moral obligations. If the claim of any Band in respect of any particular land is to be decided as a justiciable issue and not a political issue, it should be so considered on the facts pertinent to that Band and to that land, and not on any global basis.' There is little reason to expect that any judicial notion of Aboriginal self-government as an Aboriginal right now protected in the Constitution or otherwise contained in the body of common law would be able to promote a global vision.[31]

In the courts, Aboriginal peoples are petitioners to outsiders; their interests are not articulated by their representatives before those who are in a position to act to promote or to reject them. They are explained in a cumbersome and costly process, largely by non-Aboriginal hired hands, to a judicial arm of government wherein the powers of the government side outweigh those of the petitioners. The dreams of Aboriginal peoples for political liberty are merged with the dreams of others. If Aboriginal dreams of political liberty are to be translated into meaningful institutions that permit the development of a global vision of political liberty within Canada, then recourse to the courts will not be sufficient. It is not to be expected, for example, that court decisions will lead to a restructuring of the basic federal institutions of this country.

The visions of political liberty currently asserted by Aboriginal people generally contain relatively little institutional detail. The immediate concern of Aboriginal leaders is to assert the legitimacy of their claims and to secure formal acceptance of them in the constitutional and institutional order. They tend to look back to history to explain the distinct character that distinguishes them from ethnic and other minorities in Canada. This overriding concern with the rational basis for a political claim leaves less time and energy for the elaboration of preferred institutional models of self-government.

The future shape of Aboriginal self-government seems bound up with the resolution of the tension between the interest of Aboriginal leaders to articulate local concerns, coupled with the narrow focus of judicially defined rights, on the one hand, and the development of a more global vision of political liberty, on the other hand. The latter depends for its success on the aggregation of all available resources on the part of the Aboriginal peoples in Canada. The resolution of this tension can only be evaluated in its particular context, a context that comprises small, impoverished Aboriginal communities scattered across the rural and remote parts of the country, and large diverse groups of relatively unorganized Aboriginal individuals living in the cities.

The context also comprises not only a narrow and locally focused judicial vision of Aboriginal rights, but an historically paternalistic governmental system that is itself initiating a devolution of administrative decision-making by various means. This process of devolution is focused either upon small communities or new Aboriginal structures that are tightly bound up within the government's own administrative apparatus. So what factors exist to promote a global approach that emphasizes the aggregation of the Aboriginal peoples' power resources?

One method of seeking to aggregate power that has been used, and that effectively counters arguments against claims for political autonomy based on notions of 'race,' is the assertion of the existence of Aboriginal 'peoples.' Aboriginal societies that can rely upon a distinct culture and historical legacy are able to claim the rights of self-determination that inhere in all historically and culturally distinct peoples. The argument has been formally articulated recently by the Dene of the North West Territories and has always been basic to the position advanced by representatives of the Métis people in the Prairie provinces. It continues to be found in declarations of rights by various groups across the country.

In this context, it is the banner of 'nationalism' that has been raised. This nationalism has not involved the marshalling of huge crowds in the city streets. Rather, the political representatives of societies which can point to a common historical and cultural legacy have relied on the idea of nationalism to promote solidarity among small geographically dispersed communities and among individuals sharing a common legacy who live in the towns and cities.

The nationalistic movement among Aboriginal peoples challenges the notion of two founding nations in the establishment of the Canadian state. Since Aboriginal peoples had virtually no say in establishing Canada, the legitimacy of Canada, not only as a constitutional entity but as a self-defined community, is under challenge. This Aboriginal nationalism is occurring at a time when the nationalism of one of the 'official founding nations' is itself causing a fundamental reexamination of the legitimacy of the existing order.

With both the Québécois and Aboriginal peoples asserting their nationalism within the political boundaries of Canada, there is bound to be some conflict between the two sides, who are uncertain about the implications of the claims of the one upon those of the other. The 'newness' of the national assertions of Aboriginal peoples arises partly from their subjugation within Canada. Formerly, when Aboriginal voices were scarcely heard on the national scene, the Québécois notion of 'the others' referred to the non-Aboriginal English-speaking majority in Canada. Recently, Aboriginal peoples have expressed particular concern in constitutional debates about the implications of the constitutional recognition of Quebec as a 'distinct society' in light of the Aboriginal peoples' own assertions of rights to self-determination and cultural survival.[32] The path to be followed by Québécois nationalism will have profound effects upon the possible routes taken by Aboriginal nationalism.

Another potential means of aggregating the power of Aboriginal groups is the creation of political solidarity among treaty signatories. Treaties were signed with many but not all Aboriginal peoples, and the location of the constituent treaty communities often cut across provincial political boundaries, and even across traditional Aboriginal cultural and political boundaries. Furthermore, the identity of the members of treaty communities has been determined by the federal government's legislated policy. This policy has not distinguished between the status of the different treaty signatories, and has stripped individuals of treaty entitlements along with the general legislated status under the *Indian Act*. This presents problems for the solidarity and self-definition of treaty groups today.

There have been, and continue to be, significant efforts at coordinating the political activities of particular treaty constituents, and indeed, of coordinating the activities of several different treaty nations. Section 35 of the *Constitution Act, 1982* recognizes and affirms not only the Aboriginal but also the 'treaty' rights of the Aboriginal peoples of Canada, and provides a constitutional mechanism for the entrenchment of self-government agreements based on renewed or new treaty agreements. Arguments have also been raised in favour of the creation of new federal unions based upon treaties.[33]

A number of pressures work against moves to aggregate collective power and action, whether in the form of nationalist movements or of treaty federalism. Among them are the circumstances of the traditionally isolated and marginalized Aboriginal communities, whose natural focus is upon local concerns, especially the desperate social and economic conditions that plague so many of them. Aboriginal political leaders must necessarily respond to the demands of their constituents, and in the present circumstances these demands tend to be either locally oriented or generalized.

Other pressures come from the government side, especially the federal government. With the increase in general popular support for greater political autonomy for Aboriginal peoples, the federal government has moved in a number of ways to devolve some of the administrative powers it has exercised to deliver public services to Aboriginal communities, especially the Indian reserve-based communities. For example, the Department of Indian Affairs has initiated a program that it calls a self-government initiative, whereby individual reserve communities, which it has agreed to call First Nations, are encouraged one by one to enter into agreements on some legislated forms of local political autonomy.[34] Critics have pointed to the obvious imbalance of power in such 'negotiations,' expressing concerns that government success in this endeavour would put an end to notions of large Aboriginal governmental institutions. Certainly, if the government were to negotiate such local agreements with the existing 600 or so *Indian Act* band communities, there would be little prospect for a renewed federalism that would include Aboriginal entities.

Other government departments have initiated 'consultation' processes that aim to provide some Aboriginal input into administrative decision-making, such as advisory boards proposed by the federal Department of Employment and Immigration in respect of employment and training initiatives.[35] Such initiatives tend to create vested interests among the Aboriginal individuals involved, and they secure Aboriginal interests in new layers of bureaucracy. Endeavours to develop broadly based decision-making structures that might match traditional consensual methods more closely come up against federally established structures that tend to refashion Aboriginal decision-making in the image of Canadian institutions. Further, since Aboriginal peoples have suffered greatly under a historical burden of inadequate education, the endeavours to which the educated Aboriginal human resources are applied are a very important factor in assessing the future direction of autonomous Aboriginal decision-making.

At the end of the day, power is exercised. It would probably require significant political power among Aboriginal peoples to force changes to the existing Canadian federal structure that would accord with their political vision, and would balance their emerging power against the well established institutions of power. At the moment the emerging sources of Aboriginal power appear to lie in the young age of the population and in prospects for significant improvements in education. These factors will combine in time with the effects of greater access to income and profit. Such long-term prospects must be balanced against the present difficult circumstances described above. In the short term, at least, it appears that Aboriginal peoples will continue to be treated as petitioners to the governments and to the courts, who will develop for them a narrow vision of protected space and some levers with which to move government policy in favour of their interests. The articulation of a broad vision lies ahead, and the establishment of new federal structures within which to develop that vision do not appear imminent.

Notes

1 Exceptionally, the Métis people in the West participated in negotiations for the entry of the province of Manitoba. The agreement for a Métis land base was not carried out, and the Métis quickly lost political power and joined the ranks of the dispossessed Aboriginal peoples. See, generally, G.F.G. Stanley, *The Birth of Western Canada* (Toronto: University of Toronto Press 1936); Paul L.A.H. Chartrand, *Manitoba's Métis Settlement Scheme of 1870* (Saskatoon: University of Saskatchewan Native Law Centre 1991).

2 In this chapter, the term 'Aboriginal' is used in reference to the particular, known groups of Aboriginal peoples such as the Cree, Dene, the Métis, Inuit, and others who live in Canada. The term is increasingly used by Aboriginal peoples to refer to themselves and also by others. Since the term has a particular, rather than a generic, meaning here, the English convention requires its capitalization. See, generally, on the terms used in reference to Aboriginal peoples in Canada, Paul L.A.H. Chartrand, 'Terms of Division: Problems of "Outside Naming" For Aboriginal People in Canada,' in the *Journal of Indigenous Studies* 2 (1991):1-22.

3 National Indian Brotherhood (NIB), 'The Indigenous People of Canada,' a report prepared for the International Conference of Indigenous Peoples (October 1975):1.

4 See, generally, Richard H. Bartlett, *The Indian Act of Canada*, 2nd ed. (Saskatoon: University of Saskatchewan Native Law Centre 1988).

5 Canada, Indian and Northern Affairs Canada, *Basic Departmental Data, 1991* (Ottawa: Minister of Supply and Services December 1991).

6 George Manuel and Michael Posluns, *The Fourth World: An Indian Reality* (Don Mills: Collier-Macmillan 1974).

7 In 1984 the prime minister of Canada himself listed the following statistics derived from a government survey:
   • life expectancy is ten years less than for the population as a whole;
   • violent deaths are three times the national rate, while suicides, particularly in the 15-24 year age group, are more than six times the national rate;
   • between 50 and 70 per cent receive social assistance;
   • one in three families lives in overcrowded conditions, and less than 50 per cent of Indian houses are properly serviced, compared to a national level of more than 90 per cent.
   (Extracted from the speech of Prime Minister Pierre Trudeau at the 1984 constitutional conference on Aboriginal matters; reproduced in Menno Boldt and J. Anthony Long, eds., *The Quest for Justice: Aboriginal Peoples and Aboriginal Rights* (Toronto: University of Toronto Press 1985), 148). These statistics refer to the status Indian population. For other, more recent statistics, see, e.g., N.H. Lithwick, Marvin Schiff, and Eric Vernon, *An Overview of Registered Indian Conditions in Canada* (Ottawa: Indian and Northern Affairs Canada 1986); Katherine Graham, *An Overview of Socio-Demographic Conditions of Registered*

Indians Residing Off-Reserve (Ottawa: Indian and Northern Affairs Canada 1987). Indications are that conditions of other Aboriginal peoples are not significantly different.

8 This perception is a strong theme in the submissions made by Aboriginal people to a recent Manitoba provincial inquiry into the administration of criminal law as it pertains to Aboriginal people. The report of that inquiry is published as *Report of the Aboriginal Justice Inquiry of Manitoba: The Justice System and Aboriginal People*, Commissioners: Associate Chief Justice A.C. Hamilton and Associate Chief Judge C.M. Sinclair (Winnipeg: Manitoba Queen's Printer 1991).

9 See Brad W. Morse, ed., *Aboriginal Peoples and the Law: Indian, Métis and Inuit Rights in Canada* (Ottawa: Carleton University Press, revised 1989), Chapter 10.

10 Mary Ellen Turpel, 'Aboriginal Peoples and the Canadian Charter: Interpretive Monopolies, Cultural Differences,' in Richard F. Devlin, ed., *First Nations Issues: Canadian Perspectives on Legal Theory Series* (Toronto: Emond Montgomery 1991), 41-73.

11 See ss. 25 and 35 of the *Constitution Act, 1982*, being Schedule B of the *Canada Act 1982* (UK), 1982, c.11 .

12 In 1990, the Canadian army was used by the Province of Quebec to crush organized blockades of roads by Mohawks in the area of Montreal. The incident received wide public media coverage, including international attention, and several books have been written about the events. See, for example, Jacques Lamarche, *L'été des Mohawks* (Montréal: Les éditions internationales Alain Stanke 1990).

13 Christian Dufour, *The Canadian Challenge/Le Défi Québécois* (Halifax, NS, and Lantzville, BC: Institute for Research on Public Policy and Oolichan Books 1990).

14 J.C. Smith, 'The Concept of Native Title,' *University of Toronto Law Journal* 24 (1974):1-16.

15 Peter A. Cumming and Neil H. Mickenberg, eds., *Native Rights in Canada*, 2nd ed. (Toronto: Indian-Eskimo Association of Canada in association with General Publishing 1972), part II.

16 See, for example, *Calder* v. *AGBC*, [1973] S.C.R. 313 and *Guerin* v. *R.*, [1984] 2 S.C.R. 335.

17 James Youngblood Henderson, 'The Doctrine of Aboriginal Rights in Western Legal Tradition' in Boldt and Long, *The Quest for Justice*, 185 at 185.

18 Ibid. See also, for a criticism of the role of the courts, Michael Mandel, *The Charter of Rights and the Legalization of Politics in Canada* (Toronto: Wall and Thompson 1989), esp. 287 ff.

19 Henderson, 'The Doctrine of Aboriginal Rights.'

20 See, generally, on defining Aboriginal groups of people, D.N. Sanders, 'The Bill of Rights and Indian Status,' *UBC Law Review* 7 (1972):81.

21 For a current elaboration of this mistaken view, see Gordon Gibson, 'Let's not use racism to tackle native needs,' *Globe and Mail*, 1 June 1992, A19).

22 Sally Weaver, 'Federal Difficulties with Aboriginal Rights Demands,' in Boldt and Long, *The Quest for Justice*, 139 at 142.

23 Bryan Schwartz, *First Principles, Second Thoughts: Aboriginal Peoples, Constitutional Reform and Canadian Statecraft* (Montreal: Institute for Research on Public Policy 1986), p. xvii.

24 Will Kymlicka, *Liberalism, Community and Culture* (Toronto: Oxford University Press 1989).

25 Ibid., 250.

26 Joseph Magnet, 'Collective Rights, Cultural Autonomy and the Canadian State,' *McGill Law Journal* 32 (1986):170 at 174.

27 See Kathcrine Swinton, 'Competing Visions of Constitutionalism: Of Federalism and Rights,' in K.E. Swinton and C.J. Rogerson, eds., *Competing Constitutional Visions: The Meech Lake Accord* (Toronto: Carswell 1988), 279.

28 See Will Kymlicka, 'Liberalism and the Politicization of Ethnicity,' *Canadian Journal of Law and Jurisprudence* 4 (1991):239-56.

29 Per Wilson, J. in *Morgentaler v. R.*, [1988] 1 S.C.R. 30 at 164.

30 *Kruger v. R.* (1978), 75 D.L.R. (3d) 434 at 437 (SCC) (BC).

31 But see Brian Slattery, 'First Nations and the Constitution: A Question of Trust,' *Canadian Bar Review* 71 (1992):261-93.

32 These concerns are discussed by David Hawkes and Brad Morse, 'Alternative Methods for Aboriginal Participation in Processes of Constitutional Reform,' in R.L. Watts and D.M. Brown, eds., *Options for a New Canada* (Toronto: University of Toronto Press 1991), 163; and see Joan Cohen, 'Aboriginals confront Quebec,' *Winnipeg Free Press*, 19 March 1992, A7).

33 See, for example, Andrew Bear Robe, 'Treaty Federalism,' in *Constitutional Forum* 4 (1992):6 (Edmonton: Centre for Constitutional Studies, University of Alberta).

34 See generally Wendy Moss, *Indian Self-Government*, Current Issue Review 89-SE (revised 8 July 1991) (Canada, Library of Parliament Research Branch).

35 Employment and Immigration Canada, *Pathways to Success: Aboriginal Employment and Training Strategy: A Background Paper* (Ottawa: Minister of Supply and Services 1991).

Part Three:
The Economics of Federalism

9

Is Federalism the Future?
An Economic Perspective
Kenneth Norrie

Introduction

Is federalism the future? Many observers of the current European scene apparently think so, albeit from two quite different perspectives. Understood as involving a transfer of sovereignty from national governments to Brussels, federalism is often touted as the future for those Western European nations struggling with the challenge of implementing the Maastricht Treaty provisions. Understood as involving the devolution of sovereignty from the centre to the regions, it is frequently advanced as the future for those Eastern European nations (and even some of the Western ones) beset with deep-seated ethnic divisions.

The apparent anomalies do not end here. National governments in Italy, Spain, the UK, and even France are facing demands for increased local political autonomy at the same time as they are considering arrangements that will transfer additional powers to Brussels. Conversely, the new nations of Eastern Europe and the former Soviet Union are expressing interest in economic associations even though membership would act to curb their recently acquired sovereignty. Canada may be exploring ways to devolve authority to provinces, but it also recently signed free trade agreements with the United States and Mexico that limit its national policy flexibility.

The implication of these developments, to some observers at least, is that the nation state is on the wane.[1] National governments suffer by being too big to carry out the little public sector tasks that touch the daily lives of citizens, and too small to carry out the big tasks required of governments in an increasingly global environment. Local governments can manage the little things more effectively, the argument goes, while supranational organizations can better manage the others.

This interpretation of recent events raises a number of questions. First, and most obviously, how legitimate is it? Is the nation state really waning in the face of increased internationalism and increased localism? A casual recounting of the evidence certainly makes it seem so, yet we must remember that integration in Europe is not complete, and still faces a number of challenges from established nation states. Nor is the trend to devolution certain, for even in Canada outside Quebec there is considerable opposition to further decentralization.

Second, if the nation state truly is becoming the redundant order of government, what are the forces behind this development? Why is it, suddenly, both too big for some purposes and too small for others? The usual response to this question is globalization, but this answer simply raises another set of questions. What are the links between globalization and political change? How does globalization, however defined, act to reduce the legitimacy of national governments, while at the same time increasing that of regional and supranational ones?

Third, what are the implications of these political changes, if true, for important societal goals such as equity or democracy? Nation states now bear much of the responsibility for these functions. Will the new political groupings pick up responsibility for them, or will the goals be abandoned along with the institutions? Can decisionmakers take steps to ensure that the changes are as benevolent as possible?

The chapters in this section focus on the economic dimensions of these issues. This overview chapter surveys two sets of economic concepts which, it is argued, can be brought together to help understand the connections between globalization and current political trends. The first set is from the familiar integration literature, the purpose of which is to set out the determinants of the potential real output gains from economic association. Whatever else its effects, globalization is clearly altering the opportunities for interregional and international specialization and exchange. The other reference is to recent work on economics and organizations[2] that attempts to relate institutional choices to economic opportunities. This literature is mostly concerned with the organization of private sector institutions, but it can be usefully adapted to complete the link from globalization to political change.

The next section of this chapter briefly outlines the links between potential aggregate real output and the processes of market and policy integration, followed by a more detailed exploration of some principles of institutional design drawn from the economics and organizations literature. These concepts will then be used to ask when federalism is the optimal choice of governance structure. Finally, the two sets of principles will be put together to address, in a highly tentative way, the question that forms the title of this chapter: is federalism the future?

Principles of Economic Integration

The attraction of economic integration was demonstrated some decades ago, spurred by developments in postwar Europe.[3] The basic message can be simply put: economic integration is valued because the potential aggregate real output of the member economies is greater when markets are integrated than when trade and factor movements are restricted by explicit and implicit government policies. In general, the larger the geographic span of the economic association and the more comprehensive its degree of integration, the greater are these potential gains. However, even the simplest schemes for market integration require some degree of policy harmonization among members.

Aggregate Output and Market Integration

Market integration increases potential aggregate real output by enhancing the ability of goods, services, capital, and labour to move freely among member economies. It is normal to express this phenomenon, known as market integration,[4] in terms of a continuum of economic associations. The first stage is a free trade area. Members agree to remove all explicit restrictions on trade between or among themselves of both a tariff and a non-tariff nature, although each reserves the right to impose whatever restrictions it wishes on trade with non-members. In principle, goods and services can move as freely between or among countries as they can within any one of them.

Free trade increases potential real output because it permits specialization and division of labour. One of the most venerable propositions in economic theory is that aggregate production possibilities are expanded when each country specializes in production activities for which it has a comparative advantage, and trades with other countries for goods and services for which it has a comparative disadvantage. If the member economies are small, and there are significant economies of scale in production, the potential gains from specialization and trade are even greater.

There are also potential dynamic effects of an economic union. Firms in each economy are subjected to the 'chill winds' of competition. To survive, they must devote more effort to containing costs, and more resources to research and development. Membership in the free trade area gives them greater incentive to innovate,[5] and access to a larger network for the diffusion of technology and ideas.[6] As Brander notes, 'even modest increases in the growth rate brought about by increased innovation will swamp the "static" gains from trade liberalization.'[7]

The larger the geographical area covered by a free trade area, the greater are the potential real output gains. This result follows because the greater the geographical span of a free trade area, the more likely there are to be gains from specialization and scale economies, and the greater are the potential dynamic benefits. These considerations prompted the expansion of the European Community beyond the original six members, as well as the expansion of the North American free trade area to include Mexico.

Potential real output gains are also greater the more complete is the degree of market integration. Thus a free trade area will often adopt a common external tariff, thereby becoming a customs union. The benefits here are mainly administrative. In the case of a simple free trade area, there is an incentive for non-members to export first to a low tariff member, and then to re-export to a high tariff one free of any restrictions. The only recourse for a free trade area is to specify and then administer a complex set of domestic content provisions. Adopting a common external tariff makes this measure unnecessary.

The third step in the continuum is a common market, defined as a customs union with the additional feature of free mobility of capital and labour. Members agree to remove explicit restrictions on the movement of workers, and on savings and investment. Like commodities, factors can move as freely between nations as they can within them. Factor mobility complements free trade by allowing members access to the real output gains from specialization and scale economies.

Market integration does not necessarily increase potential real output. The theory of second best states that removing one type of barrier, such as a tariff, in an economy that is already distorted in other ways (taxes, transport subsidies, and so forth) is not necessarily efficiency-enhancing. Trade liberalization may actually serve to decrease efficiency to the extent that existing barriers serve to offset other distortions in the economy.

A related qualification to the proposition that trade liberalization increases aggregate real output is that any market integration beyond a simple free trade area can involve trade diversion rather than trade creation. Trade diversion occurs when participation in a regional trading bloc results in a country's imports being shifted from lower cost non-member sources to higher cost partner sources. The partner's products are competitive only because they face no tariff, while the non-member products still do. The importing country is worse off in this case as it pays more than it needs to for imports.

The potential real output gains from market integration are not fixed for all time, of course. They will change as technology alters transport and communication costs, or as commercial ties with non-members evolve. Further, the changes can go in either direction. Economic association may become attractive where it was not previously, resulting in new associations, new members added to existing ones, or increases in the degree of integration of current ones. Conversely, existing unions may see their basis for integration erode over time. Members may fall away as a result, or the degree of integration may loosen.

Shifts in the potential benefits from market integration thus serve as the first factor to look for in attempting to understand current political developments in each of the areas of the world under consideration. What is happening to the potential real output gains from market integration? Is there any reason to think there are important changes under way? If so, are these economic changes consistent with the apparent political shifts? Do these shifts point to increased economic integration where it appears to be under way, and to disassociation where it is a force?

Market Integration and Policy Integration

Market integration removes explicit restrictions on the free movement of goods, services, capital, and labour, but it does nothing about an almost endless list of implicit barriers. Separate currencies are an impediment to commerce because they impose transactions costs on trade and introduce an element of exchange risk. Different regulations with respect to safety, the environment, product labels, education and training, and securities are barriers because they reduce the ease with which products or factors can move across borders.

It is predictable, therefore, that members of a common market arrangement will consider harmonizing rules and regulations wherever possible, to remove these implicit barriers to trade. Measures such as common safety and environmental standards are known as policy integration, to indicate that they are intended to promote trade and factor flows actively rather than merely to outlaw explicit barriers to them.[8]

There are other advantages to policy harmonization beyond facilitating trade and factor flows. The larger the group, for example, the more power it may have in international trade negotiations. Further, members can often share the costs of certain public goods with large-scale economies even though they remain completely separate political entities. Common efforts with respect to defence, large-scale water diversion projects, and even transportation infrastructure come to mind immediately. Economic associations may also feature insurance schemes to insulate member economies from the worst effects of cyclical fluctuations.

An economic association that features positive integration measures is known as an economic union. It is common to posit such an arrangement as a fourth step in the integration continuum, logically following and distinct from the earlier stages. This characterization makes little practical sense, however, as Pelkmans notes.[9] Even the simplest form of market integration – a bilateral free trade area – involves some degree of policy harmonization. As the degree of market integration expands, so too does the need for further policy harmonization. A customs union, by definition, adds a common external tariff schedule. A common market arrangement requires attention to banking regulations, health and safety regulations, mutual recognition of professional and technical accreditation, and so forth.

Further, within each stage of market integration there is considerable choice as to the degree of policy harmonization to be sought. Domestic content rules for a free trade area can be simple, or they can be complex and exhaustive. Dispute resolution procedures can involve anything from informal and ad hoc negotiation to judicial-like enquiry. Members can agree to recognize each others' product and safety standards and professional certifications, or they can attempt to devise a common set.

There is, therefore, no single stage called an economic union, but rather, a continuum of associations, ranging from those with minimal formal harmonization of economic policies to those with quite extensive arrangements. The common feature is the commitment to positive measures to promote trade and specialization.

Principles of Institutional Design

Once governments opt to harmonize policies in the interests of facilitating market integration, they face a series of further challenges. They must negotiate the terms and conditions of the economic arrangement. Then they must administer it on an ongoing basis to ensure that it operates as intended. Finally, they must devise ways to resolve the disputes that will inevitably arise. Just as market integration cannot exist without policy harmonization, neither can policy integration exist independently of some type of overall governance structure.

How should members of an economic association choose a governance structure? Are some arrangements more suitable than others? Is there one that is most suitable? In particular, when is federalism the optimal choice?

One approach to answering these questions is suggested by the title of an influential book in the burgeoning literature on economics and organizations, *Markets and Hierarchies*.[10] Williamson defines market transactions as those which 'involve exchange between autonomous economic entities,' whereas 'hierarchical transactions are ones for which a single administrative entity spans both sides of the transaction, [and] some form of subordination prevails.'[11]

Williamson is concerned with the organization of private sector economic activity, the 'economic institutions of capitalism' as he terms them in a later work.[12] The distinction between market and hierarchy is clearly relevant, however, to the present topic as well. Economic relations among sovereign national governments can be thought of as 'exchange between autonomous economic entities.' Interest in federalism, then, is akin to asking whether an hierarchical arrangement might not be a superior organizational form. Interest in political devolution within an existing nation state, conversely, is like asking whether there is an advantage in replacing a hierarchical decision-making structure with one involving more interaction among autonomous economic entities.

Markets and Hierarchies: The Vertical Integration of Firms

The best way to illustrate the determinants of the choice between markets and hierarchies is by reference to an example that illustrates the economics and organizations approach at its best. Consider the case of a firm deciding how to acquire an intermediate input into production. It has three choices: purchase the input on the spot market, contract for it with another firm, or produce it internally by integrating vertically, that is by merging with the potential supplier.

The incentive is to choose the option that minimizes overall transactions costs, where this term is understood to refer to the opportunity costs of the real resources used in carrying out the transaction. The choice thus depends on the nature of the input. If the product is standard and relatively homogeneous, such as wheat or flour, the firm will likely secure it on the spot market. Products of this type are widely available, and price will be a good indication of quality. There is no reason to enter into a more complex supply arrangement.

The more uncertainty there is with respect to one or more features of the input, however, the more important it is for the firm to have some control over it. Thus, the firm's choices are to arrange a formal contract with a supplier, or to produce it internally. A contract sets out the terms and conditions under which the good or service is to be provided. The transactions costs involved are the initial ones of reaching the agreement, and the ongoing ones of ensuring that the terms of the contract are met. The easier it is to reach an agreement, and then to monitor performance and ensure compliance with it, the lower are these costs.

In most instances, it is impossible to specify all contingencies. Contracts are necessarily incomplete. Inevitably then, parties to a contract will be forced to modify agreements subsequently to take account of unforeseen events. This renegotiation can be very costly, particularly when the possibility for opportunistic behaviour exists. If the terms of the contract are vague, one or both parties may try to take advantage of the uncertainty in the bargaining. The more likely this behaviour is, the greater are the costs of transacting in this manner.

Opportunistic behaviour in turn is most likely when specialized assets are involved. A supplier making a custom product which has no other readily available buyer could suffer greatly in the event of a contract dispute. In other cases, it may be the buyer who is in the position of hostage. The input may be crucial to its own output plans, and it may have no alternative suppliers in the event of a contract dispute.

Vertical control can reduce the costs of such disputes by placing the resolution mechanism within the firm. The managers of the parent firm may be able to resolve disputes among subsidiaries more easily than can managers of separate entities using the courts and other devices. The possibility of reducing transactions costs in this manner thus becomes an important determinant of the decision to integrate vertically, and a predictor of when such mergers will take place.

Vertical integration comes with a cost. The larger the firm, the greater is the difficulty of administering it, and the higher, therefore, are the internal transactions costs. Further, there is a monitoring problem within the firm. Managers face the constant challenge of ensuring that subsidiary units operate in the best interests of the firm overall. They can monitor their actions, which is costly; alternatively, they can attempt to institute an incentive scheme that induces subsidiaries to operate in the interests of the firm.[13]

The merger decision thus comes down to comparing the costs of transacting by contract between firms compared to the costs of organizing production within the firm. In general, the more difficult it is to specify the terms of a contract completely, and the more specific the obligations of the parties to the agreement, the greater is the possibility of opportunistic behaviour, and thus the more likely it is that preference will be given to vertical integration. Conversely, the more difficult it is to monitor performance internally, or to create a system of incentives that will align the interests of principal and agent, the more likely firms are to continue to rely on contracts.

When Is Federalism the Optimal Choice of Governance Structure?

Federalism qualifies as an hierarchical institutional arrangement by Williamson's definition, while looser forms of association qualify as relations among autonomous entities. Thus it is appropriate to use these principles to ask: when is federalism the optimal choice of governance structure?

The Importance of a Credible Commitment to Free Exchange

If economic agents are to be induced to operate across political boundaries, they must understand the rules and practices governing the exchanges. One of the uncertainties they face is an abrupt change in trade policies in one or both jurisdictions. The more they fear this possibility, the more precautions they have to take. The costs of attempting to allow for the effects of these contingencies may offset a significant portion of the real output gain. In the extreme, they can be so high as to preclude altogether an otherwise efficient transaction.

The challenge for the members of an economic association, then, if they wish to take advantage of the real output gains economic integration can provide, is to reduce the possibility of unforeseen policy changes as much as possible. This feature is particularly true when the opportunities for exchange require firms to commit, up front, to specialized production facilities. The more credible this guarantee to liberalization can be, the less is the uncertainty surrounding the transactions; hence, the lower are the transactions costs to firms or other agents of completing the exchanges, and hence the greater is the likelihood that output-enhancing economic arrangements will occur.

Private economic agents are not the only ones affected in this manner. Governments, too, must make extensive, and often expensive, commitments to an economic union prior to any benefits being generated. These outlays may well determine the ultimate success of the association. There may be a need for new transportation or communication infrastructure, for example, or for a program to develop new work-force skills. The more certain participating governments are that the economic union will actually proceed on the terms agreed to, the more likely they are to undertake these important projects. Conversely, the more uncertain the future administration of the agreement is, the less likely are these investments to occur.

This requirement explains the attraction of institutions that have the effect of constraining the actions of individual governments. Operating an economic association on a government-to-government basis, issue by issue, would be very costly, tying up high-level political and administrative resources better used elsewhere. More importantly, it would expose the economic association to the vagaries of lobbying by vested interests with access to political authorities. Firms would need to allow for potentially disruptive changes in the terms and conditions of operating across political boundaries in their input and output decisions.

One alternative to direct state-to-state contact on an ongoing basis is to negotiate the basic terms of the association in this fashion, but to leave the day-to-day administration to a tribunal. Administration costs can be lower because of the specialized knowledge of the tribunal's members, but the main benefit is the greater certainty that comes with removing decision-making from the political arena. The more autonomy the tribunal has over interpretation, and the more consistently it interprets and applies the rules, the more the process will be isolated from the uncertainties of lobbying at the political level. The more secure firms are in this respect, the more freedom they have to ignore political boundaries when looking for supplies or markets, and hence the greater are the possible gains from integration.

If greater certainty yet is important for appropriating the benefits from integration, there are further options. Members can delegate broad policy authority, as well as administrative responsibility, to the central agency. Each will have some representation in this agency, and they may retain some general right of ultimate veto, but otherwise they agree to cede their authority in these areas. The benefit is the greater certainty of economic agents on both sides of a border as to the rules and their probable interpretation. The cost, which of course is the source of the economic gain, is the loss of local political autonomy.

If we think of the central agency as a layer of government, we have described a confederal arrangement. The central agency is ultimately the creation of the member states. Sovereignty, in the form of an ultimate veto, lies with the local governments. But subject to this constraint, the central agency operates independently in the areas under its control.

Federalism as the Ultimate Credible Commitment to Free Exchange

If greater certainty yet is sought, members may go beyond a confederal arrangement, and agree to give up their right of ultimate veto in the relevant policy areas. More formally, sovereignty over these functions is transferred to the central agency, while in other areas, it is retained at the regional level. This is the arrangement we know as federalism, with each order of government having ultimate authority over a specified set of policy functions.

The attraction of federalism, from this functional perspective, is its ability to promise greater certainty yet regarding the terms and conditions of economic exchange. Federalism can serve as the ultimate credible commitment to economic liberalization. Governments can signal to economic agents in this way their intention not to impose subsequent costly and disruptive restrictions on exchanges that cross political boundaries. The commitment is credible because local authorities have formally surrendered their ability to intervene.

The analogy with vertical integration is clear. Merger is attractive when it is difficult to negotiate complete contractual arrangements between firms. Centralized decision-making may be a way of lowering the costs of setting out the terms and conditions of exchange, and of resolving disputes. Similarly, when the credibility of the commitment to free exchange is an issue, the costs of supporting economic integration may be lower if the responsibility for managing the arrangement is assigned to a central authority rather than left to contractual arrangements among local governments.

There is a potential monitoring problem in a federal system, just as there is for managers of a vertically integrated firm. Once responsibility for management of the economic association is centralized, the behaviour of local political authorities may change. They face a different set of opportunities and constraints, and a new environment for strategic interaction. If each local authority operates in what it considers to be its own best interests, a natural assumption, it is easy to think of circumstances where the policy choices are inconsistent with the best interests of the economic union overall.

If the association is to function efficiently, this problem must be overcome. Some way must be found to ensure that local policies that impinge on interregional or international exchange are consistent with the general thrust of national ones. One solution is for the central authorities to monitor local actions directly, and to intervene as needed to prevent barriers to exchange from arising. This route can be very costly, and the more so the more comprehensive the economic association is.

The alternative solution, as in a vertically integrated firm, is to devise a set of incentives that will bring the actions of local decisionmakers more in line with overall interests, without having to monitor them directly. The extensive literature on principal-agent relationships is relevant here. How can the central government use the tools at its disposal – for example, fiscal transfers – to best advantage? What fiscal structure is most compatible with the efficient operation of the economic union?

Distributional Considerations: Another Rationale for a Federal Arrangement

The transactions cost approach to economic association outlined thus far focuses on economic efficiency exclusively. As Dow points out, however, it is only legitimate to emphasize economic efficiency as the determinant of institutional choice if utility can be costlessly transferred among participants.[14] Specifically, it must be possible to make side payments or participation bribes as required to induce the full cooperation of all members. The minimum cost governance structure will clearly dominate in this circumstance, since it is always possible to 'bribe' important but reluctant members into participating.

If it is not possible to make transfers among members, however, the link between economic efficiency and the choice of governance structure is broken. There may well be governance structures that dominate on economic efficiency grounds, but which are, nonetheless, rejected because they cannot attract key participants. The structures that survive will be those that allow key participants to obtain a satisfactory return, even if these forms are demonstrably less efficient than one or more alternatives.

Dow identifies two sets of circumstances when participation bribes may not be possible. The first involves the phenomenon of non-contractible investments. Suppose there is a production coalition that is demonstrably more efficient than any other arrangement, but which requires one or more members to make specialized prior investments. If those affected can make prior contracts for the distribution of the rents, these investments will be made, and the coalition will be brought into being. If it is impossible to contract in this way, however, the investment will not be made, and the coalition will not emerge. It will be replaced by one that can offer a better guarantee of a return to the specialized investment, even if aggregate real output is lower as a consequence.

Dow cites externality problems as a possible second source of difficulty in making the requisite transfers. One example is an arrangement that will provide benefits to future members who, because they cannot be identified with any certainty today, cannot be made to contribute to the costs of the project. Another situation is an arrangement where current members without a veto can be deprived of their rents by a reorganization forced on them by a sub-coalition.

Dow's critique of the transactions cost approach to institutional choice is particularly relevant to the case of economic associations. It is easy to think of circumstances where the most efficient arrangement involves some transfers among members. These payments might be long term and compensatory in nature, as when the formation of the association promises substantial structural adjustment to the type and location of economic activity. Alternatively, they might be short-term transfers designed to offset cyclical instability, and required because association means the loss of traditional macroeconomic stabilization tools such as monetary and exchange rate policy.

If interjurisdictional transfers are required, the more credible the commitment to them, the more likely are economic agents, private and public, to agree to participate. In this case, it may be optimal to assign responsibility for redistribution to the central agency. The reasoning is similar to that for exchange restrictions. It will be much more difficult or even impossible for individual governments to renege on these commitments. This feature provides another rationale for a federal arrangement, and another task for the central authority in it.

Is Federalism the Future?

Why Transfer Sovereignty Beyond the Nation State?
If the preceding sections are to be believed, nations will be tempted to transfer sovereignty beyond the nation state when each of the following conditions are met. First, the potential real output gains to market integration have increased. Second, nations must harmonize their respective

policies more completely than they have to date if they are to appropriate these gains. Third, they can achieve this policy harmonization most effectively if they replace ongoing, ad hoc, state-to-state negotiations with some form of hierarchical governance structure such as federalism. Finally, it is possible to make fiscal and other transfers among members as required.

The link to federalism begins with the phenomenon of globalization, which Nymark defines as 'the integration of markets on a world scale.'[15] He focuses in particular on the role of international businesses. 'More and more,' he writes, 'corporations must both plan and operate on a global scale. They manufacture, provide services, conduct research, raise capital and buy supplies wherever these activities can best be done, regardless of nationality.' The key feature in this definition of globalization is the recognition that goods, services, capital, technology, and even labour are now more internationally mobile. This development in turn means that the old pattern of producing a product entirely in one country, using its expertise and its supplies of capital, labour, and natural resources, and exporting it to another is breaking down. Now, materials and components may be acquired separately in several different countries, assembled in yet another by an international business, and marketed world-wide by still other firms under product mandates or other arrangements.

This new pattern of production increases the potential real output gains from specialization and exchange, which is the opportunity globalization provides. But it also increases the need for policy harmonization. The increase in the geographical span of economic transactions creates an incentive to broaden the membership of existing economic associations. The new areas of supply and the new markets will have to be brought into existing trade and investment networks. As products and factors become more internationally mobile, there is pressure, as well, to extend the degree of integration within existing associations.

The implication of these developments is twofold. A commitment to open borders is more important than ever, and whatever commitment there is must provide for the greater complexity of the exchange. The key concepts from the theory of vertical integration are instructive. We argued above that firms are drawn to consider integration when the costs of proceeding by means of contracts are high.

Globalization creates much the same set of circumstances, only with respect to international exchange. Supporting economic association by means of contracts among sovereign nations is increasingly costly: the number of participants is rising, and the ever more complex nature of the economic linkages makes it more difficult to devise a complete contract, increasing the likelihood of eventual trade disputes. The specialized production facilities involved make opportunistic behaviour by governments more costly to firms, which may suddenly, and unpredictably, be cut off from a supply relationship or a market they have spent time developing.

The alternative to contracting for a firm is vertical integration. The alternative for a group of sovereign political units is a central institution that can offer a credible commitment to the terms and conditions of economic association. These terms will obviously include freedom of movement for goods, services, capital, and labour. They may also include inter-jurisdictional fiscal transfers, as compensation or as part of an income insurance scheme.

The more difficult it is to establish the necessary credibility, the more comprehensive and binding must be the powers of the central agency. At the limit, the solution may be to transfer not just administrative authority upwards, but also sovereignty. Like a decision of a firm to integrate verti-cally, it may be efficient for nations, such as those of Western Europe, to internalize the transactions costs of supporting their economic association. The fact that this movement is apparently under way may well reflect the potential new benefits from integration that globalization provides, along with the recognition that institutions must change for the gains to be appropriated.

Integration is far from assured, however. Market integration may be an economically efficient step, and a federal arrangement may be the least costly governance structure. But these conditions alone are not sufficient to guarantee that the institutional changes will be made. The question of transfers among members must also be addressed. Will it be necessary to 'bribe' important members into participating? Can these transfers be made as required?

Why Transfer Sovereignty Below the Nation State?

Why do we observe trends in the opposite direction? Why is there pressure in Canada and elsewhere to strip the central government of much of its authority over economic management? The argument in the previous section for enhanced political integration ran from the fact of globalization to the incentive for increased market integration, to the need for increased policy integration, to the need for a new governance structure, to federalism as an appropriate model. If the reasoning is at all robust, the explanation for the interest in devolution must be that one or more of these links must be broken.

The first possibility is that in some circumstances globalization acts to reduce, rather than increase, the potential real output gains from market integration. This might be the case, for example, if trade barriers were falling world-wide, but the common external tariffs of an economic association were not following suit, or at least were not doing so as rapidly. Trade diversion can become a problem in this circumstance, even if it were not so before. If the economic structures of the members differ enough, the costs of the trade diversion may be borne unevenly, leading to regional dissatisfaction with the terms of the union.

A second explanation is that globalization has increased the desired degree of market integration as expected, but has led to a need for less, rather than more policy harmonization. The mobility of labour may have increased in absolute terms in the postwar period, but it has decreased relative to that for goods, services, capital, and technology. In part, people are tied to communities, and are reluctant to move. In part, they cannot always move even when they wish to, as these political barriers are the slowest to come down.

Formerly, access to capital and natural resources mattered a great deal in terms of the standard of living a community was able to achieve. Increasingly, however, comparative advantage rests less and less on these relative endowments. Raw materials are a smaller component of total costs typically, and firms in any case have ready access to other sources. Capital moves around the globe quickly and relatively costlessly, as do technology and business expertise.

Labour is less mobile. Differences in labour endowments among communities are more likely to exist and, if they exist, to persist. Comparative advantage thus rests increasingly on the skills and abilities of this relatively immobile factor input. A skilled and flexible labour force can give a community a cost advantage over its trading partners, while the opposite characteristics can doom it to long-run decline.

Another important factor in explaining cost differences is the local environment of rules, regulations, and business practices and procedures within which enterprises operate. A local environment that encourages savings, investment, entrepreneurial behaviour, and flexibility will allow a community to prosper in a global economy, while one that discourages these activities will only create long-run problems.

Both labour skills and the local environment can benefit from judicious policy intervention. The quality of labour depends on the commitment to education, training, retraining, and, in some instances at least, relocation assistance. Saving, investment, risk taking, and adjustment are responsive to tax and other incentives.

The ability to influence comparative advantage in this manner raises the question of where responsibility for the policies should reside. The answer turns in large measure on the degree and pattern of labour mobility. The more mobile labour is within an economic association, the stronger is the case for vesting control with the central authority. The argument is the familiar one of internalizing spill-overs and externalities. Local governments may under-invest in education and training when labour is mobile. Regions of net out-migration will be training workers for other jurisdictions, while regions of net in-migration will be content to let them do so.

If labour is immobile within an economic association, however, there is a case for devolving responsibility for education and training to the local level. There are fewer externalities to worry about, so the benefits of vesting the control with the government closest to the scene are relatively more important. This argument is frequently made for Quebec within the Canadian economic union, for example, and it might be as well for other federations that feature geographically concentrated minority groups.

A third explanation for the interest in devolution within nation states may be that the desired degree of market and policy integration have increased as expected, but there is a perception that federalism, at least as currently constituted, is not the optimal governance structure. We saw above that federalism is favoured when it is important to make a credible commitment to the terms and conditions of economic association. If the central government does not carry out this assignment effectively, or at least if it is not perceived to do so, its reason for being disappears. It is no longer the lowest cost way to administer the union and to resolve internal disputes.

A central government's credibility as custodian of the economic union will suffer if its economic policies become captive to the same vested interests that restrict the actions of local authorities. Federalism has no inherent advantage over confederalism in this event.[16] Another possibility is that the central government comes to be perceived as not representing the various local interests fairly. Economic policies will necessarily have an uneven impact in an economic union where regional economic structures differ markedly. It is important, therefore, that all parts of the union feel policy decisions are made in a fair and consistent fashion.[17]

The final explanation is the distributional issue. It may be the case that transfers among members are an important condition for the existence of the economic union, and that the central government has borne this responsibility until now, for reasons discussed above. If the terms of these transfers are being altered significantly, for whatever reason, it is natural that members will begin to question the legitimacy of the federal arrangement more generally.[18]

Conclusion

This chapter focused on the question of what lies behind the changes in political organization apparently under way in the world today. It argued that two sets of economic literature are useful in helping to understand these trends. One set looks at the conditions under which economic integration can produce potential real output gains. The other links the ability to appropriate these potential gains to the design of the institutions established to support the association. The chapter indicates briefly how these concepts can be used to analyze more rigorously the connection between globalization and political change.

Suppose the nation state truly is waning, giving way to supranational institutions at one level and local governments at another. Should this trend concern us? If our concern is with economic efficiency, and if certain of the circumstances set out above hold, the answer is clearly no. The nation state is disappearing for good reason. In the case of Western Europe, it is losing ground to supranational institutions because it cannot provide the necessary credibility of commitment to economic association that the forces of globalization require. At the other extreme, it is losing ground to local governments because it is insufficiently flexible to manage the new competitive emphasis on labour skills and local business environment, or is unable to arrange transfers among members as required.

The answer is less certain under other circumstances, however. It is possible that particular federations are showing signs of dissolving not because of any inherent problems with the federal system, but rather because of design faults, particularly in the central institutions. If dissolution results from an inability to correct these, as could well be the case in Canada at least, the consequences would be less, rather than greater aggregate real output.

The answer is also less clear on equity grounds alone. National governments have an important redistributive role in most countries, both among persons and among regions. Will the new supranational institutions play the same role? Will a more decentralized federation be able to share any surplus from association in the same manner? Some observers argue that they will: plans for European integration make provision for regional development programs, and even the most decentralist visions of Canadian federalism, such as that of the Allaire Committee, presume the continued existence of an equalization program.

It is easy to be sceptical, however. The political will to redistribute is tied closely to perceptions of shared citizenship. Europe has not developed these shared values yet, and Canada is likely to lose them as it becomes ever more regionalized. Thus the main casualties of globalization will likely be residents of poorer countries, or poorer regions within countries, who do not have the skills to benefit from globalization, who lack the ability to migrate to regions where they might acquire them, and who are less and less a part of a sharing society.

Notes

1 Thomas Courchene, 'Presidential Address: Mon pays, c'est l'hiver: Reflections of a Market Populist,' *Canadian Journal of Economics* XXV, No. 4 (1992):759-91; Richard Simeon, 'Concluding Comments,' in Douglas M. Brown and Murray G. Smith, eds., *Canadian Federalism: Meeting Global Economic Challenges?* (Kingston and Halifax: Institute of Intergovernmental Relations and Institute for Research on Public Policy 1991), 285-91; Benjamin Barber, 'Jihad Vs. McWorld,' *The Atlantic* 269, No. 3 (March 1992); Robert R. Reich, *The Work of Nations* (New York: Alfred A. Knopf 1991).
2 The symposium on organizations and economics in *Journal of Economic Perspectives* 5, No. 2 (1991) is a good recent reference to this literature.
3 B. Balassa, *The Theory of Economic Integration* (Homewood, IL: Richard D. Irwin 1961); B. Balassa, 'Types of Economic Integration,' in F. Machlup, ed., *Economic Integration, Worldwide, Regional, Sectoral* (London: Macmillan 1976), 17-31; Jacques Pelkmans, 'Economic Theories of Integration Revisited,' *Journal of Common Market Studies* XVIII, No. 4 (1980):333-54.
4 Pelkmans, 'Economic Theories of Integration Revisited.'
5 James Brander, 'Innis Lecture: Comparative Economic Growth: Evidence and Interpretation,' *Canadian Journal of Economics* XXV, No. 4 (1992):792-818.
6 R.G. Harris and D.D. Purvis, 'Constitutional Change and Canada's Economic Prospects,' mimeo, Queen's University 1991.
7 Brander, 'Innis Lecture,' 807.
8 Market integration is sometimes referred to as negative integration, and policy integration as positive integration.
9 Pelkmans, 'Economic Theories of Integration Revisited.'
10 Oliver E. Williamson, *Markets and Hierarchies* (New York: Free Press 1975).
11 Ibid., xi.
12 Oliver E. Williamson, *The Economic Institutions of Capitalism* (New York: Free Press 1985).
13 This issue is referred to as the principal-agent problem. See David E.M. Sappington, 'Incentives in Principal-Agent Relationships,' *Journal of Economic Perspectives* 5, No. 2 (1991):45-66 for a recent survey.
14 Gregory K. Dow, 'The Appropriability Critique of Transactions Costs Economics,' mimeo, University of Alberta 1992.
15 Alan Nymark, 'Globalization: Lessons for Canadian Investment Policy and the Federation,' in Brown and Smith, eds., *Canadian Federalism: Meeting Global Economic Challenges?* 183 at 183.
16 Some of the main distortions in the Canadian economic union result from federal rather than provincial government policies. See John Whalley and Irene Trela, *Regional Aspects of Confederation* (Toronto: University of Toronto Press 1985) for examples.
17 Regional fairness is a longstanding issue in Canadian political economy. See Whalley and Trela, *Regional Aspects* for examples.
18 The Canadian federal government has been altering the terms of the system of intergovernmental transfers as part of its recent budget measures, to the great dissatisfaction of the provinces. See Kenneth Norrie, 'Intergovernmental Transfers in Canada: An Historical Perspective on Some Current Policy Choices,' in

Peter M. Leslie, Kenneth Norrie, and Irene K. Ip, eds., *A Partnership in Trouble: Renegotiating Fiscal Federalism* (Toronto: C.D. Howe Institute 1993), 87-129.

10

Economic Federalism and the European Union
Tommaso Padoa-Schioppa

Introduction

The words 'federal' and 'federalism' have traditionally created great divisions in the European Community (now European Union), with emotional attitudes often prevailing over rational arguments. On two occasions, strong political leaders – Charles de Gaulle in the 1960s and Margaret Thatcher in the 1980s – greatly emphasized national pride in their efforts to regenerate the policies of their countries. This led them to antagonize the European Community, to oppose any plan involving the granting of new competencies to a supranational level, and to mock the European Commission and 'Brussels.' For these leaders, the words 'federal' and 'federalism' were synonymous with relinquishing essential prerogatives of the nation state to 'quelque aréopage technocratique, apatride et irresponsable' or to 'appointed bureaucrats.' Neither de Gaulle nor Thatcher seemed to be aware that federalism is a constitutional system that owes much to the idea of 'minimum government' in the tradition of Locke and Tocqueville, and is not a Hobbesian Leviathan or Orwellian 'big brother.'

At the risk of oversimplifying, and speaking as a layperson in constitutional matters, I would argue that federalism essentially supplements the traditional 'horizontal' division of government functions between the legislative, executive, and judicial branches with a 'vertical' division, in the sense that government powers are required for the village, the county, the region, the country, etc. Lower layers of government should not derive their power and legitimacy from higher levels but rather be founded independently on the people's will. Kant, who is often considered the father of the political philosophy of federalism, thought that only a world federation could ensure perpetual peace among nations.[1]

As to the question of how power should be distributed between different layers, the 'principle of subsidiarity' is the key. Taking the general criterion of minimum government as the guiding principle, powers would be assigned to the different levels of government according to the rule that 'the functions of higher levels of government should be as limited as possible and should be subsidiary to those of lower levels.'[2]

Federalism and the Economy

From its very beginning, the idea of 'minimum government' has had an economic as well as a political dimension: it was intended to leave individuals free not only to follow their moral and religious beliefs, but also to pursue material wealth. Thus, in the field of ideas as well as in the field of political action, the economic and political programs of traditional liberalism have always been closely intertwined, and a similar blend of economic and political elements has characterized the evolution of socialist ideas and political actions. Notwithstanding the many variants that have been proposed or tried, both economic liberalism and socialism have a body of ideas and propositions that define the basic features of the economic system and ensure consistency between the economic and political constitution of the state.

In the case of federalism, the parallelism between the economic and political strands is much less developed. This is somewhat surprising, because the general principles of federalism that I have just outlined lend themselves to straightforward application in the economic sphere. Just as federalism supplements traditional liberalism with the idea of a plurality of levels of political government, it would supplement the traditional principle of minimal economic regulation implicit in the theory of the 'invisible hand' with the idea that the level of government should be low.

Thus, for an economist, the principle of subsidiarity means that the production of public goods should be attributed to the level of government that has jurisdiction over the area in which that good is 'public.' Attribution to a higher or a lower level of government would provide an inadequate solution to the problem of public goods, because it would involve inefficiencies of various kinds. A function should be allocated to the lowest level of government at which the expected welfare gains can be reaped. Only indivisibilities, economies of scale, externalities, and strategic requirements are acceptable as efficiency arguments in favour of allocating powers to higher levels of government. While the general principle is clear cut, its application may not be so simple. Uncertainties and conflicts may arise as to the 'appropriate' level at which certain government functions should be discharged. In general, they can be resolved by a combination of two approaches: specifying in detail the respective fields of competence and adopting rules of procedure for deciding concrete cases.

I shall not try to explore here why the body of economic analysis stemming from this central proposition is so small and only just beginning to develop, but a large part of the answer probably lies in two factors: first the analytical complexity of removing the customary 'one economy, one government' assumption; and second, the scant attention paid by modern economists to the institutional dimension of policies.

The Case of the European Union

For the study of the 'economics of federalism,' the European Union represents a most interesting case, as well as an historical experience that has inspired important new ideas. Primarily, this reflects the intrinsically dynamic nature of the EU project: unlike the United States, the Union was not created by a single constitutional act. Rather, it is a process in which the attribution of government functions to a supranational level has been gradual and marked by constant efforts to strike a balance between the preservation of national prerogatives and the need for efficient community-level action. What follows is an attempt to describe the main features and developments of the Union in the context of the foregoing definition of federalism.

The European Union is not a fully fledged political union. As far as institutions are concerned, the decision-making power is weaker than that of the central government in most federal constitutions, owing to the extensive recourse still made to unanimity and qualified majority voting. Even in economic areas such as trade, agricultural, and industrial policy, where the Union has considerable power, decision-making involves long negotiations between representatives of the twelve member states. As to Union competencies, the production of typically 'federal' public goods, such as defence and internal security, is still largely the responsibility of national governments, although the Maastricht Treaty has laid the foundations – albeit in a rather hesitant way – for an extension beyond the economic and monetary fields.

Yet the Union is much more than a simple international agreement among sovereign nations. It is endowed with the three standard branches typical of government – a legislative body, an executive, and a judiciary. In many areas, particularly since the Single European Act of 1986, decision-making is no longer based on the unanimity rule. Many decisions, as well as the rulings of the Court of Justice, are directly applicable to individual citizens throughout the Union.

Unlike most existing federations, where the distribution of powers between the central government and the states is largely an historical heritage, often ultimately the result of military conquest, the allocation of competencies in the Union is the result of deliberate choices by the member states. At each step of the development of the European Union, since its creation in the early 1950s, the relinquishment of elements of national sovereignty has been assessed on the basis of common values and on grounds of efficiency in the exercise of government. It has been decided and made legally binding according to the constitutional rules of member states and, since 1958, the procedures of the Treaty of Rome.

To give an idea of how these very general principles are implemented in the economic field, I will follow the standard taxonomy of the three economic functions of government: allocation, which covers microeconomic policy instruments aimed at ensuring the efficient use of resources; stabilization, which refers to macroeconomic objectives, especially price stability, growth, and employment; and income redistribution, both between individuals and between regions.

Market Integration: Blockage and Restart

Reflecting the objective of creating a large internal market, allocation has been the main area of competence of the European Union from its early days, when it was commonly referred to as the Common Market. Again, allocation plays the crucial role in the Single Market program, the aim of which is to eliminate all physical, technical, and fiscal barriers to the free movement of goods, services, capital, and persons.

In practice, however, the Common Market was not achieved. By the end of the 1960s, the European Community had succeeded in eliminating quantitative and tariff barriers to trade and in creating a common policy in the fields of coal, steel, and agriculture, but it was still very far from being a common market comparable to national markets. The 1970s saw a reversal of the integration process, even relative to the achievements of the 1950s and 1960s: non-tariff barriers remained high and were sometimes raised, and in most countries capital controls were strengthened.

Several factors contributed to the slowing down of the integration process in the 1960s and its virtual paralysis in the 1970s. In particular, it is worth noting the strength of national sentiments and organized interests, as well as the impact of macroeconomic difficulties, which led to differentiated responses in the EC countries that conflicted with the further opening of markets. Here, however, it is necessary to draw attention to the reason that most directly concerns the issue of federalism. In my view, the deadlock in the process of European integration owed much to the concept of European integration that prevailed in those early years. In spite of the ideals that moved its founding fathers, for a long time the Community developed more like a centralized state than a federation. The implicit model was the centralized structure of government of most of the member states, rather than the principles of minimum government and subsidiarity that constitute the essence of federalism.

In most European states, with the notable exception of Germany, there is no historical or legal tradition of a vertical division of power. The guiding principle is the indivisibility of government, whereby the central government has the ultimate responsibility for every area of policy and, at best, delegates certain powers or administrative functions, or both, to regional and local authorities. In accordance with this constitutional model, it was thought that the creation of a common market implied a massive transfer of competencies to European institutions. In particular, the prevailing view was that the whole body of national laws and regulations concerning economic activity had to be redrafted on a 'harmonized' basis by EC legislators. Not only did this approach conflict with national habits and rules; it was also difficult to justify on grounds of economic efficiency. During the 1960s and the 1970s, the Community was plagued by this internal contradiction. Numerous proposals were tabled for the harmonization of national laws on various matters, including irrelevant ones such as the hours during which noisy lawnmowers could be used in urban areas. Endless negotiations took place to very little effect.

It was only after major rethinking in the early 1980s that a different approach emerged and gave new impetus to the creation of a unified market. Two main forces played a crucial role in the reassessment of the way in which the allocative function of government should be organized. The first was the intellectual climate in favour of deregulation and a reduction of the role of the state in the economy; the second was the pressure from market participants – in particular, industry – to remove existing barriers and create a common market that would revitalize the slow-growing EC economies and provide a cure for 'eurosclerosis.' In the background was the monetary and exchange rate stability the European Monetary System (EMS) had helped to restore.

The Treaty amendment of 1986, known as the Single European Act, was the legal and institutional instrument of this new era. It marked a change in the whole approach to integration by introducing the two closely related principles of minimum harmonization and mutual recognition, as well as significantly extending the application of majority voting in the approval of EC legislation.

It had become clear that the only way to arrive at a single market, short of complete harmonization, was for each member state to recognize the legal provisions and technical standards of the others. In terms of this approach, which conforms to the principle of subsidiarity, the Community would only be responsible for laying down a set of minimum rules which would make products acceptable to every other country in the Community. The purpose of the Single Market Directives is to provide these minimum rules; they do not suppress national legislation, but seek to safeguard the Community-level 'public goods' inherent in safety standards, consumer protection, and free access to markets. The convergence of national rules and regulations, which the earlier approach of complete top down harmonization had failed to achieve, will eventually be brought about by market forces and competition between national rules.

This new start marks the shift from a centralized to a federalist approach in the exercise of the allocative function of government. It should be noted that the principle of mutual recognition was first adopted in the Community by the European Court of Justice in a series of judgments, of which the 'Cassis de Dijon case' is the best known.[3]

The Problem of Tax Harmonization

One field where progress towards the single market has been slow and inadequate is that of taxation. There are two related reasons for this. The first is that there is no general agreement in academic or official circles on the level of government to which different taxation decisions should be assigned or on the degree of harmonization required by a single market. The second is that the Single Act has preserved the rule of unanimity for decisions on fiscal matters.

According to economic theory, tax decisions should be taken at the level of the public good whose production they finance; and since the production of public goods in the EU is largely at the state level, prima facie there seems to be little scope for attributing decisions on taxation to higher levels of government. This simple proposition, however, disregards the role played, for any given level of tax revenue, by the structure of taxation. In particular, the structure of national tax systems may impede the full implementation of the internal market.

This was recognized at the start of the EC. Most countries at that time had different systems of indirect taxation, and maintaining these systems would have resulted in trade distortions that contradicted the objective of a common market. Not even the harmonization of tax rates would have been sufficient. The members opted for the radical solution of abandoning their different systems of taxation in favour of a new one; the value added tax (VAT). VAT is transparent and neutral with respect to the location of production. It is also flexible enough for member countries to retain a degree of freedom to decide the rates at which the tax is levied and, to a limited extent, the base.

The distortions caused by different structures and levels of taxation are particularly important when an economic activity can be easily moved from one jurisdiction to another. This is the case for corporate taxes, labour-related taxes and contributions, and even VAT rates, although the member states have recently agreed, after lengthy negotiations, on a set of minimum rates. The main problem, however, emerges in the financial field, because the mobility of financial assets encourages tax competition, leading to the lowest level of taxation – a result that may not be desirable for the Union as a whole, since it implies excessive tax burdens on labour relative to capital, and possibly adverse effects on the distribution of net income and wealth. A certain degree of harmonization is, therefore, required in the taxation of highly mobile goods and factors of production. This is why, with the aim of avoiding tax competition, the EU countries made a commitment to achieve minimum harmonization when they agreed to liberalize capital movements in 1988. So far, however, the commitment has not been fulfilled.

Macroeconomic Stabilization: Fiscal Policy
The questions of whether and to what extent the creation of a single market requires the centralization of stabilization policies have been debated for years. The Werner Report, published in 1970, indicated that economic and monetary union would require both monetary and budgetary policy decisions to be centralized at the community level.[4] In 1992, building on the recommendations of the Delors Report,[5] the Maastricht Treaty adopted a different approach: monetary policy is to be centralized, but not budgetary policy.

According to the Treaty, economic and monetary union does not require the implementation of a common budgetary policy, but the compliance of national budgetary policies with a set of minimum rules, aimed basically at excluding monetary or privileged financing of deficits and preventing 'excessive' deficits. On strictly economic grounds, the loss of the printing press by national governments can be expected to foster fiscal discipline, and it is difficult to justify the arbitrary numbers chosen to define 'excessive' deficits in the Treaty. Several reasons have been advanced for setting rules. In a monetary union, the instability that could stem from a member government's failure to meet its financial obligations could have systemic consequences, as the debt of each government is more likely to be held abroad. In addition, to alleviate the burden of its debt, a member country might be tempted to exert political pressure on the central bank of the union to let money grow at an excessive rate. Finally, large deficits in one country could exert upward pressure on interest rates throughout the union and channel too large a share of total savings to that country at the expense of other countries and sectors.

The important point for the issues discussed here is that such budgetary rules do not imply the centralization of budgetary policy. On the contrary, they leave national governments and parliaments with complete sovereignty as regards the size and composition of public expenditure and taxation, and as regards the size of deficits, as long as they are reasonable, that is, not 'excessive.'

The implicit doctrine underlying the approach taken by the Treaty can be formulated as follows. First, greater 'federal' control over national budgets would have infringed on the general principle of subsidiarity, given that the function of the budget (whether national or federal) is to provide public goods and that, for the moment, these are seen as being predominantly national. Second, even from the point of view of the stabilization function, fiscal policy should remain national, because this is the only instrument left to stabilize the economy in the event of asymmetrical shocks across countries once they have renounced control over monetary and exchange rate policy. The experience of monetary unions without a large federal budget – such as Switzerland, Belgium and Luxembourg, and the United States before 1930 – suggests that the stabilization function can be performed efficiently through decentralized budgets.

The system designed by the Maastricht Treaty will have to pass the test of experience. It will perhaps be found that some scope for a 'federal' fiscal policy is needed – for instance, to avoid inconsistencies between the stance on monetary policy and that on fiscal policy. Should this be the case, it will be necessary to decide whether the solution should be sought in greater Union control over national budgets or a 'macroeconomic' use of the Union budget. The latter solution, in turn, would pose the problem of the size and financing of the Union budget, which will be briefly addressed later in this chapter.

Monetary Policy

The centralization of monetary policy embodied in the Maastricht Treaty is founded on the analytical proposition, confirmed by historical experience, that in an area with free trade and complete capital mobility, fixed exchange rates cannot coexist with the independent execution of monetary policy by member states. The attempt by any national authority to adopt a monetary stance different from that of other countries would immediately be defeated by capital movements that would equalize rates of return across borders. The early experience of the US Federal Reserve system showed that while in theory reserve banks had the power to change the discount rate in their own jurisdictions, in practice they were not able to create 'local' monetary conditions different from those prevailing in the rest of the country.

It should be noted that in the case of monetary policy, and in contrast to the other policy areas examined so far, it is not possible to apply the

162 Tommaso Padoa-Schioppa

principle of subsidiarity to the distribution of powers among different levels of government. In the jargon that developed in 1988-91, when monetary union was studied and negotiated, this was referred to as the 'indivisibility' of monetary policy. After all, it is no accident that the word 'central' is part of the name of the institution responsible for monetary policy.

In providing the blueprint for the single monetary policy, the Treaty creates an interesting and original structure for the monetary authority. By the start of the third phase (January 1999 at the latest), exchange rates will have been irrevocably fixed. Consequently, there will be a single monetary policy conducted by the European System of Central Banks (ESCB), which is composed of the European Central Bank and the central banks of the participating countries. Decisions on the single monetary policy and the single currency of the Union, the écu, will be taken by the council of the ESCB, in which the governors of the national central banks participate, each with one vote. The national central banks will remain subject to national jurisdictions to the extent that the latter's provisions do not conflict with those of the Treaty; they will be independent of all other national or Union institutions and will be responsible for implementing monetary policy decisions.

The ESCB will thus be a supranational institution with a fairly decentralized structure. Such decentralized structure for a federal institution is quite different from a structure in which power is shared between the federal and national levels of government, referred to above as a federal structure or a vertical division of power. In the case of the ESCB, the nation states and the federation do not share competencies; these are all attributed to the federation, which exercises them through an institution that is organized in a decentralized way. In a truly federal solution with a vertical division of powers, the national central banks would have retained a monetary power of their own, independent of that of the System.

Regional Redistribution

The principle of equity on which the redistributive function of economic policy is based has been a concomitant of allocative efficiency from the very beginning of the integration process of the EU. Indeed, at each step of the Union's history – from the Coal and Steel Community to the EEC, the EMS, the Single Act, and now the Maastricht Treaty – the opening of markets and the integration of countries' policies have been accompanied by additional measures aimed at assisting the less favoured regions and sectors.

The respective roles of the member states and the Union in redistribution have been debated at length. The approach followed by the Union has two important features: first, Union policies should not substitute but should supplement national ones; second, the two levels of government should work together. The rationale for the former feature is that the opening of markets within the Union increases aggregate welfare, but is not necessarily an improvement in the Pareto sense; some regions may turn out to be worse off, primarily because of the importance of agglomeration economies. As to the second feature – cooperation – Union action takes the form of participation in member states' policies at all levels, from project evaluation to financing and assessment.

The general objectives of the Union's structural funds are to promote development and structural change in the backward regions, defined as those where per capita income is less than 75 per cent of the Union average (about 20 per cent of the population of the Union); to restructure regions in industrial decline, in particular where the unemployment rate is higher than the Union average and industrial employment is falling; to support the training of young people; and to foster the development of rural areas.

A major issue for the redistributive function is the amount of resources involved. The EU budget currently amounts to just over 1 per cent of the Union GNP. This figure is clearly too small to produce the type of income redistribution between individuals and regions that is found in most federations. It should be noted, however, that the redistributive impact of the EU budget is by no means negligible. Ireland, for instance, receives net transfers of about 7 per cent of its GDP and for Greece the figure is 5 per cent. These amounts compare favourably with estimates of the public funds flowing directly (not through the federal tax system) from the richest to the poorest regions in European countries; in 1977, the McDougall Report estimated that in most countries these flows were between 3 and 10 per cent of the recipient regions' GNP, though they were as high as 20 per cent in some regions, such as Brittany and Northern Ireland.[6]

Since the creation of a monetary union is a further important step towards eliminating barriers within the single market, a case can be made for matching it with stronger redistributive policies of a structural nature. Indeed, agglomeration economies may cause firms to locate increasingly in the richest regions. With the adoption of the EMU Treaty, the member states have agreed to establish a new fund – named the cohesion fund – to support the four countries (Greece, Ireland, Portugal, and Spain) whose per capita income is less than 90 per cent of the Union average. The use of this fund will be conditional on the adoption of convergence programs that will meet the requirements for participating in the final stage of EMU.

Another highly controversial aspect of redistributive policies concerns the financing of the Union budget. At present, the EU obtains its resources by way of national contributions that are mostly computed on the basis of VAT and external tariff revenues. Proposals have been put forward to move towards a system based on GNP shares. In the future, I think the Union will have to move away from a system in which contributions are made directly by the member states, which inevitably leads to friction between net contributors and net receivers. In order to avoid these difficulties, the Union budget should be based on a uniform revenue system and on criteria that do not depend upon the domicile of the contributors.

Conclusion

The integration of Europe made a new start in the mid-1980s. In the last few years, a tremendous acceleration has taken place. Several factors have contributed to this, not least the disappearance of yesterday's bipolar world. One major factor has been the rediscovery of the basic constitutional principle of federalism, in which competencies are attributed to the different levels of government according to criteria of efficiency and equity.

The shift towards a federal structure is not yet explicitly recognized by all the member states, and this may be an advantage. In a preliminary version of the Maastricht Treaty, the first article included the sentence: 'This Treaty marks a new stage in the process of creating an ever closer union with a federal vocation.' In some (mainly British) political circles, federalism was interpreted as implying a greater centralization of power; in others, as a decentralization of power to subnational, regional, and local authorities. After long discussion, the reference to a 'federal vocation' was dropped. The sentence now reads: 'This Treaty marks a new stage in the process of creating an ever closer union among the peoples of Europe, in which decisions are taken as closely as possible to the citizens.' This, in my opinion, is an even stronger statement of the federal vocation of the Union. It is indeed my belief that as integration proceeds, the need to limit the power of Union institutions with respect to national and regional authorities will be stressed precisely by those whose approach to European political union is inspired by federalism.

Notes

1 I. Kant, 'On Perpetual Peace,' in *Kant's Principles of Politics*, ed. and trans. W. Hastie (Edinburgh 1891).
2 Committee for the Study of Economic and Monetary Union, *Report on Economic and Monetary Union in the European Community* (Delors Report), Luxembourg 1989, para. 20.
3 Sentence of the European Court of Justice, *Rewe-Zentrale AG against Bundesmonopolverwaltung für Branntwein*, 20 Feb. 1979.
4 Werner, P. et al., *Report to the Council and the Commission on the Realization by*

Stages of Economic and Monetary Union in the Community (Werner Report), Supplement to Bulletin II-1970 (Brussels: EC Commission 1970).

5 Delors Report, 1989.

6 McDougall, D., *Report of the Study Group on the Role of Public Finance in European Integration*, 2 vols. (Brussels: EC Commission 1977).

11

Governing European Union: From Pre-Federal to Federal Economic Integration?
Jacques Pelkmans

After more than forty years of evolution, the European Community had become what might be called a 'pre-federal' system. Following passage of the Maastricht Treaty, the question is whether what is now called the European Union will be transformed into a fully fledged federal polity. This chapter explores this question from an economic perspective, but one which is also sensitive to the broader social and political dimensions of European integration.[1] The chapter uses the economic theory of federalism to explore progress prior to Maastricht, the deepening and widening of the union arising out of Maastricht, and the further developments which will be required to move the European Union from a pre-federal to a federal economy.

Despite the political/institutional approach to federalism long advocated in the European federalist movement, European integration has actually eschewed a formal and constitutional imposition of 'federalism.' Rather, integration has generated innovative, but modest, institutional provisions, with highly circumscribed 'federal' powers for 'federal' bodies. More important, the emphasis has been on substance, including a legal framework for free movement and non-discrimination, and selected common economic policies to make the common market work properly. The deepening of these economic competencies and the widening of the scope of EU powers has been the major determinant of institutional adaptation.

'Thinking federal' still does not come naturally to many Europeans, although their acceptance of EU substantive powers has greatly increased. The heated political debate in 1991 in the UK even led to 'federalism's' being associated with 'centralization,' something federalism aims to prevent. The federalist movement in Europe consists of a tiny elite outside the mainstream. Apart from a few conspicuous attempts to force breakthroughs – all abortive[1] – federalism as a political idea has barely affected European integration. The EU will only become federal – if ever – from the bottom up and through a gradual evolutionary process. This renders an economic perspective even more significant.

European Integration and the Theory of Federalism

Any attempt to apply the classical economic principles of federalism to Europe faces four immediate obstacles.[2] First, the classical theory has concentrated on justifications for decentralization within an initially unitary state by asking what can be shifted from central to lower levels of government. This dynamic is quite different to the situation in Europe. Here, it is a matter of constructing a new set of central institutions where before there was a group of independent, sovereign countries. The primary question, therefore, is what should be centralized? How does one build an economic union?

Second, despite the progress towards completing the internal market, the Union is still a long way from achieving a fully integrated labour market. Cultural and language differences will always constrain labour mobility in Europe. Beyond that, member states show little inclination to pursue greater integration through common regulation and standards in such key areas as hiring and firing rules, minimum wages, collective bargaining, social security, housing policy, and healthcare. One result is that 'voting with one's feet' – a central element of the economic theory of federalism – remains very difficult in the EU.

Third, the EU has barely begun to assume some of the characteristics normally taken for granted in federations. There is as yet no common currency, and even if that is achieved by the end of the decade, it will not cover all member states. The EU level of government has no independent right to tax, and even the common customs code and external tariffs are implemented by the various national customs services. In addition, the Community has a very weakly developed common foreign policy and no common defence policy. These are all fundamental roles for the federal government in truly federal countries.

Finally, the EU does not have many of the institutions of federal government, directly elected by and accountable to the European Parliament and European voters. This democratic deficit has not been overcome with Maastricht. The Union does have a supreme court, which has proved highly integrationist with respect to the internal market and related economic policies. Nevertheless, given the limited scope of EU law, and the desire to avoid a 'government of judges,' the court cannot compensate for the weakness of other EU institutions. Thus, the legitimacy of the 'federal' authorities, their capacity to develop a political program, and their ability to enforce central laws is immeasurably more limited than in fully-fledged federations.

Despite these caveats, the economic theory of federalism can offer important insights into the design of further stages of economic integration. On the one hand, the theory provides criteria for the assignment of powers to the central level.[3] Local policies may be inefficient when there are high levels of externalities or spill-overs, raising the possibility of 'beggar thy neighbour' policies. Local supply of services may also be inefficient where there are large economies of scale, or where the benefits of policies are 'indivisible.'

On the other hand, the logic of integration does not necessitate the centralization of all economic functions at the central level. Indeed, the existence of different sets of preferences among voters in different locations and the difficulties of signalling these preferences to governments suggest an alternative principle, *subsidiarity*, based on the premise that if there are regional differences in preferences, a central government will fail to produce optimal policies. The implication is that assignment of responsibilities to local governments will yield a closer fit between policies and citizen preferences; hence, responsibilities should be assigned to higher levels of government only when local execution would be ineffective, inefficient, or harmful to others.

Federal Principles in a Pre-Federal Community

No Internal Frontiers

The classic theory of federalism[4] assumes that the internal market of a federation is completely free and open. In analytical terms, this means that all types of markets are covered (products, services, and all mobile factors of production) and that markets function well in the sense that there is effective competition and responsiveness to spatial differences in price, earnings, quality of life, taxation, social security, and the number and quality of public goods provided.

One can argue about the degree to which this assumption is attained in actual practice in federations such as the US, Canada, Australia, or Germany. However, there is little doubt that, until recently, the EU differed from all of them in that it maintained internal customs frontiers and – closely related – internal fiscal frontiers. It was also characterized by a much higher density of regulatory barriers.

It is important to appreciate that the original EEC treaty was 'pre-federal' in the sense that it did not aim to remove internal frontiers. Doing so leads one to expect greater responsiveness to price signals and other determinants of mobility. This is due not only to the reduced costs of doing cross-frontier business, but also to the reduction in uncertainty facing economic actors. The impact is already being felt in transportation and many other sectors, where rationalization and further exploitation of economies of scale are no longer resisted out of fear of vulnerability to frontier measures or new national requirements. Sourcing and distribution have also seen a radical boost in europeanization via procurement syndicates, chain stores, and cross-border direct investments by department stores.

The Regulatory Environment
The '1992' approach to removing regulatory barriers in the single market, while finding common solutions where regulation is considered justified, is original and may well have fruitful lessons for other federal systems. Its innovative character was prompted by two decades of frustrating and costly efforts to increase harmonization. These were characterized by painstaking detail, excessive uniformity, and decision-making by unanimity. Since 1984, the EU has gone through a painful process of learning to 'think federal' on regulatory issues. The relative clarity of the principles, as they eventually emerged, is as much the result of experience from trial and error, as it is due to conceptions developed at the outset of the 1992 program.

In systems of multi-tiered government, different views about what to regulate and what to leave to the market can be held among the constituent states and/or among the vertical layers of government. This is particularly the case if there are significant differences in the preferred level of safety, health, or consumer protection. Not only may harmonization be sub-optimal, but an overly strict application of free movement provisions may also be inappropriate. The question is what regulation should be assigned to what level of government in the union. Today's answer to this question follows from an understanding of five distinct elements: subsidiarity, free movement (of products, services, and factors of production), minimum harmonization (only for the so-called 'essential requirements'), mutual recognition, and regulatory competition among member states. This quintet dispenses with the old EU idea that liberalization always depends on or requires harmonization. The combination of the five elements and the greater utilization of qualified majority voting (instead of unanimity) has decreased the regulatory costs of harmonization enormously.[5]

The EU is now capable of finding regulatory compromises in those cases where, before 1992, an all-or-nothing decision between heavy harmonization and undistorted free trade would have been imposed. Beyond the minimum harmonization, free trade is respected via the obligation of 'mutual recognition.' Thus, the ideal of 'undistorted' free trade is pursued much less rigorously than in the past. Furthermore, it is often argued that, when national products and services (subject to national requirements) are fully exposed to competition of products and services originating from another regulatory environment (beyond the minimum EU harmonization), a dynamic process of 'regulatory competition' would be set in motion. This process would be driven by business, which would see its competitiveness threatened by more onerous regulatory requirements.

Fiscal competition is a special subset of regulatory competition. The Union has gone through a learning process, shedding the notion of far-reaching fiscal harmonization in favour of mobile taxable items – that is, the Value Added Tax (VAT), excise duties, taxation of savings and income from capital, as well as corporate taxation. After three successive rounds of proposals, the Council finally accepted a measured form of fiscal competition for VAT with a minimum of harmonization of the rates.

Finally, regulatory and fiscal competition are subsets of a wider notion gaining currency in the EU, namely that of 'policy competition.' It has increasingly been accepted that in the long run the entire policy environment is a crucial determinant of the location of firms in a large single market. Policy competition refers not merely to local taxes (and tax breaks) and regulation, but also to the stability of the social climate, the efficiency of the public administration, infrastructure and communication facilities, access to skills, adequate education facilities, and other public goods that raise the quality of life. In this respect, the EU of today is very different from that of a decade ago. There is an awareness that 'policy competition' may serve as an effective tool to produce better government. This awareness has spread from regional governments, competing for inward direct investments, to member state governments. Except for a call for high social standards and, increasingly, for high environmental quality, the emphasis is not on harmonization, but on greater autonomy to 'compete.'

Transfers and Efficiency
Ever since the Single European Act went into force, the EU has pursued policies to promote 'economic and social cohesion.' It is important to understand that (apart from a marginal impact on equity via the Social Fund) the policy is governed chiefly by efficiency, rather than redistributive considerations. This is not immediately obvious from the political debate, which has often asserted that the southern EU countries and Ireland obtained the funding for cohesion as the political price for their adherence to EC-1992.

In fact, the bulk of expenditure of the structural funds is aimed at equalizing the framework which will permit effective competition in the single market. The emphasis is, therefore, heavily on infrastructure whether physical (transportation networks, telecommunications, energy supplies, etc.) or social (human capital and retraining), as well as support for other needed reforms. In this way, the capacity of each region to seize the opportunities offered by a single market is enhanced. The transfers are, therefore, related to efficiency, and hence temporary. This is not to deny that cohesion is also motivated by the political desire to have a *stable* economic union. The two justifications accord well as long as economic performance is satisfactory.

Subsidiarity and the Single Market
Although the term subsidiarity can already be found in one article of Spinelli's 1984 draft treaty[6], it was the success of EC-1992 that pushed the principle to the forefront. The higher ambitions of the 'social dimension' and 'monetary union' to which EC-1992 gave rise outstripped most policymakers' capacities to understand a possible new institutional equilibrium. This blend of satisfaction about hard-won progress with anxiety about the pace of change and the apparent open-endedness of EC-1992 was also affected by the external dimension of EC-1992, which markedly increased the powers at the EU level. Finally, 1988 was the year of the cohesion decision, which led to a considerable increase in EU expenditure. In this climate, the federal principle of subsidiarity was embraced to enable discrimination between desirable and undesirable elements of centralization. The first authoritative attempt to employ the concept of subsidiarity was the Padoa-Schioppa Report.[7]

The concept is often misused, however, as the social dimension of EC-1992 illustrates. The modesty of the present proposals on the social dimension of EC-1992 is usually justified by invoking the subsidiarity principle. This deference to subsidiarity has prevented the single labour market from coming into being. The restrictions on product and services markets, tackled in the EC-1992 program, pale when compared to what member states do in labour markets. Nonetheless, the latter interventions are hardly touched by EC-1992. EU-level policies to bring about competition in labour markets are widely resisted, as they would disrupt the link between national social protection and the national welfare state system. This resistance creates a profound dilemma: decentralization, at the cost of having no single labour market, or overly central regulation of the labour market in the EU, which would be extremely costly. The political attachment to national labour market regulation and the welfare state has prevailed at the expense of a single labour market.

Even a functional application of subsidiarity cannot be expected to solve all the problems of assignment of powers to the two levels of government. This is so because weighing the two central criteria – spill-overs (externalities between jurisdictions) and economies of scale – often does not lead to a clear conclusion. For instance, since the Single European Act,[8] the underlying preferences of member states with respect to the environment have undoubtedly begun to converge. With greater political homogeneity and many clear instances of negative externalities, it is now claimed that subsidiarity calls for strong EU environmental powers to prevent regulatory competition and to maintain the integrity of the single market. A closer look, however, shows that the matter is much more complicated. Thus, one may centralize the highly technical and costly identification and monitoring of the problem to some degree along with the formulation of the objectives, but depending on the nature of the objective (for example, a measure of the quality of air or an emission norm to be achieved), policy implementation may sometimes be left to lower levels of government. Even the objectives need not always be set at the EU level. Depending on the spread of externalities, they may be better assigned to the world level, or to individual member states or regions, or indeed groups of regions across borders in the EU.

Assignment based on subsidiarity also hinges on the efficiency of cooperation among the member states. Thus, if member states insist (as they have done) that supervision of financial institutions, based on harmonized rules, can remain decentralized, close cooperation and permanent information exchange between the national supervisory authorities will be required. The case for centralization is stronger the higher the costs of cooperation. The point can similarly be applied to customs services, tax prevention, or the approval of new medicines.

The Economic Union in Practice
Four primary elements define the present European economic union: the single market, the rules and practices to ensure its effective operation, a set of common policies, and policies to promote economic and social cohesion.

The Single Market after 1992
The single market after 1992 consists of rules and policies at the EU level which ensure the free movement of goods, services, capital, labour, technology, and entrepreneurship throughout the Union. It will also apply to persons with EU citizenship. The basic rules are rights in the Treaty, often accompanied by or elaborated in detailed sets of obligations for member states, as well as in explicit prohibitions against certain interventions.[9] Such rules include Art. 30, EEC, which outlaws non-tariff barriers in product markets (except when explicitly allowed under Art. 36, EEC). It has its US counterpart in the 'commerce clause.' Both the US and the EU's internal markets have received strong integrationist boosts from the case law based on these rules. There is no obvious counterpart in the Canadian internal market nor in its case law; hence, 'barriers' have persisted in the Canadian market which would be outlawed in the EU single market.[10]

The first rewrite of the EEC treaty – the Single European Act, in force since

July 1987 – contains another crucial rule in Art. 8A: unlike the original EEC Treaty, it defines the internal market, thereby overcoming most of the conditions and other complications of the Rome Treaty in fields such as financial services, transportation, and capital movements. Clearly going beyond the old treaty, it unambiguously states that the internal market is 'without internal frontiers.' This has served as a powerful integrating device in the EC-1992 program.

Although it is difficult to establish when an internal market is really 'completed,' it is clear that the EC-1992 program has been highly effective. That program was based on a 1985 White Paper,[11] but in fact it has moved well beyond that to include the Single European Act, important additions such as the internal energy market, the external dimension (hardly touched in the White Paper), the social dimension (ignored in the White Paper), alterations of the method of harmonization and liberalization (for example, in taxes and technical barriers), and amendments following a few landmark rulings in the European Court.

The upshot is that the internal market was almost completed by early 1993, in the sense that the Council had taken over 95 per cent of all the relevant decisions on the White Paper list. The added ambitions, however, were not all attained. As a result, some (temporary) exemptions for specific member states in specific cases, and the extension of implementation dates for more recent directives mean that the coming into force of EC-1992 will be an ongoing process until the mid-1990s. The higher ambitions may cause legislative activity until late in the decade. This will not necessarily be smooth sailing, however, as will be discussed later in this chapter.

The Effective Operation of the Single Market

The EC-1992 program and the 'customs union plus' preceding it are necessary conditions for a single market. However, for the single market to achieve the full aims of the Treaty, it must function effectively. The main instrument is undoubtedly EU competition policy, an instrument that has gained in significance by 'deepening' and 'widening' its scope. Deepening has taken place via the 1989 Merger Control Regulation, a landmark ruling of the court on enterprises with 'exclusive rights' (for example, telecommunications and utilities), and a tightening of the control on public subsidies to business, especially to state-owned enterprises. Widening has been crucial for service industries such as banking, insurance, air transportation, and telecommunications.

It is increasingly clear that the proper functioning of the single market hinges on an optimal combination of regulation and competition policy. This is particularly sensitive in services and public procurement markets. Another lever to enhance the functioning of the market is exposure to external competition. As Jacquemin and Sapir have shown for industrial goods markets, external competitors have a greater capacity to discipline EU firms than internal competition.[12] In this respect, EC-1992 is likely to improve the functioning of the single market, because the external dimension of EC-1992 is rather liberal, substantially improving market access for third countries.[13]

Two other areas of importance to the functioning of the market are infrastructure (for example, transportation linkages, telecommunication linkages, etc.) and provisions concerning the free movement of labour within the context of nationally regulated labour markets and social security systems. Whereas the former had been tackled belatedly in the so-called 'Trans-European Networks,' in plans up to the year 2010, the latter has remained almost unrealized, to the detriment of the internal market.

Common Policies

The most important common policies of the economic union are:
- a common trade policy, completed by the EC-1992 program. Remaining national quotas have been removed, and the policy is extended to services.
- the common agricultural policy: a customs union for agricultural products with minimum prices sustained by intervention purchases and export subsidies.
- the common transport policy, which has emerged in response to the EC-1992 program. It combines liberalization (so as to create an internal market for transport services) and harmonization (of diplomas, permits, market access requirements, technical standards, and certification, and some fiscal provisions). An important strategy paper in 1992 proposed the widening of transport policy to tackle, for the first time, the relationship between transport and environment, undistorted intermodal competition, the link between transport infrastructure and the external dimension (critical, above all, for air transport).
- competition policy, which consists of four elements: prohibiting or controlling restrictive business practices among independent firms; anti-monopoly policy (called 'abuse of dominant position'); a regime curbing state aids; and one on public enterprises (which are to behave like private ones, although utilities have special rights).

Some other common policies have also been initiated. The most important are structural policies which are inextricably linked to the 'cohesion' of the economic union. A common research, technology, and development (R, T & D) policy emerged in the 1980s. This has gradually shed its bias towards nuclear research (inherited from the Euratom Treaty and its joint research centres) and now focuses on basic research for industry and agriculture. More recently, there has been a tendency to emphasize practical applicability and the link with the competitiveness of European business. The EU funds remain only a small fraction of total national outlays for R, T & D. Even if defence-related R, T & D is excluded, the EU share of spending in this area does not reach 5 per cent.

The Single Act also introduces the basis for a common environmental policy, although the main route to implement it has typically been that of harmonization of technical requirements. This is likely to change after ratification of the Maastricht Treaty: the legal basis for a common policy will be stronger, and there is also much wider political support than half a decade ago.

Cohesion of the Union

Before the Single European Act, EU specific-purpose grants were small and bedeviled with problems: a patchwork of three structural funds, which were constrained by 'juste retour' traditions, narrow scope, administrative restrictions, and limited funding. In February 1988, funding for the three structural funds[14] was doubled, and major reforms were imposed. The taboo against direct cooperation between the regions and the European Commission – bypassing the national governments – was broken.[15] In addition, there was a commitment to remove biases in other EU policies which could be detrimental to the poorer regions of the Union. A provisional assessment of this 'cohesion' suggests that the former policies have been moderately successful, but that the latter have not. For example, the Common Agricultural Policy disadvantages countries relying primarily on Mediterranean products, and the calculation of the EU budget continues, despite alterations, to weigh more heavily on the poorer members.

EMU, Maastricht Style

The Treaty of Maastricht represents a major move towards a federal economy. Its successful conclusion is remarkable because it shows that governments were prepared both to transfer and constrain the major tools of national macroeconomic policy. In the process, they also wrote what seems like an unexpectedly strict monetary constitution.

Monetary Union

The treaty lays down the following properties of the monetary union: irreversible, strict entry conditions; parallelism of monetary and budgetary policy-making in EMU; assignment based on subsidiarity; and price stability as the overriding objective. The properties of irreversibility and subsidiarity are critical to the central question of this chapter, while a minimum degree of parallelism in economic policy-making is a necessary condition for the monetary union to be stable. The strict entry conditions and the commitment to price stability determine the quality of the monetary union.

Irreversibility is firmly set out in the treaty as well as in a special protocol. Not only has a general opting-out clause been avoided, but also the timetable is such that monetary union will start at the latest in 1999,[16] although possibly in 1997. This is crucial for the political credibility of national governments, which will have to pursue often painful policies to live up to the entry conditions. Every member state is now fully responsible for joining the monetary union; it is required by the treaty to comply and cannot tinker with the Union's decision. This is, therefore, a constitutional decision.

Subsidiarity has been applied to monetary policy in the classical way: monetary policy will be centralized at the Union level and a European Central Bank (ECB) will be established, issuing the common currency – the écu – and conducting the single monetary policy. The ECB is part of the European System of Central Banks, inspired by the Federal Reserve system in the US. Not only is the ECB fully independent (the executive board being appointed for eight years, non-renewable) but also the ESCB as a whole will acquire independence. All national central banks will move towards independence before the start of monetary union (that is, either 1997 or 1999). In addition, there are obligations on the leadership of the ECB and the national banks not to seek or take instructions from any other body; conversely, national governments and EU institutions are required not to seek to influence the ESCB.

It is important to appreciate that for a number of member states, the Maastricht Treaty is not merely a transfer of monetary policy and currency to the EU level; it also represents a much greater commitment to price stability than national laws and a radical break with the tradition of subjecting monetary policy to short-term political considerations. Of course, this has become possible because of the successful anchoring function of the Deutschmark in the EMS up until German unification. It is only in the fundamental aspects of external monetary policy that Council and Commission will be able to exert influence.[17]

Budgetary Peculiarities

Compared to the monetary unions of federations, the EU does not possess such characteristics as a sizable federal budget relative to member states' budgets, the right to tax, or significant federal social spending. The EU is not allowed to run a deficit on its relatively small budget. At the central level, there is little possibility for active macroeconomic stabilization policy.

Nevertheless, a considerable degree of budgetary coordination has been agreed to, to enable the monetary union to function properly (that is, price stability is not to be undermined). This coordination has a purely monetary function; there is no relation to the structure or purpose of public expenditure. Three regimes are applied: prohibitions, the prevention of 'excessive deficits,' and the world capital market. With respect to prohibitions, member states, and the ESCB, are prohibited from financing budgetary deficits by creating money; they will not be required to come to the rescue of a member state which has borrowed excessively (no bail outs); and any privileged access of public bodies to the capital markets (including state-owned financial institutions) is ruled out.

With respect to the prevention of 'excessive deficits,' prior convergence before entry is probably more important than the build-up of an excessive deficit, once in the union. 'Excessive deficits' have been defined somewhat arbitrarily as those greater than 3 per cent of GDP.

With respect to the world capital market, financial markets, in choosing government securities, judge the creditworthiness of borrowers, including members of the EU's monetary union. Whether the deficit or the outstanding debt is 'excessive' can be left to market signals, as happens in the US states and Canadian provinces. The EU has implicitly accepted such a role for market forces in the Maastricht Treaty but not fully. It has inserted a benchmark of 60 per cent of GDP for outstanding debt; the speed and direction of the movement towards this benchmark is taken into consideration. The less than full reliance on markets reflects a conviction among EU policymakers that effective market signals may come too late and hence cause disruption and unacceptable social costs.

Due to the extreme budgetary decentralization as compared to federal economies, the monetary union will also lack a shock-absorbing mechanism. In a true federal system, a drop in income for one region or federal state will be cushioned by federal stabilizers. The tax flow to the federal fisc will drop, while the net transfers to the region through federal programs will increase. This is not possible in the EU. Therefore, the EU monetary union will have several budgetary peculiarities. Given the great appetite for budget deficits developed by some member states over the years, monetary union will not come without tears. Whether it will be stable with such extreme decentralization – that is, with domestic budgetary politics being subjected to strict EU rules and common 'surveillance' – remains to be seen.[18]

Beyond Pre-Federalism?

The foregoing analysis demonstrates that despite the amazing progress made by Maastricht, the EU is still far from being a federal entity that is somehow comparable to Switzerland. It is even less comparable to less decentralized federations such as Canada and the US, let alone Germany. Should the Union move further down the federalist road? Six issues should be borne in mind.

(1) Federal Stabilizer?

In the run-up to the Maastricht Treaty, the European Commission proposed an EU-wide 'shock absorption mechanism' to assist member states to absorb severe specific shocks. This proposal was rejected by the Council, but its economic rationale has not disappeared for individual countries: the exchange rate will be definitely lost as a policy instrument, as will an independent monetary policy. There is an EU-wide interest in preventing, or at least cushioning the impact of such shocks: it would prevent political pressure for higher transfers and enhance member states' capacities to live up to the discipline of budgetary coordination.

(2) Federal Right to Tax?

There are several arguments for giving the EU the right to tax. First, it would facilitate fiscal harmonization and limit undesirable fiscal competition when the tax basis is highly mobile. Second, it would mark a return to reliance on its 'own resources' by the Union, an idea greatly eroded by the increasing reliance on VAT and GNP-based 'national contributions.' Third, there may be efficiency reasons for collecting certain taxes at the federal level. Since the EU has no intention of pursuing redistributive objectives, other than fostering cohesion, a move to a progressive system of national contributions would suffice, so no federal right to tax is needed on these grounds.

The main obstacles are the extreme political sensitivities at the member-state level, and the practical issue of finding a revenue source which is not already taxed, and hence does not directly touch national fiscal sovereignty. Member states continue to prefer variants of 'national contributions.'

(3) Federal Social Spending

Apart from very limited outlays from the Social Fund – mainly retraining facilities for long-term unemployed, measures combating youth unemployment, and some adjustment assistance – there is no desire to consider EU-wide social security programs of any kind. On the contrary, member states' governments and labour unions have insisted on an interpretation of 'subsidiarity' which holds that social security should remain at the national level. The debate on the social dimension has been conducted solely in terms of maintaining high minimum social standards in EU and domestic regulation, thereby preempting regulatory competition in social matters. As noted, even eligibility for social security is not automatically extended to EU citizens, except when working in the country concerned and when specific – usually temporary – arrangements apply (for example, scholarships for students).

(4) A Federal Defence and Foreign Policy?
The Maastricht Treaty will strengthen the fledgling common foreign policy of the European Union. It also provides a basis for a future defence role. In the short and medium run, expectations should not be set too high. Even the initial phases of common defence are controversial and will be governed by 'géométrie variable.' The Maastricht Treaty will likely trigger a reconsideration of the diplomatic activity of EU member states and their representation on international organizations, world-wide as well as in Europe. Tensions are bound to arise among the existing member states, and these may well be exacerbated when new members join. In fact, the Danish 'No' in the June 1992 referendum on Maastricht partly arose from anxiety about the mere possibility of a European army even two decades hence.

(5) Subsidiarity and the 'Federal' Level
The Maastricht Treaty has raised subsidiarity to the status of a fundamental principle governing the European Union. This should promote a more federal way of thinking about the European Union. There is little doubt that subsidiarity is much better understood and appreciated in the Union today than before the EC-1992 program, yet the fundamental problem remains that the political logic of an (economic) integration process differs sharply from the decentralization debate in an existing federation. Lack of a feeling of nationhood and solidarity tend to carry much more weight than the usual arguments for 'centralization' in federations.[19] In fact, subsidiarity is more often than not used as a political alibi to maintain member states' powers, rather than as a constitutional principle to allocate powers to the respective tiers of government.

In a much more limited sense, subsidiarity may assume a more functional role in the EU of the 1990s. When concurrent powers exist (both at EU and member state levels), the actual use of those powers will be governed by this principle. It is this limited role for subsidiarity which has been formally enshrined in the Maastricht Treaty. It is possible that, in these cases, recourse to the European Court of Justice may be had to develop a Union doctrine on subsidiarity.

(6) Subsidiarity and the New Regionalism
One reason why EU member states are ambivalent about subsidiarity is the revival of the regions.[20] This trend is the result of several recent changes. First, since the 1988 reform of the structural funds, it has become accepted

practice for regions to deal directly with the Commission. For a long time some member states strongly resisted this, fearing that increased funding from the EU would weaken the dependence of regions on national governments. Second, in addition to Germany, three EU countries now have quasi-federal structures: Belgium, Spain, and, increasingly, Italy. Pressures to decentralize are on the rise in several other countries. This may well be interpreted as a threat in national capitals: precisely when the EU is rapidly assuming important economic and other public functions, including a common currency, decentralization could rob the central governments of member states of many of their remaining powers. Third, the tortuous developments in Eastern Europe and the CIS have fuelled a debate in some regions about special status (for example, in Scotland and Alto Adige). Fourth is the new phenomenon of 'Euregions,' cross-border agreements to facilitate cooperation and reduce the inconvenience of regulatory barriers for those living near frontiers. The legal difficulties of Euregions are formidable, yet their number is rapidly increasing. The EU has initiated a special program (Interreg) to sponsor their fledgling activities. Fifth, the Maastricht Treaty has erected a special advisory council for the regions of the EU. Although primarily a response to the anxiety of the German Länder about EC-1992 and the Maastricht Treaty, it is possible that this will enhance the capacity of regions to organize themselves as a political force. Regions have been quick to spot the potential to use 'subsidiarity' arguments both in their national capitals and in Brussels. This would be consistent with federal thinking.

Conclusion

The present European Union is still only half-way along the path to federalism. In making great progress with the EC-1992 program as well as new higher ambitions (such as the 'social' and 'external' dimensions of EC-1992), the EU has learned to adopt a series of 'federal' principles. The four principles, discussed in this chapter, are no internal frontiers, the regulatory environment, efficiency-motivated transfers, and subsidiarity as the assignment principle.

The even more ambitious Maastricht Treaty would seem to add some further federal characteristics. However, while monetary policy is unambiguously centralized, budgetary policy remains extremely decentralized. A fairly strict regime of budgetary coordination is required for the proper functioning of the monetary union itself. The budgetary part of EMU is, therefore, radically different from existing federations: the size of the EU budget remains extremely small; and the EU has no right to tax, nor to levy social charges, nor to spend on social security, nor to otherwise contemplate any form of macroeconomic stabilization policy, not even in the form of a (country-specific) shock-absorption mechanism.

The difficulties surrounding the ratification of the Maastricht Treaty show in a dramatic way the dynamic interdependence of societies that find themselves in a common process of accepting considerable constraints on their sovereignty, based on hard-won consensus among member states. For example, not only has the UK opted out of the Social Protocol of the Maastricht Treaty – a protocol adhered to by all the other eleven member states – it has also attempted to reduce the 'acquis communautaire' on the basis of a political interpretation of subsidiarity (even though the Maastricht Treaty explicitly states that the 'acquis' is accepted as given). Moreover, the UK disputes the interpretation of Art. 8A of the Single European Act (discussed above) as implying that internal frontier controls of persons should be fully eliminated.

Thus, the Union remains a special, sui generis model which seems dynamically stable, but is not yet federal. The cracks and occasional retrogressions have thus far proved to be temporary. In any event, they do not seem to undermine the core achievements of the Union. Whether the core achievements will (ever) become 'federal' is a question that should be reassessed, perhaps in ten years, when further 'deepening' and the admission of new members have occurred.

Notes

1 Neither the Hague Congress of 1948 nor the Council of Europe it generated could be controlled by the federalists (even though the movement was then at its height). See also the abortive Political Union and European Defence Community treaties of the early 1950s and the (watered-down) Spinelli Draft Treaty on European Union of 1984 which was inspiring but not 'federalist' in the traditional sense.
2 For a more detailed discussion of economic principles of federalism, see Kenneth Norrie, 'Is Federalism the Future? An Economic Perspective,' Chapter 9 in the present volume.
3 Wallace E. Oates, *Fiscal Federalism* (New York: Harcourt Brace Jovanovich 1972); D. MacDougall et al., *Report of the Study Group on the Role of Public Finance in European Integration*, 2 vols. (Brussels: EC Commission 1977); F. Forte, 'Principles for the Assignment of Public Economic Functions in a Setting of Multi-layer Government,' in MacDougall, *Report*, vol. 2; J. Pelkmans, 'The Assignment of Public Functions in Economic Integration,' *Journal of Common Market Studies* 21, No. 1-2 (September-December 1982).
4 For example, Oates, *Fiscal Federalism*.
5 J. Pelkmans, 'Regulation and the Single Market: an Economic Perspective,' in H. Siebert, ed., *The Completion of the Internal Market* (Tübingen: Mohr for the Kiel Institute of World Economics 1990).

6 Led by the federalist ex-EC Commissioner Altiero Spinelli, the European Parliament proposed a Draft Treaty on European Union which probably encouraged the adoption of the Single European Act in December 1985. Note, however, that the Draft Treaty was far from 'federal' as analyzed in the present chapter.

7 T. Padoa-Schioppa et al., *Efficiency, Stability and Equity* (Oxford: Oxford University Press 1987). See also, Tommaso Padoa-Schioppa, 'Economic Federalism and the European Union,' Chapter 10 in the present volume.

8 *Single European Act, Bulletin of the EC,* Supplement 86/2.

9 See the EEC treaty in, for example, *Treaties Establishing the European Communities* (Luxembourg/Brussels: Office for Official Publications of the EC 1978), 203ff.; and Jacques Pelkmans, 'The Significance of EC-1992,' *The Annals* of the American Academy of Political and Social Science 531 (January 1994).

10 J. Pelkmans and M. Vanheukelen, *The Internal Markets of North America, Fragmentation and Integration in US and Canada*, Basic Studies No. 16 (background report to the Cecchini Report, 'Research on the "Costs of non-Europe"') (Luxembourg: Office of Official Publications of the EC 1988).

11 See COM (85) 310 of 14 June 1985, 'Completing the Internal Market' (Brussels: EC Commission).

12 A. Jacquemin and A. Sapir, 'Europe Post-1992: Internal and External Liberalisation,' *American Economic Review* 81, No. 2 (1991).

13 J. Pelkmans, '1992-Effects on Third Countries,' in M. Hilf and C. Tomuschat, eds., *EG und Drittstaatbeziehungen nach 1992* (Baden-Baden: Nomos 1991).

14 The Regional Development Fund, the Social Fund, and the structural part of the Agricultural Fund.

15 Note, however, that member states are still crucial, since EU funding is always on a matching basis.

16 Unless only one member state would fulfil the entry conditions, which would appear to be an absurd supposition.

17 It is too early to pass judgment on how the ECB and the political authorities of the EU will find a division of labour between day-to-day operations in the currency markets (if any) and the policy with respect to exchange rate systems, voluntary pegs, etc. Given the potential influence of the écu, this is no small matter. It also complicates the accountability for maintaining price stability.

18 This chapter does not discuss the appropriateness of the package of *entry conditions* in the Maastricht Treaty, the actual impact on exchange rates in the second half of 1992, and again in 1993, and the probability of achieving monetary union, starting in 1994 with exchange rates in the EMS more in line with the fundamentals.

19 On the importance of different bases of identity, see Raymond Breton, 'Identification in Transnational Political Communities,' Chapter 3 in the current volume.

20 For further discussion, see Guy Kirsch, 'The New Pluralism: Regionalism, Ethnicity, and Language in Western Europe,' Chapter 4 in the current volume.

12

Central Asia: From Administrative Command Integration to Commonwealth of Independent States

Bakhtior Islamov

Introduction

It is common knowledge that *politically* no republic in the newly formed Commonwealth of Independent States (CIS) would like to return to old-style relations. As they began 1992, groping towards appropriate models of development within the framework of the CIS, each republic faced critical decisions about how to integrate into the world community and how to interact with its sister republics.

This chapter examines the distorted centre-republic relations which existed in the former Soviet Union, and the resulting real economic interdependence of the republics, to draw lessons for a new type of integration within the CIS. A brief overview of the Soviet system is followed by a description of the effect of centrally planned mechanisms on trade balances and national income. Finally, a framework for possible economic integration on a new basis within the CIS is suggested.

General Characteristics of Administrative-Command Integration

Seventy-odd years of Soviet history formed a so-called single, all union economic complex which was based on a specific administrative-command integration of the Soviet republics and the division of labour among them. The main characteristics of this integration were:

- a bureaucratic, overcentralized planning and financial system
- a predominance of departmental organization over regional management and independence of the economic units
- artificially and unreasonably high specialization and concentration of production
- indirect interrepublican economic relations based on strong vertical ties and governed by the centre, rather than direct horizontal ties between republics themselves
- distorted systems of prices, subsidies, grants, etc., as instruments of the

central bureaucracy for interference in trade, financial flows, income distribution, and redistribution between the centre and the republics and among the latter.

The predominant principle of the Soviet bureaucratic planning, financial, and managerial systems during all these years was a *sectoral approach*, despite the many proclamations about the necessity of combining this approach with a regional one (although there were some nominal attempts made in the 1920s (NEP) and the late 1950s and early 1960s (Sovnarkhozy)). Conforming to the sectoral approach, plans concentrated on branches (sectors) of the economy, and allocations of financial and material resources were made not by regions (or republics) but by ministries.

As a result, by 1989 almost all industry in the USSR (that is, 95 per cent) was supervised by the centre. The share of the different republics varied slightly, but did not exceed 10 per cent.[1] Decades of central planning left just one or two factories supplying the entire Soviet market with anything from tram-rails to sewing machines. Economists at the Central Economics-Mathematics Institute have calculated that of 5,884 product lines, 77 per cent were supplied by just one producer. One-third of the value of Soviet goods in 1990 was produced on single sites.[2]

Product specialization was carried to an absurd level in agriculture. The 'monoculture of cotton' of the Central Asian republics resulted in these republics producing 92 per cent of Soviet cotton fibre in 1990 (with Uzbekistan alone accounting for 62 per cent of the total). Exploitation of economies of scale and comparative natural advantage (climate, soil, water, and traditional skills in irrigation and agriculture) was offset by huge ecological and socioeconomic problems, as well as the distorted structure of production caused by centrally and administratively enforced specialization.

Product specialization in natural resources was also organized by the centre, and at the expense of complex development of the Central Asian republics, with the pumping out of raw materials to other regions as intermediary products at cheap (virtually at the cost of production) prices. Moreover, in certain instances, natural resources were imported into a republic even though they could have been produced more cheaply inside the republic itself. In 1990, for example, raw materials valued at 700 million rubles (100 million of which was transportation costs) were imported into Uzbekistan, even though over half of this could have been produced at less expense internally. In fact, the program of import substitution adopted in this republic in 1992 was projected to increase production by 250 million rubles within two years and 500 million rubles by 1995.[3]

The following section looks at how these centrally planned measures affected the republics' trade balances, both domestic and international.

Trade Balances

According to Goscomstat (Soviet State Statistical Committee) data published in 1990,[4] almost all of the republics, excluding Belorussia and Azerbaijan, had a deficit in trade balances in 1988 in terms of combined interrepublican *and* foreign trade in *domestic* prices.

The lion's share of the deficit belonged to Russia (33.3 billion (bln) rubles out of a sum of 50.4 bln rubles). The Central Asian republics had the following deficits: Kazakhstan (7.3 bln), Uzbekistan (1.8 bln), Kirghizstan (1.2 bln), and Tadjikistan (1.2 bln).

In interrepublican trade alone, five republics had positive balances (bln rubles): Russia (0.26), Ukraine (3.62), Belorussia (4.05), Georgia (0.29), and Azerbaijan (2.10).[5] The other ten republics (including all of the Central Asian republics) had interrepublican trade deficits. As a percent of Net Material Product (NMP), Azerbaijan and Belorussia gained the most – getting 19 per cent and 15 per cent of their NMP from intra-Union trade.

Foreign trade, measured in domestic prices, showed large deficits (bln rubles) for all of the republics, with the largest in Russia (33.6), Ukraine (6.6), Belorussia (2.0), and Kazakhstan (2.0). These four republics accounted for about 82 per cent of the total trade deficit in domestic prices. Measuring goods in domestic prices, however, distorts the data, as imported goods become artificially expensive.

In an effort to correct for distortions arising from administered domestic prices, Goscomstat has recalculated the export-import balances of the republics. When trade was reassessed at world market prices, both the interrepublican and foreign trade balances of Russia improved sharply, moving from a deficit of 28.8 bln rubles to a surplus of 41.3 bln rubles in 1987. This is explained by artificially low domestic prices for fuels, of which Russia is the biggest exporter internally and internationally, relative to high domestic prices of food and consumer goods, which are Russia's principal imports.

According to 1987 data, Uzbekistan and Tadjikistan each achieved a surplus of 0.1 bln rubles in foreign trade at world prices. However, at the same time, in interrepublican trade, they, as well as the majority of the republics, experienced a deterioration in their trade balance. Only Azerbaijan (apart from Russia (RSFSR) as already mentioned) had a positive balance, while Turkmenistan showed a zero balance.

Data for 1988 from Goscomstat (measured at world prices) give almost the same picture: the results were much better only for RSFSR (moving from a deficit of 33.3 bln rubles in domestic prices to a surplus of 30.8 bln rubles at world prices). Does this mean, as the *Economist* stated, 'The net result is that the Russian republic subsidizes the rest of the country to the tune of 70 bln rubles a year'?[6] One must be aware that the numbers presented cover all exports and imports of the republic, *including foreign exchange*, which is important, since more than half of the gains are connected with the distorted domestic prices paid for foreign imports. The prime minister of RSFSR, in an article published by *Pravda*,[7] suggested that 'the equivalent of trade should give to Russia additionally 24 bln rubles annually.'

When looking at the reassessments of the trade numbers, one must keep in mind certain limitations. First, technically, two balances of trade – one at domestic, the other at world prices – cannot be summed up directly, because they are calculated in different currencies: real inflated ruble, and artificial but equivalent-to-hard currency invaluta ruble introduced for calculations of foreign exports and imports. Second, conversion coefficients (ratios of domestic to foreign prices) are used for highly aggregated commodity groups. Third, principally, in my opinion, the recalculations should be limited to real export prices for the goods which had real buyers in the world markets, and, therefore, real and not hypothetical foreign prices. Such goods in the trade between sovereign republics could and should be bought for real money (hard currency) at world prices. As for other goods, which were subject to interrepublican trade and have no real market among foreign buyers, the world prices could not and should not be used. But in these cases it is necessary to use domestic prices with distortions created by turnover taxes and subsidies eliminated.

Turnover Taxes And Subsidies
The turnover tax was introduced into the Soviet administrative-command economic mechanism at the beginning of 1930. Since then it has been one of the major parts of the centrally fixed system of prices and the source of the Soviet state budget revenues. The turnover tax is the difference between retail and wholesale prices minus a national trade (wholesale and retail) margin. For such goods as petroleum derivatives, tobacco products, matches, bread, and other wheat products, the turnover tax was calculated at a fixed amount per unit of the commodity. For a few goods subject to local price regulations, the rates were ad valorem, ranging from 5 to 50 per cent of the retail price net of trade margin. A small share of products was excluded.

In 1989, almost two-thirds of revenue from the turnover tax was raised in the food and beverage industry (46.8 per cent) and light industry (17.9 per cent), with a large share derived from the sales of alcoholic beverages (mainly vodka). Estimates for 1989 indicated that on average the turnover tax amounted to 27.5 per cent of gross retail commodity sales for alcoholic beverages, with the tax revenue equivalent to 82.4 per cent of recorded consumption.[8]

Why is the problem of taxation, and the turnover tax specifically, so critical for understanding current centre-republic tensions in economic power-sharing, as well as implications for interrepublican trade and national income balances? The main reason is that it has been one of the largest sources of redistribution of value-added between the centre and the republics. In 1989, the turnover tax contributed almost one-third of Soviet state budget revenues.[9]

The republics that produced more final-demand commodities, which were sold at retail, were subject to more turnover tax and gained more share of value-added, including value-added created in previous stages of production. Conversely, the republics producing more intermediate goods (raw materials, semi-finished components) which were shipped to manufacturers at wholesale prices lost value-added. For example, more than 90 per cent of the cotton fibre produced in Uzbekistan was shipped out for manufacturing in other republics and foreign countries. The rate of turnover tax imposed on the primary processing of raw cotton was 410 to 600 rubles per ton of raw cotton, whereas products manufactured from the raw cotton obtained 1260 to 1700 rubles per ton of raw cotton.[10]

Two issues regarding the turnover tax are noteworthy: the allocation of turnover taxes between the centre and the republics, and the real adjustment of trade and national income balances in light of the contribution of each republic to value-added. The emphasis in the past has been on the first issue. The general conclusion has been that the tax has been an instrument for equalization for the least developed republics at the expense of the most developed ones.[11]

The above-mentioned example of cotton fibre versus cotton textiles helps point out, however, that while Uzbekistan retained 100 per cent of its turnover tax, this was only 10 per cent of cotton fibre production; 90 per cent was manufactured outside the region. Thus, in both absolute and relative terms, a major part of the region's value-added was shared with the centre and the other republics. This then distorts the measurement of national product.

The sum of the distortions created by the turnover taxes alone in the Soviet Union in 1988 was 6.4 bln rubles. Central Asia lost almost 3 bln rubles, while Russia, the Ukraine, and Belorussia gained a total of 5.7 bln rubles.

State subsidies (money transfers from government to enterprises or consumers) were also a large factor in creating distortions in trade and national income balances.[12] Over four-fifths of budgetary subsidies in 1988 went to agriculture. Nearly two-thirds of agricultural subsidies (40 per cent for milk and meat products alone) are used to support basic food prices, with most of the rest provided directly to farmers. The average subsidy rate (with respect to retail price) is estimated to be about 65 per cent. But, as of 1988, meat was subsidized at a 233 per cent rate, butter at a 247 per cent rate, and milk at a 171 per cent rate.[13]

Only 7 per cent of budgetary subsidies were given to heavy industry, 80 per cent of which went to the coal industry (the share of which increased markedly in the early 1990s as a result of miners' strikes). Other domestic subsidies for services (mainly housing, culture, and foreign tourism) historically remained relatively small.

The distortions in intra-union trade from state subsidies totalled 6.2 bln rubles. Almost 85 per cent of this total benefited Russia, which gained 5.1 bln rubles from production and consumption of state subsidized goods. Central Asia did not benefit from the distribution of subsidies among the republics. Kazakhstan lost 1 bln rubles; Turkmenistan lost 0.1 bln rubles; Uzbekistan broke even; and Tadjikistan benefited by 0.1 bln rubles.

In total, in 1988, the Central Asian republics, including Kazakhstan, lost about 4.0 bln rubles because of the distortions created by the system of turnover taxes and state subsidies, comprising a significant share of their value-added – 12.7 per cent of NMP in Turkmenistan, 7.2 per cent in Uzbekistan, 8.0 per cent in Kirghizstan, 6.3 per cent in Tadjikistan, and 4.4 per cent in Kazakhstan. The trade balances of these republics (especially Turkmenistan and Uzbekistan) after adjusting for these distortions changed substantially for the better.

Thus, these newly available data indicate that the turnover tax and the system of state subsidies which were thought to benefit the least developed republics (that is, the Central Asian republics) of the former Soviet Union may well have been operating, at least partially, in the other direction. There was a further measure of distortion, however, in the highly integrated republics through the measurement of the national income balances and grants system.

The National Balance and Grants System

Almost all of the republics considered themselves losers under the integrated Soviet system. Because there was no transparent picture of the multiple cross-budgetary transfers and enormous price distortions resulting from the integrated state, each republic felt it was being short-changed. The Soviet Union identified two forms of Net Material Product (NMP): national income produced, which was the sum of value-added minus depreciation in the productive sphere (industry, agriculture, construction, trade, and related transportation services); and national income used, which was the sum of consumption, the accumulation of funds, and the increase in reserves.

Respectively, each year, Soviet statistics would provide the two figures characterizing production and distribution of Net Material Product within a certain republic. The difference between national income produced and national income used constitutes the integral results of the All-Union and republican intergovernmental budgetary transfers through different channels (taxation, subsidies, grants, and profit transfers). National income balances were broader than the trade balances among the republics and reflect interrepublican value-added transfers through a centrally administered budgetary system.

Depending on whether there was a deficit or a surplus in the national income balances, the republics were divided into two groups: so-called 'donors' (NMP produced NMP used) and 'recipients' (NMP produced NMP used). According to Soviet statistics and available Western assessments,[14] all Central Asian republics were classified as long-term recipients. Between 1970 and 1989, Kazakhstan was in absolute and relative terms the largest recipient with a total sum of more than 73.2 bln rubles (having a 13-18 per cent negative balance as a share of national income). In Central Asia, only Turkmenistan possessed a positive sum of about 0.8 bln rubles over the twenty years, although in the period 1984-8, it was also a net recipient.

If Central Asia has consistently been a net recipient, with the redistribution of national income through state budgets rapidly increasing year by year (especially in the late 1980s), why has the gap in all principal economic measurements between the two groups (donor vs. recipient) worsened – not only in relative, but in absolute terms as well? One argument is that the per capita measurements have worsened because of the much more rapid growth of the Central Asian population and the less favourable age structure of labour in the area compared to the western and northern republics.

These demographic reasons are not convincing, however. Azerbaijan, another Turkish-speaking, Muslim republic, situated in the Transcaucasia is much like many of the Central Asian republics in terms of its development and demographic features (high fertility rates, a low level of urbanization, and few women in the work-force). However, according to Belkindas and Sagers,[15] for the years 1978-87 it was the third largest donor (in absolute terms) after Russia and the Ukraine, and the largest in relative terms, yielding as much as about one-quarter of its national income produced. This shows that the division of net donors and net recipients in the former USSR was artificial and not correlated with the level of development of the republics, their real production, and their consumption. One may draw incorrect conclusions, having only statistics on national income produced by the republic and national income used by its population.

The Soviet structure also had a system of grants and profit transfers. In 1989, all Central Asian republics were recipients of grants totalling 5.9 bln rubles, a huge increase over even 1985. In the 1990 state budget, the major items in Union grants to Central Asian republics are income compensation for regional differences (2.6 bln rubles), development of social infrastructure (about 3 bln rubles), and subsidies to Kazakhstan on agricultural prices (2.2 bln rubles).

Table 12.1

**Regional grants compared with losses of
Central Asian Republics on turnover taxes
and subsidies (in bln rubles)**

Republics	Losses in 1988 because of turnover taxes and subsidies	Grants in 1989
Uzbekistan	1.5	1.9
Kazakhstan	1.2	2.7
Kirghizstan	0.4	0.5
Tadjikistan	0.3	0.3
Turkmenistan	0.6	0.4
TOTAL	4.0	5.8

Source: Calculated on the basis of following sources: *Vestnik Statistiki* 3:37 and 4:49 and *European Economy* 45 (December 1990):150.

The increased role of regional grants is (like the turnover tax retention discussed earlier) viewed as having been beneficial to the Central Asian republics at the expense of the more developed republics. However, in 1989 the size of the grants to the Central Asian Republics more or less correlated with the size of their losses in 1988 because of the turnover tax and subsidy mechanism alone. Grants eliminated the subsidy on agricultural prices (which in 1990 was more than 2 bln rubles) and were even less than figures suggested by Goscomstat for adjustments in the 1988 national income balances. Thus, in essence they were a sort of income compensation to Central Asian republics for their previous year's losses on the turnover tax and subsidy system.

The last big source of distortion in prices and channels of value-added redistribution in the Soviet system was profits, which accounted for almost one-third of the Union state budget revenues. Raw materials were sold at a low price to supply the larger republics with inputs, which then profited when the finished goods were sold. Not enough data is available to analyze this phenomenon fully, so it is only mentioned as another factor in the overly integrated Soviet legacy which the newly independent republics must face.

The Role of Integration

The Soviet administrative-command mechanism created in its own manner greater internal integration than the European Union and, to a certain extent, even the United States, if one is to compare interstate (interrepublic) economic relations. In domestic prices, interrepublican trade (excluding 'nonproductive') in the USSR reached 21 per cent of GDP in 1988, greater than the EC trade in goods and services among its members (14 per cent).[16] However, while the percentage of GDP of trade of the EC members with the rest of the world was roughly the same, the Soviet republics' exports abroad amounted to barely one-quarter of the value of the interrepublican trade.[17]

In 1988 the ratio of interrepublican trade to net material product (value-added) in all republics excluding Russia was higher than the All-Union index (29.3 per cent). Central Asia, characterized by the high degree of product specialization typical of the Soviet system mentioned earlier, depended heavily on trade with the other republics (Turkmenistan, 50.7 per cent; Kirghizstan, 50.2 per cent; Uzbekistan, 43.2 per cent; and Tadjikistan, 41.8 per cent). Kazakhstan, with more balanced production, was somewhat less reliant on interrepublican trade (31 per cent). Russia (18 per cent) and the Ukraine (39 per cent) were at the low end, while Belorussia (69.6 per cent), coupled with the smaller republics in the Baltics (61-66 per cent), Transcaucasus (54-61 per cent), and Moldova (62 per cent) had the highest ratios. Although a few of the EC countries (for example, the Netherlands) reached such high ratios, intra-EC indices of the largest members were 25-50 per cent less.[18]

Looking at *foreign exports* relative to value-added, the reverse picture for the republics was true. Russia had the highest share (8.6 per cent). Among the Central Asian republics, only Uzbekistan (7.4 per cent) was close to the All-Union index (7.5 per cent), sharing second place with Estonia. As for the other republics in the area, Tadjikistan's share was 6.9 per cent, Turkmenistan's 4.2 per cent, Kazakhstan's 3.0 per cent, and Kirghizstan's 1.2 per cent. These percentages compared favourably with the export ratios of the republics of the Transcaucasus, but were somewhat lower (excluding Uzbekistan) than the western republics.

The role of interrepublican trade, under the existing mechanism of commodity and finance transfers, in the economic development of the republics can also be assessed by an analysis of the share of exports in the value of production and imports in consumption. The 1988 data show the substantial role of interrepublican trade both in production (11-28 per cent) and consumption (14-29 per cent).

The economy of small republics is much more vulnerable to shocks in mutual trade than that of the larger republics. The share of exports in production and imports in consumption are, for example, in the Baltics (24-28 per cent and 27-29 per cent), Transcaucasus (26-28 per cent), Moldova (28 per cent and 27 per cent), Russia (11 per cent and 14 per cent), and the Ukraine (16 per cent and 18 per cent). The same is true within the regions, in the case of Central Asia: Kazakhstan (12 per cent and 20 per cent), Uzbekistan (18 per cent and 24 per cent), Kirghizstan (21 per cent and 28 per cent), Tadjikistan (21 per cent and 29 per cent), and Turkmenistan (22 per cent and 25 per cent).

The role of domestic intra-Union trade in the economy of the republics was much higher than the influence of foreign trade in the Soviet republics' production and consumption. In 1988, exports were 30 per cent of the gross value of total output for the USSR, imports 64 per cent.

In comparison with market economies' integration and trade in general, the USSR share of trade among republics was fairly constant over the 1966-88 period. This shows that bureaucratic integration failed to provide progressive types of specialization and cooperation based on new technologies. The rapid increase in the exchange of unfinished goods in comparison with the general growth of trade was a direct function of the growth of commodity production and specialized enterprises with old-fashioned equipment and technology.

Slight changes in the shares of exports and imports in the economies of the different republics are better explained by changes in price structures. The trend in prices was inversely proportional to the size of export shipments, which have been growing for some goods (for example, cotton) even faster than production.

Inconsistent macroeconomic measures by the centre and unilateral steps by the republics (various forms of export restrictions, political friction, 'war of laws,'[19] meat and other food or consumer goods wars) administered shocks to all the republics. By the spring of 1991, both the centre and the majority of the republics came to the conclusion that integration and independence of the former Soviet republics required coordinated action. Unilateralism, protectionism by any republic, as well as Union inflexibility on the need for real decentralization of economic power could create stronger shocks for the newly independent republics than the 1973 oil price increases caused the major oil-importing countries.

What Is Necessary for Transition to Economic Integration on a New Basis within the Commonwealth of Independent States

Some progress has been made towards making the CIS a working entity, but none of the republics has put great effort into the creation of an effective system. Still lacking, according to G. Yavlinsky, are a comprehensive package of treaties in the main policy areas; permanent coordinating bodies capable of ensuring the functioning of a large interstate amalgamation; and structures necessary for the solution of the most critical interstate problems like those of Karabakh and Trans-Dniestria.[20]

Some breakthroughs have been made through bilateral agreements, but much needs to be done before the republics can function effectively, given their heavy reliance on interrepublican trade. Disruption of the totalitarian and overcentralized system, with a transition to a new community with a completely different relationship, requires new principles and approaches which can be summed up as follows.[21]

Political sovereignty

(1) State sovereignty for each of the republics.
(2) A stable and predictable legal system with possibly a common basis.
(3) The republics define their respective degrees of participation in their interrelationships and coordinating bodies, and their right to amendments and secession.

Economic sovereignty

(1) Property:
  (a) The wealth within the territory of each republic (its land and other natural resources; its economic, scientific and technological potential, etc.) is the material basis of its sovereignty.
  (b) The republics are entitled to their respective shares in the former property of the All-Union state (including, for example, diamonds, precious metals, reserves, and currency holdings).
(2) Taxes:
  All corporate or physical persons (and any other forms of business or taxpaying entity) within the territory of a republic are to be taxed for their and their locality's budgets exclusively.
(3) Economic relations
  (a) Interrepublican exchange is to take place in hard currency at world market prices for the goods which could be sold at that moment in the real international market; and for all other commodities, at the domestic price, with all distortions removed.
  (b) Revenues, losses, assets, and obligations from or in the foreign economic relations in which a republic engages are to be properly budgeted for in its state budget; private sector firms shall engage in foreign relations at their own risk, subject to taxation.

Economic community

(1) Common market (common intra-CIS trade regime):
  (a) Free movement of goods, people, and capital; no customs, tariff, or contingency barriers in interrepublican relations, i.e., free trade, on the basis of rational specialization and concentration of production and the optimal combination of the big, medium, and small state-owned and private businesses.

    (b) Common customs regulations to protect against outside negative influence on the common market, but not to prevent integration with the world market and its positive influence through the mechanism of competition.

(2) Common credit and financial policies:

Common hard currency reserve to meet previous Union obligations and to finance interrepublican programs. The republics are owners of their shares in this reserve fund; stabilization of the ruble by radical devaluation and achievement first of its internal and then full convertibility.

(3) Institutions – goals and functions:

    (a) Each republic is to regulate its own economy within its own territory; the coordinating or managing bodies of the common market are to act only in accordance with the authority delegated to them by the republics.

    (b) Goals: macroeconomic coordination and a common or harmonized policy to help shape the market and protect its viability.

    (c) Functions: fundamental research; common energy supply; provision and control of principal railways, pipelines, and navigation; regulation of nuclear power, communication, and information systems; common intellectual property protection, weather service, weights, measures, and other standards; common statistics and economic accounting; common emergency funds; defence and security of common borders.

Under a new political and economic environment, the main comparative social advantages of Central Asians – commitments to private ownership and enterprise – could provide them with better opportunities to overcome their socioeconomic, ecological, and other problems and to become integrated into the world community. Integration into the world economy would be facilitated, of course, if technical assistance from the G7 through the IMF and the World Bank were not limited to Russia, but involved Central Asia and the other republics as well. Highly industrialized countries could also promote the republics' transition to a market economy and democracy by establishing and building a cooperative relationship in various areas including research and education. Given the highly integrated nature of the former Soviet Union, however, the struggle to enter into the world community will be very difficult, especially for the republics of Central Asia.

Notes

1 Directorate-General for Economic and Financial Affairs, Commission of the European Communities, 'Stabilization, Liberalization and Devolution. Assessment of the Economic Situation and Reform Process in the Soviet Union,'

European Economy 45 (December 1990):75.

2 See *Economist*, 13 July 1991, 23 and *Economist*, 11 August 1990, 67.

3 *Pravda Vostoka*, 6 April 1991, 2.

4 Goscomstat, *Vestnik Statistiki*, 3 and 4 (1990).

5 The statistics that follow are from Russian statistical sources and the IMF, World Bank, OECD, and EBRD report, *A Study of the Soviet Economy*, vols. I-III (1991) in vol. 1, 225, 228, 229.

6 See *Economist*, 13 July 1991, 23.

7 *Pravda*, 5 December 1990.

8 *World Bank Report on USSR*, 'Standard Fiscal Issues' (draft paper), vol. 1 (December 1990):45.

9 Ibid., 34.

10 Z. Solokhitdinov, 'Otcenka Effectivnosti Kapital'nykh Vlozhenij V. Usloviyath Otkrytoi Ekonomiki,' *Ekonomika Zhizn* 10 (1985):17.

11 'The Central Asian Republics keep almost 100 percent of the turnover tax revenues they collect, while more industrialized regions such as the RSFSR, Ukraine, and Latvia hand over roughly half of their turnover tax receipts to the all-union budget' (Donna Bahry, *Outside Moscow* (New York: Columbia University Press 1987), 55).

12 By 1990, in fact, for the first time, domestic budgetary subsidies totalled more than turnover tax revenues (International Monetary Fund, 'Structural Fiscal Policy,' draft (1990):77).

13 Ibid.

14 Data for 1989 include only grants to the Central Asian republics from the Union budget (see *European Economy* 45 (December 1990): Table A.11). Statistics for 1970-88 are from M. Belkindas and M. Sagers, *Soviet Geography* XXXI (November 1990):640-1.

15 Belkinda and Sagers, *Soviet Geography*, 641.

16 IMF, World Bank, OECD, and EBRD, *A Study of the Soviet Economy*, vol. 1, 193.

17 Ibid.

18 *European Economy* 45 (December 1990):75.

19 'War of laws' refers to the republics' passage of laws giving priority to their laws in cases of conflict with central laws, followed by the centre passing a law invalidating those laws, and the republics reenacting their laws.

20 G. Allison and G. Yavlinsky, *Window of Opportunity: Joint Program* (Cambridge, MA: Harvard University Press 1990).

21 The general principles of the model were developed in discussions of '500 day' and other programs connected with the transition to a market economy in the Soviet republics-centre relations by the author during his visiting scholarship at Harvard in 1990-91.

13

American Federalism: An Economic Perspective

Alice Rivlin

The nation states as we have known them, including those with federal structures like the United States and Canada, are being challenged internally and externally. On the one hand, the technological revolution has shrunk distance and made us all more interdependent. Not only economic well-being, but actual survival depends on strong international cooperation and on some surrender of sovereignty to that end. On the other hand, people everywhere want more control over their own lives and over their own public services. In some places localism is having, at least temporarily, tragic consequences with no apparent solution. In others, as in the United States and Canada, the struggle is peaceful, but it is still very deep, involving basic tradeoffs between local autonomy and the control of central authority. Even in the United States, where no empire is dissolving, the recent trend is towards local and state autonomy. The movement towards greater state and local responsibility in the United States has, however, had little connection with ethnic self-determination.

The forces of global interdependence are not reversible. Nonetheless, it is very difficult for some countries, especially the United States which has been relatively self-sufficient and very powerful for a long time, to face the fact that it may have to surrender some sovereignty. Many Americans would like to turn inward, ignore the rest of the world, do our American thing within our own borders, bank with our own banks, and defend our own interests. But the revolution in technology has made total self-sufficiency impossible.

There are many benefits of globalization – from a single market for finance to an ability to learn from each other. But there are dangers as well. It is possible now to deliver lethal weapons to all parts of the globe in seconds or minutes. Economies are much more vulnerable to trade wars, to financial collapse, and to environmental damage that spreads easily across borders. Survival and world prosperity, therefore, really depend on international cooperation and on international regulation.

The global community must control the weapons of mass destruction. We have also learned in the last few years that we must have international regulation of banking practices and of atmospheric emissions. Moreover, the richer nations have an enormous stake in the prosperity of poorer ones and in helping to settle disputes before they escalate.

Does global interdependence require some kind of world government or world federalism? While many hoped for that after the Second World War, it now seems more realistic to organize ad hoc partnerships to address specific problems than to think idealistically about world government. A more likely scenario is a network of international partnerships focused on issues such as weapons control, conflict resolution, trade regimes (which one hopes, in the interest of all, will be liberalizing trade regimes), financial regulation, environmental regulation, and so forth. Each of these partnerships may differ structurally: some may be global while others are regional; some may be formal while others are more informal. But all will require delegation of various degrees of sovereignty, and they will likely become progressively more intrusive into what we used to think of as purely national matters.

Delegations of sovereignty may seem to diminish the importance of the nation state, but for the foreseeable future, international partnerships will actually make the job of governing nation states much more challenging and, hence, more important. The increasing involvement of nation states in international partnerships has implications for internal governance as well. It is very hard for leaders to play a strong role on the international scene without making enemies at home. President George Bush and Prime Minister Brian Mulroney learned that reducing trade barriers or reducing subsidies have short-run costs which may outweigh the long-range benefits in the public mind. This can cause all kinds of political difficulties. International interdependence itself fosters both popular dissatisfaction with the central government in federal systems and managerial overload at the centre. It is difficult to play a strong role on the world scene and to manage a large country at the same time. This is at least part of the explanation for the current movement towards decentralization in the United States.

There is a second force pushing for decentralizing of power: local self-determination. Federalism is a form of government designed to reconcile the conflict between central functions and the desire for diversity and local autonomy. Even longstanding successful federalisms, such as the United States and Canada, are being tested by these opposing forces. The distribution of functions between the centre and the regional governments needs constant rethinking. The essence of a federal system is dynamism, with the power and emphasis flowing back and forth, as the need dictates, between the centre and the periphery. The United States had a very weak central government for its first 150 years. The federal government was small; it dealt with foreign affairs, facilitated interstate commerce, and developed the frontier, but it did not do much else. Then roughly from 1930 to 1980, power flowed towards the centre, with people who grew up in that period beginning to think that this was inexorable.

In fact, two different movements were occurring. First was the establishment of national economic institutions, which the United States had lacked and which it found were desperately needed to cope with the Great Depression. Bank regulation and the establishment of the social security system reflect these forces. These efforts are working quite well, and most people want to maintain these national economic institutions. The second movement sought to influence what the states actually did to improve their own functions. It reflected a widespread perception that the states were not modern governments, that they were unrepresentative, and that they were sometimes racist and unprofessional. The federal solution was to grant money to the states with conditions on how they should spend it.

The flow of power to the centre and the reliance on Washington for reform eventually ran into two obstacles. The first was public backlash. President Reagan's election in 1980 reflected a popular mood that the federal government had become too big and too intrusive. Unfortunately, Reagan reduced federal funds for states and localities without sorting out responsibilities. President Reagan also made a huge fiscal policy mistake, resulting in a very large federal deficit that penalizes our economic vitality and drains the savings of the country. The deficit fostered a cutback in central government aid to the states.

The second force was not backlash, but success. The states were strengthened by federal efforts in the 1960s and 1970s. They did become more professional, more representative, and less racist. In the face of the Reagan revolution, they also took over some of the functions the federal government had been performing and became much more innovative than Washington has been for at least ten years.

This history leaves the United States with a policy dilemma. Economists are almost universally agreed (and this is remarkable for economists) on what ought to be done about the economy: we ought to eliminate the federal deficit; we ought to increase public investment and particularly improve our schools and our infrastructure; and we ought to fix our creaky and expensive health financing system. That is an agenda over which there is not much controversy. However, we have been paralyzed, especially at the federal level, in part because these actions would require a big increase in taxes at a time when there is little enthusiasm for federal taxation and diminished trust in the federal government to do things right.

One of the ways out of this situation requires rethinking our federal structure. I have proposed a set of policies that I call 'dividing the job.' This involves a return to a much stricter division of responsibilities between the federal and the state governments. The federal government ought to take on the role of fixing the health system, because it is very difficult for the states to do that by themselves. That would relieve the states of some fiscal burden. Any necessary increase in federal tax might be more saleable, because it would be associated not with the general purpose of supporting the government, but with the specific purpose of financing a reformed health system that would cover everybody and reduce the rapid growth in health costs.

The states, on the other hand, should take full responsibility for the productivity agenda – for drastic education reform, for training, for infrastructure, for housing, and for community development. Moving those responsibilities to the states would help reduce the federal deficit, but it would raise the question of where the states would get the money. One way to strengthen the state fiscal systems is a new approach to raising revenue that I call 'common taxes.' States have unequal resources, and they compete with each other. Both these problems could be alleviated with some common taxes shared on a redistributive basis. That is a revolutionary idea in the United States, but is quite common in some other federations – for example, it is the basis for the German financial arrangements.

Dividing the job would clarify who is in charge. One reason for the public's lack of confidence is simply confusion about who is supposed to do what. Some services would work better if it were clear that they were state and local responsibilities, that they had to be adapted to local conditions, and the visible officials were accountable. The current overlapping of responsibility means that nobody is quite clear who is in charge.

There are other services that work better when they are done uniformly across a nation. Social insurance is one; healthcare, or at least healthcare financing, is another. Some responsibilities, presumably, have to be joint – for example, much of the environmental problem, because some pollution spills over borders and some is purely local. Support for research and development should be joint for the same reason.

I have spelled out the case for a new division of governmental tasks between Washington and state capitals in a recent book.[1] Not everyone will agree with my particular scheme.[2] The point I hope readers will carry away, however, is that undertaking the productivity agenda and reducing the federal deficit at the same time requires some creative thinking about which level of government should do what.

One thing is certain: the way in which any federalism structures the division of responsibilities between the centre and the states in the 1990s will change again. There is no right answer: if centralization is excessive, people will protest and want to swing back. Similarly, if the pendulum moves too far towards decentralization, it will swing again. This tension is characteristic of a federal system. Indeed, it is the beauty of a functioning federal system that it can accommodate these swings and not break apart.

Notes

1 Alice Rivlin, *Reviving the American Dream: the Economy, the States, and the Federal Government* (Washington: Brookings Institution 1992).
2 For a different view, see Robert Howse, 'Federalism, Democracy, and Regulatory Reform: A Sceptical View of the Case for Decentralization,' Chapter 17 in this volume.

Part Four:
The Law and Politics of Federalism

14

New Wine in Old Bottles?
Federalism and Nation States in the
Twenty-First Century:
A Conceptual Overview

Thomas O. Hueglin

Introduction

I begin with three propositions. First, federalism and the nation state are contradictions in terms. The latter is an historical construct of centralized power monopolization, initiated by 'small groups of power-hungry men [who] fought off numerous rivals and great popular resistance in the pursuit of their own ends.'[1] The former is nothing less than its opposite, a form of decentralized political organization designed to prevent power-hungry men from assuming monopolized power. Second, federalism is the most important political device for the regulation and accommodation of the world's most burning and devastating conflicts. Without some form of federalism, the conflicts in Northern Ireland, in the Middle East, or among the nationalities of the former Soviet bloc will not go away. At the same time, federalism is merely a technical tool (*techne*) and not an end (*telos*) in itself, so there is nothing intrinsically democratic or just about political federalism. While federalism is designed to frustrate the ambitions of power-hungry groups, as has been pointed out often enough, its decentralization may instead facilitate or preserve the rule of power-hungry local elites.[2] As the great theorist of political centralization, Thomas Hobbes, observed more than 300 years ago, if the same clique occupies power at both levels of government, 'it would no whit advantage the liberty of the subject; for as long as they all agree, each single Citizen is as much subject as possibly he can be.'[3] Of course, Hobbes's argument was aimed at denouncing all forms of 'compounded' or 'mixed' government as ineffective and unstable. But his argument can be turned around: if there is some practical wisdom in the federal organization of politics, then it must be to ensure that the same clique of power-hungry men does not occupy and dominate the political institutions at all levels of government.

Third, for federalism to be a legitimate tool of effective conflict management, it must be based on legitimate organization by political communities, and the latter requires the democratic empowerment of citizens within those communities. The implication is that politics in federal states must become federalized in a societal sense, providing checks and balances over constitutional change as well as policy formation in at least three ways: by constraining national government through legislative co-determination by regional governments,[4] by reorganizing provincial political life in such a way as to allow for significant input from all relevant social groups, and by constraining both national and regional or provincial governments through national minimum standards of public services and socioeconomic guarantees that cannot be undercut. Of these three ways, the reorganization of provincial political life so as to permit significant participation by all relevant social groups is of particular importance.

With novel degrees of non-territorial fragmentation, new and non-territorial forms of representation may well be required (for example, the inclusion of some forms of conciliar or corporatist representation of organized interests in upper legislative chambers). Such fragmentation may further require the recognition of non-territorial groups of people – linguistic or racial minorities – as fully autonomous participants along with provinces or as some type of third order of government in the federal process. In other words, the provincial players of federalism must be constrained by the same principles of power-sharing they wish to impose upon the federal process of decision-making.

It is now a commonplace observation that the world has become both more integrated and more fragmented.[5] Therefore, federalism seems a natural response as regards institutionalized political organization. Integration would lead to the formation of supranational institutions coordinating regional preferences and differences, while fragmentation would require the preservation and protection of such differences at the national as well as regional and local level. What that means for federalism as a promising and adequate form of political organization is not simply which powers ought to be allocated to which level of government, but which groups of citizens ought to be empowered at which level of government. How can federalism be used wisely as an institutional tool for reorganizing the political process so that more people and groups of people are empowered by that process?

In light of these concerns, particularly that of broader and more meaningful participation in the political process, I first discuss briefly a number of examples of federal concepts and forms that in my view are inadequate as models for a new world order of integration and fragmentation, and then turn to examples that should indeed be considered as such models. Given the fact that politics in federal states often appear as not much more than a competition of vested interests in constitutionally defined fiefdoms for political and economic power, it should not be surprising that most of the latter examples are derived not from established federations, but from quasi-federal practice in political and/or social systems that are not formally federal or that are in the process of creating federal institutions for the first time.

Before beginning such a critical examination, however, another clarification is in order. The purpose of this chapter is not to denounce the models and experiences of established federalism as complete failures or travesties of the 'true' federal spirit. On the contrary, political federalism has doubtlessly made postwar (West) Germany more democratic, for example, by supplying new social movements such as the Greens with regional springboards to political authority and responsibility; it has given Canada a much envied degree of regional social stability, for example, by a regional equalization commitment that has at least helped to better (some) regional life chances; it has on occasion helped to curtail the imperial power aspirations of American presidents, for example, by at least limiting the extent of social budget-cutting in the name of a decentralizing new federalism during the Reagan presidency; and it has helped social democratic forces within the European Union to push for at least some degree of cohesive social responsibility, for example, by implementing a social charter as a tradeoff for the creation of an economic union of trade and production.

The point is that political federalism is not an *automatic* safeguard for such achievements. It can be used to promote such legitimate ends, or it can be used precisely to circumvent and prevent them from becoming part of the agenda.

Old Bottles

Switzerland

In a recent special issue of *Government and Opposition*,[6] a number of scholars raised the question whether the 'Confederatio Helvetica' can serve as a model of democratic federalism in a new world order. It is one of the mysteries of modern comparative political science that Switzerland routinely figures as an almost idealized model of democracy and federalism, when in fact thorough and critical analyses of the Swiss political system hardly exist. The verdict of the issue's contributors was ambivalent. While some argued that Switzerland's unique historical experience and political culture have created political institutions that cannot be exported, others insisted that the spirit of federalism, and its commitment to non-majoritarian forms of democracy, can and should be exported. But just what is that unique experience and culture, and what political institutions and spirit have they created?

The historical experience of Swiss federalism is not actually unique. As in the United States, the constitutional consolidation of the federal system came after a secessionist war carried on by the country's conservative patriciate against the modernizing forces of economic liberalism. The result was the constitution of 1848, and as in Canada or Germany, it was based on the historical compromise between the centralist economic interests of the new bourgeois elites and the older regional interests seeking to retain autonomy over culture, religion, and education.[7] Unlike most federations, however, the constitution was not a venerable document of first principles cast in stone, but a pragmatic workhorse that would be frequently changed and adapted to changing times. As in other federations, more and more tasks and competencies eventually came to be assigned to the federal level of government.[8]

A number of peculiarities suggest that Swiss federalism is unique, nevertheless. First, there is a strong plebiscitarian component to political decision-making, including both a legislative *referendum* and *initiative*. As a consequence, Swiss citizens are asked to go to the polls more frequently than citizens elsewhere. Between 1970 and 1986, for example, some 120 decisions were put before them in this way.[9] Second, there is a more recent trend of pragmatic decentralization. As Kloeti reports, most of the tasks constitutionally assigned to federal government have in fact been at least partially 'delegated' back to the cantonal level.[10] Third, there is a regime of strict proportionality. Its most visible and important manifestation is the composition of the federal government which includes the four major parties according to the famous 2:2:2:1 formula and which also takes account of regional and cultural-linguistic differences. As a consequence of this *grand coalition* arrangement, there is for all practical purposes no opposition to which the government would be formally accountable.

At first glance, then, it appears that Swiss federalism has found various antidotes to the traditionally recognized weaknesses of federalism elsewhere: the plebiscitarian component serves as a corrective to the heavy-handed routine of executive bargaining among intergovernmental elites, ensuring that the people's voice is not lost and even breaking deadlocks resulting from irreconcilable self-interest at the two levels of government; the practice of delegating competency from the federal to the lower government levels helps to satisfy such self-interest and enhances local flexibility in administering policies which, at the same time, remain under the control of a centrally regulated universality; the adherence to strict proportionality dampens divisive partisanship, and especially so when such partisanship appears reinforced by regional conflicts. However, this conventional picture of Swiss federalism as a nearly perfect model ready for imitation elsewhere is alarmingly deceiving.

The plebiscitarian component is more often characterized by manipulation from above than by popular input from below. The frequency of referenda and initiatives has resulted in one of the lowest voter turnouts in the Western industrialized world. Therefore, the outcome of plebiscites mostly depends on massive mobilization campaigns requiring money and media influence. With regard to both, organized business dominates all other interest-groups. This domination is facilitated by the exceptionally high degree of centralization of organized business. The most influential *Vorort*, for example, represents 108 sections of more than twenty different branches of the Swiss secondary and tertiary economy.[11]

Organized business also controls the media to a considerable extent. The control mechanism here is advertising money in a small national media market. When the left-liberal *Tages-Anzeiger* published an analysis of the influence the corporate sector had exercised in the defeat of a 1977 popular initiative concerning air pollution control, for example, car importers collectively withdrew advertisements worth millions of Swiss francs. Similar concerted actions have frequently accompanied the plebiscitarian process.[12]

Plebiscitarian manipulation is ultimately facilitated by the country's demographic composition, as well as by constitutional provisions. Constitutional changes, for example, subject to a mandatory popular referendum, require a double majority of the population at large and of the population in at least half of the cantons. Thus, a majority in fourteen of the smallest cantons can block a constitutional amendment, or, in other words, 20 per cent of the population can in theory block a decision supported by 80 per cent.[13] Add the notoriously low general degree of voter participation, and referendum campaigns inevitably come down to a battle among a few crucial groups affected by the decision.

The plebiscitarian component in Swiss federalism can hardly serve as an encouraging model of how to leaven the executive elitism embedded in the intergovernmental process with popular input. The delegation of central powers back to lower levels of government, on the other hand, appears to be a promising corrective to the inefficiencies and inflexibilities of the federal duplication of government and administration. In Germany, for example, most general legislation is made at the federal level, but its detailed specification, administration, and implementation is left to the Länder. Citizens are spared expensive dual layers of federal *and* provincial administration, but the division of powers – between central legislation and local administration – is maintained.

In Switzerland, this division of powers is crucially undermined by the overlapping accumulation of public office between the three levels of government. About 10 per cent of the members in the two chambers of the Swiss national legislature are members of cantonal or city governments, and local government presidents routinely sit in cantonal legislatures.[14] The suspicion inevitably arises that the process of power delegation is largely driven by personal-interest collusion at all levels of government, and that this collusion will, in Hobbes' words, 'no whit advantage the liberty of the subject.'

The full extent of power and office collusion in Switzerland only emerges when what the Swiss themselves refer to as 'militia democracy' is taken into consideration. What 'militia' stands for is an old and venerable concept of honorary participation in public office. Swiss parliamentarians are not paid a salary. Compensated for their expenses only, they are considered part-time politicians on an honorary basis.

In practice, of course, they have long since been turned into 'semi-professionals.'[15] Reimbursement comes in the form of multiple board memberships. Of the 244 deputies in both houses, 82 per cent at one point occupied a collective 'total of over 1,000 directors' jobs,' representing some 15 billion Swiss francs, or one-third of 'all the social capital of all the limited companies registered in Switzerland.'[16] In other words, they receive remuneration from the private sector they come to represent. They do their business mainly in the 400 or so hearing commissions that dominate the policy process, and it is perfectly normal that a hearing, say, on banking law will be stacked with representatives of the large banks, or on nuclear reactors with the board members of the energy sector. This is why Hans Tschaeni, one of the country's leading journalists, speaks of the Swiss legislature as a 'cartelized fortress' deformed by 'militia entanglement.'[17]

The better known military militia system also makes it a male fortress. With voluntary military activity the inevitable price of a political and economic career, the militia army provides the bonding glue for a political system of 'male societies'[18] of power and influence. A typical member of the ruling cartel may hold office at both levels of government, he will be a president or board member of one or several of the country's leading industries, and he will hold the rank of reserve officer in the militia army. Typically, his soldiers will be his employees. It is not surprising, therefore, that women gained the national vote only in 1971. Gender-*apartheid* in Switzerland is not an accidental Alpine anachronism, routinely acknowledged with a wink and a chuckle by the world's predominantly male political-science community.

The system of strict proportionality also ensures that the influence of organized labour remains limited. Tied into an accord for industrial peace or 'voluntary restraint' with business since 1937 and coopted into the ruling cartel of the multiparty Federal Council since 1943, unions and socialists have traded the independent representation of working class interests for a share of political power as well as (more modest) access to the pecuniary sinecure of multiple board memberships. One consequence of that cooption is their complicity in Switzerland's labour policy of sustaining near full employment via the 'flexible' regulation of a large and nearly rightless migrant work-force. Simply put, Swiss unions acquiesce in a policy that imports and exports workers according to the fluctuations of the business cycle, because that policy exports unemployment to the migrant workers' countries of origin and thus sustains the employment and income stability of their Swiss members.

Add to this the overlapping memberships in public office, and a pattern of power collusion emerges that eclipses the formal provisions of federalist power separation. Moreover, adherence to principles of strict proportionality appears far less as a device for subordinating partisanship to the principles of federalism than a mechanism to intensify the grip of a small ruling elite on the overall system. Because the Swiss appear increasingly uninterested in honorary public office, no longer do the many take turns in administering the few functions of a minimal state, but rather the few share among themselves a multitude of functions through the channels of an 'incestuous interlocking of political, economic and military hierarchies.'[19]

Swiss federalism does play a significant role in the spatial allocation of fiscal resources and in the proportional accommodation of cultural diversity. But other than from a rather narrow institutionalist perspective, there is little that could serve as a federalist model for the empowerment of more people and groups of people. The growing distemper of Swiss citizens over environmental scandals, military expenditure, and gender discrimination, and the continuing divisiveness over the inevitable prospects of European integration indicate that Switzerland, rather than providing such a model, must finally develop one.

The United States
Switzerland may be an exceptional case, but it is hardly a unique one. Endless is the list of books that have been written about 'capital corruption' in the United States. They are read, sometimes even with praise and enthusiasm, and then they are put aside and everybody returns to business as usual.[20] The difference is that a large country like the United States usually can afford to tolerate a few dissenters, like court jesters who prove the 'liberalism' of their rulers, whereas a small country like Switzerland cannot. Consequently, authors like Jean Ziegler in Switzerland earn the scorn of the entire nation, while Amitai Etzioni in the United States can calmly report isolated responses from 'patriotic' readers accusing him of un-American activities.

It is not necessary to reiterate the well-documented influence that powerful corporate 'PACs' (political action committees) in the United States have upon the selection and electoral success of – mostly conservative – political candidates.[21] More interesting and revealing is the direct influence of corporate America upon the policy process itself. Given the weakness of party control and discipline in Congress, lobbyists do not attempt to influence partisan behaviour, but the votes of each individual member. They can do so because the legislative process has drifted from a system of some twenty standing committees, each responsible for a fairly broad policy field, to a jungle of perhaps as many as 180 subcommittees in each house. This pattern of subcommittee fragmentation 'simplifies the lobbyist's task of controlling legislation. It offers the special-interest group its special-interest subcommittee.'[22]

This system of private sector influence is doubtlessly more fragmented than the much more concerted Swiss one, and it, therefore, allows some degree of economic pluralism. Corporate America may not like this often cumbersome degree of fragmentation, but it is the price to be paid in a country where pluralism remains the dominant form of ideological legitimacy. As E.E. Schattschneider observed some time ago, however, it is a 'pluralist heaven' with a 'strong upper-class accent' because 'probably about 90 per cent of the people cannot get into the pressure system.'[23] A related phenomenon is the uncontrolled growth of mostly conditional grants-in-aid, which still dominate intergovernmental relations despite all presidential efforts to curb their budgetary impact through successive rounds of proclaimed *new federalisms*. The chaotic waste of fiscal intergovernmentalism may paradoxically be a result of centralization. Due to the historical victory of the supremacy clause over the Tenth Amendment, the federal government dominates all legislation in a system of 'permissive federalism,'[24] leaving for state legislation only what the national power calculus of Congress, Presidency, and Supreme Court agrees to discard for ideological and/or budgetary reasons. As in the private sector, state and local governments have to engage in a fragmented competition for scarce fiscal resources. In short, American federalism hardly appears to be a promising model for a federal future that would empower more citizens and groups of citizens in a world of fragmentation and integration.

Canada, Germany, and Eastern Europe

Similar arguments could be made with regard to Canada and Germany as well. The point to be made here, however, is merely that both federations appear to be in dire need of reorganization. German reunification has added five new and impoverished Länder to a federal system thus far notorious for its centripetal homogeneity. Moreover, the social costs of their precipitate inclusion have begun to tear apart the legendary social consensus upon which both industrial corporatism and federal cooperation had been built. In Canada, the faith of the populace in executive deals, such as the Meech

Lake and Charlottetown Accords, is at an all time low. Moreover, the traditional sense of what constitutes 'political community' appears to be seriously eroded. Representatives of the separatist Parti Québécois, for example, attempt to legitimize their quest for (more) self-determination by simplistically identifying a francophone nation with Quebec's provincial borders, thus brushing over Aboriginal and other non-francophone interests in the province. And finally, both countries are currently driven by the deregulatory desire of their business elites for continental market integration, although the faith of their populations in a new world order of open borders may be wearing thin. Fragmentation and integration appear far more as antagonistic forces than as complementary and reconciliatory ones.

In the post-communist world of Eastern Europe, on the other hand, federalism as a creative force of neighbourly coordination is nowhere apparent. As in the case of the Habsburg Empire at the end of the First World War, the old nationalisms clash with unmitigated intransigence. Hungering for a quick market-fix, their goal is separate and accelerated access to the European Union, not federal self-coordination. It seems that any notion of mutual sharing is mistakenly equated with the old collectivist tyranny.

Even within the former Czechoslovakia, the country with perhaps the most 'westernized' sociocultural tradition, 'federalism' has failed. Led by the Thatcherite economics minister Klaus, the wealthier Czechs saw federalism mainly as an obstacle to rapid market integration. The poorer Slovaks have been led to independence after their demands for slower and more differentiated economic liberalization were met with indignation by the Bohemians, who quickly conjured up past Slovak Nazi collaboration, rather than engaging in serious discussion about viable forms of socioeconomic federalism. The division of the country appears to stem from the inability of political leadership on both sides to formulate a compromise that would actually help the people in a time of tremendous upheaval and change.

The European Union

On both sides of the Atlantic, the image and model of the quasi-federal European Union draws envious attention. This is mainly for two reasons, which are not very different from those that led to the emergence of various federalized, territorial nation states a century earlier: one is the prospect of further profit maximization through market integration (now continental instead of national); the other is the 'building,' rather than 'dis-building,' dynamic of European federalism.[25] In short, the rationale, as emphasized in countless editorials in *The Economist*, for example, is not very different from that driving Bismarck's Germany or Sir John A. Macdonald's Canada a century earlier: economic growth legitimizes everything, and if the only way of getting it is a federalist political compromise, so be it.

Of course, the European Union *has* been a most successful model of federal integration. It has brought peace and considerable prosperity to (many) Europeans, and it has indeed provided a fairly new alternative model of *con*federation building that the world, as well as some established federations, can perhaps learn from. At the same time, its contribution to the empowerment of more citizens and groups of citizens appears doubtful at best. Thus far at least, one of the most advanced industrial regions of the world has mainly succeeded in creating an integrated agricultural market, not a common industrial strategy. The Common Agricultural Program (CAP), now under growing international pressure and reluctant internal review, has led to absurd levels of overproduction and waste, to regulated discrimination against other regions of the world that depend much more on agriculture than does the EU, and, in particular, to the destruction of independent family farms by European agribusiness.

In short, what is called a 'market' is in reality a misnomer for political regulation by dominant interests. The consequences are often absurd and demeaning. In Florence, for example, the lower classes can no longer afford to buy tasty tomatoes at local markets. Instead, they have to eat the tasteless industrial products of northern Europe which, on the other hand, are now available all year round. Or consider the fact that there is not a single cow left anywhere near Rome, and that Romans are instead supplied with milk by several dozens of tractor trailers that travel every night from somewhere in the Bavarian-Swabian Alps.

European economic analysts insist that one of the beneficial consequences of 'Europe Inc.' has been a reduction of regional disparities.[26] However, what these analysts measure as regional disparities are, in fact, national data. And indeed, Spain, Italy, and Greece have undoubtedly benefited from EU membership. But the benefits are distributed unevenly *within* those countries. In Spain, for example, Catalonia is now one of the fastest growing regions in all of Europe. But agricultural reforms in southern Spain have been cancelled owing to EU pressure, and the trend towards regional socioeconomic equalization has been slowed or even reversed. Behind the required harmonization of national economic performance en route to Europe 1992 and beyond, new prospects of regional inequality loom large.[27] Given the magnitude of regional disparities in the EU, even its revised structural fund and regional aid programs remain a mere pittance.

The main socioeconomic consequence of European integration has undoubtedly been the formation of a new and wealthy European middle class operating out of a few growth regions and metropolitan centres that begin to have more in common with each other than with the countries in which they happen to be located. For the rest of the European populace, the prospects are far less spectacular. In particular, European market integration has not, as some have suggested in the North American free trade debate, led to the creation of jobs. In fact, EU unemployment figures have remained stubbornly above OECD rates. A major expression of the newly reinforced peripheral misery is the voluntary or forced back-migration of large work-forces from rapidly restructuring growth centres.

Given these European socioeconomic realities, is the EU model of federal community building a model for the future? The answer must be the same as the one given at the outset of this chapter: it may or may not be, according to how it is used.

EU federalization has progressed in three phases:[28] from unanimity rule among the member states, to qualified majority voting in all market-related matters, and, in anticipation of the creation of political union, to the extension of qualified majority voting to most other matters of Union policy, especially social matters. The latter commitment was significantly diluted at the Maastricht Summit on European Union. John Major's Britain, for example, now appears fully committed to the prospect of a federalized 'Europe Inc.,' but remains stubbornly opposed to an extension of suprana-tional authority over social policy. Opposition to Maastricht was strong in both Denmark and France. It seems clear that there has been considerable (social democratic) opposition to the market-driven agenda of European federalization within some of the member states, and that the federalization of Europe must partly be seen as a political attempt to circumvent such opposition. Inasmuch as the Germans appear willing to incorporate their polity into a fully federalized Europe, one cannot help thinking that this may be a half-conscious political calculation since they will doubtless continue to dominate that community economically.

Because of the strong social democratic tradition in Europe, however, which is sorely lacking in the context of the North American free trade debate, the European Union has, in fact, moved one step closer to the binding regulation of European social norms and standards. It has also taken some significant steps towards the development of a legitimate institutional framework for defining political community, as well as a more democratic political process, again in contrast to the Canada-US Free Trade Agreement, where the dispute settlement mechanism is merely a minimal form of inter-executive conflict resolution. In other words, the European Union has at least the potential to be a promising model for a new world order.

New Wine

Managing Intergovernmental Relations
Ever since Richard Simeon published his seminal dissertation on Canadian federalism as a system of 'federal-provincial diplomacy,'[29] the Canadian

debate has revolved mainly around the mismatch of *interstate* and *intrastate* federalism.[30] The main argument has been that the lack of intrastate federalism in Canada (that is, representative bicameral co-determination of the provinces in the federal legislative process) has brought about an unhealthy degree of interstate federalism (intergovernmental deals among executive elites at both levels of government).

But all hopes to move Canada away from its reliance on intergovernmental bargaining have thus far been premature, if not in vain. The political price paid for the introduction of a limited Triple E Senate in the Charlottetown Accord (as demanded mainly by Alberta) would have been a significant devolution of powers from Ottawa to the provinces (as demanded by Quebec), resulting in more intergovernmental agreements, and the institutionalization of annual First Ministers' Conferences. Canadian intergovernmentalism, it seems, is a consequence of divergent provincial aspirations, not of faulty constitutional design. Federal-provincial diplomacy or *confederalism* may yet prove to be the most promising form of political coordination, and especially so among highly asymmetrical communities.

The lack of legitimacy attributed to First Ministers' Conferences in Canada mainly stems from the fact that provincial participants come with a mandate that is not only problematic in democratic terms, but also limited in juridical substance. Nevertheless, they engage in an intergovernmental exercise more appropriate to agreements among relatively autonomous or *confederated* political units. In the Canadian case, this exercise is part and parcel of a national federal legislative and constitutional process that substitutes for the lack of intrastate federalism – hence, its emphasis on universality and the insistence on equality for all provinces (an insistence that betrays the asymmetrical nature and reality of Canadian Confederation).

A comparison with the European Union may prove instructive. There, the ultimate legislative power rests with the Council of Ministers, even more so since the adoption of the Maastricht Treaty. In other words, the European Union is a quasi-federal *unicameral* system with an upper house, organized as a federal council of governments, but without a lower house (as the European Parliament to date does not possess significant legislative powers of decision-making and control). The decision-making process in the Council of Ministers is not unlike that of First Minsters' Conferences in Canada, typified by late night marathon sessions behind closed doors.[31] As in Canada, the Council has been criticized for its lack of politically representative legitimacy. A main difference is, of course, that the European Council members still represent (nearly) sovereign nation states, whereas Canada's provincial premiers represent constituencies with limited legislative authority. However, the comparison is instructive, because it leads to a reconsideration of the interstate model of federalism in general. It can be argued that it is not a priori undemocratic to base the decision-making process of the European Union primarily on intergovernmental agreements among (democratically elected) government representatives. These agreements are mainly made on the basis of consensus, unanimity, and/or qualified majorities, and they would appear legitimate at least as long as the European nation states continue to be the main collectivities in European politics, shaping the identities of their citizens as well as the direction of politics.

As Fritz W. Scharpf has pointed out,[32] there are essentially two 'models of federalism,' one following the American pattern of institutional power separation, the other more like the West German pattern of interlocking (intergovernmental) power. From the beginning, the Union has been based institutionally much more on the latter model. The decisive difference between the American and the German model is the following: while federal competencies in the United States are formally independent of state cooperation, and such cooperation is in constitutional terms based on 'voluntary concessions' of the federal government, the praxis of West German federalism requires the (qualified majority) consent of the Länder governments in all important acts of legislation, and the implementation of such legislation by the Länder administrations. The execution of federal competencies is in other words 'de facto dependent on the Länder governments.' The European Union constitutes a similar case of institutionalized 'political interlocking,' because 'important policy tasks have been transferred to the next higher institutional level, whereas policy formation and implementation remained tied to the unanimous agreement of the member-governments.'

In this comparative perspective, Canada's federal system is clearly constructed upon the second model of interlocking intergovernmental power. Its notorious legitimation deficit, on the other hand, appears to stem from two constitutional inconsistencies with that model. First, in comparison with German federalism, the intergovernmental players in Canada derive their authority from unmitigated majority-party rule at each level of government. Due to the odd mixture of Westminster parliamentarianism and federalism, the process of consensus building only begins at the intergovernmental bargaining table, whereas proportional representation and coalition building in Germany already laid the grounds for compromise within each level of government. It is this German system of multiple compromise requirements which enhances the overall representative legitimacy of the intergovernmental process.[33]

Second, in comparison with European confederalism, the allocation of powers in Canada is based far more on concurrency than on functional division. Due to the odd distribution of powers in the original *British North*

America Act of 1867, itself the expression of English and French Canada's diametrically divergent societal conceptions at the time, federal and provincial governments often appear to compete for the same powers, whereas the member states of the European Union simply delegate limited functions to the European level of administration.[34]

If Canada's historic mix of unity and diversity of asymmetrical communities precludes a decisive constitutional move to either intrastate federalism or interstate confederalism, Canadians may simply have to live with the status quo. Short of a complete breakup, at least between Quebec and the rest of Canada, however, they may consider accepting the de facto asymmetry of the Canadian Confederation and allowing for a renewed process of asymmetrical federation 'building' rather than 'dis-building' under forced principles of symmetry. A promising model of legitimate federation building to look at may be Spain, where the democratization process after Franco's death in 1975 allowed for a bottom-up process of regional self-determination that included the formulation, and constitutional recognition, of asymmetrical packages of powers for the seventeen autonomous communities.[35]

Spain

Basically, the 1978 constitution allowed for three different paths towards the quasi-federal devolution of the former centralized nation state. It gave an 'accelerated' and almost immediate right of autonomy to the three *distinct* historical regions of Spain: the Basque country, Catalonia, and Galicia. It allowed all other regions to achieve the same degree of autonomy, if so desired, via a slower and more complicated constitutional route. Finally, it provided a third compromise path for Andalusia, a region that did not constitute an historical nationality, but where popular support for accelerated autonomy was exceptional.

All processes had to be initiated by the historical regions themselves. In these three regions, existing pre-autonomous bodies would draft their own autonomy statutes. After consideration by a constitutional committee of the Spanish Cortes, each statute would be submitted to a referendum within the region. Other regions had to initiate the process with the active support of all provincial councils and two-thirds of municipal councils. A statute of autonomy then had to be drafted by an assembly comprising provincial council delegates as well as deputies and senators elected to the national Cortes.

Statutes had to be passed by the Cortes before the region could assume a limited package of autonomous rights, including the organization of self-government, housing, environmental protection, cultural affairs, social welfare, and tourism. After five years, it would proceed to the same full autonomy status as the historical regions, however, assuming differentiated packages of power ranging from various degrees of fiscal autonomy to the right to conclude international treaties.

This process of autonomy building allowed for considerable degrees of asymmetry resulting in 'special relationships' with Madrid, such as special tax autonomies and/or a particular emphasis on education, culture, and language. Generally speaking, however, and contrary to the more clearly defined and symmetrical division of powers in the classical federal state, the regions of Spain were not only able to decide freely whether they wanted to assume the status of autonomous communities (they all did), but more importantly, they could decide on the level of autonomy desired, as well as a time-frame for progression to full autonomy.

The result has been a rather complex organization of quasi-federal institutions and arrangements with a high conflict potential, especially in the field of fiscal redistribution and equalization. The ultimate goal of a 50:25:25 split of public sector spending between national, regional, and local governments has yet to be fully realized. The overseeing body is a consultative Fiscal and Financial Council composed of the finance ministers of the communities, as well as the state finance minister and the minister for public administration. In the assessment of one of the seven 'fathers' of the 1978 constitution, Jordi Solé Tura, the Spanish compromise has been, and continues to be, a difficult one, marred not only by the old forces of the right – whether nationalist or separatist – but also by the internal divisions among the new governing left.[36]

Nevertheless, the Spanish road to regional autonomy has been a highly innovative one. It is the technocrats of politics, as well as some neo-liberal proponents of authoritative governments presiding over free markets (the ones Solé Tura fears might eventually undermine the careful compromise required in Spanish politics) who assume that democratic governance should be easy and straightforward. Especially for post-communist Eastern Europe, the Spanish example, and not the American or German one, should provide new models and ideas of political, economic, and sociocultural renovation.

Solé Tura's assessment of the Spanish experiment also makes clear that it is, after all, an experiment in territorial federalization only. By distinguishing between political regions and sociocultural nationalities (a distinction the Parti Québécois in Canada obviously still has to learn), and by pointing to other forms of intraregional as well as interregional fragmentation (such as class, partisanship, or ethnicity), he raises the issue of unity and diversity, integration and fragmentation, once again. Two remaining issues can, therefore, be identified: the empowerment of non-territorial political communities within the framework of territorial federalism on the one hand, and the provision of a national (or even supranational) set of universally binding norms on the other, assuming a continued commitment to some form of cohesion.

Towards Multi-Dimensional Federalism?

With regard to class, it has long been conventional wisdom that only centralized collective action can overcome the monopolization of politics by dominant economic elites. Industrial unionism was an historical response to that monopolization, and, at least initially, so was communism. An argument can now be made that decentralized solidarity and action gain strategic importance when national markets appear less dominated by nationally based corporations, and nation states are less capable of regulating industrial relations. Regionally and locally de-centred structures and organizations of collective solidarity may indeed appear as a promising model of social empowerment.

The idea of power-sharing must be extended to the socioeconomic realm of production and work. After the Second World War, workers' co-determination laws were established for large enterprises in several European countries. Given the growing importance of small-scale and flexible production in post-industrial economies, institutionalized forms of co-determination must be extended to the level of small business as well. New forms of more cooperative capitalist management and industrial democracy are already being explored in several industrial states.[37] They ought to be extended, in particular, to local levels of investment and production. Such forms of co-determination need to be embedded in representative and accountable decision-making institutions that, in fact, lead to the empowerment of all participants, and not to the formation of regional crisis cartels into which subordinate social forces are pulled by business elites using the blackmail of investment location.

This is precisely a matter of socioeconomic federalism. General statutory frameworks regulating industrial relations at the national or even international level must guide flexible and autonomous regulation at the regional and local levels. Co-determination councils with advisory and/or veto powers at both levels of government would have to complement territorial institutions of federalism.

There is no reason why the circle of participants within such structures could not be extended even further. Together with business and labour, women's organizations, environmentalist and consumer groups, and organizations representing racial and/or linguistic minorities could be added to a structure of conciliar decision-making.

The main argument against any functional scheme of interest- representation has always been that it cannot be all-inclusive. Some dominant interests will be included, and all others not.[38] Apart from the fact that conventional systems of territorial representation are hardly all-inclusive except in a purely formal sense, this argument is not convincing. First, there is no reason why the idea of federalism cannot be extended to non-territorial collectivities with exclusive characteristics. Indeed, as Richard Simeon states in this volume, suggestions have surfaced in the Canadian debate to concede 'provincial status' collectively to the bands of native peoples scattered across the country or even to the francophones living outside Quebec.[39]

Second, in cases of less exclusive and/or overlapping collectivities (along the lines of class, gender, and race, for example), compulsory membership could be replaced by voluntary membership. Individuals could choose to which of the various collective constituencies they want to belong, and groups of individuals would be free to constitute new constituencies, albeit not on a whim, but under the auspices of carefully crafted procedural regulation, perhaps similar to the provisions for second-tier autonomization in the Spanish constitution. In the case of multicultural societies, the overall or federal state would then no longer appear as a 'nation state' but as a 'nationality state.'

The idea is not nearly as new as it may seem. It was in fact conceptualized by Karl Renner at the turn of the century as a solution to the disintegration of the multinational Habsburg monarchy,[40] and it was implemented for the German and Jewish minorities in Estonia between 1925 and 1940.[41] The main principle was one of 'cultural community' (*Kulturgemeinschaft*), instead of 'territorial community' (*Siedlungsgemeinschaft*), which allowed each individual 'personal autonomy' in the choice of nationality and, accordingly, the strand of representation.

Here, once again, lies the conceptual basis for a peaceful reorganization of the multinational orbit of Eastern Europe in particular. But during a recent newspaper interview in Prague, my references to these arrangements in the old Habsburg monarchy were the only ones to be carefully omitted from the printed version. In a post-communist world, obsessed with bland notions of standardized territoriality and homogenized market liberalism, this was obviously not a popular message.

The Need for Universal Norms

The concept of federalism is essentially one of power-sharing, and not one of exclusive power allocation to one or other level of government. With a more confederal division of powers, and a larger diversity among the member units of a federation, therefore, some universal bond of common norms and mutual control appears to be the sine qua non of federalism. Most federal constitutions specify not only a binding framework for the establishment of governmental institutions and their powers, but also include a charter of inalienable individual or human rights. Under conditions of socioeconomic fragmentation and confederal decentralization, however, a 'social charter' ought to ensure inalienable standards of social existence as well – of adequate food, shelter, healthcare, and education. Even from an economic point of view, the disappearance of such standards seems undesirable, and some form of social charter seems to be the only effective way of maintaining them.[42] A social charter was proposed in the Maastricht Treaty, for example, to protect against the further erosion of 'existing minimum programs,' or even to promote the improvement of social 'minimum security.' Its purpose is the protection of workers and structurally weaker regions in the context of continental economic integration.[43]

The conceptual basis for the provision and implementation of universally binding social norms in federal systems is the principle of *subsidiarity*. In the context of Canadian federalism, a social charter would identify a general framework of 'minimum standards.' Provinces would be empowered to comply with these standards flexibly, on the basis of extant programs or new programs adapted to specific regional needs. Only if they failed to do so would the federal government have the right to proceed with regulation *subsidiarily*. Obviously, such a provision needs some form of enforcement, including the possibility of individual appeals to the court system and some form of intergovernmental judicial review by the Supreme Court. That does not necessarily mean permanent intergovernmental litigation. In Canada, again, and unlike in the United States, the Supreme Court can be asked to render legal opinions before the stage of litigation is reached.

In a globalizing as well as interregional world of trade and competition, finally, the main problem may not be the *internal* violation of standards by an individual political community, but their erosion under the *external* pressure of market competition. Moreover, international trade regulations may press all participants into increasingly standardized codes of socioeconomic and cultural behaviour that run counter to the idea of federalist diversity. But, as Marjorie Griffin Cohen has argued, trade must not inevitably 'demand uniform economic behavior from all countries.' The notion that 'the actions of a nation [or subnational political community] in its own boundaries cannot be directed by trade laws' is an essential political assumption from a federalist perspective. Federalism in a trade context, therefore, not only means the guarantee of internal socioeconomic autonomy, but also some safeguards against external constraints upon that autonomy. Cohen refers to the imposition of 'social tariffs' as a way of 'preventing huge capital shifts from wealthy to poor countries,' and quoting from a recent position paper of the Canadian federal New Democratic Party, 'Putting People First,' she elaborates that 'standards should be incorporated within the GATT and the OECD ... to allow countries to limit, or levy tariffs on imports from countries which do not meet minimum standards.'[44] In other words, the idea and model of federalism must be extended to trade relations as well.

Conclusion

The centralized territorial nation state, whose form still predominates, is an invention of the nineteenth century, and the beginnings of the kind of market it was to organize and protect date back to the eighteenth century. Clinging to this venerable model of political and economic organization in a post-industrial age of subnational fragmentation and globalized flexibility appears outright anachronistic. It is the stuff of unimaginative political science and economics textbooks, the continuing legacy of a dominant ideology that has served power-hungry men so well for so long.

In a documentary on the plight of native peoples in Canada,[45] after exploring the diversity and misery of living conditions as well as political expectations, the late Barbara Frum asked a representative of the Assembly of First Nations how a solution to the pressing political demands of native peoples was possible when their expectations differed so much from region to region, and almost from band to band? The answer was more remarkable than most of the expert voices at the round tables of Canadian constitutional conferencing taken together: it is only white man's understanding that there always and unimaginatively has to be one solution to so many problems, she said. We can easily see many solutions to many problems.

Notes

1 Charles Tilly, 'Western State-Making and Theories of Political Transformation,' in Charles Tilly, ed., *The Formation of National States in Western Europe* (Princeton: Princeton University Press 1975), 635.
2 William H. Riker, *Federalism: Origin, Operation, Significance* (Boston: Little Brown 1964).
3 Thomas Hobbes, *De Cive* (London 1651; Oxford: Clarendon Press 1983), VII.IV (108).
4 This is the classical provision of checks and balances in federal states, typically organized as either *intra-* and *inter*state federalism.
5 See among many Charles Maier, ed., *Changing the Boundary of the Political* (Cambridge: Cambridge University Press 1987).
6 *Government and Opposition* 23, No. 1 (1988).
7 See Ulrich im Hof, 'Die Geschichte der Schweiz,' in Landeszentrale für politische Bildung Baden-Würtemberg, ed., *Die Schweiz* (Stuttgart: Kohlhammer 1988), 61-4.
8 See Ulrich Kloeti, 'Political Ideals, Financial Interests and Intergovernmental Relations: New Aspects of Swiss Federalism,' *Government and Opposition* 23, No. 1 (1988):93-6.
9 Rolf Nef, 'Die Schweizer Referendumsdemokratie,' in *Die Schweiz*, 163.

10 Kloeti, 'Political Ideals,' 93.
11 See Peter J. Katzenstein, *Corporatism and Change* (Ithaca: Cornell University Press 1984), 112-13. *Vorort* is Switzerland's largest business organization.
12 See Hans Tschaeni, *Wer regiert die Schweiz?* (München: Piper 1987), 127-32.
13 On the whole question see Franz Lehner, 'Consociational Democracy in Switzerland: A Political-Economic Explanation and Some Empirical Evidence,' in *European Journal of Political Research* 12 (1984):30.
14 See Tschaeni, *Wer regiert die Schweiz?* 78-9, and Leonhard Neidhart, 'Die Schweizer Konkordanzdemokratie,' in *Die Schweiz*, 140.
15 On the concept of militia democracy, see Alois Riklin, 'Milizdemokratie,' in *Staatsorganisation und Staatsfunktionen im Wandel, Festschrift für Kurt Eichenberger* (Basel: Helbing & Lichtenhahn 1982), 41-57.
16 Jean Ziegler, *The Awful Truth* (New York: Harper & Row 1976), 108-15.
17 Tschaeni, *Wer regiert die Schweiz?*.
18 Ibid., 14.
19 Jean Ziegler, *Die Schweiz wäscht weisser* (München: Piper 1990), 174-5.
20 See Amitai Etzioni, *Capital Corruption* (New Brunswick: Transaction Books 1988).
21 See, among many, Theodore J. Eismeier and Philip H. Pollock III, *Business, Money, and the Rise of Corporate PACs in American Elections* (New York: Quorum Books 1988).
22 Michael Parenti, *Democracy for the Few* (New York: St. Martin's Press 1980), 226.
23 E.E. Schattschneider, *The Semi-Sovereign People* (New York: Holt, Rinehart and Winston 1960), 31-5.
24 See Michael D. Reagan and John G. Sanzone, *The New Federalism* (New York: Oxford University Press 1981), 175.
25 See Richard Simeon, 'Canada and the United States: Lessons from the North American Experience,' Chapter 16 in this volume.
26 Personal interviews at the IFO-Institut in Munich, summer 1989.
27 See *Papeles de Economia Espanola* 45 (1990):25-61.
28 See G. Bruce Doern, *Europe Uniting: The EC Model and Canada's Constitutional Debate* (Toronto: C.D. Howe Institute 1991), Chapter 2.
29 Richard Simeon, *Federal-Provincial Diplomacy: The Making of Recent Policy in Canada* (Toronto: University of Toronto Press 1972).
30 See, among many, Donald V. Smiley and Ronald L. Watts, *Intrastate Federalism in Canada* (Toronto: University of Toronto Press 1985).
31 As in Canada, and despite formalized voting procedures, its strength stems from the participants' ability to reach consensus on the basis of compromise.
32 Fritz W. Scharpf, 'Die Politikverflechtungs-Falle: Europäische Integration und deutscher Föderalismus im Vergleich,' *Politische Vierteljahresschrift* 26, No. 4 (1985):324-50.
33 The German model of multiple consensus and compromise now appears challenged by the process of reunification and the incorporation of six new Länder with dramatically different socioeconomic and cultural status.
34 It has always been the hope and prediction of the functional integration school that the process of step by step functional integration would eventually lead to a qualitative jump into full-fledged supranationality – and hence a decisive move from inter- to intrastate federalism. The ultimate fate of the Maastricht Treaty

may decide this issue for a long time to come.

35 The following summary is mainly taken from Peter J. Donaghy and Michael T. Newton, *Spain: A Guide to Political and Economic Institutions* (Cambridge: Cambridge University Press 1987), Chapter 7.

36 Jordi Solé Tura, *Nacionalidades y Nacionalismos en España* (Madrid: Alianza Editorial 1985).

37 See M. Donald Hancock, John Logue, and Bernt Schiller, eds., *Managing Modern Capitalism* (New York: Praeger 1991), especially Part II.

38 See Charles W. Anderson, 'Political Design and the Representation of Interests,' in Philippe C. Schmitter and Gerhard Lehmbruch, eds., *Trends Toward Interest Intermediation* (Beverly Hills: Sage 1979), 293.

39 Simeon, 'Canada and the United States.'

40 See Robert A. Kann, *Renners Beitrag zur Lösung nationaler Konflikte im Lichte nationaler Probleme der Gegenwart* (Wien: Verlag der Österreichischen Akademie der Wissenschaften 1973).

41 See Carl J. Friedrich, 'The Politics of Language and Corporate Federalism,' in Jean G. Savard and Richard Vigneault, eds., *Les Etats Multilingues, problèmes et solutions* (Québec: Les Presses de l'Université Laval 1975), 227-37.

42 See the study of Lars Osberg for the Government of Ontario, *The Economics of National Standards* (Halifax: Dalhousie University 1991), especially 62-5.

43 See Doern, *Europe Uniting*, 36-9.

44 Marjorie Griffin Cohen, 'Social Democracy – Illusion or Vision?' *Studies in Political Economy* 37 (1992):158-9.

45 Canadian Broadcasting Corporation, *The Journal*, 'Legacy,' December 1991.

15

Federalism and the Nation State: What Can Be Learned from the American Experience?

Samuel H. Beer

'The most difficult problem in the world today,' said George Shultz recently, 'is governing over diversity.'[1] The former American secretary of state was referring primarily to the ethnic conflicts that have torn apart the Yugoslav federation. Those horrors constitute one of the more grotesque failures of federalism in the contemporary world. The passions are so irrational and the barbarity so inhuman, however, that it is out of place to blame them on a mere institutional failure. One must doubt that any constitutional order could have contained this tidal wave of value-laden emotion.

Dr. Shultz also had in mind other places where, although politics follows a more moderate course, ethnic diversity has led to regional tensions irreconcilable with federalism. This is odd, suggesting that an institution designed to accommodate such differences has in fact exacerbated them. Where a population sharing certain characteristics occupies a particular territory, it is plausible to believe that both fairness and peace will be promoted if this people have the governmental powers to protect and foster their way of life. In principle, for instance, such an arrangement should enable francophone Quebec to indulge its provincial values, while also enjoying the advantages of the continental economy of Canada and the greater influence of the confederation in international relations. In Western Europe, a similar division of authority would seem to make it possible for these countries to remain nations, and yet also to share in the greater prosperity and power realized by a federal Europe.

Reason points in this direction, yet in both cases national sentiments get in the way. I recall a conversation between two shop girls in Canterbury about the tunnel under the English Channel. They recoiled from the prospect of greater intercourse with the continent. 'The point about being an island,' said one, 'is that you are different, isn't it? You don't want to be like other people.' Her 'point' had been expressed in grander language by General de Gaulle. The supreme task of a political leader, he asserted, is to protect and develop the 'personality' of his nation, for which purpose he must adamantly defend national sovereignty, the right to self-definition, 'le droit à la différence.'[2]

Federalism seems to make such good sense for Canada and for the European Union. Yet ethnicity – that sharing of values and a belief in common descent which gives a set of persons an identity as a people – may well inspire nationalism and the demand for political self-determination. Such an attachment of a people to a state, or to their aspiration for a state, threatens the rational harmonies of federalism. The diversity that justifies a division of governmental authority then works to undermine that allocation. Although the magnitudes are vastly different, the same conflict of reason and passion impedes federal cooperation for greater prosperity, security, and liberty in Canada and the European Union as in post-communist Yugoslavia and Soviet Russia – hence, the commonplace in both continents that the nation state is the enemy of federalism.

The American experience must shake the plausibility of this familiar generalization. In the United States, nationalism is an indispensable support of federalism. Such success as the US has enjoyed as a federation owes much to its being a nation state – indeed, the first nation state.[3] A comparison with Canada will bring out these distinctive features of the American system. My argument, however, is not meant to suggest that American federalism is to be preferred as a model generally. Precisely because of its difficulties and the Canadian way of coping with them, Canada may be a better guide to what will happen and to what ought to be done.

Both countries have their serious ethnic problems. Their federal systems, however, have responded in quite different ways: the American by drawing ethnic groups into the hurly burly of pressure politics at the centre; the Canadian by diverting them into extra-parliamentary government-to-government negotiations. Each method offers instruction as to how ethnicity may be managed. Their experience also drives home the continuing importance of the passions of nationalism to the success or failure of a state and, more broadly, the importance of political culture as a force shaping institutions and behaviour.

The American/Canadian comparison will occupy most of my attention. I will then ask what light these contrasts throw on the nature of and prospects for the European Union, concluding with some brief speculations regarding the far more severe problems of federalism in Eastern Europe.

Two Theories of Federalism[4]

I start from the conventional definition of federalism as a political system in which a territorial division of authority between a general government and several regional governments is constitutionally established. It is not just decentralization, but decentralization with a constitutional basis. This definition is broad enough to embrace significant variations which lead to sharp controversies between advocates for these differences. In the United States, although less important than in Canada, these controversies sometimes become prominent. For instance, when President Reagan took office in 1981 he proclaimed a 'new federalism.' Its main thrust was to cut back on the activities of the federal government – and, indeed, of all levels of government – by reducing or eliminating a large number of federal programs, the principal cuts falling on aid to state and local governments.[5] The president judged these activities to be inefficient, unnecessary, and harmful. He also claimed that they were improper under the Constitution – not in the strict sense that they violated specific provisions of our fundamental law, but in the larger sense that they offended against the true meaning of the document.

In his first inaugural address, accordingly, President Reagan promised to 'restore the balance between levels of government.' He made clear his reliance upon a certain theory – the compact theory – of the Constitution to justify his reforms. 'The Federal government,' he declared at one point, 'did not create the states; the states created the Federal government.'

This allegation did not pass without comment. Professor Richard B. Morris of Columbia called the compact theory 'a hoary myth about the origins of the Union' and went on to summarize the evidence showing that 'the United States was created by the people in collectivity, not by the individual states.' No less bluntly, Professor Henry Steele Commager said President Reagan did not understand the Constitution, which asserts that it was 'ordained' by 'We, the People of the United States,' not by the states severally. An ardent liberal, he argued that this view of the origin of the Constitution justified and even mandated the new purposes served by federal power in recent times.

This bout of rhetorical fisticuffs between the president and the professors reflected a conflict of ideas and values which goes back to the beginning of the republic, and which informed the most serious crisis of our first century, the Civil War. In that struggle, President Reagan's view, the compact theory, was championed by Jefferson Davis, the president of the seceding South. Under the Constitution, which he termed no more than a 'close alliance,' 'each state, was in the last resort the sole judge as well of its wrongs as of the mode and measure of redress.' On the other hand, the first Republican president espoused the national theory. 'The Union,' said Abraham Lincoln, 'is older than any of the states, and in fact, it created them as States ... The Union and not the States produced their independence and their liberty ... The Union gave each of them whatever of independence and liberty it has.' There could, therefore, be no constitutional right of secession, nullification, interposition, or, indeed, of what some have called 'massive resistance' by any one or more states.[6]

In these same years, the Canadians were establishing their own federal system. With regard to both theory and history, they accepted the Southern account of the American conflict. The Conservative leader, John A. Macdonald, recoiling from the tragedy of the war, attributed it to the weakness of the central government and of the federal bond in a union which had been formed by a compact among sovereign states. Liberal reformers likewise traced the conflict to 'the idea of the United States constitution ... that the central government is a delegated government, deriving its powers from the "sovereign" states which go to make up the Union.' 'The Canadians,' writes Robert Vipond, 'believed that the "Calhoun doctrine," by which they meant the view that the Constitution is really a covenant among sovereign states, had furnished "the secession with an exceedingly plausible argument."'[7]

The Canadian framers, therefore, gave their new federal government much stronger legal powers than those possessed by the American federal government. The words of the *British North America Act* of 1867 were more than adequate to establish a centralized federal system. What emerged during the next half century or so, however, was a far weaker central government and more fissiparous federation than the American.

The blame for this outcome is often put on the Judicial Committee of the Privy Council (JCPC), the final court of appeal in questions of constitutional interpretation until 1949. The weakening of Ottawa by judicial review stands in marked contrast with the strengthening of Washington during the same period by a Supreme Court appointed by a long line of Republican presidents.[8] The provincialist tilt of the JCPC is undeniable, but the arguments of the provincial rights movement also prevailed throughout wide sectors of public and governmental opinion in Canada. This success was achieved not only in the judicial process, but also, as Robert Vipond has observed, 'in the larger process of defining a distinctive Canadian political culture.'[9]

In comparison with the American experience, what was missing in Canada was not only a nationalist court, but also and especially an equivalent of the meta-legal theory which in the United States shaped the way courts, governments, and the voting public understood and construed the law of their Constitution. It is ironic that the theory which did gain acceptance in Canada and which provided a background of constitutional interpretation was in its essentials the anti-national, states' rights outlook which many Canadians had seen as the malign influence leading to the American Civil War.

At the time the American Constitution was being founded, the advocates of the two approaches, the compact and national theories, shared similar political values. Both were democratic, or to use the less demanding word, republican, being champions of government by the many rather than by the few and believing that popular government was the best safeguard of individual liberty. They differed over the question of scale. Compact theorists held that self-government was feasible only in a small society. A big republic, they believed, would be reduced to conflict and impotent confusion by the diversity of interests and ideas among its citizens, leading ultimately to caesarism. The small republic, on the other hand, would be able to govern itself coherently and to agree on how to protect the rights and liberties of its citizens, thanks to its homogeneity. Government would be 'closer to the people' in the sense not merely that citizens would be physically nearer to one another, but rather that their interests would be more in harmony and their sympathies stronger and more intimate. For these reasons, in the words of Anti-Federalists, such a polity would have 'individuality,' or as we would say today, it would be more of a community.[10]

Morally and politically self-sufficient, small communities would need to band together by compact with others in order to protect themselves against foreign enemies. But this did not undermine the basic claim that the small state was the proper seat of self-government and freedom. Coming down from Machiavelli and Montesquieu, this small republic theory provided the intellectual basis for the opposition to the Constitution at the Philadelphia convention and during ratification. After its defeat in those encounters, moreover, it acquired a second life as a way of construing the Constitution, which culminated in the formidable polemic of John C. Calhoun. 'The very idea of an American People, as constituting a single community,' he said in a climactic challenge to nationalism, 'is a mere chimera.' On this intellectual foundation Southern speakers based their powerful and coherent case for secession and states' rights.[11]

The Federalists attacked both elements of the compact theory. If such an agreement were the basis of central authority, they argued, the autonomy of the member states would render it incapable of maintaining order at home or security abroad, as demonstrated by the sad history of the country under the Articles of Confederation. The idea that won the day for them, however, was their critique of the small republic theory. Granting that the bigger country would be more diverse, they turned the argument of the Anti-Federalists on its head: diversity would be a more secure ground for political and individual liberty. The classic exposition is James Madison's Tenth *Federalist* paper. Since no polity can ever be perfectly homogeneous, he observed, smallness of scale simply sets the stage for a narrow-minded majority to oppress the minority.[12]

The way to reverse the tendency to the 'tyranny of the majority' inherent in the small republic, continued Madison, is, therefore, to 'extend the sphere' of government so as to 'take in a greater variety of parties and interests.' Madison believed that such heterogeneity would avert the danger of the factious majority, but he did not expect, let alone hope, that pluralism would paralyze government. On the contrary, like his nation-building co-author Alexander Hamilton, Madison looked forward to an activist government at the centre which would not only safeguard the rights of all citizens, but also pursue what he called a 'more enlarged plan of public policy.' Government would be majoritarian, but as he wrote in his great summarizing paper no. 51, thanks to 'the great variety of parties, interests and sects' in the extended republic of the United States, 'a coalition of a majority of the whole society could seldom take place on any other principles than those of justice and the general good.'[13]

Madison had great hopes for such non-factious, civic majorities. Such a coalition was not a mere collection of individuals, but a body of citizens sharing 'principles' which, as expressions of justice and the general good, were worthy of general assent. His analysis, therefore, demonstrated how the citizens of the extended republic could achieve unity out of diversity; in other words, how they could act as the 'one people' which in Jefferson's declaration had made itself independent. The people display their sovereignty in two roles. They are the 'constituent sovereign' which ordains the Constitution and thereby creates the federal system of government in which both levels, state and federal, derive their authority from the same source. As the political force, moreover, which governs according to those rules, they exercise a limited constitutional power as the 'governmental sovereign.'[14]

How Madison expected the people to perform in their capacity as governmental sovereign brings out the principal function of the states in the scheme of national federalism. In *Federalist* 46, Madison sets out to answer critics who said that under the proposed Constitution the general and the state governments 'in their efforts to usurp the authority of each' will be 'uncontrolled by any common superior.' Accusing these adversaries of the Constitution of having lost sight of 'the people,' Madison wrote:

Notwithstanding the different modes in which [the federal and state governments] are appointed, we must consider them as substantially dependent on the great body of the citizens of the United States ... The federal and State governments are in fact but different agents and trustees of the people constituted with different powers, and designed for different purposes ... The ultimate authority wherever the derivative may be found, resides in the people alone ...

In no way contradicting his often asserted proposition that the checking process depends in the first instance upon the rivalry of the two sets of office-holders, Madison does not make this competition the conclusive control on who will prevail. Explicitly, he declares that 'whether either, or which of them, will be able to enlarge its sphere of jurisdiction at the expense of the other ... will not depend merely on the comparative ambition or address of different governments,' but rather '*in every case*' (my emphasis) will 'depend on the sentiments and sanction of their common constituents.'[15]

Thanks to their ambition, the office-holders at both state and federal levels will seek to protect and to extend their jurisdictions. The decisive fact in determining the outcome of these contests, however, will not be some merely mechanical balance, but the intervention of 'the great body of common constituents' – that is, the voters at both levels of government. When the citizens intervene to turn back some abuse – for instance, to use the state governments to correct the federal government – they are part of the 'checks and balances' of the system. But in the Madisonian scheme, the people intervene not only to correct, but also to direct, one or the other level of government. As an activist and nation builder, Madison perceived how these intergovernmental controls could be used to shape and direct federal, as well as state action. For example, he perceived how state laws could serve as models for federal legislation, in one instance painting a scene of 'the skilful individual in his closet, with all the state codes before him' compiling 'a law on some subject of taxation for the whole Union.'[16]

This capacity of the common constituents to use the states for larger national purposes was pointed out by other commentators on American government. In 1888 James Bryce, in his *American Commonwealth*, noted how 'federalism enables a people to try experiments which could not safely be tried in a large centralized country.' This function of the states, characterized in the phrase 'laboratories for experimentation,' was later given wide circulation by justices Oliver Wendell Holmes, Jr., and Louis D. Brandeis. This positive, national function of the states, as Madison's perceptive speculation indicates, was inherent in federalism on the American plan.[17]

'*Divide et impera*, the reprobated axiom of tyranny,' wrote Madison, 'is under certain qualifications, the only policy, by which a republic can be administered.' National federalism makes that principle serve the cause of popular government by reversing the roles of governors and governed. Now the governed divide their governors for the sake of the people's interests. The object of the controls of the federal system is not merely to preserve the 'constitutional equilibrium' between the federal and state governments. It is primarily to enable the common superior of both, the people, to intervene at either level in order to promote justice and the general good. This division of power makes the governed the arbiter between the two sets of governors and the champion of the people's rights and interests within each.[18]

This function of the states in the defence of liberty is their primary rationale, but they also serve the purpose of economic welfare. In the distribution of governmental powers, according to Madison, the state governments have the care of certain 'local and particular interests' while the federal government deals with 'the great and aggregate interests' of the nation. This rule is much the same as the criterion followed by advocates of 'fiscal federalism' today when they use the distinction between 'internalities' and 'externalities' to allocate functions to levels of governments in order to maximize utility.[19]

The makers of the Constitution believed they had reason on their side. While they recognized that at the time popular sentiment was weighted on the side of localism, not nationalism, they expected that the benefits of greater liberty, security, and prosperity under the new order would shift the attachment of its citizens towards the centre. Yet the framers were also acutely aware of the fragility of reason. According to Madison, no matter how rational the design of the Constitution, such a scheme would 'not find it a superfluous advantage to have the prejudice of the community on its side.' This need was widely perceived at the time. Thoughtful people recognized that the young republic would have to enlist the affections of its citizens as well as their prudent idealism.[20]

Supplementing Madison's appeal to reason, James Wilson of Philadelphia, his colleague in the Federalist cause, presented a more robust solution. Hardly inferior to Madison and Hamilton as an architect and spokesman of the new regime, Wilson was as ardent a supporter of democracy as of nationalism. The link between the two was his conception of how participation transforms values. As the extended republic widened the scale of choice of the voters, said Wilson, their preferences would be similarly transformed, generating 'the most endearing connection among the citizens' and 'the most powerful, and at the same time, a most pleasing bond of connection among the citizens and those whom they select for their different offices and departments of government.' In Wilson's account, the expansion of affectual attachment occurs in the process of self-government and because of it. Citizens come to love the country they are creating.[21]

To the question of whether reason can be an effective substitute for nationhood, the answer of the American framers is 'No.' Reason must rule, they say, but rationality alone is not enough to secure that result. A regime which seeks to embody the rational universals of liberal democracy must, according to them, also enjoy the support of the public affections associated with nationhood.

How Canada Coped

In the Canadian experience, the national theory, which has played such a dominant role in American origins and development, has had no influence on thinking about federalism and on the political culture which has shaped how the confederation actually worked. In the United States, for more than half a century before the Canadian confederation, the conflict of the national and the compact views was the axis of political controversy, culminating in Lincoln's elaboration of the national theory as the legal ground for employing federal military force to put down the Southern rebellion. In Canada the speeches and writing of John A. Macdonald, the leading figure in the founding of the confederation, reveal no recognition of Lincoln's argument.[22] Like Lincoln, he would welcome reasoning that supported a strong central government. But in the situation Macdonald faced and on the premises by which he understood it, there was more than one cause for his not attempting to use the Lincolnian argument to reach that conclusion.

For one thing, he, like other founders, was a monarchist. When Macdonald and others spoke of Queen Victoria as 'our Sovereign Lady,' this was not mere colonial sycophancy. In the British constitution, as then understood, the monarch, not the people, was the source of authority. The conventions of 'responsible government,' of course, obliged the monarch to exercise that authority only on the advice of the ministers, who were themselves held to account by a parliament elected by a substantial and growing electorate. The principle of royal sovereignty, however, excluded any appeal to popular sovereignty in the American style. Its presumptions were further strengthened by the Civil War, which, according to Macdonald's biographer, marked, for many English-speaking Canadians, 'the final stage in the discredit of democracy and republicanism.'[23] The intention of the Canadian framers was to establish not popular government, but responsible government, which they were confident would, in the spirit of Victorian liberalism, ensure 'constitutional liberty' for all.[24]

Transferred to Canada, moreover, this model of 'responsible government' gave the executive at both levels of government the broad authority of the British cabinet over the legislature. Hence, both federal and provincial cabinets could make agreements with one another which credibly committed their respective law-making bodies. When the electorates represented in these legislative bodies were united by distinct and opposing concerns, the dominance of their executives made it natural for citizens to press their demands through them. Cabinet government, in short, fitted nicely with the political tendencies of Canada's two main ethnic groups, the British and the French, to relate politically to one another as separate communities, not as individual citizens of one sovereign state.

While monarchism excluded democratic thought along American lines, the existence of these 'two nations' stood in the way of American-style nationalism. It is hard to imagine Macdonald matching the exalted rhetoric of John Jay in the second *Federalist* paper, where he hailed the Americans as 'one united people,' nor could he have spoken of Canada with the emphasis George Washington gave to the coda of his Farewell Address proclaiming the American union to be 'an indissoluble community of interest as *one nation*.' And no more than the French of Lower Canada would the British of Upper Canada have applauded such sentiments. 'We desire self-government,' declared the voice of Liberal reform in Ontario, the Toronto *Globe*, speaking for both communities in 1864, 'in order that the separate nationalities of which the population is composed may not quarrel.'[25] Although Macdonald did conceive of the Canada of the future as sufficiently one in political terms to be called a 'nation,' he recognized that it would remain divided into ethnically different and separate 'nationalities.'[26] As shown by his cooperation with Cartier, he had learned the lesson of Lord Durham's failed experiment in assimilation and had come to accept '*la survivance*' which Cartier and his French compatriots sought above all things.[27] The absence of the American versions of both democracy and nationalism meant that the fundamental law of Canada could not announce that 'We, the People ... do ordain and establish' the new frame of government.

Since it was the authority of the Queen in Parliament that delegated to each level of government its legal powers, neither of these could alter the allocation. To that extent, the new system was federal in the same sense as the American Constitution. A fatal defect of that document in Macdonald's eyes, however, was that by enumerating the powers of the federal government and leaving the residuum to the states, the Constitution implied that the states were sovereign.[28] Reversing that logic, the *British North America Act*, therefore, was so drafted as to enumerate certain powers for each level, but explicitly to leave the vast residuum to the federal government. This imbalance of power was clinched by the further provision that the specific grants were made to the provinces 'not so as to restrict the generality' of the basic authority of the federal government 'to make Laws for the Peace, Order and good Government of Canada.' Even more important, although the federal government could not formally alter the powers delegated to the provinces, it was authorized by its rights of reservation and disallowance to decide when the provinces had exceeded their powers and to take action to nullify such abuse.[29] This power of veto, it may be observed, Madison had sought stubbornly and in vain to have the Philadelphia convention give to the federal government.[30] In Canada, as in the US, a court was given what might be considered the final authority to judge the constitutionality of laws of both levels of government.

There was an age when within the British Empire the aristocratic and monarchical claim of the Westminster parliament to an overriding authority was mightier by far than democratic or republican pretensions. In the eighteenth century, sentiments of deference to the Crown still gave to the laws that abundant support in public affections which Edmund Burke thought indispensable to any stable regime.[31] At the time of the *British North America Act*, this old claim still had considerable weight. In his *English Constitution*, published the same year the Act was passed, Walter Bagehot described this reality, simultaneously reflecting in the liberalism of his analysis the rising power of the democratic idea.[32]

In Canada during the years that followed, the movement for 'provincial rights' deployed this idea to reverse the imbalance of power established by the 1867 Act. The story is a remarkable instance of the power of political culture, specifically the meta-legal theory of compact federalism embedded in popular attitudes, radically to determine the meaning of laws and to shape the institutions established by them.[33] In essence, the plot is that in the competition for democratic legitimacy the provinces had a case and the federal government did not. They had the edge because it was they which, as colonies, had from the 1830s initiated and carried on the struggle for self-government. Philosophically, their claim to democratic legitimacy was grounded in the small republic theory. Because they were homogeneous communities, their advocates argued, much in the manner of the American Anti-Federalists, that the provinces were the primary and proper seats of self-government and liberty.[34] Diversity was between, not within such bodies politic. This internal homogeneity, moreover, was also ethnic, since it was understood to mean not only common values, but also common descent from ancestors sharing a common culture.

Starting from the small republic premise, the provinces were virtually obliged to argue 'contractualism,'[35] the second leg of compact theory. Evidence for this argument dating from the founding is thin. Surely, the most telling circumstance in favour of the provincial case was the undeniable fact, widely recognized at the time, that only the entente between the leaders of the two nations, Macdonald and Cartier, made confederation possible. Although not put forward until 1869, compact theory had a solid foundation in reality.[36] Thus supported by theory and practice, the claim to 'provincial autonomy,' as Vipond concludes, became 'a legitimate, durable, indeed constitutional value' which continued and continues to inform debate.[37] In the controversy over constitutional reform in the past thirty years or so, it is the inarticulate premise leading all parties to agree that any fundamental change must be unanimously accepted by the provinces.[38]

In this manner the greater provincialism of Canadian political culture and the greater nationalism of American political culture shaped the marked differences in political institutions and political behaviour in the two federations. One of these differences, a 'truly distinctive' feature of modern Canadian federalism, as Vipond remarks, is 'its dependence at almost every level – from program operation to high level constitutional rearrangement – on negotiation between governments.' This informal, pervasive process, termed 'executive federalism' by Donald Smiley and 'federal-provincial diplomacy' by Richard Simeon, has been not only distinctive, but also effective.[39] It can be traced in the practices of Canadian politics from the earliest times – for instance, in the system of 'double majorities' of the pre-Confederation union and, indeed, in the Macdonald-Cartier entente itself – to more recent years when its rapid growth and development after the Second World War demonstrated its capacity to cope with the demands of modernization. Thanks to this unwritten constitutional innovation, which has given rise to over 500 intergovernmental conferences and meetings a year,[40] Canadian federalism, despite a continuous state of crisis for more than a generation, has repeatedly falsified predictions of its imminent demise.

We can see the differences between the American and Canadian federal systems by comparing how they respond to subnational pressures, specifically the pressures of ethnic diversity. In the American system these pressures have direct access to central decision-making. Regional and local economic interests across the nation are brought to bear on the legislative process in Washington.[41] Blacks have used their electoral power to secure federal protection of their civil rights and further measures offsetting discrimination. In contrast with Canadian practice, the federal government deals directly with local governments, and routinely uses state governments to carry out federally formulated programs.[42] Federal-provincial diplomacy, on the other hand, as the term implies, gives the centre nothing like so dominant a position. The process is much more a matter of bargaining between autonomous powers – so much so that in some cases when the outcome requires federal legislation, the national body does little more than ratify the agreement between governments.[43]

Policy matches process in the two countries. In the United States, the conflicts rooted in ethnicity are no less severe and no closer to final solution than in Canada. It is a simplification, but not a great one, to say that the principle on which Americans have tried to base their solution is integration, while the Canadian principle has been the opposite. By this I mean not the contradictory of 'disintegration,' but the contrary of 'segregation' or 'disengagement,' as Canadians may prefer to term it. Francophone Quebec seeks equality by means of separation verging on independence, while the champions of black Americans, rejecting the doctrine of 'separate but equal,' seek equality of rights verging on equality of results. For Americans this doctrine of equal rights for all – 'colour blind' justice – follows from the presumptions that they are one people, one nation, all of whose members are entitled to the same 'blessings of liberty,' the greatest of the 'great objects' of the Constitution. Quebec, on the contrary, seeks equal status and treatment as a separate social and political entity, a 'distinct society,' a line of argument which naturally and almost inevitably entails a distinctive set of rights. Insofar as compact theory has priority in Canadian political values, this demand is logical. It differs from the doctrine of uniformity of rights upheld by American liberalism and likewise departs from the intention of the Canadian framers expressed in Macdonald's similarly liberal doctrine of 'constitutional liberty.'[44]

One cause of this discrepancy is political culture. Another is the contrasting patterns of ethnicity. In Alan Cairns's classification, the American pattern is diffuse, the Canadian pattern concentrated; more precisely, in the United States the black minority is dispersed among the states, while in Canada the francophone minority constitutes an overwhelming majority in one province.[45] From the days of the legislative union that concentrated pattern, exhibited in both British Upper Canada and French Lower Canada, made for a direct relation of each of the two ethnic groups to the central government. This relationship, further facilitated by cabinet government at both levels, developed into the model of federal-provincial diplomacy. Given these two distributions of political resources, it makes sense in the first case that the ethnic minority will use its regional government as an instrument to win advantages from the central government, while in the other case, since the group will be dispersed as a minority in each of a number of regions, it will look to its leverage in national politics for protection of its rights against regional majorities. In both cases the distribution of the group shapes political behaviour in the same form as the ideal pattern of political culture.

Thus the United States model tends towards centralization of decisions and uniformity of policy, while the Canadian model tends towards decentralization of decisions and asymmetry of policy. What light do these contrasts of process and policy throw upon the long continuing controversy in Canada over constitutional reform?

The Failure of Mega-Constitutional Politics
Much has been written recently about the differing 'visions' of Canada which, it is said, have informed, and even incited, this controversy. Various

and conflicting as these visions may be, however, all reflect the compact and none the national theory, American style.[46] The nineteenth-century conception of the 'two founding nations,' French and British, remains strong in Quebec and in Ontario and eastern Canada generally. What is sometimes said to be a new view – that Canada consists of ten provinces of equal constitutional status – has been voiced especially in the opposition of the West to the Charlottetown Accord's recognition of Quebec as a distinct society entitled to a special status in the confederation. As a principle of federalism, however, that view also implies 'contractualism,' the proposition that the constitutional bond uniting the provinces is a compact among separate polities.

The strength of this premise was reflected during negotiations over the method of ratification of the Accord. Although the federal government had intended to avoid the paralyzing requirement of unanimity, this sensible precaution was dropped in favour of the rule that the referendum must be passed by popular majorities in all provinces. Reflecting on this lapse, Robert Vipond has remarked that 'it is amazing how some version of the compact theory has made a comeback in this country.'[47]

One might conclude that the compact theory is the problem. If we look at the practical consequences of this idea in the constitutional history of Canada, however, its considerable merits appear. Given the balance of power between the two founding nations, it is hard to see how the centralized structure of the 1867 Act, with its implicit British dominance, could have lasted. As the rationale for the dismantling of these impractical provisions of law, compact theory did good service. In the more relaxed framework created by this gradual adjustment, Quebec, as Richard Simeon has observed,[48] shared abundantly in the social and economic progress of the federation.

After the Second World War, to be sure, the old conflict sharpened and deepened, as continuing modernization gave Quebec the incentive and the resources for a new phase of self-assertion. The rise of secular Quebec nationalism in the 1960s, Vipond writes, triggered a series of challenges to the stability of the political system and established the urgency of basic constitutional reform.[49] If compact theory may be blamed for this new tension, it must also be credited with generating a corrective for its own shortcomings, when in the following years, federal-provincial diplomacy expanded so greatly as to become a major feature of constitutional structure. Insofar as this process resembles international rather than intranational relations, as John Meisel suggests,[50] it enables the separate actors to settle conflicts and achieve their respective aims by bargaining rather than rule-making, by trading advantages rather than by agreeing on a common program.

As both observers and participants have reported, the process was a considerable success in social, economic, and fiscal matters. Its outcomes sometimes involved special treatment for Quebec, yet the policies adopted in the 1960s have also been acclaimed by that champion of pan-Canadian effort, Pierre Trudeau.[51] As a method of constitutional reform, however, federal-provincial diplomacy was far less successful. Repeatedly in the 1960s and 1970s these negotiations ended in stalemate, Quebec being the great holdout. While writing a book on Canadian federalism during this period, Donald Smiley recalls that he twice stopped work because of his fear that the federation would not last as long as it would take to finish the manuscript.[52]

In light of these disappointments, the more recent failures of the Meech Lake and Charlottetown agreements in 1990 and 1992 looked like success, in some respects indeed 'a truly remarkable achievement,' as the premier of Ontario said of the latter.[53] Both were unanimously agreed upon by the federal government and all by the governments of all ten provinces, the great accomplishment in both cases being the assent of the Quebec government, which had been denied to all previous efforts from the Fulton-Favreau and Victoria Charter attempts of 1964 and 1971 to the passage of the *Constitution Act* in 1982. With Meech Lake coming so close to unanimous ratification with the legislatures of only two of the smaller provinces failing to act, the question demanding explanation is the far greater defeat of the Charlottetown Accord in a national referendum which voted it down by a substantial popular majority, the Yes vote carrying only four provinces and one territory, while the No vote carried six provinces, including Quebec, and one territory.

On the face of it, the disparity of outcomes is puzzling, since the 1992 attempt was altered in both message and medium in response to the main criticisms of the 1990 effort. The proposed reform was made more inclusive, special regard being shown not only to the claims of Quebec, but also to those of the Western provinces, as in Senate reform, and to the claims of the Aboriginal peoples, as in the recognition of a considerable degree of self-government. The criticism of the Meech Lake process as secretive and elitist had been even more severe than the criticism of the proposal itself. In response, the process by which the 1992 proposal was discussed, agreed, and ratified was made far more participatory. The final decision was rendered not by provincial legislatures, but directly by the voters, the proposal submitted to them itself having issued from an unparalleled measure of consultation among the federal government, a joint committee of the parliament, provincial, territorial, and Aboriginal representatives, academics, speakers for interest-groups, and ordinary citizens. Yet this more inclusive and more participatory approach was defeated even among those very constituencies, Quebec, outer Canada, and the Aboriginal peoples, to whom it had been especially directed, a culminating failure of more than a quarter of a century of effort to bring about comprehensive constitutional reform.

From this record, some observers infer that the clue not only to the disparity between 1990 and 1992, but also to the long saga of failure of constitutional reform is the nature of the effort itself. The fatal flaw, to use a term of Peter Russell's, is 'mega-constitutional politics' – Canada's preoccupation not simply with constitutional reform, but with fundamental and comprehensive change.[54] Donald Smiley elaborated essentially the same objection in his criticism of 'administrative rationality,' a failing he particularly attributed to Pierre Trudeau.[55] Its misleading premise was that 'the aim of policy should be stated at a high level of generalization with more specific aims controlled by broader ones.' If they follow this premise, parties to a negotiation will attempt to solve a particular problem by seeking agreement on a general principle under which a solution is subsumed, quite possibly only to find, when they have discovered such rationales, that they confront intractable conflicts of principle with one another. The pursuit of rationality in this manner will have heightened and widened the conflict, while a benign neglect of principle in favour of attention to the particulars of the case might have enabled the parties to arrive at a tradeoff satisfying both sides. And even if there is no real conflict of principles or visions, the search for agreement on general principles may bring to mind the particulars of other possible conflicts and thereby arouse fear and suspicion sufficient to block agreement. Something of this sort does seem to have happened in 1992. Although the voters had been assailed by a barrage of arguments embodying broad principles and appealing to different visions, many voters seem to have judged the accord by the parochial fear that it would put their province at some disadvantage.[56]

Alan Cairns makes a similar point in his regret that Canadian elites had failed to develop a conception of 'a living constitution' as a mode of conduct 'embedded in the evolving habits and values of successive generations.'[57] In practice, if not theory, that had been the method of piecemeal adjustment by which the constitution of Canada had developed since 1867 and which had produced the saving innovation of federal-provincial diplomacy.

But can constitutional adjustment in any mode, comprehensive or piecemeal, cope with the passions of ethnicity? When one samples the rhetoric of Québécois self-assertion, one may well hear a distant echo of the value-laden emotions destroying constitutional order in Eastern Europe.

The Paradox of Modern Ethnicity
Ethnicity is an aspect of culture that entails a distinctive sort of political behaviour. Like any culture group, the members of the ethnic group share

certain beliefs about the individual and the world. They also have a special sense of history, a belief that they are descended from people who in the past similarly shared this culture and lived as a community. This belief in a biological tie to family, clan, kindred, or tribe, further strengthens the solidarity of the group. While making the ethnic group more cohesive, this belief also makes it more exclusive. Such ethnic-driven nationalism, as daily proved by the self-destructive behaviour of the states emerging from the communist regimes of the Soviet Union and Yugoslavia, can only with great difficulty be constrained by a stable constitutional and international order.

Nationalism, however, need not be ethnic. Some elements of culture are not ethnic, and these may be transferred from one person to another, as the values and virtues of one group are adopted or vicariously appreciated by other groups. Nationality so constituted is, therefore, intrinsically open to accepting new members. Even if free of ethnic pretensions, however, the narrowly homogeneous political culture will be harsh towards internal deviance and uncomprehending towards foreign diversity. If we are to find a cultural basis for constitutional and international order, we must turn to the universal principles of modern liberal democracy.

Now comes the paradox. These principles of liberal democracy, born with modernity, will flourish, one would expect, with the progress of modernization. Greater independence, mobility, and communication should break up old ethnic solidarities as common interests and wider understanding grow. Yet, in fact, ethnicity, an archaic force deeply hostile to liberalism, has achieved its great prominence in social and political analysis only recently. One sees this in the history of the term. While 'ethnic,' 'ethnology,' and 'ethnography' go back to the nineteenth century, 'ethnicity,' as a term needed to identify a broad and powerful social force was coined only a few years ago.[58] As in rhetoric, so also in behaviour. In Canada, the interprovincial conflict, although dating back to the early nineteenth century, flared up in its present acute form only in the 1960s while Quebec was moving away from its agrarian traditionalism towards an urban, commercial, and professional outlook more characteristic of its old antagonist. While the cultural gap was being closed, the political gap widened.

In a pioneering work on ethnicity, which has become authoritative in the field, Glazer and Moynihan have supplied a key to this puzzle.[59] The rise of the welfare state, they point out, has made government the source of a wide array of benefits for groups suffering from disadvantages, intended or unintended, which can be attributed to the attitudes and institutions of the society. Where ethnic minorities still live less well than the rest of the society, the general commitment of the welfare state to levelling-up is, in effect, an invitation to such groups to claim redress by government action. Success incites imitation – in the US, for example, the removal of disadvantages by blacks encouraged the members of other ethnic groups to organize and act politically for similar benefits.[60] Hence, despite the homogenizing effect of modernity on ethnic differences, their assertion has become more pronounced. The Canadian experience bears out the hypothesis, the first discussion of francophone Canadians as an 'ethnic class' taking place as recently as 1962, a time of rapid progress in economic and social modernization in Quebec.[61]

Yet this dark cloud of speculation has a silver lining. A basic insight of the Glazer-Moynihan analysis is that ethnicity today can function not only as an end in itself, but also as a means to other ends, in particular the eminently modern end of increase in the wealth of the nation. Quebec fits the hypothesis. It was once very much the traditionalist society, trying, above all, to fend off outside interference with *la survivance*. Its recent large and detailed demands for decentralization, however, were not sought simply in order to protect certain old practices of church, family, and language. Far more emphatically they were advanced as conditions necessary for the further progress of this affluent exemplar of up-to-date corporatistic capitalism, sometimes referred to as 'Quebec, Inc.' Modernization has made Quebec, in fact, a far less distinct society than it was in the not too distant past.[62] As Vipond notes, the nationalism inspiring Quebec's surge of self-assertion after the Second World War was secular. Yet that same process of modernization has also added to the resources Quebec can muster when bargaining for concessions from the rest of Canada in the name of its distinctness.

The gist of this analysis is that the differences between Quebec and the rest of Canada, and indeed among all the provinces today, are not so much conflicts of value as differences of interest and, therefore, amenable to appeals to rational calculation. So viewed, one would expect the process of bargaining which led to the Charlottetown Accord to start with the statement of sharply opposed positions by the parties. And so it was, as one can see if one compares the far-reaching decentralization proposed by the 1991 Allaire Report of the Quebec Liberal Party with the managerial centralism advocated in the federal government's proposals later that year in *Shaping Canada's Future Together*. As participants in a rational bargaining process, moreover, one would also expect the negotiators to recognize the necessity of maintaining the confederation and, therefore, in the course of their negotiations to make very considerable concessions. Again, this happened, as the centre gave up its managerial dream and Quebec scaled back its famous list of twenty-one devolutionary demands to a half-dozen or so.

Even in the demands of the moderates, not to mention the tough talk of the separatists, Quebec had threatened secession. The issue was sharpened once more in 1994 with the election of the Parti Québécois with its commitment to holding a referendum on sovereignty before the end of 1995. Whether or not the referendum will succeed remains in question. Support for sovereignty is strong, and the ability of the new government to shape events in partnership with its federal allies, the Bloc Québécois, should not be underestimated. A good deal of evidence points the other way: even the PQ talks about the need to maintain extensive economic linkages, and public opinion surveys show that the commitment to outright independence is still a minority view, and that many Quebecers continue to hold a profound attachment to Canada.

One may doubt that there will be further negotiations in the mega-constitutional mode. Piecemeal adjustment by the bargaining processes implied by the logic of compact theory and inherent in the structure of federal-provincial diplomacy is more likely. In those processes the greater resources of a modernizing Quebec are balanced by its recognition of the advantages of a close connection with the rest of Canada. Reason, if not nationalism, therefore, may well lead to another of those cobbled-up compromises, which, despite distressing appearances, have enabled Canada in general, and Quebec in particular, to thrive as peaceful, lively, and modern societies. In the cultural context of liberal democracy, compact theory as well as national theory can produce a viable federalism.

But does this bland case study, to use Cairns' adjective,[64] offer much guidance as to the future of federalism in other polities, such as the European Union or the Russian Federation?

The Future of Federalism in the European Union

Both ethnicity and federalism figure in the thought that shaped the European Union. The preamble of the Treaty of Paris of 1951 looked forward to 'a broader and deeper community among peoples long divided by blood.' The rhetoric does not seem out of place when *La Marseillaise* still sings of watering the fields of France with the *sang impur* of foreign invaders and the *jus sanguinis* still determines German citizenship. In the minds of the principal architects of the Union, Jean Monnet and Robert Schuman, the solution of these ancient antagonisms was 'a European federation.'[65]

Since these hopes were expressed, a very considerable centralization of power has taken place and promises to continue. A familiar refrain of federal theory is echoed in the commitment to 'subsidiarity' as a principle which will prevent interference by the central bodies in matters that can be better handled by the governments of the member states. The constitution of the Union is evolving in the British rather than the Continental manner, step by step, sometimes by the explicit provisions of a treaty, sometimes informally and incrementally by legislative and administrative practice. In this ever closer union, reason, which clearly points towards some form of fiscal federalism,[66] seems to be winning over passion. However, the Maastricht Treaty aroused in some member countries a fearful resistance, reminiscent of the reaction to mega-constitutionalism in Canada.

Some champions of union have thought that Europe could follow the American model. The difficulty, as pointed out repeatedly by many observers, is that there is no 'one European people,' but rather, as stated in the preamble to the original Treaty, several 'peoples.' As Guy Kirsch notes, European integration is a 'child of reason, not emotion,' leading to the formation of a suprastate, not a supranation.[67] While individuals will affirm their support for integration when questioned by public opinion surveys, the Union was not founded on a surge of pan-European sentiment comparable to the 'whig party' of American origins or the nationalist movements of eighteenth- and nineteenth-century Europe. Today it still numbers few 'impassioned Europeans,'[68] lacking the base for a pan-European politics which would give legitimacy to its governing bodies. As in its origins, the Union is an elitist, not a populist operation.

This does not mean that the Union must fail or that it cannot be federal. While we do not see a supranational Europe, we do see a Europe of nation states, identifying and pursuing its common interests by a process of continual negotiation, which, as Richard Simeon suggested some years ago, greatly resembles federal-provincial diplomacy.[69] Bureaucratic and business elites throughout Europe, motivated not by some long-run 'ideology of Europe,' but by immediate concrete interests, have often nudged their governments into responses to administrative and economic problems which, over time, add up to even closer integration.[70] One step in centralization may have unintended side-effects which call for further centralizing action. For example, in the single market exchange rate instability interferes with the increase of trade; this in turn leads concerned elites to move their governments towards monetary union.

Both experience and analysis, however, show that this spill-over mechanism depends on a larger context. Depending on that context, the same side-effect may be decentralizing rather than centralizing. In the summer of 1992, for instance, agreement to a fixed exchange rate under the ERM obliged Britain to raise its interest rates so high as to aggravate an already serious unemployment problem. In response, Britain took the decentralizing step of withdrawing from the agreement. In general, a policy convergence has been a necessary condition of the major steps towards closer union.[71] But the differences arising from the distinctive history and values of different nations still retard progress towards a federal regime.

To what extent are these cultural restraints ethnic? All the countries of Western Europe did have an ethnic past, in the sense that the territories where these peoples now reside were once inhabited by a vast array of kinship groups each of which, considered individually, might be considered as having a homogeneous culture. The rise of the typical nation state of Western Europe, however, is the story of its emergence from such a multi-ethnic population. By various means, most of them not very gentle, the modern nation states of Britain, France, Germany, Italy, Spain, and so on created in each country from such a multi-ethnic background a uniform system of law and custom. Yet within each, much of the old variety survived and, despite modernization, still survives.

As both cause and effect of this ethnic assimilation, liberal democracy became the dominant regime. Its aspiration to impersonal standards of justice and its inclination towards toleration and accommodation – its appeal to reason – enhanced the ability of these states to cope with the passions of ethnic prejudice. They also prepared these states for cooperation with one another. The liberal democracy of the political cultures of the nation states of Western Europe is the indispensable ground for the rise and progress of the Union. Cultural constraints on closer union are substantial. But judging by its record over the past generation, the Union has much the same capacity for compromise which, expressed in federal-provincial diplomacy, has for so long sustained the bargaining process and asymmetrical outcomes of Canadian federalism.

The Failure of Federalism in Eastern Europe
In Eastern and Central Europe the failure of federalism is pervasive, from the horrors of 'ethnic cleansing' in Bosnia-Hercegovina to the 'velvet divorce' of the Czech and the Slovak republics, and including the disintegration of the Soviet Union and the internal threats to the Russian Federation itself. The causes are far too complex and obscure to be fully addressed here, but the contribution of cultural factors to this dangerous and tragic dissolution bears directly on the relation of ethnicity and federalism. Ethnicity is notoriously the justification offered for internal separatism and external conflict. In this mind-set, the major premise is the claim of both common descent and a homogeneous culture; the minor premise is the theory of self-determination that any social body so defined has the right to sovereign independence. The consequence of this fatal syllogism is the defeat of both constitutional and international order.

In the Soviet Union and its satellites, as Alan Cairns points out, the breakdown of central communist control led to 'an explosion of ethnicity.'[72] In the late 1980s the Soviet Union was seized by what one Russian observer termed a 'separatism mania,' as its constituent republics broke away from the centre, regions from republics and cities and districts from regions.[73] By the end of 1990 all fifteen union republics had declared themselves sovereign or independent. When the USSR was disbanded in December 1991, a new and far looser association termed the Commonwealth of Independent States was formed, consisting of eleven of the former republics. In their rejection of the CIS, the three Baltic states, which had been the first to leave the Soviet Union, were joined by Georgia and in October 1992, by Azerbaijan. Within the individual republics, moreover, interethnic violence broke out in Armenia, Azerbaijan, Moldavia, Georgia, and Central Asia.

The background to these centrifugal disorders was the existence, in the area embraced by the USSR, of some 100 ethnic groups, twenty-two with populations over one million. Moreover, they were so dispersed in their geographical locations that it would have taken the most monstrous gerry-mander to make up a federal scheme which allocated one and only one ethnic group to each jurisdiction. The typical republic included, alongside a dominant ethnic majority, a number of ethnic minorities, themselves also prone to seek autonomy. In Georgia, for instance, the South Ossetians and Abkhazians both demanded independence by right of self-determination. The Moldavians, having successfully claimed sovereignty for the republic in which they were overwhelmingly the majority, brutally suppressed the demand for autonomy by the Gagauz, a small Turkic-speaking Christian minority. The Armenians went to war with the Azerbaijanis over the Nagorno-Karabakh enclave which they cherish as the centre of their ancient culture. In Ukraine, as Dr. Vassylenko notes,[74] the integrity of the state is threatened by separatist movements in the Crimea, Novorossiya, and the Kryvorizko-Donetska, and Carpathian republics.

The fissiparous aspirations which motivated this resistance to union were commonly informed by historical memories which harked back several centuries to a distant past when clan and kindred were major social forma-tions. For each group these memories had supported the sense of a common life during generations of oppression by one another and especially by great empires, culminating in the totalitarian control of communism. While the reaction against that control fed hostility towards even the milder forms of political union implied by federalism, the doctrine of ethnic self-determi-nation professed in the formulae of Soviet political theory and Soviet constitutions legitimated a separatism without limit.

Comparison with Western Europe, however, shows that the motivating ideas went much deeper. The dominance of authoritarian empires well into the modern period is an important factor. As Dr. Vassylenko observed, until the beginning of the twentieth century, 'a majority of the nations of Central, Eastern and southern Europe were deprived of statehood,' surviving as nothing more than 'components of three empires – the Russian, the Aus-trian-Hungarian, and the Ottoman empires.'[75] 'National identities' as well as 'national conflicts' remained 'frozen and suppressed during communist rule,' as indeed they had been for centuries under previous imperialisms.

By contrast, in Western Europe the medieval dream of empire was brought to an end by the nation state, which, as we have seen, provided the basis for the rise of liberal democracy. There, as in North America, states inspired by its values have displayed the capacity for the toleration and cooperation required by federalism. One might have thought that the considerable dispersion of ethnic communities in Eastern Europe, when released by glasnost, would have led to similar outcomes. But neither the favourable ethnic pattern nor the ideology of Marxism could produce a cohesive political culture. In the absence of liberal democracy, 'the melting pot simply did not work,' to quote Reneo Lukic.[76] Today in the successor states of the communist empire, liberal democracy and its expression, a stable federal regime, have a chance, but only a chance, against the blinkered thrust for self-determination fuelled by the disintegrating forces of an archaic ethnicity.

Conclusion

Any approach to government which in theory or practice fails to take into account the passions of politics is bound to fail, but political passions can also be enlisted in support of rational structures and rational governance. The austere rationality of the economist's model of fiscal federalism is not likely to be realized in practice, yet federalism in various looser forms often makes sense for large polities. Sometimes, as in the case of the United States, the public affections of the nation state may be not only compatible with, but also strongly supportive of a federal regime. Structures more in the style of compact federalism can also thrive as peaceful and prosperous polities, as Canada shows and the European Union promises to show.

It is fundamental that, as in these instances, the passions of political identification be embedded in a culture of liberal democracy. The great nation states of the West have been the progenitors and today are the bearers of these values. In this role their nationalism has been an indispensable foundation for federalism. To be sure, there is a nationalistic passion that is intrinsically hostile to federalism. This is the passion for a state founded on cultural homogeneity and ethnic purity. That nationalism is a threat not only to federalism, but to all forms of constitutional and international order.

Notes

1 Interview, *MacNeil/Lehrer NewsHour*, PBS, 8 December 1992: transcript no. 4515.
2 Quoted in Anne Sa'adah, 'Sovereignty and Citizenship: What Can the Old France Tell Us about the New Europe?,' in Linda Miller and Michael Smith, eds., *Ideas and Ideals: Essays on Politics in Honor of Stanley Hoffman* (Boulder, CO: Westview Press 1993).

3 Edward Millican, *One United People: The Federalist Papers and the National Idea* (Lexington KY: University Press of Kentucky 1990), 14, 41, 49.
4 The discussion of American federalism in this section comes from my book, *To Make A Nation: The Rediscovery of American Federalism* (Cambridge, MA: Harvard University Press 1993).
5 Timothy Conlan, *New Federalism: Intergovernmental Reform from Nixon to Reagan* (Washington: Brookings Institute 1988), 3, 97-111, and Chapter 8, passim.
6 Abraham Lincoln, *Collected Works*, ed. Roy P. Basler (New Brunswick, NJ: Rutgers University Press 1955), vol. 4, 434-5; Jefferson Davis, *Messages and Papers of Jefferson Davis and the Confederacy*, ed. James D. Richardson (New York: Chelsea House-R. Hector 1966), vol. 1, 35.
7 Robert C. Vipond, *Liberty and Community: Canadian Federalism and the Failure of the Constitution* (Albany: State University of New York Press 1991), 25, quoting the Toronto *Globe*, 1 August 1864. What I say on Canadian intellectual history comes largely from this splendid work.
8 On how the Supreme Court in this period 'facilitated a concentration of governing authority,' see Stephen Skowronek, *Building a New American State; The Expansion of National Administrative Capacities, 1877-1920* (New York: Cambridge University Press 1982), 41. On the JCPC's reduction of federal power by its interpretations of ss. 91 and 92 of the *British North America Act*, see Anthony H. Birch, *Federalism, Finance and Social Legislation* (Oxford: Clarendon Press 1955), 158-62.
9 Vipond, *Liberty and Community*, 9.
10 Beer, *To Make A Nation*, 237-43.
11 Ibid., 8, 86-92, 219-24, 316-17.
12 Ibid., Chapter 8, esp. 255-61.
13 Ibid., 257-64.
14 Ibid., 245, 314, 323, 338.
15 Ibid., 295-301.
16 James Madison, *Federalist 71*; Beer, *To Make A Nation*, 306.
17 James Bryce, *American Commonwealth* (New York: Macmillan 1888, 1924), vol. 1, 353, Holmes J. dissenting in *Truax v. Corrigan*, 257 US 312, 344 (1921), Brandeis J. dissenting in *New State Ice Co.* v. *Liebmann*, 285 US 262, 311 (1932).
18 Letter to Thomas Jefferson, 24 October 1787 in James Madison, *The Papers of James Madison*, ed. Robert A. Rutland et al. (Chicago: Chicago University Press 1975), vol. 10, 214.
19 Beer, *To Make A Nation*, 293-5.
20 Ibid., 357-9.
21 James Wilson, *The Works of James Wilson*, ed. Robert G. McCloskey (Cambridge, MA: Harvard University Press 1967), 788-9; Beer, *To Make A Nation*, 360-5.
22 See especially Macdonald's speeches in the Quebec conference of October, 1864, in G.P. Browne, ed., *Documents on the Confederation of British North America* (Toronto: McClelland and Stewart 1969) and in the Legislative Assembly of 1865 in *Parliamentary Debates on the Subject of the Confederation of the British North American Provinces* (Quebec: Hunter Rose 1865).
23 Donald G. Creighton, *John A. Macdonald: The Young Politician* (Toronto: Macmillan 1952), 320.

24 Quoted in Kenneth McNaught, *The Pelican History of Canada* (Harmondsworth: Penguin Books 1976), 134. See also Vipond, *Liberty and Community*, 132, on 'legal liberalism' in mid-nineteenth century England.
25 Vipond, *Liberty and Community*, 27.
26 *Parliamentary Debates*, 44, 45; Creighton, *John A. Macdonald*, 369, n. 31; McNaught, *The Pelican History of Canada*, 118.
27 Nicely summarized in McNaught, *The Pelican History of Canada*, 127-33.
28 *Parliamentary Debates*, 33; Browne, *Documents*, 95; Jennifer Smith, 'Canadian Confederation and the Influence of American Federalism,' *Canadian Journal of Political Science* 21 (1988):444.
29 *British North America Act*, s. 90.
30 Beer, *To Make A Nation*, 291, 301.
31 Edmund Burke, 'Reflections on the Revolution in France,' *The Writings and Speeches of Edmund Burke*, ed. Paul Langford (Oxford: Clarendon Press 1981-), vol. 4, 147.
32 Walter Bagehot, *The English Constitution*. World's Classic Series (London: Oxford University Press 1928). See his discussion of the continuing importance of the traditional 'dignified' parts of the constitution (the monarchy and the House of Lords) in contrast with the modern 'efficient' parts (the cabinet and the House of Commons).
33 Vipond, *Liberty and Community*, passim, summarized at pp. 44-5 and 191.
34 Ibid., Chapters 3 and 4, esp. 87-90.
35 Ibid., 5.
36 Ibid., 43. See also Norman McL. Rogers, 'The Compact Theory of Confederation,' *Canadian Bar Review* IX, No. 6 (1931).
37 Vipond, *Liberty and Community*, 3.
38 See below, p. 237.
39 Vipond, *Liberty and Community*, 73; Richard Simeon, *Federal-Provincial Diplomacy: The Making of Recent Policy in Canada* (Toronto: University of Toronto Press 1972), Chapter 5; Donald V. Smiley, *Canada in Question: Federalism in the Seventies*, 2nd ed. (Toronto: McGraw-Hill Ryerson 1976), Chapter 3.
40 Canada, *Shaping Canada's Future Together: Proposals* (Ottawa: Ministry of Supply and Services 1991), 41.
41 See the discussion of various types of coalitions in S. Beer, 'The Modernization of American Federalism,' *Publius: The Journal of Federalism* 3, No. 2 (Fall, 1973).
42 See the discussion of the intergovernmental lobby in Beer, 'The Adoption of General Revenue Sharing: A Case Study in Public Sector Politics,' *Public Policy* 24, No. 2 (Spring, 1976):166-71.
43 Simeon, *Federal-Provincial Diplomacy*, 61, 87.
44 Vipond, *Liberty and Community*, Chapter 5, passim.
45 Alan Cairns, 'Constitutional Government and the Two Faces of Ethnicity: Federalism is Not Enough,' Chapter 2 in this volume.
46 Yet I must report that what seems to me the true note of democratic nationalism was struck by Premier Clyde Wells of Newfoundland, one of the most acute thinkers among Canadian political leaders, when during the debate on the Meech Lake proposals, he declared: 'The Constitution belongs to the people of Canada – the ultimate source of sovereignty in the nation.' Quoted by Michael

Harris (Conservative) in a debate on constitutional reform in the Legislative Assembly of Ontario, 20 September 1992, 2247.

47 Robert C. Vipond, 'Seeing Canada Through the Referendum: Still a House Divided,' unpublished, February 1993, p. 25. The words quoted are from a letter to me dated 23 February 1993.

48 Richard Simeon, 'Canada and the United States: Lessons from the North American Experience,' Chapter 16 in this volume.

49 Vipond, *Liberty and Community*, 1.

50 John Meisel, 'Introduction' in Simeon, *Federal-Provincial Diplomacy*, viii.

51 'Trudeau to Robertson, So Where Is the Demagogy?' *Globe and Mail*, 21 October 1992.

52 Donald Smiley, *Canada in Question: Federalism in the Seventies*, 2nd ed. (Toronto: McGraw-Hill Ryerson 1976), viii.

53 Premier Bob Rae, Legislative Assembly of Ontario, 20 September 1992, 2241-2.

54 Quoted in Vipond, 'Seeing Canada Through the Referendum,' 26, n. 2.

55 Smiley, *Canada in Question*, 49-52, 74-9.

56 Vipond, 'Seeing Canada Through the Referendum,' 19.

57 Alan C. Cairns, 'The Living Constitution,' LXXVII, *Queen's Quarterly* 4 (1970):4, quoted in Smiley, *Canada In Question*, 51.

58 Nathan Glazer and Daniel B. Moynihan, *Ethnicity: Theory and Experience* (Cambridge, MA: Harvard University Press 1975), attribute the first use of the term to David Riesman in 1953.

59 Ibid.

60 Ibid., 25.

61 Ibid., 269.

62 For example, in Hugh MacLennan's classic on interwar Canada, *Two Solitudes* (Toronto: Macmillan 1945).

63 See Simeon, 'Canada and the United States.'

64 Cairns, 'Constitutional Government.'

65 Robert O. Keohane and Stanley Hoffmann, *The New European Community: Decisionmaking and Institutional Change* (Boulder, CO: Westview Press 1991), 87.

66 For further discussion, see Tommasso Padoa-Schioppa and Jacques Pelkmans (Chapters 10 and 11) in this volume.

67 See Cairns and Kirsch (Chapters 2 and 4) in this volume.

68 John S. Ambler, quoted in Mark Kesselman and Joel Krieger, eds., *European Politics in Transition*, 2nd ed. (Lexington, MA: D.C. Heath 1992), 749.

69 Simeon, *Federal-Provincial Diplomacy*, 299-300.

70 For a summary of the functionalist in contrast with the intergovernmental view, see Keohane and Hoffman, *New European Community*, 10-25.

71 Ibid., 23-5.

72 Cairns, 'Constitutional Government.'

73 Nicolai Petrov and Leonid Smirnyagin, quoted in Kesselman and Krieger, *European Politics*, 603.

74 Volodymyr Vassylenko, 'Disintegration of the Soviet "Federation" and the "Federalization" of Ukraine,' Chapter 20 in this volume.

75 Ibid.

76 Quoted in Cairns, 'Constitutional Government,' p. 23.

16

Canada and the United States: Lessons from the North American Experience

Richard Simeon

Canada and the United States are the two oldest, most stable, and arguably most successful federations in the world. Modern federalism was invented by Americans, and adopted, with significant variations, by Canada in 1867. Each was born in the desire to bring pre-existing political entities in British North America together into a single political unit, while maintaining the autonomy of the founding communities. Each also became the vehicle for building nations which eventually spanned continents. But each federal country has evolved in different ways. In the United States, centripetal forces tended to predominate, so that some commentators are led to wonder if the United States is still fully federal. In David Walker's phrase, it is a 'nation-centred' federalism.[1] In Canada, despite an initially much more centralized constitution, centrifugal forces have tended to predominate – so much so that the very survival of the country as a federation has often been in question.

Thus the two countries, despite their many similarities, politically, culturally, and economically, offer a rich variety of experience which may offer lessons for the applicability and utility of federalism, or federally inspired models, in other settings.

The American and Canadian Models of Federalism
First, however, it is important to note some broad differences between the United States and Canada in the institutions and practices of federalism.

Canada is a parliamentary federation; the US a congressional one. This difference has large consequences for the operation of federalism in the two countries. In the United States, power at the national level is shared between president and Congress; and in Congress, the weakness of the party system and party discipline further disperses power. 'Divided government' is not only a feature of politics in Washington, but also in an increasing number of states.[2] In Canada, the fusion of executives and legislatures, combined with strong party discipline, renders both national and provincial governments much more centralized.

This, along with the smaller number of Canadian provinces, powerfully contributes to the distinctive Canadian pattern of intergovernmental relations known as 'executive federalism'[3] and to policy-making through direct intergovernmental bargaining which has been labelled 'federal-provincial diplomacy.'[4] Intergovernmental relations in the US are far more fluid and diverse, played out in a myriad of program-oriented policy networks involving congressional committees, bureaucratic agencies, and state and local agencies – marble cake or fruit cake federalism.[5] 'Summit diplomacy' plays a central, though increasingly contested role in Canada, but a relatively minor one in the United States. The rhetoric of Canadian federalism sees provinces and Ottawa as a partnership of equals; American writers, by contrast, talk of the 'intergovernmental lobby.'

This in turn is reflected in the intergovernmental fiscal and policy relationships: Canada has many fewer shared-cost, conditional, or grant-in-aid programs; those it has, involve far less detailed federal control and supervision, and a much larger proportion of federal transfers to the provinces take the form of unconditional grants.[6] The concentration of power in provincial executives has also meant far fewer relationships between Ottawa and municipal governments than in the US, despite the fact that in both countries local governments are constitutionally creatures of the states or provinces. More generally, C.E.S. Franks argues that the 'diffusion of contacts and exchanges in the United States blunts the force of the gaming element and the competition for legitimacy that is prominent in executive federalism.'[7]

A second fundamental consequence of congressional versus parliamentary federalism is that 'intrastate federalism' – the representation of regional and local interests within the national governments, and the balancing of these and the national interest at the national level – plays a far stronger role in the US. Both systems are bicameral. In the US, however, there is equal representation of the states in the Senate (as distinct from equality among regions in Canada); the US Senate is elected, in contrast with the federally appointed Canadian Senate, which is thus unable to play a distinct, autonomous role in regional or provincial representation; and weak party discipline ensures that members of both houses of Congress are able to play a visible role in representing local interests within Congress. Canadian Members of Parliament are much less able to play this role. This difference greatly inhibits the ability of the national parliament to act as the arena for the balancing and accommodation of regional and national interests, and powerfully strengthens the role of provincial governments as advocates of provincial interests, even within national policy-making.[8]

This difference has led some scholars to assert that this is in itself a sufficient explanation for the much greater concentration on regional and intergovernmental conflict in the Canadian federation.[9] The exclusion of provincial interests from the centre, it is argued, transmutes regional into intergovernmental conflict and vests influence in provincial politicians with an interest in sustaining this conflict and strengthening provincial powers. It is also argued that the weakness of intrastate mechanisms in Canada subordinates the interests of less-populated regions and provinces to the interests of the majorities found in the large provinces of central Canada. Both these arguments underlie the recent drive for Senate reform in Canada.

Another important institutional difference was that, with the Bill of Rights, the US federation was from the start a 'chartered' federation. Canadian federalism, until the passage of the *Charter of Rights and Freedoms* in 1982, was not. The Bill of Rights was from the beginning a powerful affirmation of the rights of individual citizens, as against governments at either level. This was both a powerful centralizing influence, and a force to ensure that US political discourse, at least after the Civil War, was more focused on individual rights than it was on federalism or the rights and interests of state or regional collectivities. The adoption of the Canadian Charter was a powerful stimulus to the reorientation of Canadian political debate in the same direction. It too was a powerful nationalizing instrument; and it identified and gave status to a range of collective interests – gender, Aboriginal peoples, multicultural groups – which challenged the way in which federalism privileged territorially based divisions.[10] The Canadian federal system is thus in the process of working out the tensions among the three logics of federalism, parliamentarianism, and the *Charter of Rights*. While similar tensions are not unknown in the United States, they have very largely been worked out in favour of the predominance of national norms, whether expressed through Congress or the Supreme Court.

Especially in recent years, the US court has placed few limits on the scope of federal power and its ability to impose standards on the states. Despite the fact that the US Constitution contains only a short list of federal powers while reserving all others to the states, the courts have granted virtually unlimited scope to congressional authority; there are few legal limits (though important political ones) on the reach of federal power. Federalism is to be defended in the political arena, though there are some hints that the current US Supreme Court is giving renewed weight to the federal principle.[11] By contrast, the courts – until 1949 the Judicial Committee of the Privy Council in Britain – took a constitution which on its face is highly centralist and interpreted it to expand provincial powers and constrain the federal power. More recently, in a number of crucial decisions, the Canadian

Supreme Court has self-consciously sought to balance federal and provincial authority, responsive to increased federal powers in some respects, but careful not to open the door to unrestricted federal invasion of provincial jurisdiction.[12] In general however, the Canadian Supreme Court remains a much more active umpire of the federal system than does the US court.

The greater federal authority in the US takes a number of forms – a virtually unlimited power to spend on state and local matters, a virtually unlimited ability to preempt state action, especially by virtue of the trade and commerce power, and the ability to impose regulatory requirements on state governments – what has been called 'cooptive federalism' or 'regulatory conscription,'[13] and by Reagan and Sanzone 'permissive federalism.'[14]

The institutional differences between American and Canadian federalism are reinforced by patterns of political cleavage in the two countries. Provincial identities and loyalties appear to be considerably stronger in Canada than the United States. In this, institutions and attitudes interact: regionalism fosters strong assertive provinces; strong assertive provinces foster regional interests and identities.

All these differences combine to explain why, by most measures, Canada is a considerably more decentralized federation than is the United States, why Canadian politics is far more focused on the politics of region, why intergovernmental relations are so much more prominent in Canadian policy-making, and why federalism, national unity, and the constitution have been *the* preeminent issues for governance in Canada while, at least since the Civil War, they have tended to be of secondary importance in the United States. With this background, let us turn to the implications of federalism for community, democracy, and governmental effectiveness, the fundamental themes identified in the Introduction to this volume.

Federalism and Community

In Canada, the institutions of federalism parallel and reinforce the historically dominant socioeconomic cleavages; they cut across them in the United States. Nowhere is this more clear than in the most fundamental division in each country: race in the United States, language in Canada. French-speaking Canadians are concentrated in Quebec, where they constitute the large majority. The rest of the country, with the exception of New Brunswick, is overwhelmingly English-speaking. African-Americans, by contrast, are widely distributed across the country; in no state or region are they a majority. This difference has profound consequences for federalism, and for the ways in which the politics of race and language are played out.

From the outset, issues of community have been at the heart of the Canadian federal experience. The political deadlock between French and English-speaking communities in the united provinces of Canada was primary impetus for the larger British North American union of 1867 in the first place. It was the desire of Quebecers to maintain autonomy in the social and cultural spheres which dictated a federal model for the new country. It was their previous existence as distinct political communities which led to the reluctance of the Atlantic provinces to join the federation. As the country expanded to the Pacific, the federal model itself helped 'construct' provincial communities in provinces such as Manitoba, Saskatchewan, and Alberta.

Since then, federalist debate in Canada has focused primarily on the community dimension; until recently, debate in terms of effectiveness, efficiency, and democracy have been much more muted. The issues have been phrased in terms of 'province building' versus 'nation building'; 'centralization versus decentralization'; 'one Canada' as a single national community versus Canada as a 'community of communities'; a bi-national or bi-communal view of Canada as a partnership of 'two founding peoples' versus Canada as a federation of ten equal provinces.[15] Thus Canadian federalism does not embrace and institutionalize a single vision of the Canadian political communities; rather, the matter has been hotly contested throughout Canadian history.

The continuing ability of Canadian federalism to reflect, accommodate, and reconcile alternative images of community is now under question from a variety of sources. First is Quebec, where the driving force has been the growth, since the early 1960s, of the sense of the province as a distinct, secular, French-speaking national society, in which the provincial government is the primary, if not the only, legitimate political expression of that society. Federalism is to be judged in terms of its capacity to permit the full development of this society without the values of the country-wide majority being imposed on it. Virtually all Quebec-based elites, whether federalist or *indépendantiste* accept these as the fundamental premises. Canada is a bi-communal polity, a partnership of two linguistic communities, one centred on the Quebec government, the other, more diverse, reflected both in the federal government and in the other provincial governments. As a distinct national community, the province is in a different category from the other provinces.

Within this framework, a broad range of constitutional alternatives has been proposed. They include the symbolic recognition of Quebec as a 'distinct society' within the federation, a Quebec veto over constitutional change, greater powers for the province in areas deemed critical to its economic, social, and linguistic development, and strict constitutional limitations on the ability of the federal government to intervene in Quebec's areas of jurisdiction through the spending power or other devices.

These proposals all presume Quebec's continued participation in the federal union. *Indépendantiste* or sovereignist proposals to break the federal mould include the two-unit confederal model expressed in the term 'sovereignty-association' and outright independence, with or without continued economic and perhaps political linkages with the rest of Canada.

Recent constitutional history in Canada has revolved largely around these issues. Failure to agree on modest constitutional changes in 1971 was followed in 1976 by the election of the sovereignist Parti Québécois and its subsequent 1980 referendum seeking a mandate to negotiate sovereignty-association with the rest of Canada. The defeat of the referendum, and the promise of a 'renewed federalism,' led to another round of constitutional debate, culminating in the passage of the *Constitution Act, 1982*. That amendment gave Canada a domestically based constitutional amending formula and the *Charter of Rights and Freedoms*, but made no concessions to the Quebec-centred image; and indeed weakened it in some respects.[16]

Despite this set back, Quebec nationalism appeared to be in sharp decline after 1982. In these circumstances, the government of Conservative Prime Minister Brian Mulroney, elected in 1984, sought to bring Quebec back into the Canadian 'constitutional family.' The result was the 1987 Meech Lake Accord, which contained a number of elements central to the Quebec federalist position: recognition of Quebec as a distinct society, a Quebec veto, limits on the federal spending power, constitutional recognition of Quebec's right to three judges on the Supreme Court of Canada, and shared authority for the province in immigration. A number of other provisions addressed the concerns of other provinces.

As is well known, the accord, the first major test of the amending formula which Canada had enacted in 1982, failed.[17] Two provinces failed to ratify it in the required three-year time period. But more generally, the accord generated broad and intense opposition throughout the rest of Canada. Its failure was thus widely regarded in Quebec as a profound rejection of its fundamental objectives, added to the exclusion which had occurred just five years earlier.

The resulting sense of betrayal which led to a rapid rise in *indépendantiste* sentiment, an escalation in the demands for increased autonomy, even among federalists, and a new strategy designed to force the Rest of Canada (ROC) to respond. This included a commitment to a referendum on sovereignty in the fall of 1992, combined with a refusal to participate in further intergovernmental constitutional discussion. It was up to the rest of Canada to 'make an offer' and it was widely believed that it would do so only under the threat of a referendum.

The result was yet another round of negotiations culminating in yet another accord, the Charlottetown Agreement and a subsequent national referendum, in October 1992. The agreement was defeated by a clear majority, both in the rest of the country and in Quebec, where it was widely regarded as providing insufficient recognition of Quebec's distinctiveness and its demand for increased autonomy. 'Mega-constitutional politics' had failed.[18]

This recitation suggests that the answer to the question of whether federalism has facilitated the management of linguistic cleavages in Canada should be 'no.' Throughout Canadian history, and especially since the 1960s, the country has been in the throes of almost continual constitutional crisis. The independence movement has grown; the Parti Québécois now forms the government in Quebec, and is committed to an early referendum. And, in the most striking recent development, the *indépendantiste* Bloc Québécois contested the 1993 federal election, winning fifty-four seats and the status of official opposition in the Canadian parliament.

At another level, however, the answer might be more positive. After all, the federation has managed to survive over a long period. Quebec has been the central force ensuring that the Canadian federal system is in some ways the most decentralized federation in the world. Quebec has been able to use the institutional, political, and financial resources which federalism provides to build a powerful national society, and to become, in Andrew Stark's terms, 'the most powerful sub-state government in the OECD.'[19] It has been able to develop distinctive economic, linguistic, and social policies, with relatively few constraints from the centre. These policies have helped to erase the economic inequality between francophone and anglophone citizens in Quebec,[20] to erode anglophone domination of major economic institutions, and to create, with the assistance of the Quebec state, a powerful Québécois business class, known as 'Quebec Inc.' Its weight in the central government has ensured national policies sensitive to Quebec aspirations, and fostered limited – and still controversial – extension of language rights and government services to francophones outside Quebec. Arguably, Quebec's economic, social, and linguistic security as a small minority on the North American continent has been stronger within the Canadian federation than it would have been as a small independent state.

These differing assessments are reflected in Quebecers' responses to federalism. While electing nationalist governments in the province – whether federalist or *indépendantiste* – Quebecers have, at least until 1993, consistently elected strong federalists to represent them in Ottawa. They continued to give massive support to Prime Minister Pierre Trudeau, even though his career was committed to an unrelenting attack on Quebec nationalism. This ambivalence towards federalism is reflected in surveys which show that on most values and substantive issues – with the vital exceptions of language and political status – the policy differences between Quebecers and non-Quebecers are small and declining. More generally, support for outright 'separatism' or 'independence' has been highly variable, and has always been a minority view in Quebec, until it reached 50 per cent in 1990 in the wave of post-Meech anger.[21] 'Softer' autonomist options like 'sovereignty' and 'sovereignty-association' have always commanded greater support, at least in part because they seem to imply some continued participation in the Canadian political system. Finally, surveys reported by Maurice Pinard conclude that while Quebec voters are far more likely to self-identify as Québécois, rather than 'Canadian' or 'French-Canadian,' six out of ten also feel 'profoundly attached' to Canada.[22] Thus, despite the many tensions in the current situation, the potential for a successful accommodation is there, and the final verdict on the ability of the federal system to reconcile Quebec and the rest of Canada is by no means in.

Nevertheless, the recent experience illustrates a number of dilemmas with respect to federalism and the management of linguistic divisions in Canada. First, federalism entrenches, perpetuates, and institutionalizes the very divisions it is designed to manage. It is Janus-faced; its virtues are also its vices. Federalism provides Quebec *indépendantistes* with the institutional and organizational resources to achieve independence. While independence would provoke economic and political turmoil in both Quebec and the rest of the country, few doubt the institutional capacity of an independent Quebec. As Stéphane Dion notes, within federalism Quebec is already a 'quasi-state.'[23]

Second, federalism, as several other writers in this volume point out, does not address the problem of minorities within minorities. At a minimum, in order to meet this problem some form of minority language rights is essential. An alternative approach, advocated by some anglophone as well as Québécois scholars, is to bring the linguistic boundaries into line with the political ones, with a 'territorial' approach to language use on the Swiss or Belgian model.[24]

Third, just as federalism depends on a balance of identities and loyalties between a given cultural community and the larger political union, so also it depends on a division of powers which divides authority so that the minority retains the powers essential to its sense of community, and the national political system retains the powers relevant to the whole country. This is not an easy balance to achieve. One interpretation of recent Quebec constitutional challenges is to argue that social and economic change in Quebec has rendered obsolete the balance of powers reflected in the 1867 Constitution. That division broadly reserved social and cultural matters to the provinces and major economic powers to the centre. As Quebec modernized, and as the policy agenda changed, the distinction broke down. Quebecers also sought much greater control over their economic lives, calling for jurisdiction over the whole range of economic and social policies, all of which were deemed important to the preservation and enhancement of the group.[25]

The most difficult barrier to reconciling Quebec with the rest of Canada, however, is the fundamental clash between the dualist, or 'two founding peoples' conception of the country, and rival conceptions. The rest of Canadian society is itself increasingly diverse and fragmented, with a number of ideological cross-currents which are in tension with Quebec, with each other, and with important elements of the existing federal system.[26] First, bi-nationalism, with its implications of special status, clashes with the view of Canada as a collection of at least ten 'distinct societies,' and that the constitution should reflect the juridical and political equality of all provinces. Numerous provisions of the 1867 constitution and subsequent political practice respond to the distinct characteristics not only of Quebec, but of other provinces as well. Nevertheless, 'provincial equality' has become a potent rallying cry against any form of special status for Quebec.

This tension plays out in debates about 'symmetry' versus 'asymmetry' in the division of powers. Asymmetry suggests that the federal system should be designed to ensure each provincial community powers suited to its particular needs. Two versions have been advocated in recent years. First is the use of constitutional devices which enable any province to exercise distinct powers, whether by 'opting out' of federal programs, delegating powers between Ottawa and individual governments, or designating certain powers as 'concurrent with provincial paramountcy.'[27] Such devices appeal because they might facilitate the acquisition of distinct powers by Quebec, while maintaining the principle of provincial equality. Critics argue that other provinces might indeed also choose to exercise the additional powers, thus rendering Canada a diverse chequer-board of different regimes, and powerfully dissuading the federal government from initiating new policies.

Provincialist views have also been expressed in arguments for a greater measure of intrastate federalism in Canada. These claims now focus on reform of the Canadian Senate to make it a more effective voice of provincial interests at the centre, and to temper the overwhelming weight of Ontario and Quebec in the House of Commons.[28] While earlier proposals focused on representation of provincial governments, on the model of the German *Bundesrat*, more recent proposals have centred on the call for a 'Triple E Senate' – elected, equal, and effective.[29] Advocates argue that such a Senate would not only ensure a national government more sensitive to the interests of smaller provinces, but also that it would potentially undercut the claim of provincial executives to be the sole effective representatives of the provincial interest and to exercise an important role in national policy-making. There are, however, important objections to the Triple E model. Equal representation, given the huge differences in provincial populations, represents a major departure from proportionality; and the more effective a Senate became, the more it would challenge the British parliamentary model of responsible government and majority rule. Moreover, such intrastate solutions have little attraction for Quebec. The Charlottetown Agreement did provide for an elected, equal Senate. The 'effectiveness' of the proposed body was much disputed, but it was designed in such a way as to maintain the House of Commons as the dominant legislative body in Ottawa.

Debates between the Ottawa-centred, province-centred, and bi-national visions of Canada have traditionally dominated constitutional discourse in the country. But these federalist concerns have come into increasing conflict with a third set of conceptions of community in Canada. The adoption of the Charter was a fundamental constitutional change which embodied an attack on the premises both of federalism and parliamentarianism. It explicitly conferred rights on individual citizens as against governments. Since the Charter, Canadian constitutional politics have been as much about citizens and governments as they have been about the relationships between governments. The Charter also gave recognition and status to collectivities which cut across provincial lines – women, multicultural groups, the disabled, and Aboriginal peoples. Many of these groups have argued that federalism is a direct barrier to their political effectiveness.

Their mobilization was a decisive factor in the defeat of the Meech Lake Accord, seen as a solution to the traditional issues of federalism – Quebec and the role of the provinces. Many saw it as a potential threat to the rights which they had gained in the Charter. They also saw its limitations on the federal spending power – and the possibility of further decentralization of powers in other areas – as a future barrier to Ottawa's ability to generate progressive social policy. The 'roving Canadianism' of the Charter-Canadians, as Cairns describes them,[30] was especially hostile to the implications of Quebec as a distinct society. These developments profoundly challenged the traditional assumptions of constitutional debate, and dramatically expanded both the range of issues on the constitutional agenda and the groups who believed they have a major stake in the outcome. For example, in debates about Senate reform, some of these groups asked why reform should concentrate only on how better to represent provinces; why not design a Senate to reflect the other elements of diversity, such as race and gender?

Federalist assumptions have also been challenged by the claim of the Aboriginal peoples to the 'inherent right to self-government.' Reminding Canadians that they were the original founders, the First Nations, they challenge the idea of Quebec as a distinct society by arguing that in all practical meanings of the term, they have at least as strong a claim. Most fundamentally, they claim a right to self-government and at least a share of sovereignty.

Thus Aboriginal peoples asserted their right to a full presence at the constitutional table and to a consideration of Aboriginal self-government alongside, and equal to, other constitutional issues. In the 1992 negotiations, Aboriginal representatives and the governments of the two northern territories were full participants co-equal with the governments of Ottawa and the provinces.

While Aboriginal claims are on their face hostile to federalist assumptions, it can also be argued that federalism opens the way to effective self-government within the federation. It is a system based on divided sovereignty, with a division of powers, multiple levels of government, mechanisms for equalization, and machinery of intergovernmental relations. Federalism legitimates shared loyalties and identities. All these are tools with which to fashion Aboriginal self-government as a third order of government in Canada.[31] Such a model would greatly depart from the known forms of federal government, but would be entirely consistent with the underlying premises of federalism as a political idea.

In sum, we see a bewildering kaleidoscope of competing identities played out on the constitutional stage. The traditional tensions associated with federalism have not disappeared, nor have they been resolved. Indeed, the 1993 election results, which not only brought separatists into the federal parliament, but also saw the Reform Party, a largely Western-based conservative populist party, win fifty-two seats, underlined the continued salience of these issues. But cutting across them are the alternative, non-territorial dimensions of identity which have recently come to prominence. The result is a complex, unmanageable constitutional agenda. However, the defeat of the referendum has for the moment removed the constitution from centre stage, and turned attention to alternative arenas and more informal mechanisms for adaptation in the Canadian federal system. Constitutional debate is unlikely to be renewed unless and until a decisive vote for sovereignty in Quebec forces it back on to the table.

This discussion of community has focused entirely on Canada. This is not to argue that many of the same issues – especially those associated with the mobilization of new social movements, the greater representation of minorities and Aboriginal rights – have not played prominent roles in the United States. But because the federalism issues in the United States are largely settled, because the major divisions are not territorially centred, and because the US Constitution has not itself been in question, these conflicts have been played out in different forums, especially Congress and the courts. Moreover, in Canada, the divisions of language and region have been decentralizing forces; in the US the dominant cleavage of race has been centralizing as African-Americans turned to federal authority to challenge the racist policies which were a central component of 'state's rights.'

Ironically, while many of the newly mobilized groups in Canada fundamentally challenge federalism, the way they have been mobilized, the terms in which their demands are phrased, and the arenas in which they have been expressed have all been profoundly shaped by Canadian federalist discourse. In the United States the 'national' version of federalism triumphed over the compact version[32]; in Canada, multiple visions continue to compete.

Federalism and Democracy

If Canadian federalism is debated, justified, and criticized primarily on the basis of competing images of community, American debate on federalism has tended to focus much more strongly on the version of democracy embedded in it. Federalism, to the founders, was part and parcel of the larger model of limited government, checks and balances and restraint on the tyranny of the majority.[33] More recent theoretical defences of US federalism have been cast in similar terms. In addition, writers like Vincent Ostrom[34] argue for other democratic virtues of federalism: it promotes the existence of smaller governments, closer to, and, therefore, in principle more accessible to citizen participation than larger, more remote government. Smaller governments competing to offer a variety of alternative 'packages' of services increase the chances of a better 'fit' between citizen preferences and policy outcomes.

While these are powerful virtues, they are associated with a particular view of democracy, one relatively hostile to majority rule. They may also bias government responsiveness in favour of the better off. To the extent business is more mobile than citizens, and wealthier citizens are more mobile than poorer ones, the competition may well be 'downwards' to lower tax rates, weaker environmental rules, and the like. This is a powerful argument for central funding of major redistributive programs, and for national standard-setting in areas where the regulated interests are mobile.[35] In addition, the virtues of decentralized decision-making may be vitiated if the governments of some units lack the financial resources effectively to carry out the responsibilities assigned to them. This raises the question of redistribution or equalization.

The US model of national standard-setting, through grant-in-aid programs, use of the trade and commerce power, and other devices is considerably more powerful than it is in Canada. 'National standards' and how to implement them in a highly decentralized system have been a major feature of recent constitutional debates in Canada. In the US, there are few if any legal or constitutional restrictions on the federal establishment of national standards; hence variations stem more from political factors.

With respect to equalization, Canada has acted more strongly than the US. Important elements of redistribution are built in to a number of federal programs such as unemployment insurance, and into shared cost programs such as Established Program Financing. While some redistribution is built in to US programs, and while some recent changes have sought to reallocate competencies to make Washington more responsible for redistributive programs and the states more responsible for allocative decisions and service delivery, redistribution has less impact than in Canada. The Canadian-American difference is replicated at the state-local and provincial-local levels – with, for example, the provinces assuming a greater proportion of funding for local school boards, with the result that disparities in the capacity to provide equal education in rich and poor districts are less than in the United States (though American disparities are currently under vigorous attack in courts and legislatures).

There is no US parallel to the Canadian equalization program. Unconditional federal transfers to the poorer provinces are designed to ensure provincial ability to provide reasonably comparable services to their citizens at reasonably comparable levels of taxation, a commitment enshrined in s. 36 of the *Constitution Act, 1982*. This goes a long way towards standardizing per capita provincial revenues, despite large differences in underlying revenue capacity. Thus, the US tends to emphasize national standards, and Canada to stress equalizing provincial fiscal capacity.

An additional issue for the relationship between federalism and democracy focuses not on the existence of multiple governments but on the ways they interact through the machinery of intergovernmental relations. In the US, as mentioned at the outset, this interpenetration is managed through a multiplicity of program-specific policy networks. Congress and its committees play an important role in developing and overseeing these relationships. Perhaps as a result, there has been little discussion of a 'democratic deficit' in American intergovernmental relations. In Canada, by contrast, executive federalism has come under severe attack on democratic grounds. It is alleged, in Smiley's classic formulation[36], to limit citizen participation, enhance governmental secrecy, exclude important groups, and cloak policy debates in the arcane and obtuse language of fiscal arrangements. In particular, it blurs the accountability to citizens built in to the parliamentary system, because of the confusion about who is responsible for what and the opportunities for shifting blame. Fiscal accountability is eroded because the federal government transfers funds to provinces whose spending it cannot control, and provinces spend funds which they are not responsible for raising.

Criticism of the 'democratic deficit' of executive federalism was central to the debate on the Meech Lake Accord. It was reached in the classic executive federalism model – eleven first ministers meeting behind closed doors, and there had been little public discussion prior to the intergovernmental meetings. Once reached, the accord required ratification under the amending formula enacted in 1982, which had introduced indirect citizen involvement through the requirement of legislative ratification. However, legislatures were to have no opportunity to modify the agreement, since to do so would require a new round of intergovernmental negotiation and the risk of unravelling it.

This procedure was widely regarded as fundamentally illegitimate. It had excluded all the constitutional stake-holders except governments, and then rendered public debate a sham. The resulting hostility was a major reason for the failure of the Meech Lake Accord, which strongly shaped the subsequent debate. Recognizing the imperative of conducting a more open process in the next round, governments sought to involve citizens and groups more deeply. Thus, in the recent round, there was extensive public consultation, followed by the national referendum. Critics continued to argue, however, that, despite the participation of Aboriginal groups, the crucial negotiations took place in the traditional intergovernmental forum.

The consultative innovations in the recent constitutional discussions raise some questions about democratic participation. There is no doubt they have broadened the process of constitutional discussion. The puzzle is whether they have also rendered it unmanageable: successful in challenging the monopoly of government elites, but perhaps less able to ensure compromise and reach agreement. Thus federalism raises some important dilemmas for democratic politics. Some arise from the distribution of powers among governments, others from the necessity of achieving cooperation and coordination between them.

Federalism and Governmental Performance

Just as with the relationship of federalism to democracy, so there is a complex literature on the implications of federalism for public policy and governmental performance, summarized in Chapter 9 of this volume by Kenneth Norrie. Again, there is an American-Canadian difference here: Beer points out that in the US an 'instrumental view' of federalism has permeated the debates[37]; in Canada, while such concerns have also been common, in recent decades they have been clearly subordinated to the discourse on community and the constitution.

In both countries, federal institutions face a number of important policy challenges. First, there is federalism and globalization. Global forces now reach over national boundaries to directly impact on state and local communities and their governments; simultaneously, federalism projects itself into the national arena. The impact of these forces is likely to be greater the more regionally differentiated an economy is to start with. Hence they appear to have had a greater effect on Canada than the United States. They have tended to exacerbate regional inequalities (while reducing the capacity of the federal government to deal with them) and to reduce the importance of trade and economic linkages within the country relative to linkages of each region and province outside the country. This has important implications for the capacity to develop 'national' economic policies, for the ability to sustain cross-country political and social linkages, and for the continued commitment to regional equalization. [38]

On the other side of the coin, in both countries there has been a great increase in the international activities of states and provinces, in the form of investment and trade promotion offices around the globe, state and provincial encouragement of exports, and state and provincial tax and regulatory efforts to create favourable investment conditions. States and provinces have become significant international actors. Earl Fry notes that forty-one states had 120 offices in twenty-four countries in 1991, twice that only five years previously. More states have offices in Japan than in Washington. There has been an 'enormous increase' in state economic development activities, in export promotion and financing, and a wide variety of incentives to attract capital.[39] This tendency is likely to increase, though fiscal restraint within state and provincial governments may slow the expansion.[40]

These developments pose a number of important questions for the future of the two federal systems. First, increased global competition focuses attention on economic efficiency and productivity, and the possible consequences of federalism for that. In Canada, this has lent strength to a longstanding debate on the 'economic union,' and the extent to which non-tariff trade barriers among provinces within Canada impair the capacity to develop larger, more integrated firms, better able to compete in global markets. There is agreement that a multitude of such internal barriers exist, but much less on the aggregate costs of such measures or their impact on competitiveness as compared with other factors affecting it.[41] The economic union has been an important part of recent discussions, both in terms of strengthening s. 121, which guarantees free movement of goods within the country, in order to apply it to the other factors of production, and in terms of clarifying the federal role in managing the economic union. Many participants, however, have been concerned to ensure that any such measures preserve government capacity to promote regional development and achieve social goals, and that no redefinition opens the door to an unlimited expansion of federal power or imposes severe constraints on provincial capacity to manage economic affairs. There is little inclination in Canada to replicate the unlimited economic powers of the US federal government under the trade and commerce clause.

In addition, in Canada there has been considerable hostility to enshrining market-oriented values in the constitution. Many have argued that the 'social union' – the preservation and enhancement of Canada's social programs – should also be protected in the constitution, through a 'Social Charter' or 'Covenant' akin to the European model. While the economic union, as such, has not achieved such prominence in American debates, there are concerns about interstate competition for investment, and the impact of a highly uncoordinated taxation system. Indeed, cross-border coordination issues are particularly common in the US since so many metropolitan areas spill over state lines.

Given the ever increasing importance of international trade, and the involvement of provincial policies with international rules, another important federalism issue in Canada is the treaty power. In the US, state involvement in treaty-making is achieved through the intrastate mechanism of Senate ratification. Once that happens, treaties are self-executing, applying equally to federal and state governments. In Canada, however, despite the federal power to negotiate treaties, federalism cuts in at the implementation stage. Ottawa does not have the power to implement treaties whose provisions trench on provincial jurisdiction. Many critics have argued that this hampers Canadian participation in international trade negotiations and have called for reform. In the Canadian context, there is little chance of approval of a blanket federal power to implement treaties. More likely is an arrangement in which the provinces' participation in international trade negotiations is traded off against their role in ratification.[42]

Finally, globalization raises a more general question: is greater central dominance within the country the implication of greater interdependence within the world? Is globalization yet another dimension of modernization whose requisite is centralization? Does it require a federal government both more able to speak authoritatively for Canada abroad, and more capable of promoting adjustment and managing the economy at home?

Or is the implication the reverse, that globalization undermines central governments and the traditional powers (tariffs, fiscal and monetary policy) that they have exercised more than it does provincial powers? Are states and provinces perhaps better equipped to be flexible, experimental, and innovative in adapting and adjusting? If so, how is this to be reconciled with the need to address problems such as the environment which transcend provincial and national borders, and to develop regimes to regulate the activity of corporations and other groups whose scope also extends beyond borders? What are the implications for redistributive policies?

A few years ago, it is likely that the most common answer, on both sides of the border would have been centralist. Recently, however, there is a growing consensus that the answer is no. In the United States, for example, David R. Beam argues that 'under conditions of global competition and rapid technological change, a large nation composed of multiple political and economic centers, each striving to secure its own economic advantage, will be better able to advance the welfare of its citizens than a large nation dominated by a single political and economic center.'[43]

Alice Rivlin[44] similarly calls for a 'restructuring' of federal-state responsibilities, with a broad devolution to the states of responsibilities for the 'productivity agenda,' including education and skills training, childcare, infrastructure, and economic development. Washington, she argues, cannot possibly mobilize the community support, business-labour cooperation, and policy coordination that successful industrial policy requires. Governors and mayors are much better placed to do so. 'The best chance of having a successful industrial policy in a country this size is to have a lot of communities, states and regions competing with each other to improve their own economic prospects.'45 Washington should focus on broad redistributive policies, including healthcare, and on managing international relations.

Where once the tendency was in favour of central responsibility, commentators in both the US and Canada appear to have adopted the idea of 'subsidiarity' much discussed among Europeans. This suggests that responsibilities should be assigned to the smallest feasible unit.

Canadian scholars such as Tom Courchene have long argued in this vein.[46] Kenneth Norrie has argued that the federal government should be responsible for major redistributive policies, but that the provinces should be responsible for 'place prosperity.'[47] Writing from a radically different political perspective, Thomas Hueglin speaks of the 'irrationality of unilateral federalism in a complex industrial society that is nationally fragmented, regionally inter-dependent and internationally dependent.'[48] Like Rivlin, Canadian observers have suggested that coherent industrial policies, involving cooperation among the major economic actors, are much more likely at the provincial level than at the national level where the interests to be accommodated are so much more diverse. The Canadian model for such provincial strategies is Quebec Inc.

Fiscal Federalism
Finally, both Canada and the US face important challenges arising out of the need to manage federations in an era of fiscal crisis. In both countries, transfers to states and provinces represent a significant share of total federal spending; in both, such transfers represent a large proportion of provincial and state revenues. In both, as well, conservative national governments have sought to reduce the size of the federal government and to transfer responsibilities to the state and local levels. They have also had to grapple

with massive central debts and deficits. One result is the 'cascading' of fiscal problems from one level to the next. Thus in the 1980s, under the Reagan administration, federal transfers to the states as a proportion of GDP declined quite sharply, reversing a long period of steady growth.[49] The Reagan administration also sought to increase state and local freedom of action by consolidating and simplifying grant-in-aid programs, with their detailed program supervision. Congressional opposition, however, sharply limited the achievement of the 'new federalism.'

Similar concerns motivated the Canadian federal government, though the decentralizing thrust had at least as much to do with meeting provincial concerns as it did with neo-conservative ideas. In its early years, the Mulroney government largely isolated the provinces from deficit-reducing efforts, but since 1988, there have been significant measures to restrain the rate of growth in federal transfers to the provinces, and a capping of welfare-related payments to the wealthier provinces.[50] Thus, in important respects the fiscal crisis has been recreated at the state and local level in both countries, as subnational governments experience not only reduced revenues of their own, but also increases in spending requirements. The problem appears especially acute for US states and localities, since they tend to have less revenue-raising capacity than Canadian provinces, and in many cases have constitutional limits on their ability to spend more than they raise. In addition, citizen participation in initiatives and referenda on taxation and other matters have limited states' ability to raise revenue, thus focusing restraint even more on the expenditure side.

Hence there is a tension in the decentralizing efforts of both the Reagan-Bush 'new federalism' and in the recent Canadian approach to decentralization. In both, the rhetoric of empowering states and provinces is accompanied by limits on transfers, and by a willingness to flex federal muscle where necessary. We see increased fiscal pressures on states and provinces but, at the same time, a considerable opening up of the policy space in which they can act. Thus, despite the legal dominance of the centre – which leads some to question the continuing legal autonomy of the states – there has also been a surge of innovation at state and local levels in a host of policy areas, along with considerable strengthening of state institutional capacity.[51] Richard Nathan talks of a 'paradox of devolution.'[52] Rather than reducing governmental activity generally, as President Reagan hoped, his approach instead sparked 'the resurgence of the state's role in American federalism.'[53]

Nevertheless, in both countries, the word 'crisis' has been used to describe current federal-state or federal-provincial fiscal relations. If spending responsibilities and revenue-raising continue to be devolved to the states, then inequalities in fiscal capacity will become more pressing, especially in the absence of any American equivalent of the Canadian equalization program. In Canada, on the other hand, there are increasing doubts as to whether the existing equalization program can be sustained at current levels. Hence, in both countries, there is growing discussion of alternative financing mechanisms.[54] In both countries, the issues of the division of powers and fiscal federalism are very different from those associated with the previous era of expanding governments at both levels. We have shifted from the federalism of growth to the federalism of restraint. Fiscal crisis means that the conflicts arise not from federal 'intrusions' into state or provincial jurisdictions that stem from the central power to spend, but rather from the exercise of the 'dis-spending power.' Both countries need to rethink the appropriate roles of federal and provincial governments. Again, this is an incremental scattered process in the United States, in which the principles of federalism itself do not loom large. In Canada, the division of powers has been a major element in the constitutional debate, but one largely subordinated to the larger community-oriented questions discussed earlier. However, in both countries, there does seem to be declining confidence both in the capacity of central governments to act effectively and in the efficacy of the complex machinery of cooperative federalism. Hence, there is an increased desire to reestablish a clearer sense of the roles and responsibilities of each order of government and to reduce the costs of overlapping and duplication.

Conclusion

Both North American federal systems face some pressures in common: the need to adapt federal institutions to an increasingly diverse and fragmented domestic society and to the influences of an increasingly interdependent global political economy. But at the same time, they offer very different models, both in their structure and their political dynamics. They also face different challenges. If the Canadian danger is a slide into 'centrifugal disequilibrium,' the danger in the US is 'centripetal imbalance.'[55] The cost for the US, Walker argues, is overload and paralysis at the centre, as all the dimensions of social and economic diversity are played out in Washington; the cost for Canada is continuing uncertainty about the survival of the federation.

Nevertheless, there is some convergence in the federalism debates in the two countries. In Canada, there has been a resurgence of interest in intrastate federalism. In the US, federal cutbacks and paralysis along with increased state institutional capacities have contributed to a limited, but significant increase in the vitality of state governments. And both countries face similar dilemmas as they seek to rationalize federal and state activities, deal with issues of fiscal federalism, and rethink the roles of the different orders of government.

Notes

1 David Walker, 'The Contemporary Condition of American Pluralism: A Comparative and Chronological Assessment' (Washington: Advisory Commission on Intergovernmental Relations 1985, mimeo), 2.
2 Morris Fiorina, 'Divided Government in the States,' in Gary W. Cox and Samuel Kernell, eds., *The Politics of Divided Government* (Boulder, CO: Westview Press 1991), 179-202.
3 The term was invented by Donald Smiley. See his *Constitutional Adaptation and Canadian Federalism Since 1945*, Royal Commission on Bilingualism and Biculturalism, Document No. 4 (Ottawa: Queen's Printer 1970).
4 Richard Simeon, *Federal-Provincial Diplomacy: The Making of Recent Policy in Canada* (Toronto: University of Toronto Press 1972).
5 For a summary, see R. L. Watts, 'Centralization, Decentralization and Non-Centralization in Canada and the United States' (paper presented at conference on Comparative Federalism, Dartmouth College, June 1989).
6 Ibid., 36-7.
7 C.E.S. Franks, 'Decision Processes and Decision Rules: Canada's Problem?' (paper presented to the Western Political Science Association, Reno, NV, 1991), 17.
8 For an excellent review of this literature, see Donald V. Smiley and R.L. Watts, *Intrastate Federalism in Canada*, Research Studies of the Royal Commission on the Economic Union and Development Prospects for Canada, vol. 39 (Toronto: University of Toronto Press 1986).
9 This thesis is powerfully argued by Roger Gibbins, in *Regionalism: Territorial Politics in Canada and the United States* (Toronto: Butterworths 1982).
10 These ideas have been most fully worked out by Alan Cairns. See, for example, *The Charter Versus Federalism: The Dilemmas of Constitutional Reform* (Montreal and Kingston: McGill-Queen's University Press 1992).
11 For one example, see *New York Times*, 6 May 1992, A1.
12 See, for example, Peter H. Russell, 'Bold Statecraft Based on Questionable Jurisprudence,' in Peter H. Russell et. al., *The Court and the Constitution* (Kingston: Institute of Intergovernmental Relations 1982), 1-32.
13 See Timothy Conlan, *New Federalism: Intergovernmental Reform from Nixon to Reagan* (Washington: Brookings Institution 1988), 235.
14 Michael D. Reagan and John Y. Sanzone, *The New Federalism*, 2nd ed. (New York: Oxford University Press 1981), Chapter 4.
15 For a history of Canadian federalism exploring these ideas, see Richard Simeon and Ian Robinson, *State, Society and the Development of Canadian Federalism*, Research Studies of the Royal Commission on the Economic Union and Canada's Development Prospects, vol. 71 (Toronto: University of Toronto Press 1990).
16 For assessments, see Keith Banting and Richard Simeon, eds., *And No One Cheered: Federalism, Democracy and the Constitution Act* (Toronto: Methuen 1983); Roy Romanow, John Whyte, and Howard Leeson, *Canada Notwithstanding ...* (Toronto: Carswell 1984); and Guy LaForest, 'Quebec Beyond the Federal Regime of 1867-1982,' in R. L. Watts and Douglas Brown, eds., *Options for a New Canada* (Toronto: University of Toronto Press 1992), 103-22.
17 For assessments see, among others, Patrick Monahan, *After Meech Lake: An Insider's View* (Kingston: Institute of Intergovernmental Relations 1990); Richard

Simeon, 'Why Did the Meech Lake Accord Fail?' in R.L. Watts and Douglas Brown, eds., *Canada: The State of the Federation 1990* (Kingston: Institute of Intergovernmental Relations 1990), 15-40; LaForest, 'Quebec.'

18 The phrase is Peter Russell's, whose *Constitutional Odyssey*, 2nd ed. (Toronto: University of Toronto Press 1993) is the best overall survey of constitutional negotiations in the contemporary period.

19 Andrew Stark, 'English-Canadian Opposition to Quebec Nationalism,' in R. Kent Weaver, ed., *The Collapse of Canada?* (Washington: Brookings Institution 1992), 123.

20 Between 1977 and 1992, the gap between English and French-speaking workers in Quebec declined from 8.2 to 1.9 per cent. In Canada as a whole, however, the gap *increased* from 9.9 to 14.1 per cent. Statistics Canada data cited in Alanna Campbell, 'Hopes for Bilingualism Unrealized,' *Globe and Mail*, 23 March 1994, A1, A7.

21 See Stéphane Dion, 'Explaining Quebec Nationalism,' in Weaver, ed., *The Collapse*, 86-7.

22 Cited in Dion, 'Explaining,' 86-7.

23 Ibid., 102.

24 See comments by Jean LaPonce and Robert Young in Richard Simeon and Mary Janigan, eds., *Toolkits and Building Blocks: Constructing a New Canada* (Toronto: C.D. Howe Institute 1991).

25 For a powerful statement of this view, which would leave few policy areas in the hands of the federal government, see Parti liberal du Québec, *Un Québec Libre de ses choix* [The Allaire Report] (Quebec: PLQ 1991). The PLQ has since shifted to a position more supportive of the constitutional status quo. For a very broad review of Quebec opinion in the aftermath of Meech Lake, see Commission sur l'avenir politique et constitutionnel du Québec [Belanger-Campeau Commission], *Rapport* (Quebec 1991).

26 See Andrew Stark, 'English-Canadian Opposition,' for one attempt to chart these currents. See also Cairns and Jenson (Chapters 2 and 7) in this volume.

27 For a detailed review of these options, see David Milne, 'Equality or Asymmetry: Why Choose?' in Watts and Brown, eds., *Options*, 285-308.

28 Others have focused on the composition of the House of Commons and on proposals to reform the electoral system to ensure a closer match between seats and votes. See, for example, William P. Irvine, *Does Canada Need a New Electoral System?* (Kingston: Institute of Intergovernmental Relations 1979).

29 For a review of the many proposals, see R.L. Watts, 'The Federative Superstructure,' in Watts and Brown, eds., *Options*, 308-36.

30 Alan Cairns, 'Constitutional Change and the Three Equalities,' in Watts and Brown, eds., *Options*, 80.

31 For an elaboration of this argument, see Richard Simeon, 'Federalism and Canadian Political Values,' in David Hawkes, ed., *Issues in Entrenching Self-Government* (Kingston: Institute of Intergovernmental Relations 1987), 49-56.

32 See Beer in this volume.

33 Samuel Beer, *To Make a Nation: the Rediscovery of American Federalism* (London and Cambridge, MA: Harvard University Press 1993).

34 Vincent Ostrom, *The Political Theory of the Compound Republic* (Lincoln, NE: University of Nebraska Press 1987).
35 See, for example, Robin Boadway, 'Constitutional design in a Federation: An Economist's Perspective,' in Watts and Brown, eds., *Options*, 237-57.
36 Donald V. Smiley, 'An Outsider's Observations on Federal-Provincial Relations among Consenting Adults,' in Richard Simeon, ed., *Confrontation and Collaboration: Intergovernmental Relations in Canada Today* (Toronto: Institute of Public Administration of Canada 1979), 105-13.
37 Samuel Beer, Preface to Conlan, *New Federalism*, xiv.
38 See, Thomas J. Courchene, *Rearrangements* (Oakville: Mosaic Press 1991), Chapter 3; Richard Simeon, 'Globalization and the Canadian Nation-State,' in G. Bruce Doern and Bryne Purchase, eds., *Canada at Risk? Canadian Public Policy in the 1990s* (Toronto: C.D. Howe Institute 1991), 46-58.
39 Earl Fry, 'Trade and Investment Promotion in the United States: New Frontiers,' in Douglas M. Brown and Murray Smith, eds., *Canadian Federalism: Meeting Global Challenges* (Kingston: Institute of Intergovernmental Relations 1990), 239-55. For a review of Canadian practices, see other chapters in this volume.
40 For example, Ontario recently closed its offices overseas – though restating its commitment to aggressive promotion policies abroad.
41 The most thorough study was prepared by the Royal Commission on the Economic Union and Canada's Development Prospects, *Report*, vol. III (Ottawa: Supply and Services 1985).
42 For a thorough review, see Douglas M. Brown, 'The Evolving Role of the Provinces in Canadian Trade Policy,' in Brown and Smith, eds., *Canadian Federalism*, 81-128.
43 David R. Beam, 'Reinventing Federalism: State-Local Governmental Roles in the New Economic Order' (paper presented to the American Political Science Association, 1988, mimeo), 16.
44 Alice Rivlin, *Reviving the American Dream: The Economy, the States and the Federal Government* (Washington: Brookings Institution 1992).
45 Ibid., 120.
46 Courchene, *Rearrangements*, Chapter 5.
47 Kenneth Norrie, 'Intergovernmental Transfers in Canada: An Historical Perspective on Some Current Policy Choices,' in Kenneth Norrie, Peter M. Leslie, and Irene Ip, eds., *A Partnership in Trouble* (Toronto: C.D. Howe Institute 1993), 87-129.
48 Thomas Hueglin, 'The End of Institutional Tidiness: Trends of Late Federalism in Canada and the United States' (paper presented to the American Political Science Association, Washington 1984).
49 See Conlan, *New Federalism*, Chapter 8 and passim.
50 See Peter M. Leslie, 'The Fiscal Crisis in Canadian Federalism,' in Norrie, Leslie, and Ip, eds., *Partnership*, 1-86.
51 See Conlan, *New Federalism*, 228ff.
52 Richard P. Nathan, 'Federalism: The Great Composition,' in Anthony King, ed., *The New American Political System*, 2nd ed. (Washington: American Enterprise Institute 1991), 231-61.

53 Ibid., 243.
54 Rivlin, *Reviving the American Dream*, Chapter 8; Norrie, 'Intergovernmental Transfers'; Leslie, 'The Fiscal Crisis.'
55 Walker, 'Contemporary Condition of American Pluralism,' 78.

17

Federalism, Democracy, and Regulatory Reform: A Sceptical View of the Case for Decentralization

Robert Howse

Introduction

In a wide range of recent policy literature,[1] decentralization of political and economic power is advocated as a means to government that is more democratic, more efficient, and more sensitive to individual and community preferences.[2] Often, federalism is viewed as the obvious instrument of such decentralization. Typically, what is implied is a prescription for greater devolution or delegation of powers in states that are already federal, or the creation of new federal structures in the case of unitary states.

Much of the new-found enthusiasm for federalism as an instrument of decentralization has emerged in the context of policy debates about reform of the mature regulatory and social welfare state in advanced industrial democracies such as the United States and Canada, which are characterized by longstanding federal arrangements. Today, however, the case for federalism as an instrument of decentralization is often made in vastly different social and political contexts, whether the project is structural economic reform in developing countries[3] or the transition to market economics and liberal democratic politics in the former communist countries of Central and East Europe,[4] where (not surprisingly) the legacy of state centralism has led to intense interest in the devolution of political and economic power.

This essay takes a critical look at this new-found enthusiasm for federalism as a solution to the supposed failings of central governments. I intend to develop three lines of argument. First, it is far from clear that in mature federal states such as Canada and the United States further devolution or delegation of power to federal sub-units is likely to result in more democratic, more liberal, or more efficient government. Second, many of the arguments for decentralization upon which the case for devolution of powers is based would more logically imply a transfer of power not to lower levels of government but to non-governmental actors, whether through privatization or contracting of delivery of services to community or non-profit organizations, or the use of incentive-based as opposed to centralized command-and-control-type policy instruments. Third, in the context of many developing countries and Newly Liberalizing Countries in Central and Eastern Europe, there may be particular costs and obstacles to decentralization through federalism which have been often neglected by advocates of federalism as a general policy prescription.

None of these three lines of argument is intrinsically opposed to federalism. Rather, my aim is to challenge the dogmatic bias towards decentralization through federalism which characterizes much contemporary discussion about policy reform, and to point those who are seriously preoccupied with questions of policy reform, whether in North American or other contexts, towards scholarship on federalism that examines the costs as well as the benefits of decentralization, and which takes a subtle and contextualized approach to the allocation of powers and the design of federal structures.

Democracy, Federalism, and Decentralization

Common to many mature liberal democracies is a deep crisis in the legitimacy of representative democracy as we know it. Voting in national elections – the formal means to express the democratic will – is often perceived as yielding very weak citizen control over, or influence upon, policy outcomes. While the election does, in some circumstances, give citizens a chance to make a clear programmatic or moral statement, more routinely the contemporary electoral process has yielded to the brokerage of votes by a cynical machine of party professionals, media consultants, and pollsters.[5] Often set in contrast to this malaise in formal democratic institutions is the promise of the new grassroots politics, characterized by the proliferation of organized advocacy groups[6] that are outside the party system (for example, environmental organizations, women's rights groups, or groups to advance the concerns of the disabled). These groups, which in fact span the entire ideological spectrum, do not have any *formal* democratic legitimacy, since they are not elected by anyone, and the leaders may not even be elected by the members at large of the group itself. However, advocacy groups have bred or are breeding a new generation of democratic politicians, insistent that their concerns be heard. Advocacy groups frequently look to principles to ground the legitimacy of their influence, and thus invite a real debate about the ends of politics and of policy.[7]

The groups' leaders often have qualities of leadership and insight vastly greater than those observed among the elected politicians (of *all* parties). As Tom Kent suggests, 'whether your main concern is the environment or women's issues or aboriginal rights or the Constitution or almost any other issue, you can have far more sense of effective involvement within an advocacy group than within a political party.'[8]

The promise of a new kind of democratic politics, driven in significant measure by such groups and movements, has been eloquently expressed by Czech President Vaclav Havel:

> Their authority certainly cannot be based on long-empty traditions, like the tradition of mass political parties, but rather on how in concrete terms, they enter into a given situation. Rather than a strategic agglomeration of formalized organizations, it is better to have organizations spring up *ad hoc*, infused with enthusiasm for a particular purpose and disappearing when that purpose has been achieved.[9]

Often the promise of grassroots, advocacy group-driven democratic politics is identified in the literature as dependent upon the devolution of political power to lower levels of government, where the networking and grassroots organization characteristic of such a politics would appear to be easier and less costly to undertake.[10] However, just as smallness can expand opportunities for a direct citizen voice in politics, it can also create obstacles. Politics at a national level in a pluralistic liberal democratic society normally involves taking into account diverse and often conflicting interests. In smaller and more homogeneous communities, the contest between opposing ideas and interests may be much less vigorous, thereby resulting in a more impoverished process of democratic debate and deliberation.

The Problem of Majority Tyranny

This leads to concerns about the protection of minorities from majority tyranny. Undoubtedly, in some circumstances devolution of powers to federal sub-units can be seen as an essential protection against the tyranny of a national majority. This is especially the case in federations where an ethnic or religious group is a marginalized or disadvantaged minority within the nation as a whole, but is able to constitute a majority within a federal sub-unit.[11] In many other circumstances, however, government on a national scale will be less susceptible to majority tyranny, precisely because national political outcomes are likely to reflect a greater diversity of opinions and interests. As John Stuart Mill suggested, 'as different opinions predominate in different localities, the opinion which is in a minority in some places has a majority in others, and on the whole every opinion which exists in the constituencies obtains its fair share of voices in the representation.'[12]

The Canadian experience is indicative of the danger of making broad generalizations about whether grassroots democratic politics is likely to work better at the subnational or national level. The progressive social forces that led to the establishment of medicare and other core programs of the Canadian social welfare state met with their first successes in several of the provinces. On the other hand, in other provinces, vested economic interests were able effectively to stymie these movements, and it was through *federal* government involvement that the entitlements of a modern social welfare state were extended to the entire country.[13]

As Mill noted more than a century ago, 'What pretends to be local self-government, ... is, too often, selfish mismanagement of local interests by a jobbing and *borné* local oligarchy.'[14] In some provinces of Canada, even today, economic power – including ownership of land and industry – is heavily concentrated in the hands of a few families,[15] a factor which may explain in part the observation that many environmental activists (particularly those concerned with industrial pollution) place their main hopes in federal environmental control, even with respect to relatively localized pollution problems.[16] Griffen suggests, in the context of a study of developing countries, 'it is conceivable, even likely in many countries, that power at the local level is more concentrated, more elitist and applied more ruthlessly against the poor than at the centre.'[17] Similar observations are to be found in more recent works by Smith[18] and Slater.[19]

The Costs of Democratic Activism

An additional concern is the cost of effectively exercising democratic voice. A particular group may not be strong or numerous enough within a federal sub-unit to organize politically and bring to bear influence on the sub-unit's policies. If the group can pool its resources nation-wide and concentrate its effort on influencing democratic outcomes at the national level, it may be able to achieve a great deal more.

Recent empirical research in the context of Reagan-era 'new federalism' in the United States tends to support this analysis. Wolman and Teitelbaum studied the relative impact of different interest-groups in Washington and in each of the fifty states, and concluded, 'overall a widespread decentralization would imply that certain interests – the poor and labour, especially – would be disadvantaged relative to other interests in low-income states and in states with a higher percentage of poor people or minorities.'[20] Scott makes a similar analysis with respect to environmental regulation in Canada:

> The environmental movement as a whole seeks economies of scale. It is less costly for a national group to learn about, compare and criticize national standards than for many provincial groups to perform these functions for diverse provincial standards ... Indeed by concentrating their pressure they may be able to persuade the federal government to set standards on international bases and methods. Success in this means their signalling costs under Ottawa are less than under the provinces.[21]

Advocates of decentralization are often insensitive to these economies of scale because of their assumption that many citizen interests are in fact aggregated or concentrated geographically, thereby making collective action on a national scale difficult or impossible. It is a complex exercise, however, to determine which of citizens' politically salient concerns are, in fact, geographically localized or defined. In an era characterized by mass communications at both the national and international levels, by large-scale migration, and by an increasingly pluralistic view of human identity(ies), the range of an individual's interests, views, and preferences that are definitively linked to membership in a particular subnational or even national[22] community is becoming increasingly narrow.[23] Many of the most pressing concerns that unite citizens in political action – the global environment, gender, and children's rights are some examples – are not geographically localized. Residence in a particular federal sub-unit is likely to say little about my views on such concerns, or how important aspects of my identity should be expressed in politics.[24]

The response of advocates of competitive federalism[25] is that federalism can generate packages of public goods that differ from sub-unit to sub-unit, and people can be free to move themselves or their businesses to the sub-unit with the package that best reflects *their* preferences, just as they can shop around for consumer goods. But, of course, some people in a given society are likely to be much more mobile geographically than others, and in addition, the notion of 'packages' may finesse a very difficult problem. What if my concerns about gender equality are best reflected in the policies of sub-unit A, but my economic philosophy is much more consistent with that of sub-unit B? While I can choose to buy my socks at store A and my shirts at store B, I cannot easily be a citizen of both sub-unit A and of sub-unit B.[26]

Federalism as a Second-Best to Direct Democracy

Often, federalism has been viewed as a 'second-best' to the *polis*, a human community where citizens can actually practise town-hall democracy, or where every citizen at least has some personal acquaintance with each other citizen, or the potential for such acquaintance.[27] While it is highly unrealistic under modern circumstances to aim at a federal sub-unit of this size,[28] nevertheless, it has also been argued, most forcefully by Tocqueville,[29] that a greater degree of public-spiritedness is likely to be found within smaller units of government, given that they are concerned more directly with the day-to-day interests of the ordinary citizen. It is difficult to reconcile this hypothesis with the empirical evidence that, for example, in the United States today voter turnouts in subnational elections are usually considerably lower than in national elections.[30] Susan Rose-Ackerman notes with respect to federalism in the United States that 'much citizen participation in state and local activities results from requirements in federal statutes and regulations. These requirements indicate that national politicians believe the ideal of citizen participation to be undervalued by state and local officials.'[31]

In fact, contrary to Tocqueville's assumption, it may be that public-spiritedness requires a certain distance from one's immediate interests and concerns that is supplied by the loftier or grander goals more characteristic of politics at the national level. Precisely *because* local, subnational politics is more likely to be dominated by those motivated by the protection of their personal stake in the community (property, schools, etc.), there may be less room for a transcendent common good that can attract and form public-spirited citizens.

What, however, characterizes the new social movements that I have argued constitute much of what is vigorous in my own country's public life, and that Havel identifies as the future of democracy, is both their devotion to greater and more abstract good *and* their capacity to conduct political deliberation and association at the *national*, and even sometimes at the *international* level.[32] While such groups do organize citizens and promote initiatives at the community level, they also bring people together throughout the country. They promise the individual, through association, an opportunity to affect the public life of a vast nation.

We are discovering that the fax machine,[33] and in general, cheap long-distance rates and discount airfares, are powerful facilitators of national political deliberation. And it is far from clear, in Canada at any rate, that the new kind of national political deliberation is of lesser quality than that within smaller communities. Perhaps it is too early to make a definitive judgment, but it may be time to question seriously the communitarian rhetoric about smallness and closeness.[34] Meaningful political participation and associative public action may well not depend on citizens sharing the kinds of ties and relationships typical of individuals who grow up together in a relatively small and homogeneous community.[35]

What are the implications for federalism of these observations concerning the democratic defects and limits of decentralization? First, where a policy area is such that it generates common concerns among citizens throughout the nation, devolution of responsibility for that policy area to the sub-units may well undermine rather than extend the possibilities of citizen voice in the determination of policy. Second, just as a dogmatic identification of decentralization with democracy is misguided, so equally would be a dogmatic preference for centralization. Where citizens' interests *are* genuinely local, or happen to be concentrated in a particular community, these interests may well be marginalized in the national political calculus, but much better reflected by smaller units of government. While a federalism driven by a dogmatic choice for decentralization is likely to reduce the possibilities of democratic participation and voice, a federal order designed to counter majority tyranny at both the national level and within subnational communities may well have a democratic potential superior to that of a unitary state, in that citizens can organize and seek a public reflection of their needs and interests at more than one level of government.[36]

Achieving this democratic potential, however, would seem to point less to decentralization of exclusive powers over policy fields, than to maintaining a wide range of concurrent or shared jurisdictions, where each government is free to respond to citizen demands within a given policy area. Under this kind of concurrency, if citizens are unable to persuade one level of government to respond to their needs, they have the opportunity to appeal to the other level for action.

Ultimately, concurrency may create its own set of democratic drawbacks. Often both levels of government will end up being active in the same broad policy field, in the short term leading to greater overall responsiveness to citizen demands, but in the longer term blurring or confusing the lines of policy accountability as policy initiatives begin to multiply and overlap.[37] When citizens are no longer clear about who to praise or blame for policy outcomes, democratic accountability suffers.[38] At the same time, the complexity of governance in contemporary societies is likely to require considerable flexibility in the allocation of policy responsibilities between governments, further reinforcing the logic of concurrency. Many challenges and tasks of government, whether environmental protection or retraining workers to meet the demands of global competition, are likely to have both local and national aspects.

Managing interdependence in governmental responsibilities in a manner that preserves or enhances federalism's democratic possibilities is a crucial challenge of legal and institutional design, one that in my view is not being adequately met in many contemporary federations.[39] Instead, the most typical response to interdependence has been to resort to what is often called 'executive federalism.' This involves complex intergovernmental agreements, usually negotiated in secret by senior bureaucrats and ministers, which have an immense impact on policy outcomes. These outcomes may well reflect the power relationships between those at the table as much or more than the democratic will of either the national constituency, or the sub-unit constituencies. As well, the elite nature of executive federalism processes tends to result in the marginalization of grassroots advocacy or public-interest groups.[40] Indeed, executive federalism itself may be said to be a significant part of the crisis of representative democracy itself in federal unions – whether Canada,[41] the United States,[42] or the European Union.[43]

Reinvigorating the Democratic Possibilities of National Government
In comparison to the complex institutional design issues that may need to be solved if federalism is to fulfil its democratic potential, many of the measures that can be taken to enhance the responsiveness of central governments to democratic participation and voice seem relatively straightforward. For instance, the Canadian experience suggests that access of advocacy groups and social movements to public funding (or at least to tax deductible private contributions) would be a positive measure, as would the support of nation-wide public affairs television and radio as a forum for national democratic deliberation.[44] The use of independent commissions to monitor and assess governmental performance in particular policy areas, such as trade and industrial policy[45] or social welfare entitlements, may also improve the quality and impact of democratic deliberation, especially where such institutions are directly open to participation by a full range of advocacy groups and of individual citizens.[46]

Strengthening democracy at the national level is especially important as an increasing number of policy fields have direct implications for action at the international level, where (with few exceptions) nation states remain the major actors. The historian Michael Howard has made the important point that internationalism or supranationalism does not imply that democratic life at the national level is of lesser importance, but rather that national democratic institutions should be strengthened. 'Otherwise,' suggests Howard, 'the elites who participate in these supranational enterprises, be they politicians, industrialists, financiers or intellectuals, will be seen as out of touch with and irrelevant to the needs of the ordinary people at the grass roots.'[47]

I doubt that weak national governments, and even less, smaller communities, will have the capacity to make these elites accountable. I doubt, as well, whether smaller communities can have much effective voice in shaping the terms and conditions of globalization, whether they are set in the boardrooms of multinational corporations, or at what remain even today interstate negotiations in which the larger powers are usually observed to wield the greatest influence on outcomes (the GATT/WTO, the OECD). While in some circumstances, it may be possible to contemplate a genuine representative democracy at the supranational level (for example, the European Parliament),[48] and while (as noted above) some public-interest groups may be able to operate at the international level, in general the level of the nation state remains the essential, practicable locus of democratic control over supranational outcomes.

Efficiency and Respect for Diversity
Among the mature industrial democracies, the traditional regulatory and

social welfare state has been under attack for some time (and not just from neo-conservative or libertarian critics) for its rigid, centralist solutions to human problems that instead require sensitivity to diversity among individuals and communities.[49] Here, the critique of the nation state focuses not on the defects of the democratic process but on the inflexible policy instruments it supposedly generates. As well, in the case of newly liberalizing and democratizing countries throughout the world, centralism is often identified with a legacy of tyranny and oppression.

Two kinds of federalist solution have often been proposed to address the evils of centralism. The first is devolution of regulatory authority to the federal sub-units; the second is a kind of administrative decentralization where the sub-units deliver or implement federal policies or conduct their own policies, but according to national standards.

Do policies of federal sub-units display greater flexibility and efficiency than those of the national government, and are they less likely to be of a traditional 'command and control' character? Despite all the rhetoric identifying federalism and decentralization with efficiency, there is very little concrete empirical evidence on the matter. Some of the most promising experiments with incentive-oriented policy instruments (such as the adoption of tradeable pollution permits by the US Environmental Protection Agency, or the Canadian government's Ecologo environmental labelling program) have been undertaken by national governments in federal states, not the sub-units, in areas where *both* levels of government possessed the legal jurisdiction to be active. In other areas, as is the case with industrial policy in the United States, subnational governments have been responsible for many of the most promising and innovative experiments in policy-making over the last decade.[50] However, this must be viewed against the background reality that during this period in the United States there was an ideological commitment at the federal level to *in*action in the areas in question.

Offloading the Responsibilities of National Government

In some instances, one may be justified in suspecting that the enthusiasm of national governments for the rhetoric of decentralization and devolution is rather narrowly self-interested – unable or unwilling to make the difficult institutional and redistributive choices needed to reform and reinvigorate the central state, they have sought a way of dumping their problems on other governments. These lower levels of government may lack the resources, infrastructure, and indeed the political will to do the job, and so the budget and program cuts are passed on in turn to the municipalities. This was characteristic of Reagan-era federalism in the United States,[51] and explains as well a number of decentralization initiatives in developing countries.

The case of Mexico, as described by Lowder, is particularly instructive:

> The hidden agenda [of decentralization] emerged when the financial and legal underpinning did not materialize ... ; the fiscal base of municipalities enshrined in those laws was probably never sufficient but, in any case, has seldom been distributed on an equitable basis within states. Even when implemented, municipalities did not have the equipment or staff to assume the new responsibilities ... Clearly, these circumstances permit the blame for lack of adequate provision to be shifted to new levels of government, which, however, have little real autonomy over the type or level of service they provide.[52]

Similar phenomena have been noted with respect to the decentralization of governmental power in Colombia,[53] Brazil,[54] Hungary, and Russia.[55]

Efficiency, Fiscal Autonomy, and Competitive Federalism

The experience of decentralization in these countries need not, of course, be attributed to the failure of the federalization/decentralization model as such, but rather to the failure to transfer adequate resources along with policy responsibilities. True decentralization, along the lines of the competitive federalism model, implies that both taxation and expenditure functions be transferred to lower levels of government.[56]

Even where the underlying intent is not to offload responsibilities, governments may have strong reasons for not accompanying devolution of authority over expenditures with a full transfer of revenue raising responsibilities and capacities. There is a range of countervailing considerations that favour centralized revenue raising.[57] These include the importance of a national fiscal policy in macroeconomic stabilization[58]; limited tax collection and enforcement powers of lower levels of government[59]; the possibility of a 'race to the bottom' as jurisdictions cut taxes competitively to attract or retain investment; and the natural inclination of central governments not to surrender voluntarily the 'power of the purse.' In addition, and most fundamentally, different subnational jurisdictions are likely to have widely differing tax bases, leading to the possibility that – contrary to the theory of local public expenditure – policy diversity will be as much a product of differences in income as of differences in preference. For these reasons, decentralization of policy responsibilities has rarely gone hand in hand with decentralization of revenue raising capacities and responsibilities. Transfers from the federal government of actual tax revenues raised centrally, or a *combination* of equalization payments and tax room, have been much more prevalent.[60]

These transfers have, however, rarely preserved local autonomy over expenditures, which is the essential goal of the decentralization model of local public expenditure. While unconditional equalization payments aimed at compensating for a weaker tax base do, in theory, preserve this autonomy, in practice it will often be politically difficult to maintain a commitment to raising vast amounts of revenue from taxpayers nation-wide, without some control of outputs. In order to get the political 'credit' for equalization, the central government must be able to ensure that some national minimum levels of services are delivered across the federation, regardless of regional disparities. Thus in the Canadian context, although unconditional equalization payments are an important feature of fiscal federalism, they are strongly and importantly linked in the public mind with national standards in social programs, which are in fact more directly related to various *conditional* grants.[61]

As well, a significant moral hazard exists with respect to federal sub-units spending money that has been raised by the national government. Since the sub-unit governments are not fully accountable to their own taxpayers, or to lenders such as bond-holders, for the federal funds which they spend, these governments will be less likely to exercise fiscal prudence. As Bird suggests, the effect of fiscal transfers is 'almost invariably to break the nexus between expenditure and revenue responsibility and thus to reduce ac-countability to some, and often a considerable, extent.'[62] Indeed, these problems may even persist where revenue raising has been decentralized, unless the federal government makes credible commitments not to bail out federal sub-units in a fiscal crisis. On the other hand, failure to act as a lender or cashier of last resort may result in the collapse of essential public services in the sub-unit concerned, thereby producing unacceptable redistributive consequences, and in some federations, dangerously exacerbating regional and ethnic tensions as well.[63]

In addition, more general problems exist with respect to compensating sub-units directly for new policy responsibilities that have been transferred to them. Even where the central government may be prepared to transfer an appropriate portion of revenues equivalent to what it spends now on the programs in question in each sub-unit, these transfers are unlikely to reflect the costs of training and hiring new personnel, and otherwise creating an appropriate delivery infrastructure at the subnational level. Unless the central government is prepared to make redundant the federal civil servants currently responsible for the programs in question (politically difficult or legally impossible in many countries) or transfer them to the sub-units, a devolution in policy responsibilities may actually lead to increased bureau-cratic waste by further bloating central administrations with unnecessary cadres. Finally in a number of countries undergoing economic transition, both in Central and Eastern Europe and in the developing world, recommendations for decentralization should take into account the scarcity of technology and competent personnel to implement the new market-oriented legislation and policies. Decentralization that entails the duplication of bureaucracies and delivery infrastructures at the subnational level may well squander the scarce resources available for the implementation of policy reform.

Reforming National Policies to Respond to Diversity
On the positive side of the equation, it is important to recognize that national governments need not conduct their policies in a manner that is insensitive to diversity. For example, national governments increasingly deliver services, such as job counselling or shelters for battered women, in partnership with community organizations able to provide programs and tailor them to quite diverse needs and requirements.[64] Moreover, by funding a variety of experimental programs designed by community groups or non-profit organizations, the national government can create laboratories of democracy and competition for better policy solutions without decentralization to lower levels of government.[65] Many of the policy instruments that have emerged as a response to the critique of central administration, or command and control regulation,[66] do not have inherent properties that make them more amenable to introduction at the subnational than the national level. For instance, taxes and charges on pollution can be implemented at the national level. Moreover, national governments can act in partnership with national and supranational actors, such as major corporations, or national advocacy associations, or national or multinational trade unions in seeking cooperative approaches to basic challenges, such as worker adjustment to global competition. Inasmuch as the relevant non-governmental actors themselves act on a national scale or the national stage, *national* government is likely to be closer to them than governments of the sub-units.

A related point is that major shifts in policy often require considerable scope for redistribution.[67] Here, I am referring not to the issue of fiscal equalization discussed above, but to the need to distribute the costs and benefits of certain specific major initiatives, such as the restructuring of national industries for privatization and liberalized trade. The wider the taxpayer base over which these adjustment costs can be spread, the more likely the initiative's political acceptability will be.

Administrative Delegation
The need for continued exercise of power at the national level is sometimes seen as reconcilable with the benefits of decentralization through techniques of delegation, where the lower level of government participates in

the delivery or design of specific programs under federal authority or general federal direction. Indeed, some proposals go beyond delegation, to allow for the exercise of federal power only with the consent of and under such terms and conditions as are agreeable to the sub-unit(s) (in the Canadian context, the notion of provincial paramountcy).

While in some particular instances delegation may be desirable, as a general recipe for better government it has very serious drawbacks. First, it is quite likely that the lower level of government will have its own priorities, and these may conflict with the national concerns that drive the initiative. Second, by setting up the lower level of government as the intermediary between the citizen and the national authorities, delegation tends to interfere with direct public participation in, and identification with, national policy outcomes.[68] Third, to return briefly to an earlier theme in this paper, delegation threatens democratic accountability – it is hard to identify one government that can be held responsible for the failure (or success) of the policies in question.[69]

As suggested earlier, the more attractive alternative is to decentralize delivery below the lower level of government, below bureaucracy altogether, to individual citizens and groups of citizens – community and advocacy-group run daycare centres or employment counselling facilities, shelters, and hostels for the homeless.[70] Monitoring and enforcing national standards with respect to lower levels of government would probably be more difficult than with respect to many community-level non-governmental actors, since governments (at both political and bureaucratic levels) have strong interests in the assertion of power and authority unrelated to the specific goals or causes in question, and since they like to consider themselves equal co-sovereigns with the national government.[71]

Conclusion

In this brief essay, I have attempted to question the fashionable view that decentralization through federalism is a route to better government. Depending on the policy context, as well as the basic economic, political, and social circumstances of the country concerned, decentralization may or may not result in government that is more democratic, more efficient, and more respectful of individual and community preferences. As John Stuart Mill observed in his *Autobiography*, dogmatic biases for and against decentralization are twin evils in policy-making.[72] In Mill's words, it is time to insist 'with equal emphasis upon the errors of both sides.'[73] The general bias towards decentralization through federalism reflected in much contemporary policy literature should be replaced by a much more contextual and cautious approach, sensitive to the costs as well as the benefits of decentralization, and particularly to the complex institutional design issues that must be solved if the benefits of decentralization are to be realized. Despite the contemporary rhetoric of globalization and decentralization, many of the pressing policy challenges of our time can only be tackled if *national* governments directly face the responsibility for democratic renewal and for the required adjustments in the relationship between the market and the state and between the state and the individual.

Acknowledgments

In developing the ideas in this essay, I benefited greatly from conversations with Vojtech Cepl, Ron Daniels, Arthur Fish, Richard Janda, Karen Knop, Don Lenihan, Wayne Norman, Michael Trebilcock, and Rob Yalden. My greatest debts are to Kathy Swinton, whose searching editorial comments have strengthened greatly the manuscript, and to Deborah Coyne, with whom I have carried on an enormously instructive conversation about federalism over the last five years. Lara Friedlander made incisive comments on a draft that have improved it greatly and also provided excellent research assistance. I alone, of course, am responsible for errors, shortcomings, and the views expressed.

Notes

1 See, for example, W. Robson, *Dynamic Tensions: Markets, Federalism, and Canada's Economic Future* (Toronto: C.D. Howe Institute 1992); T. Courchene, *In Praise of Renewed Federalism* (Toronto: C.D. Howe Institute 1992); D. Osborne and T. Gaebler, *Reinventing Government* (Reading, MA: Addison-Wesley 1992); D. Osborne, 'A New Federal Compact: Sorting Out Washington's Proper Role,' in W. Marshall and M. Schram, eds., *Mandate for Change* (New York: Berkeley and Progressive Policy Institute 1993); D. Rondinelli and J.R. Nellis, 'Assessing Decentralization Policies in Developing Countries: A Case for Cautious Optimism,' *Development Policy Review* 4 (1986):58.

2 For a largely sympathetic elaboration of the critique of the modern regulatory state that informs this interest in decentralization, see R. Howse, J.R.S. Prichard, and M.J. Trebilcock, 'Smaller or Smarter Government?' *U. of Toronto L.J.* 40 (1990):498.

3 See D.A. Rondinelli, J.S. McCullough, and R.W. Johnson, 'Analysing Decentralization Policies in Developing Countries: A Political-Economy Framework,' *Development and Change* 20 (1989):57.

4 See, for instance, T. Pangle, *The Ennobling of Democracy* (Baltimore: Johns Hopkins University Press 1991) at 155, and the policy developments in NLCs themselves, discussed in R.M. Bird, 'Local Government Finance: A Neglected Dimension of Transition' (paper presented at the conference on the Post-Communist Transformation: Emerging Economic, Legal, and Business Implications, University of Toronto Faculty of Law, 17 October 1992).

5 A useful discussion of the problem in the Canadian context is T. Kent, *Getting Ready for 1999: Ideas for Canada's Politics and Government* (Halifax: Institute for

Research on Public Policy 1989), Chapters 2 and 3.

6 Recognition of the importance of such groups in maintaining the quality of democratic deliberation is not, however, altogether new. Consider the following observation of de Tocqueville 'De notre temps, la liberté d'association est devenue une garantie nécessaire contre la tyrannie de la majorité. Aux États-Unis, quand une fois un parti est devenu dominant, toute la puissance publique passe dans ses mains; ses amis occupent tous les emplois et disposent de toutes les forces organisées ... : il n'y a pas de pays où les associations soient plus nécessaires, pour empêcher le despotisme des partis ou l'arbitraire du prince, que ceux où l'état social est démocratique.' *De la démocratie en Amérique*, in J.-C. Lamberti and F. Mélonio, eds., *Alexis de Tocqueville* (Paris: Laffont 1986), 192-3.

7 Although often maligned as special interest-groups, in fact many of these organizations assert a conception of the public interest that transcends the narrow material interests shared by their membership. On this aspect of the new social movements, see S.D. Phillips, 'Of Public Interest Groups and Sceptics: A Realist's Reply to Professor Stanbury,' *Canadian Public Administration* 36 (1993-94):606 at 612-16.

8 Kent, *Getting Ready for 1999*, Chapter 2.

9 Václav Havel, *Living in Truth* (London: Faber 1987), 118.

10 See, for example, C.H. Neu Jr. and J. Ethredge, 'Community-Sensible Governance: The Emerging Political Reality of the 21st Century,' *National Civic Review* 70 (1991):381 at 389.

11 Even in this instance, however, devolution of powers is not necessarily an adequate solution, because a group that is a minority in the nation as a whole but a majority within a sub-unit, may exercise majority tyranny at the sub-unit level over other groups that are minorities *within* the sub-unit. This difficulty is discussed at length in R. Howse and K. Knop, 'Federalism, Secession, and the Limits of Ethnic Accommodation,' *New Europe Law Review* 1 (1993):269.

12 J.S. Mill, 'Considerations on Representative Government,' in *On Liberty and Considerations on Representative Government* (Oxford: Basil Blackwell 1948), 191.

13 See, in general, K.G. Banting, *The Welfare State and Canadian Federalism*, 2nd ed. (Kingston and Montreal: McGill-Queen's University Press 1987), Chapter 5.

14 J.S. Mill, *Autobiography* (London: Penguin 1989), 151.

15 See in general, R. Morck, 'On the Economics of Concentrated Ownership' (paper presented at conference on Canadian Corporate Governance: A Multidisciplinary Perspective, C.D. Howe Institute, Toronto, 10-11 February 1994).

16 See A. Scott, 'Piecemeal Decentralization: The Environment,' in R. Boadway, T. Courchene, and D. Purvis, eds., *Economic Dimensions of Constitutional Change*, vol. 1 (Kingston: John Deutsch Institute for the Study of Economic Policy 1991), 292-3. Scott's own explanation for this phenomenon emphasizes the greater costs of lobbying provinces, rather than the greater difficulty of attaining voice for environmental concerns in a political process (for example, in New Brunswick or Nova Scotia) largely controlled by concentrated economic interests. See the next section of this chapter on the issue of costs.

17 K. Griffin, 'Economic Development in a Changing World,' *World Development* 9 (1981):221 at 225. See also, B.C. Smith, 'Measuring Decentralization,' in G.W. Jones, ed., *New Approaches to the Study of Central-Local Government Relationships*

(Aldershot: Gower 1980), 137-51.

18 B.C. Smith, *Bureaucracy and Political Power* (Brighton: Wheatsheaf 1988), 217.

19 D. Slater, 'Territorial Power and the Peripheral State: The Issue of Decentralization,' *Development and Change* 20 (1989):501.

20 H. Wolman and F. Teitelbaum, 'Interest Groups and the Reagan Presidency,' in L.M. Salamon and M.S Lund, eds., *The Reagan Presidency and the Governing of America* (Washington DC: Urban Institute Press 1985), 329.

21 Scott, 'The Environment: Piecemeal Decentralization,' 292.

22 As will be suggested below, national governments are the principal actors on the global stage, and, therefore, critical to advancing citizen concerns that are not defined by the national community itself.

23 These observations are not contradicted by the fact that ours is also an era characterized by the resurgence of ethnic nationalism. As Stéphane Dion has argued in a brilliant essay on contemporary Quebec society, nationalism may be understood as a form of reaction or resistance to the *reality* that human identities are becoming increasingly less fixed in terms of geographical locality or ethnic group membership. Stéphane Dion 'Le nationalisme dans la convergence culturelle: Le Québec contemporain et le paradoxe de Tocqueville,' in R. Hudson and R. Pelletier, eds., *L'engagement intellectuel Mélanges en l'honneur de Léon Dion* (Sainte-Foy: Les Presses de l'Université Laval 1991).

24 Katherine E. Swinton, *The Supreme Court and Canadian Federalism: The Laskin-Dickson Years* (Toronto: Carswell 1990), 207-8.

25 Ronald J. Daniels, 'Should Provinces Compete? The Case for a Competitive Corporate Law Market,' *McGill Law Journal* 36 (1991):130 (Daniels is, however, sensitive to the limits of competitive federalism in those many policy areas where personal movement is necessary to realize the potential of competition); Frank H. Easterbrook, 'Antitrust and the Economics of Federalism,' *Journal of Law and Economics* 26 (1983):23; Charles M. Tiebout 'A Pure Theory of Local Expenditures,' *Journal of Political Economy* 54 (1956):416.

26 A variant of the argument for competitive federalism suggests that its merit lies less in the competition for votes than in the possibility of generating a variety of policy experiments or different approaches to the same problem in the various federal jurisdictions. The most successful approaches will then come to be emulated by the other jurisdictions, or taken up by the federal government itself (see D. Osborne, 'Introduction,' in D. Osborne, ed., *Laboratories of Democracy: A New Breed of Governor Creates Models for National Growth* (Cambridge, MA: Harvard Business School Press 1988), 2-3). Increasingly, however, policy analysts in areas such as industrial policy or labour policy look as much to other countries' experiments in these areas as to the diversity of experiences within their own country in order to find models for innovation.

27 Benjamin Barber, *Strong Democracy: Participatory Politics for a New Age* (Berkeley: University of California Press 1984), esp. 249-51.

28 Of course, the argument might be that a sub-unit could be small enough that the elites know each other personally and can conduct political deliberation without the intermediation typical of mass national-scale politics. However, this in itself can lead to a kind of very strong 'corporatism' or politics of elite accommodation that in the end defeats the goals of democratization.

29 See Tocqueville, *De la démocracie en Amerique*, in Lamberti and Mélonio, eds., *Alexis de Tocqueville*, Part I, Chapter 5. For a good discussion of the Tocquevillean argument, see C.H. Zuckert, 'Reagan and That Unnamed Frenchman (De Tocqueville): On the Rationale for the New (Old) Federalism,' *Review of Politics* (1983):421; and C. Millon-Delsol, *L'État subsidiare: Ingérance et non-ingérance de l'État: le principe de subsidiarité aux fondements de l'histoire européenne* (Paris: PUF 1992), Chapter 5.
30 See H. Wolman, 'Decentralization: What It Is and Why We Should Care,' in R.J. Bennett, ed., *Decentralization, Local Governments, and Markets: Towards a Post Welfare Agenda* (Clarendon Press: Oxford 1990) 34-5. I am in agreement with Wolman's further observation that much more empirical work needs to be done on the relative quantity and quality of participation at national and subnational levels of government in both centralized and decentralized systems.
31 S. Rose-Ackerman, *Rethinking the Progressive Agenda: The Reform of the American Regulatory State* (New York: Free Press 1992), 166.
32 Alan Gilbert, 'Must Global Politics Constrain Democracy? Realism, Regimes and Democratic Internationalism,' *Political Theory* 20 (1992):1.
33 For an interesting discussion of the role of the fax (in the context of the democratic revolutions in the communist world) see Albert Wohlstetter, 'Le fax vous rendra libres,' *Commentaire* 52 (1990):679.
34 Michael J. Sandel, *Liberalism and the Limits of Justice* (New York: Cambridge University Press 1982), 58-65.
35 See also R. Howse, 'Retrenchment, Reform, or Revolution? The Shift to Incentives and the Future of the Regulatory State,' *Alberta Law Review* 31 (1993):455.
36 See Swinton, *The Supreme Court and Canadian Federalism*, 172-3; A. Breton, 'Supplementary Statement,' in Canada, Royal Commission on the Economic Union and Development Prospects for Canada, *Report*, vol. 3 (Ottawa: Minister of Supply and Services 1985), 486-526; R. Howse, *Economic Union, Social Justice, and Constitutional Reform: Towards a High but Level Playing Field* (Downsview, ON: York University Centre for Public Law and Public Policy 1992), 43.
37 Jean Marensin suggests, in the context of decentralization in France, 'la proliferation dans notre pays de pouvoirs locaux concurrents, et chacun soucieux de maintenir sa clientèle, la multiplication des comités, associations, organismes professionnels de toutes sortes, les procédures complexes qui s'établissent entre ces différentes instances, ... pourraient bien signifier, à terme, un recul de la démocratie dans la mesure ou la démocratie – comme les plantes des sous-bois – a besoin de clarté; cela signifie en tous les cas un recul du libéralisme au sens classique.' J. Marensin, 'Libéralisme et centralisme en France et en Angleterre,' *Commentaire* 56 (1991-92):735.
38 See P.E. Trudeau, 'Federal Grants to Universities,' in P.E. Trudeau, *Federalism and the French Canadians* (Toronto: Macmillan 1968), 79-80.
39 No shortage of proposals exists for institutional reform, but these involve quite sophisticated exercises in institutional redesign, often unachievable except in the context of fundamental constitutional reform. For some of the proposals advanced during the recent, failed round of constitutional negotiations in Canada, see R. Janda, *Rebalancing the Federation Through Senate Reform: Another Look at the Bundesrat* (Downsview, ON: York University Centre for Public Law

and Public Policy 1992); R. Howse, *Economic Union, Social Justice, and Constitutional Reform* (Downsview, ON: York University Centre for Public Law and Public Policy 1992), Part V; J. Nedelsky and C. Scott, 'Constitutional Dialogue,' in J. Bakan and D. Schneiderman, eds., *Social Justice and the Constitution: Perspectives on a Social Union for Canada* (Ottawa: Carleton University Press 1992), 59-84. For a clear and forceful presentation of the difficulties in subjecting processes of intergovernmental co-decision to effective democratic control, see P. Monahan, *The Meech Lake: The Inside Story* (Toronto: University of Toronto Press 1991), 249-51.

40 In the Canadian context, a number of empirical studies have been undertaken on the interrelationship between executive federalism and such groups. For an overview, see F.J. Fletcher and D.C. Wallace, 'Federal-Provincial Relations and the Making of Public Policy in Canada: a Review of the Case Studies,' in R. Simeon, ed., *Division of Powers and Public Policy* (Toronto: University of Toronto Press 1985), 177-91.

41 See Howse, *Economic Union, Social Justice and Constitutional Reform*, Parts II, V, and VI.

42 See M. Derthick, 'Up-to-Date in Kansas City: Reflections on American Federalism,' *PS: Political Science and Politics* 25 (1992):671, particularly at 672-3.

43 See J. Pinder, 'The European Community, the Rule of Law and Representative Government: The Significance of the Intergovernmental Conferences,' *Government and Opposition* 26 (1991):199.

44 Deborah Coyne has emphasized the importance of a national all-news channel operated by public television (CBC Newsworld) in facilitating the opening up of the constitutional debate in Canada to a wider range of groups and individuals. See D. Coyne, *Roll of the Dice: Working with Clyde Wells During the Meech Lake Negotiations* (Toronto: Lorimer 1992), 78-9.

45 For a proposal along these lines, see M.J. Trebilcock, M. Chandler, and R. Howse, *Trade and Transitions: A Comparative Analysis of Adjustment Policies* (Routledge: London 1990), Chapter 6.

46 I wish to emphasize that these measures should not necessarily include an abrupt change in the formal emphasis of representative democracy on legislative institutions and political parties – that is, towards the use of national referenda and plebiscites or towards formal interest group representation in political institutions. In fact, these latter more radical shifts could lead to a new kind of rigid formalism that simply implies a different set of instruments for the manipulation of democratic outcomes by a (slightly different) set of elites.

47 M. Howard, *The Lessons of History* (New Haven: Yale University Press 1991), 164.

48 For a sober assessment of the difficulties with this enterprise, see A. Legaré, *La Souveraineté est-elle dépassée? Entretiens avec des parlementaires et intellectuels français autour de l'Europe actuelle* (Montreal: Boréal 1992), particularly the interviews with Luc Ferry and Paul Thibaud.

49 C. Sunstein, *After the Rights Revolution* (Cambridge, MA: Harvard University Press 1990), esp. Chapters 1-3; Howse, Prichard, and Trebilcock, 'Smaller or Smarter Government?'

50 See, for description and balanced evaluation of many of these experiments, Osborne, ed., *Laboratories of Democracy*; see also, R. Scott Fosler, *The New Economic*

Role of American States: Strategies in a Competitive World Economy (New York: Oxford University Press 1988).

51 See Zuckert, 'Reagan and the Unnamed Frenchman,' 436-8.

52 S. Lowder, 'Decentralization in Latin America: An Evaluation of the Achievements,' in A. Morris and S. Lowder, eds., *Decentralization in Latin America* (1992), 190-1.

53 See F. Uribe-Echevarria, 'The Decentralization Debate in Colombia: Lessons From Experience,' *Planning and Administration* 6 (1986):10-21.

54 A. Shah, *New Fiscal Federalism in Brazil*, Discussion Paper No. 124 (Washington DC: World Bank 1991).

55 Bird, 'Local Government Finance,' 19.

56 See D. Rondinelli and J.R. Nellis, 'Assessing Decentralization Policies in Developing Countries: A Case for Cautious Optimism,' *Development Policy Review* 4 (1986):58-9, defining decentralization as 'the transfer of responsibility for planning management, and raising and allocation of resources from the central government and its agencies' to lower level government or private sector actors.

57 The following discussion owes much to a criticism by Katherine Swinton of some of my earlier work on federalism. For an overlapping but somewhat different list of explanations for the centralization of revenue raising capacity, see R. Bird, 'A Comparative Perspective on Federal Finance' (paper presented at conference on The Future of Fiscal Federalism, Queen's University, Kingston, Canada, 4-5 November 1993), 9-10.

58 See R. Boadway, *The Constitutional Division of Powers: An Economic Perspective* (Ottawa: Economic Council of Canada 1992), 42-3.

59 I. Ip and J. Mintz, *Dividing the Spoils: The Federal-Provincial Allocation of Taxing Powers* (Toronto: C.D. Howe Institute, 1992), at 7.

60 Bird, 'A Comparative Perspective on Federal Finance,' suggests that most federal countries assign 'more tax revenue than expenditure to the federal government' (at 9).

61 In fact, traditionally, the formal conditions on many of these grants have amounted to much less than a comprehensive set of national standards, but this has not been the public perception. In consequence, as fiscal and other pressures have led to greater manifest diversity in provincial programs, popular interest in imposition of clearer national standards has grown. For a clear explanation of federal-provincial fiscal relations in Canada, see Boadway, *The Constitutional Division of Powers*, Chapter 3. See also, Howse, *Economic Union, Social Justice and Constitutional Reform*, 108-13.

62 Bird, 'A Comparative Perspective on Federal Finance,' 11.

63 Some policy analysts who display a general preference for decentralization do, to their credit, nevertheless see strong arguments along the lines discussed in this paper for retaining basic social expenditure or 'entitlement' programs as a central government responsibility. See, for example, A. Rivlin, *Reviving the American Dream: The Economy, the States and the Federal Government* (Washington DC: Brookings Institution 1992), Chapter 9, 'Social Insurance: A Federal Priority.'

64 In the context of American federalism, Fosler for example makes a strong case for federal government involvement in labour market training, but notes: 'While federal involvement in the human capital field is necessary, however, such

involvement must differ in content and style from the way the federal government has approached this and related fields in the recent past. In particular, rather than relying on command and control mechanisms, the federal government could usefully [adopt an approach that] ... recognizes the need to mobilize and enlist a wide assortment of actors – from different levels of government and from both the public and private sectors.' R. Scott Fosler, 'Human Capital Investment and Federalism,' in D.W. Hornbeck and C.M. Salamon, eds., *Human Capital and America's Future: An Economic Strategy for the '90s* (Baltimore and London: Johns Hopkins University Press 1991), 311.

65 For example, in the United States some proposals that have caught the attention of policy advisors to the Clinton Administration would involve competitive bidding for job training and apprenticeship funds by a variety of sub-governmental actors, including unions, private firms, and community organizations. See T. Kolderie, R. Lerman, and C. Moskos, 'Educating America: A New Compact for Opportunity and Citizenship,' in W. Marshall and M. Schram, eds., *Mandate for Change*, 140-1. These actors are perhaps much *more* likely than local and state *bureaucrats* to respond rapidly to financial incentives, as they themselves directly benefit from the award of a grant, and, moreover, from the success of the program.

66 For a general survey of these instruments, see Howse, Prichard, and Trebilcock, 'Smaller or Smarter Government?'

67 For an argument that a strong state with significant redistributive capacities may be a requirement of economic liberalization in developing countries, see S. Haggard and C.-I. Moon, 'The South Korean State in the International Economy: Liberal, Dependent, or Mercantile?' in J.G. Ruggie, ed., *The Antinomies of Interdependence: National Welfare and the International Division of Labour* (New York: Columbia University Press 1983), 148-50. For a similar argument about the importance of redistributive capacity for liberalization in the context of the Newly Liberalizing Countries of Central and East Europe, see R. Daniels and R. Howse, 'Reforming the Reform Process: A Critique of Proposals for Privatization in Central and Eastern Europe,' *NYU Journal of Int. Law and Politics* 25 (1992):27 at 66-70.

68 Tocqueville emphasizes the crucial importance of a direct relationship between the citizen and the federal authorities: 'La puissance d'un gouvernement fédéral réside donc bien moins dans l'étendue des droits qu'on lui confère, que dans la faculté plus ou moins grande qu'on lui laisse de les exercer par lui-même: il est toujours fort quand il peut commander aux citoyens; il est toujours faible quand il est réduit à ne commander qu'aux gouvernments locaux.' A. de Tocqueville, *Rapport sur 'La Démocratie en Suisse' de Cherbuliez*, in *Oeuvres (I)* (Paris: Gallimard (Bibliothèque de la Pléiade) 1991), 635 at 650.

69 For a very good discussion of the problems that delegation and interdelegation between different levels of government are creating for transparency and accountability in the Russian Republic, see C.I. Wallach, *Fiscal Decentralization: Intergovernmental Relations in Russia*, Studies of Economies in Transformation, Paper No. 6 (Washington DC: World Bank 1992), 27-46.

70 As Havel suggests, 'The sovereignty of the community, the region, the nation, the state – any higher sovereignty, in fact – makes sense only if it is derived from

the one genuine sovereignty – that is from the sovereignty of the human being, which finds its political expression in civil sovereignty.' V. Havel, 'In a Time of Transition,' in *Summer Meditations* (Toronto: Lester Dennys 1992), 33.
71 This is not to say that conflicts of interest may not also exist between non-governmental actors and the national government; only that in the case of inter-governmental conflicts, the power struggle between governments is likely to exacerbate the problem.
72 Mill, *Autobiography*, 150-1.
73 Ibid.18.

18

Federalism, the Charter, and the Courts: Rethinking Constitutional Dialogue in Canada

Katherine Swinton

Introduction

Comparative experience indicates that there is no ideal model of federalism. In order to enshrine a federal bargain within a constitution, each state must resolve many issues: the allocation of powers or functions between levels of government, the design of central and regional institutions, and the extent and method of protection for individual and collective rights. The conclusions, reflecting the political and social forces unique to each country, must then be captured, at least in part, by legal language, in order to delineate and safeguard the bargain. Yet even at this point, difficult tradeoffs must be made between the need for flexibility and the desire for certainty.

While some might think that the major work of constitutional design has been completed with approval of the legal text, the process is, in fact, just beginning, for language can never be absolutely precise, and does not apply itself. As a result, the exercise of interpretation in the resolution of disputes inevitably changes the content of a constitution, both in the initial, groundbreaking cases in the courts and over time, as the words of the document take on different meanings to different interpreters.

This chapter deals with the challenges of constitutional interpretation in Canada, where the courts have long played a creative role in resolving disputes about the jurisdiction of federal and provincial governments under the *Constitution Act, 1867*. More recently, they have been given the daunting task of melding concepts of federalism, parliamentary government, and citizens' rights as a result of the entrenchment of the *Canadian Charter of Rights and Freedoms* in the constitution in 1982.

The Charter was a major change to Canada's constitutional framework and, thus, to the role of the Supreme Court of Canada. Yet more than a decade after the Charter came into effect, there is still much debate and uncertainty about its meaning, especially with regard to the proper balance between individual and collective rights. As well, there is, inevitably, controversy about the proper relationship between the judiciary and elected legislatures. This chapter examines the way in which debates about the meaning of the Charter and the Supreme Court's likely treatment of proposed constitutional language became an important factor in recent efforts to reform the federal system.[1] Moreover, the Charter has had an indirect effect on the types of issues included in the constitutional agenda and the process of constitutional reform. The lesson is clear: the Charter has enriched the concept of constitutionalism in Canada, making the process of constitutional reform and, indeed, governance within the existing federal system more complex. It has also demonstrated, once again, that the process of constitution-making does not end with drafting, but continues in often unanticipated and controversial ways in the courts.

Federalism and the Canadian Constitution[2]

The Canadian constitution, as drafted, set out detailed lists of legislative powers said to be 'exclusively' assigned to the federal and provincial levels of government, with only two areas of power designated as concurrent and with the residual power left to the federal government.[3] This allocation of powers appeared to contemplate a strong central government.[4] There was no express provision for judicial review to umpire this distribution of powers; indeed, a 'dispute settlement' mechanism used frequently in the early years to resolve conflicts between federal and provincial governments was the exercise of the federal powers of reservation and disallowance.[5] However, judicial review coexisted as an alternative forum to deal with disputes, and it soon replaced the federal powers.

As to the constitutional protection of rights, there was little concern shown in 1867, with only limited provisions to protect denominational school rights in certain situations[6] and the use of the English and French languages in certain federal and Quebec institutions.[7] Otherwise, the main sources of protection for individual and minority rights were to be found in parliamentary democracy and in the arrangements of the federal system itself.[8]

The constitution on paper looks very different from the constitution in operation in Canada, largely because of judicial interpretation and political arrangements made to deal with evolving policy needs. Because the constitution set out a list of exclusive legislative powers for each level of government, the courts could be asked to characterize a law as lying outside the assigned authority of the legislature which passed it,[9] and instead to classify it within the list of powers of the other level (or to invoke the residual power if the law did not fit within the enumerations). Inevitably, laws can be characterized as falling under more than one head of power,[10] thus requiring the courts to decide whether the subject matter of the impugned law should fall within the exclusive jurisdiction of one government (the 'watertight compartments' approach) or be open to treatment by both governments (the double aspect or concurrency approach).

Not surprisingly, as time went on, fitting laws within the detailed heads of power in the constitution became more difficult, since the constitution reflected the policy concerns of the framers, while modern areas of public policy, such as the environment, could be addressed under many heads of federal and provincial jurisdiction. In elaborating doctrines to aid in the application of the distribution of powers, the courts necessarily became 'constitution makers,' even though judges describe their role as that of being 'guardians' of the constitution.[11] They are constrained by the language of the constitution and subsequent case law, but the generality of the words and the conflicting images of federalism generated by them still leaves much scope for judicial creativity. Inevitably, judges are guided, in part, by their own image of the needs and values of the Canadian federal system: concerns for effectiveness in public policy, for externalities that might flow from provincial jurisdiction, for the symbolism of certain allocations, and for the effect on particular aspirations of the national or provincially based community.[12]

The result of judicial review, first through the Privy Council and since 1949 through the Supreme Court of Canada,[13] has been a rich jurisprudence that embellishes the general words of the constitution, often in ways different from that contemplated by some of the framers. For example, the apparently unrestricted federal power to legislate with regard to 'trade and commerce' was narrowed in early cases to interprovincial and international trade and commerce, leaving 'intraprovincial trade' to the provinces under the property and civil rights power.[14] The 'peace, order and good government' clause has been interpreted to encompass three functions: a residual power (allowing the federal government to deal with matters not covered by the heads of power set out in the constitution), an emergency power, and a 'national dimensions' power, that allows parliament to deal with matters that have taken on national significance, even if these matters were once within provincial jurisdiction.[15]

Judicial review has also been partly responsible for the erosion of 'watertight compartments,' although not without some early resistance in the Privy Council. Nevertheless, even that body recognized in its early interpretations of the constitution that many subjects of public policy did not fit neatly into only one category of legislative power, despite the apparent desire for tidiness espoused by the Fathers of Confederation; inevitably, there were 'double aspects' to the subjects covered by many laws.[16] Increasingly, overlapping jurisdiction became the norm in recognition of the interdependence of governments.[17]

While the courts developed doctrinal principles to guide in the interpretation of the constitution, it would be misleading to suggest that they adopted one approach for all time. They have applied their jurisprudence creatively, evolving new doctrines at different periods in the life of the country, allowing periods of greater and lesser centralization. Thus, the restriction of the federal trade and commerce power to international and interprovincial trade has been relaxed somewhat with the use of the 'necessarily incidental doctrine' that allows some regulation of intraprovincial activity.[18] More important, potentially, is the development of the 'general regulation of trade' doctrine, used to uphold the federal competition law.[19]

Judicial interpretation not only altered the distribution of powers between the two levels of government, but also affected the operations of the federal system and relations between governments through the courts' approach to the constitutionality of various instruments of public policy. Most important was their hands-off view of the federal taxation and spending powers. Under the constitution, the federal power to tax in s. 91(3) of the *Constitution Act, 1867* is unrestricted, and the courts generally do not question the policy reasons for particular tax deductions, credits, and exemptions, even though such measures can influence policy in areas that are otherwise within provincial jurisdiction.[20]

Coupled with this broad revenue generating capacity is the federal power to spend, even within areas of provincial jurisdiction and with conditions attached. The spending power has been a key tool for the federal government to influence policy in areas within provincial jurisdiction – most obviously, social assistance, post-secondary education, and healthcare. While the provinces have legislative jurisdiction over these areas, their revenue raising capacities have not kept pace with their legislative responsibilities, especially in the 'have less' provinces. This gap has been bridged by the federal government's stepping in with the spending power, sometimes placing conditions on the use of the funds, sometimes leaving the dispensation largely to provincial discretion. In addition, the spending power has been used extensively to fund grants to individuals and institutions in areas that would otherwise be, at least in part, within provincial legislative jurisdiction, such as training or culture.[21]

While the legality of this power has never been challenged directly before the Supreme Court of Canada, the Alberta Court of Appeal upheld it in *Winterhaven Stables*, noting that federal spending in provincial areas of jurisdiction was constitutional, provided that the spending was not, in substance, really regulation in provincial field of jurisdiction.[22] The Supreme Court of Canada indirectly supported the power in the *YMHA* case.[23] The results are not surprising: in practical terms, the power is crucial to the functioning of the Canadian federal system. In support of this permissive attitude towards the spending power, the judges have distinguished between the coercive elements in regulation and the lack of coercion associated with spending.[24]

In sum, judicial interpretation has shaped the content of the constitution, both through direct interpretation and through approval of devices or mechanisms which allow political institutions to respond to the changing needs of the country. The latter go beyond taxation and spending to include administrative delegation,[25] and a restricted view of what constitutes paramountcy or conflict between federal and provincial laws.[26] Some have argued that one should not overestimate the role of judicial review in the life of a federal system; equally, it is important not to underestimate its impact in the allocation of jurisdiction and bargaining power in intergovernmental relations.[27]

With the *Charter of Rights* has come a new instrument through which the courts may constrain the actions of federal and provincial governments. Once again, the judges have embarked on a creative process in interpreting the document and assessing its place in a constitution also built on principles of parliamentary government and federalism.

Rights Protection and Federalism

While federalism and protection of rights can be seen as distinct elements of the constitution, serving different ends, they are, in fact, interdependent in a number of ways. True, federalism seems to emphasize the interaction of territorially defined units of government, while bills of rights are designed to protect individuals or groups from certain actions by both levels of government. But federalism, too, can serve as a vehicle to protect the autonomy of a national minority group which constitutes a majority within a territorial unit (as in the case of French-speaking Canadians in Quebec).

Similarly, a bill of rights, while usually seen as a brake on governments in the interests of individuals and minorities, will be shaped by the history of and diversity within a particular federal system, both in its initial content and subsequent interpretation. This has clearly been the Canadian experience. One reason for the entrenchment of the *Charter of Rights* was to correct what many felt was a serious flaw in the constitution, the lack of protection for individual rights. However, other reasons for entrenchment were more closely entwined with federalism. Indeed, a major motivation of Prime Minister Trudeau and his government, in pushing for the Charter, was a desire to curtail aggressive 'province-building' activity and rhetoric throughout the 1970s, not only in Quebec, but also in Alberta, Saskatchewan, and Newfoundland. The Charter provided a possible vehicle to counter the centrifugal force of province-building. Ideally, it would act as a focal point for national identity, since citizens across the country would share the same rights, safeguarded by a national institution, the Supreme Court of Canada.[28] In addition, certain rights were specifically drafted to address particular problems in the federal system. The guarantee of interprovincial mobility rights in s. 6 was an effort to check provincial discrimination against non-residents, especially in employment,[29] while the minority language education rights in s. 23 were intended to curb Quebec's restrictions on English language education and to promote a pan-Canadian vision of bilingualism.

In retrospect, the Charter has had an immense impact on Canadian life and law, although not exactly in the ways desired by the Trudeau government. The legal impact has been significant, for the courts have been much more activist than many would have contemplated in 1982, especially given the experience under the *Canadian Bill of Rights*.[30] While some decry an apparent trend towards conservatism in the Court in recent years, the judges continue to use the Charter to constrain government activity in important ways, and in so doing, they are developing a distinctively Canadian jurisprudence of rights.[31]

The Canadian Charter begins with a general limitation clause in s. 1, stating that the rights and freedoms guaranteed in it are subject to such 'reasonable limits prescribed by law as can be demonstrably justified in a free and democratic society.'[32] The rights subsequently set out include a range of civil and political rights, including an expansive right to equality in s. 15, as well as some specifically Canadian provisions dealing with the use of the English and French languages.[33]

In interpreting the Charter, the judges have had to assume a creative role, in some ways similar to their work in interpreting the distribution of powers, but without a rich jurisprudence to guide them in their first attempts. Not surprisingly, this has generated a vigorous debate about appropriate methods of interpretation, especially in regard to the issue of reasonable limits on Charter rights.[34] The Supreme Court set out the approach to be used early on in *Oakes*, requiring courts to consider both the importance of the government's objective in limiting rights and the proportionality between the means used and the ends sought.[35] One issue that remained unclear was the degree to which the courts would be sympathetic to arguments that provincial laws failed to meet the *Oakes* test because they varied from laws in other provinces or at the federal level. Inevitably, courts in a federal system must decide the degree to which diversity across jurisdictions is a value to be recognized or preserved in the interpretation of rights.

Another related problem arises when the interests of different groups conflict, especially when one group is a minority within a province (such as the anglophones or Aboriginal groups in Quebec), and it challenges actions taken by the majority group within the territory, especially when that majority feels itself a minority in a broader context.[36] The rights claim will often be seen by the governing majority as a threat to their autonomy and their group rights that the federal system was meant to safeguard.

It can be argued that both consideration of diversity and solicitude for the majority's interests are inappropriate, for reasons explored more fully in the following section of this chapter.[37] Nevertheless, concerns about the federal system and the importance of collective interests have inevitably crept into some Charter cases. For example, the Supreme Court has relaxed the *Oakes* test, recognizing that the 'least restrictive alternative' aspect of the proportionality criterion under s. 1 was too rigid. Since Charter rights like freedom of expression and religion have been very broadly interpreted, the Court understood that there could be a range of justifiable limits on those rights under s. 1 consistent with Charter values and Canadian traditions.[38] Moreover, the Court has suggested that there should be greater judicial deference in cases where the state mediates among competing interests, especially among vulnerable groups, than there should be in the legal rights area, where the individual is often in conflict with the state.[39] Yet despite this recognition that there can be a wide range of reasonable limits on rights, the Court also holds that there is a core of rights which is universal and which must not vary from province to province, most obviously in the application of some of the legal rights in the criminal process.

In a few cases decided by the Supreme Court of Canada there has been explicit mention of the values of federalism, as in *R. v. S.*, an equality rights case, where Dickson C.J., for the Court, expressly noted the value of diversity, even within the criminal justice system (an area of federal jurisdiction).[40] At other times, there is no express reference to federalism, but the impact of an interpretation of s. 1, leaving significant room for legislative variation, has the effect of preserving the diversity in public policy across jurisdictions that federalism values.

Overall, the Supreme Court's Charter jurisprudence has not resulted in the significant centralization of power that some had predicted. Nevertheless, the Charter has been a useful legal tool to defend minorities, especially those linguistic minorities for whom Prime Minister Trudeau felt special concern. The Court has been generous in its interpretation of minority language education rights in s. 23[41], and it did strike down Quebec's language laws restricting the use of English on signs and in firm names.[42] However, in doing so, the Court also acknowledged, under s. 1, that Quebec had a legitimate interest in promoting an image of the '"visage linguistique" of Quebec [that] would reflect the predominance of the French language.' The Court's quarrel was with the proportionality of the legislation, particularly the outright ban on the display of other languages, not the desire of the French-speaking majority in the province to preserve and promote its language.[43]

In sum, the interaction of federalism and the *Charter of Rights* is complex, and the proper values to be employed in the interpretation of rights are the subject of vigorous and ongoing debate. Inevitably, then, the Charter played a significant role in efforts at constitutional reform of the federal system.

The Charter, Federalism, and Constitutional Reform

Since the 1960s, the existing constitutional order has been subject to constant challenges, most consistently from Quebec, where many nationalists argue for some form of sovereignty-association with Canada, while many federalists call for decentralization of powers, most particularly through constraints on the federal government's spending power. To date, successful efforts at renewal have not responded to Quebec's demands. The only constitutional amendment to the distribution of powers in that thirty-year period dealt with natural resources, in the form of a new s. 92A, added to the *Constitution Act, 1867* to win the support of the Western provinces for the 1982 constitutional amendment package.

Other significant constitutional changes in the 1982 package included a domestic amending formula for the constitution and the entrenchment of the *Canadian Charter of Rights and Freedoms* just described. While welcomed by many, the changes came about despite the opposition of the Quebec government, with the result that they have been portrayed as inimical to that province's interests. The most obvious sources of grievance lay in the termination of Quebec's historic veto in the amending process and the Charter's constraints on provincial legislative action, especially in regard to language policy designed to protect the primacy of French.[44]

A major effort to redress this feeling of rejection and, in the words of Prime Minister Mulroney, 'to bring Quebec back into the constitutional family,' was the 1987 Meech Lake Accord, a proposed constitutional amendment that tried to respond to five key demands from Quebec.[45] The failure to have it approved by the constitutional deadline of 23 June 1990 was seen as a further rejection in Quebec, despite the fact that the Accord received approval of the legislatures of eight provinces with over 90 per cent of the population.

A new constitutional round then began. In January of 1991, the constitutional committee of the Quebec Liberal Party issued a report demanding a drastic realignment of the distribution of powers in the Canadian federal system. Twenty-two powers were listed as ones that should be exclusively provincial, while only four powers were to be left exclusively federal (defence, interprovincial equalization, customs and tariffs, and currency and common debt).[46] Shortly thereafter, the Bélanger-Campeau Commission, a committee of legislators and representatives of various interests, reported, with the key recommendations that two committees be established, one to consider 'binding offers' from Canada and the other to consider sovereignty, and that a referendum on sovereignty be held by 26 October 1992.[47]

These demands from Quebec set in motion a new effort at constitutional amendment. A federal set of proposals was issued in September 1991.[48] While Quebec's agenda was clearly the catalyst for reform, the negotiations were constantly described as the 'Canada round,' in an effort to emphasize that it was not only Quebec's interests that were being considered, but also those of Aboriginal peoples, the smaller provinces seeking Senate reform, and those seeking a realignment of the distribution of powers to respond to new pressures. Following an intense debate over several months, the Charlottetown Agreement was reached by first ministers and the leaders of the four major Aboriginal associations in August 1992. It contained a complex set of proposed constitutional amendments, subsequently rejected in the national referendum on 26 October 1992.

Much has been and will be written about the Meech Lake and Charlottetown rounds. In the remainder of this chapter, I focus on how the Charter and attitudes towards the courts influenced the course of debate. I start from the premise that the Charter has had important symbolic, as well as legal effects on the Canadian constitutional order. It has reinforced the political consciousness of certain groups, described by Alan Cairns as 'constitutional minoritarians' – that is, groups who are minorities or, in the case of women, a slim majority, but like the other minorities disadvantaged by the operation of the political system.[49] The Charter has provided members of these groups with a new tool to wield in the policy process, through litigation or the prospect thereof. As well, the lobbying effort prior to 1982, which led to the inclusion of a series of equality provisions much more elaborate than those desired by governments, constituted an important consciousness-raising exercise, as well as a training ground for further political action.[50]

But well beyond those groups the Charter has had an important impact. It is a potent symbol of the value of rights in Canadian society (although there is some disagreement whether the Charter protects only individual rights, or collective rights as well). As such, it has an important influence in policy debates, both with regard to process and substance, often reorienting discussion around non-territorial identities.[51] The remainder of this chapter looks at the impact of the Charter on the constitutional reform agenda and debate.

Rights Talk

Post-Charter, the language of rights has infiltrated constitutional reform discussions about government powers and appropriate institutions, most notably in the debate about the Canadian social and economic union.[52] The initial reform proposals put forward by the federal government in 1991 recommended a common market clause to safeguard the freedom of movement of persons, capital, products, and services across provincial and territorial boundaries, the aim being to limit damaging non-tariff barriers within the country.[53]

This prompted others to argue for inclusion of a 'social charter' or 'social covenant' that would recognize certain positive social and economic rights in the constitution, such as a right to adequate housing, medical care, education, and other items.[54] One of its functions would be to constrain the free market emphasis of the proposed mobility clause (and, it was hoped, provide a cushion against the effects of the Free Trade Agreement with the United States and other international trade instruments). As well, it could provide an instrument to counter federal government efforts at retrenchment in social policy. Still others saw a social charter as a new legal tool to use to promote social justice and redistribution in Canadian society.

Such proposals generate serious theoretical and institutional questions, although too often such issues have not been adequately confronted in a country in which constitutional reform has been characterized by pragmatism more than principle. Should the constitution emphasize the *empowerment* of governments in the distribution of powers, leaving it to the political process to determine the content of social and economic policy in accordance with the needs and demands of the time, or should it enshrine a particular social or economic vision? If new rights are to be included in the constitution, how should they operate in a federal system? For example, the definition of a non-tariff barrier is potentially wide-ranging and, thus, potentially at odds with the concept of federalism which accepts a degree of diversity in public policy (and, therefore, consequent burdens on mobility).[55] Similarly, how would a social charter, especially one including positive rights, work in a federation where federal and provincial governments share responsibility for social policy – the former often intervening only through the spending power, while the provinces have primary constitutional responsibility, but not necessarily the funds to act?

Ultimately, the Charlottetown Agreement proposed only a statement of principles to which governments aspired in the Canadian social and economic union, to be monitored by a mechanism to be established through federal-provincial negotiations. Thus, there was some shift from the rights focus of early discussions, but not necessarily a return to total pragmatism. At least there was an agreement on broad statements of collective aspirations, although governments were still left with the ultimate authority to work out the policy tradeoffs necessary in meeting them.

Fear of Judicial Activism

With proposals for entrenchment of further rights came a debate about the appropriate institutions to enforce those rights. While some of the social charter activists argued for judicial enforcement of the new charter, most (including the Ontario provincial government which had launched the concept) were vigorously opposed. In part because of experience with judicial activism under the existing Charter, there were misgivings about the courts' suitability for these new roles and a preference for a non-judicial (and preferably political) monitor, such as a reformed Senate or a council of experts.

Distrust of courts emerged in other areas as well. Rather than embark on a detailed redesign of the distribution of powers, as initially demanded by Quebec, the debate focused on a very modest set of powers for reallocation. More importantly, the emphasis was on intergovernmental agreements, which could be used to define federal and provincial responsibilities in these and other areas, sometimes with legislative oversight. While there would undoubtedly be arguments by lawyers about the meaning of the terms describing these mechanisms and the ongoing scope of federal and provincial powers, it could be expected that most of this debate would occur outside the courts in intergovernmental negotiations.[56]

The final area in which fear of courts emerged was in relation to the recognition of the inherent right to Aboriginal self-government. Governments were generally opposed to making such a right immediately justiciable, preferring a negotiation route to the achievement of self-government. Indeed, the initial federal proposals would have postponed justiciability for ten years. However, efforts to circumscribe the judicial role ultimately were less successful than governments might have hoped, since, had the Charlottetown Agreement succeeded, there would likely have been much litigation over the interrelationship between the federal, provincial, and Aboriginal governments, about the interpretation of the *Charter of Rights* when applied to self-governments, and the use of the notwithstanding clause.[57]

Clearly, there are lessons here. Governments often wish to keep the courts out of constitutional issues, but they can never remove courts completely, for the addition of new words to a constitution inevitably generates debates about their meaning and their interaction with existing parts of the document, while relaxed rules of standing for constitutional challenges in recent years have given citizens and interest-groups many more opportunities to litigate.

The Primacy of the Charter

The growing rights consciousness has brought with it frequent challenges to the predominance of federalism in constitutional discourse, and a constant vigilance to ensure that there is no erosion of the principles set out in the Charter. Unfortunately, there is still little consensus about what the Charter says, which can make it difficult to determine whether there has been encroachment on Charter rights.

This lack of consensus was most clearly demonstrated by the controversy surrounding the distinct society clause proposed in the Meech Lake Accord, which would have added a new provision to s. 2 of the *Constitution Act, 1867* requiring that the constitution be interpreted so as to recognize the fundamental characteristics that Quebec is a distinct society and that there are two constitutionally recognized linguistic groups in Canada. Women's groups in English-speaking Canada, in particular, argued strongly that the clause posed a threat to women's equality under the Charter. Others opposed it because the recognition of the interests of one group seemed to threaten their vision of a uniform system of individual rights in Canada.[58] Still others, such as the representatives of Aboriginal peoples, quarrelled not with group rights per se, but with the limited number of groups recognized. Yet many others, for reasons explored more fully below, argued that the clause did not change the way in which the Supreme Court was already interpreting the Charter or add new restrictions to rights.

A similar debate emerged in relation to the proposed Canada clause of the Charlottetown Agreement. Again, s. 2 of the *Constitution Act, 1867* would have been amended, this time to set out a long list of fundamental characteristics to use in the interpretation of the constitution, again including Quebec's distinct society and linguistic duality, but also, among others, gender, racial, and ethnic equality and the recognition of individual and collective rights. Again, there was a heated debate about the interpretation of this clause, with some arguing that it threatened to change the Charter's guarantees substantially: first, by creating a hierarchy of principles to use in its interpretation;[59] second, by derogating from individual rights in favour of groups; and third, by conferring new powers on governments.[60]

Others, as in the Meech Lake round, profoundly disagreed, arguing that the fundamental characteristics clause set out principles which the courts could – indeed, already did – take into account in interpreting the scope of reasonable limits under the Charter.[61] Moreover, they argued that the Charter already recognized both individual and group rights (e.g., in guarantees of Aboriginal and language rights and the affirmation of multiculturalism). Rather than adding new principles or creating a hierarchy, the clause required judges to consider these items (often the subject of more precise reference elsewhere in the constitution), in determining reasonable limits on rights. While the words of a constitutional text clearly matter, the judicial task is, nevertheless, far from a minute mechanical examination of which principle comes first in the clause or document. It requires a balancing of many individual and collective interests in the context of a particular case, drawing on the whole text, as well as history and the values of a particular society at a particular point in time, as experience with the 1867 *Constitution Act* has shown.

A similar debate about potential encroachment on the Charter emerged with regard to the guarantee of the inherent right to Aboriginal self-government. While it was proposed that those governments would be subject to the Charter, they would have had the power to override the rights in accordance with s. 33, although with such modifications 'consistent with the purposes of the requirements of that section, as are appropriate to the circumstances of the Aboriginal peoples concerned.' This power to override, plus the failure to include Aboriginal self-governments within the democratic rights provision in s. 3 (which guarantees the right to vote in federal and provincial elections), were attacked by some, including the Native Women's Association of Canada, as a serious derogation from the Charter.

Again, responses varied, turning in part on a debate about interpretive principles, which then influenced conclusions about whether there was an encroachment on the Charter. Some representatives of Aboriginal associations, especially within the Assembly of First Nations, argued that the Charter would inappropriately affect Aboriginal groups, because its individual orientation is inconsistent with Aboriginal beliefs in collective rights.[62] Others defended the proposed arrangement, arguing for a more nuanced and culturally sensitive interpretation of the proposal that could attempt to bridge some of the concerns of different groups. For many, it seemed inappropriate to impose the Charter's democratic rights provision, drawn from a tradition of Westminster-style parliamentary democracy, on Aboriginal groups seeking to develop or revive their own traditions of decision-making (often far more sensitive to individual interests, since decisions are often made by the consensus of the group[63]).

Moreover, the failure to apply s. 3 of the Charter would not have left the decision-making of Aboriginal governments unchecked by the Charter. Both in the application of the reasonable limits section and s. 33, courts were invited to determine whether the decision-making process was fair – whether to support arguments that a limitation on a right was reasonable in a free and democratic society (s. 1), or that the override in s. 33 had been exercised in a manner consistent with the purposes of that section. One would hope that judges applying the Charter would be sensitive to cultural differences, as some in the Supreme Court of Canada have been in recent cases.[64] However, the courts were never being asked to ignore the basic guarantees and principles of the Charter in this proposed structure, and they would be unlikely to do so.

I leave to another time a detailed examination of these arguments. My point here is the broader one about lessons for the constitutional reform process. The debate among the commentators on the proposed changes and their impact on the Charter revealed several things. First, there is an active debate among legal scholars and lawyers, in particular, about the meaning of the Charter and the way in which it should be interpreted. Specifically, there is deep division about whether the Charter does include group rights, whether s. 1 requires a balancing of individual and community interests, and the proper sources for interpreting Charter guarantees. Each observer has started from a set of premises and readings of judicial decisions, and sometimes the opinions reached cannot be said to be clearly right or wrong, in part because there is still so much uncertainty about the meaning of the Charter. As well, it is clear that individual judges bring different philosophies about methods of interpretation and the appropriate degree of activism, and this increases the uncertainty about the future. This inevitably creates confusion among the public and suggests that it will be extremely difficult to change the constitution in the future if there is any conceivable possibility that the Charter may be affected.

Indeed, we are faced with the dilemma that various groups opposed to proposed constitutional changes are often seeking a guarantee that the Charter or other parts of the constitution will not be interpreted in a manner inimical to their own interests. Yet history has taught us that there can be no absolute certainty – whether in respect of the constitution as it now stands or in relation to proposed new constitutional provisions – as long as judges have discretion in interpreting the words of the document.

Second, and perhaps ironically, the debate about the substance of the proposed reforms will not go away with the specific Charlottetown proposals, since many elements of the Canada clause will surface anyway in Charter litigation, usually under s. 1. The legitimacy of considering them and the weight to be accorded them will be the subject of ongoing debate about the degree to which rights do and should reflect a distinctive Canadian tradition of blending a concern for the individual with a recognition of the importance of community. My own reading of the decisions of the Supreme Court of Canada suggests that there is a distinctive jurisprudence emerging, which is sympathetic to the claims of various communities for recognition and protection.[65] At the same time, there is no doubt that the Court, while sympathetic to diversity, will also safeguard a core of rights which will have the same content throughout the nation. Nevertheless, the jurisprudence will be constantly vulnerable to attack by those who do not share the same set of interpretive principles and pluralist values that many of the judges espouse.

The third lesson from recent experience is a political one about the role of experts in society. While elites debated the *legal* meaning and impact of various constitutional proposals, that debate was not solely a neutral, apolitical exercise. This is partly because law and politics inevitably intersect in a debate about constitutional reform, whether in relation to the Charter or any other provision, since any exercise in legal interpretation requires value judgments and rests on certain premises about law and its meaning. This was evident in the debates about the distinct society clause and the Canada clause. Many of those who opposed the distinct society provisions or the Aboriginal right to self-government did so out of a strong sense of liberalism – that is, a faith in individual autonomy and an opposition to group rights and 'special' status.[66] Often, those who supported such clauses were more sympathetic to principles of communitarianism, based on their reading of Canadian history and/or commitments to pluralism. While the rights of the individual remained important to them, they also emphasized the importance of groups to individual identity and experience. Thus, their debates about the meaning of the Charter and the proposals were often grounded in different philosophic and political beliefs. However, many non-experts may not realize the underlying political values that overlap with the legal premises, making it important that experts engaged in public debate try to separate their arguments about what ought to be from what is, especially in their interpretations of the constitution, or, at least, that they be explicit about the values, premises, and political commitments they bring to their assessments.

Clearly, in any future efforts to reform the federal system, there are real risks associated with any measure that can be interpreted as touching the Charter. The complexity of Charter jurisprudence alone makes it difficult for the public to understand the nature of the debate about the implications of any proposal. The confusion inevitably generated becomes even greater if the public does not understand that the legal debate itself rests on profound disagreements about legal method, judicial interpretation, and the enduring values of the Canadian state.

Conclusion: Courts and Constitutions
The evolution of any constitution through judicial interpretation is a creative, albeit sometimes controversial exercise, as Canadian experience shows. The task becomes even more complex when a constitution historically dominated by principles of federalism and parliamentary supremacy is recast with the addition of a constitutional bill of rights, for new legal dilemmas emerge concerning the meaning of individual rights in a federal system, of universalism versus diversity, and the salience of group claims based on territory when weighed against those of minorities within those territories. Entrenchment not only changes the problems before the courts,

but affects political consciousness and activity as well, which is demonstrated in calls for institutional reform, including the restructuring of the courts and other processes for constitutional change.

Canadian federalism and the Charter have only latterly begun to work out their relationship. The recent efforts at constitutional reform indicate that this can be a difficult exercise. While those efforts failed to generate formal constitutional amendments, many of the contentious issues involving the Charter will not go away. The interface between federalism and the Charter, between individuals and groups, will emerge in future court cases. And while there is not yet a constitutional right to Aboriginal self-government, there are a number of self-government agreements in operation which will, at some point, bring forward for judicial consideration the determination of the proper balance between individual and group rights. A constitution is a living document which will inevitably change, and judicial interpretation will always be a creative component of that process.

Acknowledgments

I am grateful to Karen Knop and Richard Simeon for helpful comments on an earlier draft.

Notes

1 Canada has had two unsuccessful attempts at ratification of constitutional amendment packages in recent years: the 1987 Meech Lake Accord and the 1992 Charlottetown Agreement, rejected in a national referendum on 26 October 1992. Both are described below.

2 The leading textbook of constitutional law is P.W. Hogg, *Constitutional Law of Canada*, 3rd ed. (Toronto: Carswell 1992). A much briefer overview is found in K. Swinton, 'Federalism Under Fire: The Role of the Supreme Court of Canada,' *Law & Contemporary Problems* 55 (1992):121.

3 Section 91 sets out the exclusive federal powers, after introductory words that state the federal parliament has authority to legislate for 'the peace, order and good government of Canada.' These words are the basis for the federal residual power. Among the more important heads of federal power enumerated are trade and commerce (91(2)), criminal law (91(27)), and a number of powers relating to the economy, such as banking, interest, and copyrights. The provincial powers are set out in ss. 92 and 93 and include property and civil rights and education. The concurrent powers are agriculture and immigration (s. 95), and old age pensions and supplementary benefits (s. 94A), the latter added by a constitutional amendment.

4 Indeed, this has long been a strongly held view among many English-speaking Canadians. An historical treatment is found in A. Cairns, 'The Judicial Committee and Its Critics,' *Canadian Journal of Political Science* 4 (1971):301.

5 Sections 55-57 and 90 of the *Constitution Act, 1867*. These provisions, while still part of the law, have long fallen into disuse.

6 Section 93 of the *Constitution Act, 1867*. At the time of confederation, there were only four provinces, and the terms of union for the remaining six varied in certain ways. Provisions with different wording regarding denominational education were made for the provinces of Manitoba, Alberta, Saskatchewan, and Newfoundland as they entered confederation.

7 Section 133 of the *Constitution Act, 1867*. Similar provisions regarding language were extended to Manitoba on its entry into confederation (*Manitoba Act, 1870*, 33 Vict., c. 3, s. 23, confirmed by the *Constitution Act, 1871*).

8 J.R. Mallory, 'The Continuing Evolution of Canadian Constitutionalism,' in A. Cairns and C. Williams, eds., *Constitutionalism, Citizenship, and Society in Canada* (Toronto: University of Toronto Press 1985), 51 at 94.

9 Provincial laws were also open to attack on the basis that they were in conflict with a federal law and, therefore, should be held inoperative under the rule of federal paramountcy – a judicially created rule discussed below at note 26.

10 For example, is a law regulating dumping of wood waste in waters frequented by fish to be characterized as in relation to fisheries (federal jurisdiction) or the logging industry and pollution in a province (provincial jurisdiction)? See *Fowler v. R.* (1980), 113 D.L.R. (3d) 513 (S.C.C.).

11 The Court describes its role in similar words in *Reference re Language Rights Under the Manitoba Act, 1870* (1985), 19 D.L.R. (4th) 1 (S.C.C.) at 19-20.

12 I have discussed this at length in K. Swinton, *The Supreme Court and Canadian Federalism: The Laskin-Dickson Years* (Toronto: Carswell 1990).

13 The Privy Council was the final court of appeal for Canada until 1949, when the Supreme Court of Canada, until then an intermediate court of appeal, assumed the role of final court.

14 *Citizens' Insurance Co.* v. *Parsons* (1881-82), 7 A.C.96 (P.C.) at 113. The result of this case and its progeny was to confer jurisdiction on the provinces over many important economic activities and to curtail federal action in these areas to some degree – e.g., in relation to labour relations, competition, and product marketing and standards. Because of the doctrine of precedent, these cases have had a long-term impact on the jurisprudence, although the Supreme Court can overrule earlier case law and has done so.

15 *R.* v. *Crown Zellerbach Canada Ltd.* (1988), 49 D.L.R. (4th) 161 (S.C.C.) at 184. This case upheld federal jurisdiction over marine pollution, even within provincial boundaries, under the peace, order, and good government clause.

16 For example, while the federal government had the power to address the evils of intemperance, the provinces could still regulate the hours of establishments serving liquor (e.g., *Hodge* v. *R.* (1883-84), 9 A.C. 117 (P.C.)).

17 Technically, as pointed out by Beetz J. in *Bell Canada* v. *Quebec (Commission de la santé et de la sécurité du travail)* (1988), 51 D.L.R. (4th) 161 (S.C.C.), there are only three areas of 'concurrent' power (at 231). In fact, though, there is a great deal of overlapping law, with both governments dealing with matters such as business practices, securities, trust companies, and healthcare. There may be differences in the policy instruments available to each (for example, the federal government may have to use a criminal law form or tax measures to deal with certain matters, such as securities, while the other can regulate directly), but there is much overlap in policy and prescription – hence, 'concurrency' in lay

terms.

18 *Caloil Inc.* v. *A.G.Can. (No. 2)* (1971), 20 D.L.R. (3d) 472 (S.C.C.).

19 *General Motors of Canada Ltd.* v. *City National Leasing* (1989), 58 D.L.R. (4th) 255. Until this case, the federal government had relied on the criminal law power to legislate with regard to competition, which placed constraints on the type of remedies that it could employ. In particular, it had not been able to use civil remedies such as damages. The area of greatest doctrinal manoeuvre has been the interpretation of the federal residual power, the 'peace, order and good government' clause (above, note 15). While some welcome the flexibility these doctrines give to the distribution of powers, others, especially in Quebec, fear that the flexibility inclines in one direction only – towards greater powers for the federal government.

20 The Privy Council did strike down an unemployment insurance levy in *A.G.Can.* v. *A.G.Ont. (Unemployment Insurance Reference)*, [1937] A.C.207, on the ground that this was not a taxation measure, but a regulation similar to an insurance premium integral to a public insurance program and, therefore, beyond federal jurisdiction. The result was overturned by a constitutional amendment in 1940, making unemployment insurance a subject of federal jurisdiction (s. 91(2A)), while the courts subsequently have been loathe to find a tax measure unconstitutional (see for example, *Reader's Digest Association* v. *A.G.Can.* (1965), 59 D.L.R. (2d) 54 (Que. C.A.)).

21 A brief overview of the role of the spending power and some of the controversy surrounding its use is found in K. Banting, 'Federalism, Social Reform and the Spending Power,' *Canadian Public Policy Supplement* 14 (1988):S81.

22 *Winterhaven Stables Ltd.* v. *A.G.Can.* (1988), 53 D.L.R. (4th) 413 (Alta.C.A.) at 433.

23 *YMHA Jewish Community Centre of Winnipeg* v. *Brown* (1989), 59 D.L.R. (4th) 694 (S.C.C.) at 705-06.

24 This is not uncontroversial. See, for example, A. Petter, 'Meech Ado About Nothing? Federalism, Democracy and the Spending Power,' in K. Swinton and C. Rogerson, eds., *Competing Constitutional Visions: The Meech Lake Accord* (Toronto: Carswell 1988), 187; and A. Lajoie, 'The Federal Spending Power and Meech Lake,' in ibid., 175.

25 Generally, governments can delegate extensive powers as long as they employ the right tools, such as administrative delegation, conditional legislation, or incorporation of the law of another jurisdiction by reference (see, for example, *Coughlin* v. *Ontario Highway Transport Board*, [1968] S.C.R. 569.) In contrast to the sympathy for delegation, the Supreme Court has refused to find the federal government bound by intergovernmental agreements, holding that the doctrine of parliamentary supremacy allows parliament to change the terms of such agreements unilaterally (*Reference: re Canada Assistance Plan (B.C.)* (1991), 83 D.L.R. (4th) 297 (S.C.C.)).

26 Essentially, the Supreme Court allows both federal and provincial laws to operate so long as there is no express conflict (that is, an individual cannot obey one law without violating the other) (*Multiple Access Ltd.* v. *McCutcheon* (1982), 138 D.L.R. (3d) 1 (S.C.C.) at 23-4) or, more recently, a serious interference, by a provincial measure, with the operation of the federal law (*Bank of Montreal* v. *Hall* (1990), 65 D.L.R. (4th) 361 (S.C.C.) at 385: 'dual compliance will be impossible when

the application of the provincial law can fairly be said to frustrate Parliament's legislative purpose').

27 Patrick Monahan has downplayed the importance of judicial review in the Canadian federal system, because governments have generally been able to find a way around unfavourable court decisions (*Politics and the Constitution* (Toronto: Carswell 1987), 239-43). While he is correct to caution against assigning undue weight to the courts, it is important not to undervalue their role, for their decisions affect bargaining power in federal-provincial relations and require the use of certain policy instruments when others might be more suitable and effective. Moreover, some of the solutions to a court decision have been constitutional amendments – a not insignificant move, especially in light of the difficulty of formal constitutional change.

28 This is discussed in P. Russell, 'The Political Purposes of the Canadian Charter of Rights and Freedoms,' *Canadian Bar Review* 61 (1983):30 at 31-35; R. Knopff and F.L. Morton, 'Nation-Building and the Canadian Charter of Rights and Freedoms,' in Cairns and Williams, eds., *Constitutionalism, Citizenship and Society in Canada*, 133 at 144-50.

29 The federal government's objective had been a much stronger protection for the Canadian economic union, as demonstrated in its 'pink paper,' *Securing the Canadian Economic Union* (Ottawa: Minister of Supply and Services 1980).

30 Some assessment of the impact of the Charter is found in G. Beaudoin, ed., *The Charter Ten Years Later* (Cowansville: Blais 1992). Alan Cairns's article, 'Reflections on the Political Purposes of the Charter: The First Decade,' gives a useful perspective on the political impact (at 161). See also F.L. Morton, P.H. Russell, and M.J. Withey, 'The Supreme Court's First One Hundred Charter of Rights Decisions: A Statistical Analysis,' *Osgoode Hall Law Journal* 30 (1992):1.

31 The Charter has had its greatest impact in the criminal law area, both in matters of substance and procedure. Although some describe decisions upholding legislation as conservative, in fact some of the more important decisions of the Court are those which preserve what some would regard as progressive legislation – for example, *R. v. Keegstra* (1990), 61 C.C.C. (3d) 1 (S.C.C.) (hate propaganda law); *R. v. Butler* (1992), 89 D.L.R. (4th) 449 (S.C.C.) (obscenity law).

32 Thus, the model for the Charter is found in European and international instruments, which contain limitation provisions, rather than the American Bill of Rights, with its apparently absolute guarantees.

33 The content is as follows: s. 2, fundamental freedoms; ss. 3-5, democratic rights; s. 6, mobility rights; ss. 7-14, legal rights; s. 15, equality rights; ss. 16-23, language rights. There are also interpretive provisions giving special weight to Aboriginal rights (s. 25), multiculturalism (s. 27) and gender equality (s. 28).

34 For a sampling of this debate, see D. Beatty, *The Canadian Production of Constitutional Review: Talking Heads and the Supremes* (Toronto: Carswell 1990); L. Weinrib, 'The Supreme Court of Canada and Section 1 of the Charter,' *Supreme Court Law Review* 10 (1988):469; A.C. Hutchinson and A. Petter, 'Private Rights/Public Wrongs: The Liberal Lie of the Charter,' *University of Toronto Law Journal* 38 (1988):278; R.J. Sharpe, 'A Comment on David Beatty's "A Conservative's Court: The Politicization of Law,"' *University of Toronto Law Journal* 41 (1991):469.

35 *R.* v. *Oakes* (1986), 26 D.L.R. (4th) 200 at 227.

36 While the case of the French Canadians in Quebec comes first to mind, the debate about the application of the Charter to Aboriginal self-governments indicates that this problem can arise in other situations where there is tension between the interests of individuals and groups or between groups.

37 See below. Essentially, the arguments are based either on a belief in universalism (i.e., rights should not vary from province to province) or on a conception that the Charter protects individual rights, not those of groups.

38 *R.* v. *Edwards Books & Art Ltd.* (1986), 35 D.L.R. (4th) 1 (S.C.C.) at 44. See also *R.* v. *Downey* (1992), 90 D.L.R. (4th) 449 (S.C.C.) per Cory J. at 466: 'Yet the proportionality test can and must vary with the circumstances,' and at 468: 'the determination as to whether the extent of the infringement is proportional to the legislative objective involves a balancing of societal and individual interests.'

39 *Irwin Toy Ltd.* v. *A.G.Que.* (1989), 58 D.L.R. (4th) 577 (S.C.C.) at 625-6. The Court there upheld a law restricting the use of advertising directed to children and setting the age limit at those under thirteen years of age. Part of the attack rested on the argument that a lower age limit should have been used. The Court's rejection of the argument leaves legislatures with a wide discretion in deciding the appropriate group for protection.

40 *R.* v. *S.(S)* (1990), 77 C.R. (3d) 273 (S.C.C.) at 299: 'The division of powers not only permits different treatment based upon province of residence, it mandates and encourages geographical distinction.'

41 *A.G.Que.* v. *Quebec Association of Protestant School Boards* (1984), 10 D.L.R. (4th) 321; *Mahe* v. *Alberta* (1990), 68 D.L.R. (4th) 69 (S.C.C.). Both were cases interpreting the minority language education provision, s. 23. While I describe the Court's approach as positive, some members of linguistic minority groups disagree, pointing to the restrictive approach that the Court has taken to the interpretation of language guarantees. See, for example, the passage from Beetz J.'s reasons in *Société des Acadiens du NB Inc.* v. *Association of Parents for Fairness in Education, Grand Falls Dist. 50 Branch* (1986), 27 D.L.R. (4th) 406 at 425: 'This is not to say that language rights are cast in stone and should remain immune altogether from judicial interpretation. But, in my opinion, the courts should approach them with more restraint than they would in construing legal rights.' This followed a statement that 'unlike language rights which are based on political compromise, legal rights tend to be seminal in nature because they are rooted in principle.'

42 *Ford* v. *A.G. Que.* (1988), 54 D.L.R. (4th) 577 (S.C.C.).

43 Ibid., at 627-9. The result of the case was the exercise by Quebec of the power in s. 33 of the Charter to override the decision – that is, to implement the measure notwithstanding the Charter.

44 For a critique from a Quebec nationalist perspective see P. Fournier, *A Meech Lake Post-Mortem: Is Quebec Sovereignty Inevitable?* (Montreal: McGill-Queen's University Press 1991).

45 Those demands, registered in the famous 1986 Mont Gabriel speech, were: a veto on constitutional amendments, constitutional recognition of Quebec as a distinct society, constitutional assurance that Quebec would have three seats on the Supreme Court with a role in selection, constitutional recognition of

Quebec's role in immigration policy, and controls on the federal spending power in areas of provincial jurisdiction.

46 Quebec Liberal Party, *A Quebec Free to Choose* [Allaire Report] (Montreal 1991), 38.

47 Quebec, Commission on the Political and Constitutional Future of Quebec [Bélanger-Campeau], *Report* (Quebec 1991), 79-82.

48 Canada, *Shaping Canada's Future Together: Proposals* (Ottawa: Minister of Supply and Services 1991).

49 See, for example, A. Cairns, 'Constitutional Minoritarianism in Canada,' in R. Watts and D. Brown, eds., *Canada: The State of the Federation 1990* (Kingston: Institute of Intergovernmental Relations 1990), 71.

50 The process, which resulted in a stronger equality guarantee in s. 15, bolstered by a further commitment to gender equality in s. 28, is described in C. Hosek, 'Women and the Constitutional Process,' in K. Banting and R. Simeon, eds., *And No One Cheered: Federalism, Democracy and the Constitution Act* (Toronto: Methuen 1983), 280.

51 It is difficult to know how much of the talk about rights and citizen empowerment is Charter-driven in Canada and how much it is a reflection of similar forces in other countries that emphasize citizens' rights and the importance of group identities and claims to representation.

52 Rights concern also affected debates about the impact of various proposals on the Charter, the demands for participation by various groups in constitutional discussions, and the debate about guarantees of gender equality in the Senate. The impact on the Charter is discussed below.

53 See the federal proposals to amend s. 121 of the constitution, above, note 48, p. 43.

54 The moving force behind this proposal was the Ontario government, which issued a paper, *A Canadian Social Charter: Making Our Shared Values Stronger* (Toronto: Ministry of Intergovernmental Affairs 1991).

55 See, for example, the debate about barriers in J.R.S. Prichard with J. Benedickson, 'Securing the Canadian Economic Union: Federalism and Internal Barriers to Trade,' in M. Trebilcock, J.R.S. Prichard, T. Courchene, and J. Whalley, eds., *Federalism and the Canadian Economic Union* (Toronto: Ontario Economic Council 1983), 3.

56 I have argued elsewhere that the approach builds on the tradition of executive federalism in Canada. See K. Swinton, 'Packaging Powers,' in D. Brown and R. Young, eds., *Canada: The State of the Federation 1992* (Kingston: Institute of Intergovernmental Relations 1992), 145.

57 Section 33 of the Charter permits federal and provincial legislatures to override certain rights in accordance with certain conditions. This clause would have applied to Aboriginal self-governments.

58 There is much literature on this debate. For an early exchange of the arguments, see K. Swinton and C. Rogerson, eds., *Competing Constitutional Visions: The Meech Lake Accord* (Toronto: Carswell 1988).

59 This argument rested in part on the order in which the characteristics were set out and the fact that many sub-clauses stated that Canadians were committed to certain objectives, but 'Canadians and their governments' were committed to

linguistic duality.

60 This argument rested on s. 2(4) which stated that the section did not derogate from existing legislative powers. This was said to be a sign that s. 2(1), the fundamental characteristics clause, increased governments' powers by expanding the range of defences under the Charter. See, for example, Lorraine Weinrib, 'Legal Analysis of Draft Legal Text,' (mimeo, 21 October 1992), 6.

61 See, for example, *Ford*, above, note 42.

62 See, for example, M.E. Turpel, 'Aboriginal Peoples and the Canadian Charter: Interpretive Monopolies, Cultural Differences,' *Human Rights Year Book* 6 (1989-90):3.

63 M. Boldt and J.A. Long, 'Tribal Philosophies and the Canadian Charter of Rights and Freedoms,' in M. Boldt and J.A. Long, eds., *The Quest for Justice: Aboriginal Peoples and Aboriginal Rights* (Toronto: University of Toronto Press 1985), 165 at 169.

64 For an example in the Supreme Court of Canada, see *R. v. Sioui* (1990), 70 D.L.R. (4th) 427 (treaty interpretation).

65 This is true in *Keegstra*, above, note 31; *Ford*, above, note 42; and Aboriginal rights cases such as *Sioui*, above, note 64; and *R. v. Sparrow* (1990), 70 D.L.R. (4th) 385 (S.C.C.).

66 See, for example, D. Coyne and R. Howse, *No Deal* (Hull: Voyageur Publishing 1992), especially Chapter 1.

19

Central and Eastern European Federations: Communist Theory and Practice
Viktor Knapp

Introduction

The failure of the Soviet, Yugoslav, and Czechoslovak federations cannot be understood properly without some knowledge of the theory and practice of socialist federalism in Central and Eastern Europe. From a broader perspective, this background may provide the Western student of federalism with new insight into the influence of ideology and politics on the federal idea.

This chapter outlines two frameworks for classifying and analyzing federal states, and uses these frameworks to discuss the theory and practice of the Central and Eastern European socialist federations (CEE federations). It groups federations first by geopolitical region and situates the CEE federations within one of the three major groups. The chapter classifies federations second by historical origin – how and why the federation came into being – and analyzes the CEE federations in this light. Having located the CEE federations within these geopolitical and historical frameworks, the chapter then compares them to those of other geopolitical regions. Finally, the chapter discusses the similarities and differences between the CEE federations themselves.

Federations Classified by Geopolitical Region

Federations can be broken down geopolitically into three large groups:
(1) American, with its prototype the USA, which served as a model for the formation of federations in South and Central America and Canada
(2) Western European, the prototype of which is the Swiss federation, which naturally did not exert as much influence in Europe as the US federation did on the American continent, the era of federations in Europe having come only after the Second World War
(3) Central and Eastern European, which will form the subject of this chapter.
   Apart from these basic geopolitical regions, which are discussed in this

volume, there are federations in other regions. These federations have some unique features and some features common to all federations. The most important of these federations are Australia, whose genesis resembles that of the Canadian federation, and India and Nigeria, which are based partly on ethnic elements or tribal elements and which suffered or still suffer from the political problems specific to ethnically based federations.

The Central and Eastern European Geopolitical Region
The geographic region of Central and Eastern Europe comprises the federations of Austria and the former Soviet Union and Czechoslovakia. This geographic demarcation, however, does not lend itself to reasonable abstraction and differentiation. The Central and Eastern European geopolitical region is a political rather than a geographic area. It would be erroneous to include Austria which, in spite of its position at the very centre of Europe, clearly belongs to the Western European region. On the other hand, the former Yugoslavia, although it was a southern European state and a considerable distance from Central or Eastern Europe, is often included in the Central and Eastern European region. Politically, however, the Yugoslav interpretation of the Marxist concept of the state differed considerably from the Soviet interpretation adopted by other formerly socialist countries and was not concerned with the concept of federation as the means of solving the national problem.

The Central and Eastern European federations were, thus, defined by their political character and theoretical basis, rather than by their geographical position. Although both of these criteria have been consigned to history by the political changes dating from the end of the eighties, in particular the collapse of Soviet Union and the disintegration of Yugoslavia, they have, nevertheless, left their traces on the present. All three of the former federations of this region are endeavouring to detach themselves from this geopolitical region and to 'return to Europe' or 'enter Europe.' Despite these aspirations, they are still linked by their history and by the need to find methods and forms of overcoming it. And it is the very necessity of overcoming this common history that constitutes the political reason for the persistence of a specific Central and Eastern European geopolitical region.

The Central and Eastern European geopolitical region is broader than the three above-mentioned countries. It also includes Poland, the former German Democratic Republic, Bulgaria, Hungary, and Romania, as well as Albania and the newly independent states (or successor states) of the former Soviet Union, Czechoslovakia, and Yugoslavia.

As far as federations are concerned, however, the Central and Eastern European region consists of the former socialist federations, which we shall call the 'CEE federations.' At present, this denomination has a double meaning. It concerns both the former socialist federations before the political upheaval and these same states as transformed into a number of successor states by the collapse of communism. For the sake of brevity we shall not distinguish between these two meanings.

Federations Classified by Historical Origin

Historically, federations originated in various ways. Some originated synthetically, that is, through the association of several states or self-governing territories to form a federal state (federation). This was the case particularly with the oldest federations: the Swiss federation (then confederation), the US federation, and the Soviet federation after 1922. Others originated analytically, that is, by the internal division of an initially unitary or undivided state to form a federation. As far as contemporary European federations are concerned, this process occurred after the Second World War in the Federal Republic of Germany (and after the unification of Germany, in the former German Democratic Republic as well), Austria, and then in Czechoslovakia and Belgium.

The political motives associated with the historical origins of federations are diverse and are also manifest in the contemporary internal organization of federations. Initially federations had the character of alliances, that is, groupings of diverse states or self-governing territories into units that were politically, militarily, and possibly also economically stronger. This was typical of the oldest federations, Switzerland and the United States.

Another important political motive was the solution of the national problem in multinational states or states which had arisen from the association of different ethnic groups in a common state.

Some federations were formed by the amalgamation of historical provinces or colonies of a certain state and their reconstitution as a federal state. Last but not least, some federations originated in administrative decentralization or the decentralization of state power.

There are also federations of mixed character whose internal organization shows the application of more than one of the above-mentioned principles. By way of example we can mention Canada; the structure of Canada corresponds more or less to historical territories, yet the ethnic element comes strongly to the fore in the province of Quebec. Another example is the Federal Republic of Germany, whose member *Länder* partly correspond to historical geopolitical units (for example, Bavaria, Saxony) and were partly constituted anew.

In the CEE federations the ethnic factor represents both the principal and decisive political motive for and the common denominator in their origin.

That does not mean, however, that the CEE federations are the only plurinational or multinational federations. There are others, but in these other federations the significance of the ethnic factor is different. A situation similar to that in the CEE federations exists in Belgium, where the plurinational character of the country has been the principal and decisive motive for the transformation of the formerly unitary state into a federation. In contrast, in states such as Switzerland and Canada, the ethnic factor, while of some importance, was not the decisive motive for the origin of the federation, and federalism in these countries was not used to solve the nationality problem. Another multinational federation, the USA, came into being without any regard to the ethnic structure of the population of the country, and its internal organization has been completely independent of its ethnic structure.

Let us add that, on the one hand, there are federations where the ethnic problem does not exist at all (for example, the Federal Republic of Germany) and on the other hand, there are plurinational or multinational unitary states in which the ethnic problem was solved differently, for example, by regional organization or legislation on ethnic minorities.

History and Theory of the CEE Federations

In order to understand better the present-day problems of the CEE federations, let us describe briefly their history and the theory of their social function.

Two of the CEE federations originated by means of the above-mentioned 'analytical' method (Soviet Union and Czechoslovakia), combined with the 'synthetic' method in the former Soviet Union after 1922, and one by the 'synthetic' method (Yugoslavia).

The analytical element in the origin of these federations lies in the fact that the original states in the territories in which the federations (Russia, Czechoslovakia) arose were generally unitary states. A particular feature of this historical process is the fact that the federations did not originate through the simple decomposition of previous states. Rather these states were first destroyed by revolution, and new states of a new social type and new federal form were then established on their territories. Yugoslavia, like Czechoslovakia, arose from the ruins of the Austro-Hungarian monarchy; as a federation, however, it came into being 'synthetically,' as an amalgamation of the former kingdoms of Serbia and Montenegro and some Austro-Hungarian provinces.

The original federalization of Russia took place in a rather confused revolutionary situation which, due to civil war and foreign intervention, became even more confused shortly thereafter. Federalization first took place in part of the territory of the former Russian Empire – the part populated mostly by the Russian nation. Thus the Russian Socialist Federative Soviet Republic (subsequently the Russian Soviet Federative Socialist Republic) emerged as the kernel of the future Soviet Union. This federalization first took place immediately after the October Revolution in 1917 through the Declaration of the Rights of Nations of 15 November 1917, which had the character of a political declaration. The Declaration of the Rights of the Working and Exploited People of 25 January 1918,[1] adopted by the Third All-Russian Congress of the Soviets, in addition to being a political declaration, served as the first constitution of Soviet Russia.

In article 1 of the Declaration of the Rights of the Working and Exploited People, Russia was proclaimed a republic of soviets (councils) of workers, soldiers, and peasants' deputies, while it was expressly stipulated that the Russian Soviet Republic is established on the basis of a free union of free nations, as a federation of Soviet national republics. An almost identical formulation can be found in the resolution of 28 January 1918 of the same Congress of the Soviets, 'On the Federal Authorities of the Russian Republic,' which laid the foundations for the central authorities of the then federal state power and state administration.

The Russian Socialist Federative Soviet Republic (RSFSR) was later joined by other Soviet republics[2] that arose on the territory of the former imperial Russia. By the treaty of 30 December 1922,[3] these republics associated themselves with the RSFSR to form the Union of Soviet Socialist Republics (USSR). That Union began as a federation of four member states (two of which were themselves denominated as federations): the Russian Socialist Federative Soviet Republic, the Ukrainian Socialist Soviet Republic, the Belorussian Socialist Soviet Republic, and the Transcaucasian Socialist Federative Soviet Republic (what would later become the Soviet Socialist Republics of Georgia, Azerbaijan, and Armenia). Other Soviet republics subsequently joined the Union of Soviet Socialist Republics, resulting in a Union with fifteen member states.

Yugoslavia[4] was established in 1918 as the Kingdom of Serbs, Croats, and Slovenes, which in 1929 adopted the official name of the Kingdom of Yugoslavia. It was a constitutional monarchy. The origin of socialist federation in Yugoslavia coincided with the revolutionary renewal of the Yugoslav state. The first Yugoslav constitution which declared the establishment of the Yugoslav federation, was the Constitution of 31 January 1946 of the then Federative People's Republic of Yugoslavia (FNRY).

Czechoslovakia at first remained a unitary state even after the communist take over in 1948. The Constitution of 1948 afforded the Slovak people some autonomy but retained the unitary character of the Czechoslovak state. This character was also retained in the Constitution of 1960. It was not until the adoption of the Constitutional Act on Czechoslovak Federation of 1968,[5] which came into force on 1 January 1969, that Czechoslovakia was transformed into a federal state. In contradistinction to the multinational federations of the USSR and Yugoslavia, the Czechoslovak federation was a federation of only two, to quote the law, 'autonomous, sovereign nations,' the Czechs and the Slovaks. Some of the specific features of the federal system of Czechoslovakia arose from the bipartite character of the Czechoslovak federation.

The first of these federations was the Soviet Union (or, initially, Soviet Russia), whose federal structure became more or less the model for the creation of further socialist federations.

The theoretical foundations of the Soviet federation were laid down by V.I. Lenin.[6] As a theorist of the proletarian revolution and its political leader in Russia, Lenin considered federation as a method of state organization in highly concrete terms and from the viewpoint of the revolution. It follows that first he was against federation as a way for different nations to coexist in a common state. Only after the formation of the Soviet state did Lenin change his mind and consider federation to be the most suitable form for a multinational socialist state. From this perspective, he distinguished two aspects of the multinational federation: the need for the unity of the *people*, and the national and territorial autonomy of the individual *nations* within the territory of the state. Thus, in the theoretical foundations of the origin of the Soviet and other socialist federations, the unity of the people and the diversity of nations meet and merge dialectically.

It follows from this theoretical and political approach that the federal system was applied only in multinational or plurinational socialist states, such as the USSR, Czechoslovakia, and Yugoslavia, where federation was one of the fundamental legal means of resolving the nationality problem.[7] Two examples illustrate this ethnic, as opposed to historical or territorial, approach. First, the former German Democratic Republic and the Federal Republic of Germany both consisted of several historical territorial units of Germany: however, the GDR was a unitary state and the FRG a federal state. Second, the Czechoslovak federation consisted geographically of four historical territories (Bohemia, Moravia, part of Silesia, and Slovakia), but had only two member states – the Czech Republic covering the historical territory of Bohemia, Moravia, and Silesia and inhabited by the Czech nation, and the Slovak Republic inhabited by the Slovak nation.

In the former socialist countries, state sovereignty was based on the sovereignty of nations. Two fundamental principles follow from this: the equality of nations, and their right to self-determination and self-government.

In the system of former socialist federations, the dialectical principle of the unity and diversity of opposites (antithesis) was expressed in the unity of the federal state, determined primarily by the unity of federal power, and the ethnic diversity of the nations associated in the federation. This was expressly proclaimed by article 70(1) of the Soviet Constitution which stated that 'the Union of Soviet Socialist Republics is a single, federal, multinational state, formed on the basis of the principle of socialist federalism.'[8] From the perspective of state sovereignty, this relation of unity and diversity was characterized by the Constitutional Act on Czechoslovak Federation, which stated in article 1(5) that 'both Republics mutually respect their sovereignty, as well as the sovereignty of the Czechoslovak Socialist Republic; the Czechoslovak Socialist Republic likewise respects the sovereignty of the two national states.'[9] The unity of state power in the federation, that is, the inner homogeneity of the federal state, was further expressed politically in the principle of democratic centralism as applied to the political and economic unity of the state and particularly to the leading role of the Communist party in the state.

The unity and diversity of opposites was further manifest in the theory of the state and social system of the then socialist federations in the relationship between the terms 'people' or 'working people' on the one hand, and 'nation' or 'nationality' on the other. These terms were precisely distinguished in the constitutions of the relevant states. Nations and nationalities in a state may be distinguished, but the people are always one. This was expressed with particular clarity in the Soviet Constitution, which consistently differentiated between the Soviet people and the individual nations (or nationalities) of the Soviet Union. For instance, article 70(2) of the 1978 Constitution provided: 'The USSR embodies the state unity of the Soviet people and brings together all the nations and nationalities for the purpose ... '[10]

Hence, the dialectical relationship between the unity of the people and the diversity of nations, as expressed in the quoted provision of the Soviet Constitution, is the idea which clearly dominated the former socialist federations.

Distinguishing Features of the CEE Federations

The principal difference between the CEE federations and the West European and American federations was twofold. First, the social aim of CEE federations, as discussed above, was the solution of the national problem. This aim is not unique to CEE federations. As has been discussed, this aim, although it is the common denominator and the political *raison d'être* for all CEE federations, may apply to any federation, for example, Belgium.

The feature that differentiated the CEE federations from all other federations was the role of the Communist party (including for the purposes of this chapter the Association of Communists of Yugoslavia) in these federations. The role of the Communist party, its 'leading role,' which was implemented in all former socialist countries, meant that the state, although theoretically independent of the party, in actual fact was subordinated to the Communist party as the leading political force in the society. This meant that in all relevant areas of domestic and foreign policy, state power was exercised on the basis of the political decisions made by the central bodies of the Communist party, that is, the Central Committee, the Presidium of the Communist party, or both.

The controlling influence of the Communist party relates to another specific feature of CEE federations, namely, the central planning of the national economy, which was controlled from a single federal centre and also subordinated to the political decisions of the central organs of the federal Communist party.

The influence of the Communist party de facto transformed the CEE federations, as federations of socialist (Soviet) type, into their very opposite. While preserving the federal form, they actually became strictly centralized, that is, they in actual fact became unitary states with uniform, centrally controlled economies.[11] The governments of the constituent states had only limited powers in relatively unimportant matters. The same was true of the Communist party organizations of the constituent states. In reality, the governments of the constituent states were little more than executive bodies of the federal government as opposed to governments with their own competence. The highest bodies of the Communist party of the constituent states were merely the executive bodies of the central bodies of the federal Communist party.

It is also symptomatic that there was no Communist party of the RSFSR in Russia, and in Czechoslovakia there was only the Communist party of Czechoslovakia and the Communist party of Slovakia, but no Communist party of the then Czech Socialist Republic. In the RSFSR, the Communist party of the Soviet Union performed its political activities directly, without the mediation of the Communist party of the republic concerned. The same applied to the political competence of the Communist party of Czechoslovakia in the territory of the then Czech Socialist Republic.

The last-mentioned fact shows that in the Soviet Union and Czechoslovakia, 'socialist' federalism did not eliminate what it should in theory have eliminated: in the USSR, the superior position of the Russian nation over the other nations of the Soviet Union and in Czechoslovakia, the superior position (although far less manifest than in the USSR) of the Czech nation over the Slovak nation.

Similarities and Differences Between the CEE Federations
The general features common to CEE federations were features that characterized them as socialist states. The contemporary CEE federations, which

after the overthrow of communism have set out on the road from one-party monopoly to political pluralism and from a centrally planned to a market economy, are confronted with the task of overcoming these features of socialist federalism. The political transition was carried out in a short time; the economic transition to a market economy is a considerably longer process in which elements of the previous system survive for some time. In their current development, individual CEE federations are selecting various partial solutions to the above-mentioned problems. Consequently, the common (and diverse) characteristics of the CEE federations can be discussed only from a historical viewpoint with reference to the time when these federations were socialist federations and to the starting point of their current political and economic transformation.

The principal features common to the CEE federations in this respect are the very features that distinguish CEE federations from Western European and American federations: the leading role of the Communist party, which de facto turned the federation into a strictly centralized unitary state, and the social aim of the federation intended (in vain, of course) to solve the national problem in the plurinational or multinational state.

Apart from these common features, there were also common features such as the organization of the administrative structure on the Soviet model. Particularly up to the end of the 1960s, there was intensive copying of Soviet institutions in all the former socialist countries, not just the socialist federations, because of the requirement of 'approaching the Soviet Union' or of 'sovietizing' individual socialist countries under the subsequently abandoned slogan, 'the Soviet Union – our model.' Of all the European socialist countries, it was one of the CEE federations, Yugoslavia, that managed to resist this approach successfully and find its own solution on a largely common general basis.

If the common features were primarily ideological, political, and economic, the significant differences among individual CEE federations were primarily geographic, historical, and demographic. Unlike the common features, which were determined primarily by subjective motives, the differences among the CEE federations were based primarily on objective factors.

The first of these objective factors was the difference in size of the Soviet territory as compared to the Czechoslovak and Yugoslav territory. This difference resulted in the organization of the Soviet Union as a multi-level federation with three levels. On the first level, there were fifteen union republics as member states. On the second level, there were autonomous republics, which did not have the character of member states of the USSR (nor of union republics), but formed part of the state territory of some union republics. On the third level, there were autonomous regions and autonomous districts, which also formed part of the state territory of some union republics. The Yugoslav federation consisted of six member states (republics) and two autonomous regions. In this respect Yugoslavia (obviously under Soviet influence) was also a multi-level (two-level) federation.

Czechoslovakia, in contrast, was a federation of two member states, a situation that created numerous problems for their mutual constitutional and economic relations, and for the relations of both member states to the federation. The latter relations differed considerably from analogous relations in the Soviet Union with its fifteen member states and more than one hundred nations and nationalities, and in Yugoslavia with its six member states.

A second difference between CEE federations concerns their ethnic structure. The absolute majority of their population consists of Slavic-speaking people (including Muslims in Yugoslavia). In contrast to Yugoslavia, where non-Slavic-speaking enclaves were mostly in autonomous regions and were contiguous with Albania and Hungary, and Czechoslovakia, where the only politically significant ethnic group inhabiting an integral territory was a national minority, the Soviet Union had over one hundred nations and nationalities mostly without ethnic or geographic links with other states. At the same time, the numbers of the three Slavic nations on the Soviet political spectrum far exceeded the numbers of the other nations and nationalities combined. The ethnic problem in the Soviet Union, consequently, was very different from that in Yugoslavia and Czechoslovakia. Its complexity was also manifest in the disintegration of the Soviet Union, when some member states with non-Slavic populations seceded and when in the new Commonwealth of Independent States the prevalently Slavic states played a more significant political role than the Moslem states.

The aforementioned ethnic differences are connected with another difference between CEE federations, that concerning the official language. Given the fact that most of the population of the CEE federations are from Slavic nations, the languages of these nations are similar and more or less mutually intelligible within the individual CEE federation. This was the case within the former Soviet Union as regards the Russian, Ukrainian, and Belorussian languages. However, the Soviet Union also encompassed many non-Slavic nationalities with mutually unintelligible languages. As a result, where the languages of individual nations and ethnic groups had the legal status of official languages, a common official language was also required and this was traditionally Russian. In this way, the Russian language – entirely foreign to many nations – has become superior to the national languages of the non-Slavic nations. This fact accentuated the factual political superiority of the Russian nation, determined by its numbers as well as by the fact that the governmental and administrative centre of the

Union was identical to the governmental and administrative centre of the RSFSR (Moscow).

Fourth, a by no means negligible difference between CEE federations was the fact that Czechoslovakia was the only country among them with a democratic tradition that was not forgotten even during the communist era.[12] After the disintegration of the Austro-Hungarian Empire in 1918, Czechoslovakia was founded as a democratic republic and remained one, with the exception of six years under Nazi occupation, until 1948.

Yugoslavia was also founded after the disintegration of Austro-Hungarian Empire in 1918. Originally a monarchy, it became a communist state, that is, a dictatorship, after the period of Nazi occupation and resistance. Any democratic legacy in Yugoslavia, therefore, dated from the relatively liberal Austro-Hungarian monarchy and the relatively liberal Yugoslav monarchy.

The weakest democratic tradition is in the former Soviet Union. With few exceptions (notably the Baltic states of Latvia, Estonia, and Lithuania), the nations of the Soviet Union have never known democracy. The Soviet Union originated between 1917 and 1922 with the revolutionary replacement of the thoroughly undemocratic tsarism of the former Russian Empire by the dictatorship of the proletariat, which turned into not 'bourgeois' democracy but essentially undemocratic 'socialist democracy.'

This difference in democratic traditions in the CEE federations is probably also reflected in the way that these countries elected to solve the difficult political problems that arose after the collapse of communism.

Conclusion

The extinction of communist rule in the former socialist states has brought about numerous political and economic problems that are common to all of them and their successor states. At the same time, the extinction of the communist regime has meant the collapse of 'socialist federalism,' leaving the CEE federations with not only political and economic problems, but also the problem of the future directions of their member states. If certain aspects of these problems are particular to certain CEE federations, other aspects are common to all. None of the states has yet solved all its problems. Moreover, the dominant course has been set: the complete disintegration of the federation and the creation of new fully independent successor states.

Notes

1 Aryeh L. Unger, *Constitutional Development in the USSR: A Guide to the Soviet Constitutions* (London: Methuen 1981), 25.
2 For an account of the Ukrainian experience, see Volodymyr Vassylenko, 'Disintegration of the Soviet "Federation" and the "Federalization" of Ukraine,' Chap-

ter 20 in this volume, 329-31.
3 *Soviet Treaty Series*, ed., Leonard Shapiro, vol. 1 (1917-28) (Washington: Georgetown University Press 1950), 199.
4 See also Mihailo Markovic, 'The Federal Experience in Yugoslavia,' Chapter 5 in this volume, 76-7, 80.
5 William B. Simons, ed., *The Constitutions of the Communist World* (Alphen aan den Rijn, Netherlands and Germantown, MD: Sijthoff and Noordhoff 1980), 581.
6 See also Vassylenko, Chapter 20, 'Disintegration,' 329-31.
7 For a critique of this understanding of federalism, see Markovic, Chapter 5, 'Federal Experience in Yugoslavia,' 83-6.
8 Simons, ed., *The Constitutions of the Communist World*, 351 at 368.
9 Ibid., 581 at 583.
10 Ibid., 351 at 368.
11 See also Vassylenko, Chapter 20, 'Disintegration,' 331-2.
12 Compare Markovic, Chapter 5, 'Federal Experience in Yugoslavia,' 75-7.

20

Disintegration of the Soviet 'Federation' and the 'Federalization' of Ukraine

Volodymyr Vassylenko

Introduction

History has numbered federation among the forms of state organization since ancient times. Today the idea of federalism is widespread globally and is realized through various models of federation, which coexist with unitary states throughout the world. The theory and practice of federalism are constantly evolving as federalism conforms to changes in society, and as old states disintegrate and new ones are created.

Today Europe is witness to complicated processes of disintegration and formation of federal systems which are of great significance not only to that continent, but to the entire world. On the one hand, in Western Europe a new model of federalism is being formed: a federation whose members include both classical nation states and federal states such as Germany and Belgium. On the other hand, in Eastern and southern Europe the Union of Soviet Socialist Republics and the Socialist Federal Republic of Yugoslavia, federations on the socialist model, have fallen apart. The process of disintegration has led to the breakup of yet another former socialist federation situated in Central Europe, the Czech and Slovak Federative Republic.

In this connection the following question arises: which of these diametrically opposed processes is natural? Paradoxically, the answer is that both processes are.

Western Europe is a Europe of independent nation states formed many years ago. Since the Second World War almost all the West European states have developed in the context of democracy and a market economy. Political cooperation between them has been aimed at supporting an effective system of mutual security and the formation of a common market. To achieve these goals, Western European states created the supranational institutions which serve as the basis for the gradual formation of federal structures in the European Union.

In contrast, a majority of the nations of Central, Eastern, and southern

Europe were deprived of statehood for long periods of time and until the beginning of the twentieth century were parts of three empires: the Russian, Austro-Hungarian, and Ottoman Empires. Even after the disintegration of these empires, only some of the enslaved nations achieved real independence, given that soon thereafter the empire of the Russian tsars was replaced by the Union of Soviet Socialist Republics, the totalitarian empire of the communist leaders. After the Second World War almost all the states of this region fell under the domination of the USSR and developed under conditions of totalitarianism and a planned centralized economy. The Soviet, Czechoslovak, and Yugoslav models of federalism did not develop as a result of voluntary cooperation between states. Rather, they were established artificially and subjected to the ideological postulates of communism. It is for this reason that the demise of the socialist system was immediately followed by a crisis of socialist federalism.

The subject of this chapter is twofold: first, the history of the Soviet 'federation,' culminating in its disintegration; and second, the prospects for the 'federalization' of Ukraine, both in the internal context of its future political and territorial organization, and in the external context of its potential membership in European federal structures.

The History of the Soviet Federation

Pre-Soviet Attempts at Federalism
To understand the reasons for the disintegration of the Soviet 'federation' it is necessary to establish the genesis, nature, and main stages of its development. The USSR, which replaced the Russian Empire five years after its demise, was based on the idea of federalism developed in the second half of the nineteenth century by the prominent Ukrainian scholar Mykhailo Drahomanov. Drahomanov argued that the Russian Empire should be transformed into a federation of sovereign states. He suggested the concept of a free union of all Slavic and other European nations that were dominated at that time by the Russian, Austro-Hungarian, and Ottoman Empires. It is interesting to note that Drahomanov's theory was not accepted by the Bolsheviks. Calling him a 'nationalistic petty bourgeois,' Lenin stated, 'federation is harmful ... That is why we, from the very outset ... reject the idea of a federation ... Marxists, without doubt, have a hostile attitude toward federation and decentralization.'[1]

Although rejected by the Bolsheviks, Drahomanov's ideas were accepted by the Ukrainian democratic national liberation movement. After the democratic revolution of February 1917 in Russia, this movement became especially active, uniting numerous Ukrainian parties and groups. On 17 March 1917, their representatives formed the Central Rada (Council), which functioned as the parliament of Ukraine. Now headed by the Central Rada, the movement for the reestablishment of the statehood of Ukraine became especially widespread after the Second All-Russian Congress of Soviets. This communist Congress, which took place in Petrograd soon after the Russian Revolution of October 1917, formally proclaimed the right of self-determination of peoples and nations, including the right of secession.

On 20 November 1917, the Central Rada issued the Third Universal which proclaimed the founding of the Ukrainian Republic as an autonomous unitary state within Russia. The Universal stated that the territory of the Ukrainian Republic consisted of nine provinces of the Russian Empire populated mostly by Ukrainians: Kiev, Podilia, Volhynia, Chernihiv, Poltava, Kharkiv, Katerynoslav, Kherson, and Tavria regions.

The Third Universal led to the consolidation of pro-imperial communist forces both inside and outside Ukraine. In December 1917 the Bolsheviks held the First All-Ukrainian Congress of Soviets in Kharkiv, which denounced the Central Rada and proclaimed the establishment of the Soviet Ukrainian Republic. This Congress formed the government of the Soviet Ukrainian Republic, which claimed to be the only legitimate government of Ukraine. In January 1918 it began an armed struggle against the Central Rada, calling on the troops of Soviet Russia for assistance. Under these circumstances, the Central Rada was forced to turn to the Central Powers for military assistance. In January 1918 the Central Rada issued its Fourth and last Universal, which declared the Ukrainian People's Republic an independent state. In February of that year Ukraine signed the 'Peace of Bread' with the Central Powers, thereby laying the legal foundation for the entry of German and Austrian troops onto Ukrainian territory.[2]

After the defeat of Germany and its satellites in the First World War, the end of 1918 and the beginning of 1919, the territory of Ukraine once again became the arena for a fierce power struggle between the national democratic forces and the communist forces. This struggle resulted in the defeat of the government of the Ukrainian People's Republic, which at the end of 1920 found itself in exile.

Having recognized the strength of the desire of the non-Russian nations to reestablish their freedom and nation statehood, the Bolsheviks revised their position on the concept of federation and began to use the idea as an instrument to preserve a single state within the territory of the former Russian Empire. Lenin and his colleagues realized that the only alternative to secession and the disintegration of the empire was the promise of a federation.

By January 1918, the Third All-Russian Congress of Soviets had already proclaimed Russia a federation of Soviet Socialist Republics (RSFSR). Russia itself, however, did not appear to be an equal partner in this federation. It did not proclaim its own independence and, moreover, appeared to absorb the national republics that entered into the RSFSR even though these republics did so on the basis of autonomy. In contrast, the Transcaucasian Federation (TSFSR) was formed in 1922 on a different basis, with Azerbaijan, Armenia, and Georgia becoming equal subjects of this federation.

When the question of the formation of a union of all the republics was placed on the agenda, Stalin chose the federal model of the RSFSR, which embodied his well-known plan of 'autonomization,' according to which all republics would be incorporated into the RSFSR as 'autonomous' units. Stalin's plan was resisted by the non-Russian Soviet republics, especially Ukraine. This resistance led Lenin,[3] in his article 'On the Problems of Nationalities or "Autonomisation"'[4] to favour the creation of a federal union of equal republics. The political struggle surrounding the union of the Soviet republics ended with the adoption of a Union Treaty on 30 December 1922.[5] Together with the Declaration on the Formation of the USSR,[6] the Union Treaty formed the Constitution of the USSR. The formation of the USSR brought to a halt the disintegration of Russian Empire and marked the start of its transformation into the Soviet totalitarian empire.

The Soviet Federation Up to Gorbachev

The official name of the new state was the Union of Soviet Socialist Republics. Its subjects were two sovereign unitary states (the Belorussian SSR and the Ukrainian SSR) and two sovereign federal states (the RSFSR and TSFSR).[7] Its constitution provided some guarantees of the sovereignty of its members, in particular, the preservation of separate constitutions, separate bodies of state power, republic citizenship, territorial integrity, and the right of secession. From this point of view, the newly created Union resembled a confederation. At the same time, however, the Union Treaty considered the Soviet Union 'one union state' with a common citizenship and territory, and gave the all-Union bodies broad governing and administrative powers typical of a federation.

Among the principal drawbacks of the Union Treaty were: the absence of clear wording as to the precise form of the state system of the Union; the very broad and imprecise prerogatives given to the Union; the fact that republics were deprived of the right to establish their own state budgets independently; the fact that they had to follow onerous and one-sided directives on the structure of the republican administrative and governing state bodies; and the exclusive authority of the All-Union Congress of Soviets to adopt amendments to the principal provisions of the Constitution of the USSR.

As a result, it was possible to change the Constitution without the consent of the union republics, and this ultimately led to the restriction of the republics' sovereign rights. The most telling example of this was the adoption of the 1936 Constitution of the USSR,[8] which did not mention the Union Treaty and which bore the stamp of Stalin's plan of autonomization. The 1936 Constitution, known aptly as the 'Stalin Constitution,' reflected a unitary model which severely impaired the interests of the union republics. The administrative-command system that had been formed under the conditions of Stalinist totalitarianism required the extreme centralization of both the Communist party and state structures, although this system was inconsistent with normal national development.[9] Under the pretext of protecting all-Union state interests, the independence of republics was restricted, and there was a strong tendency towards unitary rule. The most extreme manifestation of this appeared in the 1977 Constitution of the USSR. Despite a reference in article 70 to the principle of socialist federalism, in reality a unitary state was formed.

The Soviet Union reached its apogee as a totalitarian communist superpower in the mid-1970s. However, it is undeniable that this period of history also initiated the decline and fall of the USSR. The communist system, according to whose postulates the state structure and social life had been organized, entered a state of deep crisis and exhausted itself.

The Gorbachev Years: The Disintegration of the Soviet Federation
The ominous symptoms of the Soviet Union's systemic crisis forced the leadership of the Communist party of the Soviet Union (CPSU), headed by Mikhail Sergeyevich Gorbachev, to proclaim in the spring of 1985 the necessity of reconstructing and reforming the political, economic, and management structures of the USSR. The Soviet 'federation' was also subjected to reconstruction. But despite all his promises, statements, and manoeuvres, Gorbachev stood for the principles of communist Russian 'great-power' chauvinism. He attempted to preserve the Soviet empire and to breathe new life into the old system, allowing only superficial and inconsistent changes. This was due to an insufficient comprehension of the profound reasons underlying the crisis of the communist system and, hence, of the need for a program to overcome the crisis.

In 1989 the Baltic republics and the democratic movements in other republics, including Ukraine, proposed the conclusion of a new Union Treaty which would serve as the legal basis for a new federation. These proposals were categorically rejected from the outset. After Latvia, Lithuania, Estonia, Armenia, and Georgia had unambiguously declared their intention to secede from the USSR, and other republics had adopted declarations of independence equivalent to declarations of secession, Gorbachev was forced to accept the idea of a new Union Treaty. Nevertheless, from 1990 to 1991 Gorbachev tried to foist on the republics drafts of a proposed Union Treaty that would have preserved the old unitary foundation. As a result, both the concept of a new federal model and that of a union of sovereign states were discredited.

Ukraine's refusal to attend the ceremonial signing of the Union Treaty on 20 August 1991 proved decisive in the struggle between the imperial structures of the old Union and the republics. It provoked the attempted communist coup d'état which began on 19 August 1991 and was defeated within two days.

On 24 August 1991, the parliament of Ukraine approved Ukraine's declaration of independence. Soon thereafter the other republics also declared their independence. The final blow to the USSR occurred on 1 December 1991, during the referendum in Ukraine, when more than 90 per cent of the Ukrainian population approved the Act Proclaiming the Independence of Ukraine of 24 August 1991.

Legally, the demise of the USSR occurred on 8 December 1991, after the signing in Minsk of the agreement between Belorussia, Russia, and Ukraine on the formation of the Commonwealth of Independent States.[10] The agreement stated that the USSR had ceased to exist 'as a subject of international law and geopolitical reality.'

Soon eight other republics of the former USSR joined the Minsk Agreement by signing a Special Protocol[11] in Alma-Ata on 21 December 1991. On the same day all eleven republics approved the Alma-Ata Declaration,[12] which stated that the Commonwealth of Independent States was 'neither a state nor a suprastate formation.'

The member states of the former USSR chose the path of independent development and the establishment of nation statehood. Each of them has since faced many difficult problems. Ukraine is among those undergoing the process of national rebirth and the creation of an independent state. One of Ukraine's most difficult problems is the introduction of a new system to administer its territory.

The 'Federalization' of Ukraine

The Internal Dimension
The present administrative-territorial system in Ukraine is obsolete; it fails to meet the current economic, political, and social needs of Ukrainian society. This system was formed under a totalitarian autocratic regime and adapted to its needs. During the period when Ukraine was part of the Soviet Union, especially after the adoption of the Stalin Constitution, its territory was divided into many more territorial-administrative units than had previously existed. As a result, traditional historical regions, formed over the course of centuries, were dismembered: the territory of Ukraine now consists

of the Autonomous Republic of the Crimea, 24 *oblasti* (regions), 480 *rayony* (districts), two cities subordinated to *oblasti*, 288 towns subordinated to *rayony*, 916 settlements, and 28,907 villages. There are more than twice as many *oblasti* as there were traditional historical regions on the territory of Ukraine.

Both historical experience and modern tendencies suggest that the present administrative-territorial division of Ukraine must be changed. The three-tier system (*oblast'-rayon*-populated locality), under which even *oblasti* lacked real rights, was well adapted to strict centralized control and subordination. It has become evident that a dictatorship of the centre impedes the normal development of society, as it fails to take into account specific regional features and runs counter to the principles of a market economy, democracy, and self-government. In Ukraine, specific regional traditions, socioeconomic factors, interethnic problems, and geopolitical factors require a new territorial organization of the state. One point of reference is the idea of a 'federalization' of Ukraine based on the division of its territory into several large self-governing lands.

Among the factors that determine the administrative-territorial division of a state, three factors are critical: geo-ethnopolitical, economic, and administrative.

The geo-ethnopolitical factor relates to the genesis and formation of new regions within the framework of state territory. Regional differences are shaped by various factors that condition people's lives. Among these factors are the specific geographical features of a region, its natural and climatic conditions, the ethnic composition of the population, the cultural and domestic traditions of the inhabitants, and the political and legal status of the territory during different periods of history.

In the course of Ukraine's history, its various regions have come to be defined according to the different ethnic composition of their populations, traditions, mentalities, and degree of national consciousness. At least nine regions can be distinguished: Volhynia, Galicia, Bukovyna, Transcarpathia, Sloboda Ukraine (on the left bank of the Dnieper), the Donets Basin (coal region), the Black Sea area, the Crimea, and Central Ukraine.

The economic factor includes parameters such as the available labour and natural resources, the level of specialization and cooperation in the production process, and the degree of development of lines of communication. Since the late 1950s Ukrainian economists have proposed different options for the division of Ukraine into economic regions. According to their proposals the number of regions could range from seven to eleven. In most variants the proposed economic regions coincide with the historical regions of Ukraine mentioned above.

The administrative factor should provide the optimal combination of efficiency and economy of governance. Under democratic conditions, it makes no sense to preserve a cumbersome and complicated system of governance whose functions will undergo fundamental changes. According to the Law on 'Local Councils of People's Deputies of the Ukrainian SSR and Local Self-Government,' the basic unit of local self-government is a settlement of any kind. Nowadays the cities do not need the trifling guardianship of *oblast'* leaders. This is yet another argument for dividing the territory of Ukraine into administrative-territorial units that are larger than the present *oblasti*.

Thus, an analysis of the geo-ethnopolitical, economic, and administrative factors supports the argument for dividing Ukraine into nine to twelve autonomous self-governing lands or regions, where autonomy would not be the national-territorial autonomy which existed under the former USSR, but a form of regional autonomy that would enable regional governing bodies to resolve the issues under their legal jurisdiction.

Although some Ukrainian politicians and publicists disagree, the transition to regional divisions should not lead to the classical type of federation, in the sense of a federation formed when the subjects of the proposed federation sign a treaty of union that transfers certain powers from the signatories to the federation as a whole.

In the case of Ukraine, the state, which is already in existence, must decide how to establish its regional boundaries and what powers to delegate to its regions. Once these powers have been delegated, there should be no further interference on the part of the central state. Such a system and the division of powers embodied therein should be enshrined in the constitution of Ukraine. In addition, there must be special laws addressing the autonomy of all regions.

In such a state system, regional authorities can be given broad powers under the constitution and laws of Ukraine, but only on condition that they respect and preserve the territorial unity of the Ukrainian state.

Nevertheless, the division of Ukraine into regions with broad rights of self-government can lead to a weakening of the unity of the state because it creates opportune conditions for organizing separatist forces. Indeed, such a menace may already exist if one considers the fact that the process of forming the Ukrainian state is unfinished, as well as the fact that acts of anti-Ukrainian chauvinism have occurred both in Ukraine and abroad. Most recently, in addition to the illegal movement for the separation of the Crimea from Ukraine, there have been appeals to form within the Ukrainian state such autonomous states as Novorossiya (New Russia), which would include the Odessa, Kherson, and Mykolaiv *oblasti*, and the Kryvyi Rih-Donetsk Republic. To neutralize these tendencies, it is necessary not only to make those who violate the law accountable for their actions, but also to reorganize the territory in such a way as to help satisfy the demands of citizens of different regions by taking into account their specific requirements. Under these conditions, a new administrative-territorial division of Ukraine would contribute to the unity of the Ukrainian people, the strengthening of the Ukrainian state, and the integrity of its territory.

Today it is obvious that the multinational population of Ukraine makes it impossible to build a Ukrainian state on the will, spirit, and consciousness of the Ukrainian people alone. To avoid separatism, democracy, the welfare of the population, and the satisfaction of the national-cultural needs of citizens belonging to different national groups must be secured. The transition to regional autonomy will be a step towards democracy, provided that autonomy is not used as a means of preserving communist regimes. The transition should be carried out continuously in accordance with a program that would extend over several years.

During the first stage of this program, it is necessary to eliminate the *oblasti* (regions) of the republic, which the Law on 'Local Councils' has deprived of power, and to establish regions with limited powers. Thereafter, in the course of establishing Ukrainian statehood, developing democracy, and strengthening law and order, it will be necessary to empower the regions gradually with additional authority.

Even today, the adoption of such a program would undermine the ideological basis of Southern Ukrainian and other separatists by providing the guarantees of a democratic state in the near future.

The External Dimension

The federal idea has a very important external dimension, owing to profound transformations in social, economic, and political life throughout the world. At present, new federal forms seem to be evolving into practical models for the political organization of interstate relations in Europe.

On the one hand, Western European countries have long been engaged in an ambitious program to complete the formation of a single market and Europe-wide political institutions, which are to be established in accordance with the Maastricht Treaty on European Union[13] negotiated in December 1991.

On the other hand, the countries of Central and Eastern Europe are trying to reconstruct their regional relations in order to replace the institutions of the Warsaw Pact, the Comecon, and the USSR. To this end, Czechoslovakia, Hungary, and Poland constituted themselves as the Visegrad Three. The republics of the former USSR declared the creation of the Commonwealth of Independent States. But in reality, both these institutions are no more than mechanisms for multilateral negotiation.

Almost all the countries of Central and Eastern Europe are searching for ways to cooperate with the West so as to become integrated into existing and future Western European structures. For the time being, the European Union, NATO, and other institutions have resisted the closer political and economic association sought by their partners from the East. This is quite understandable, given the existing level of political, social, and economic development in the former communist countries. It is also quite clear that given time and freedom, each of these countries sooner or later will find its way to democracy, a market economy, industrial growth, and prosperity, and ultimately will be ready to join Western institutions within the framework of a planned pan-European federation or confederation.

Ukraine's membership in a future pan-European union will be possible if the Ukrainian government manages to cope with its economic crisis, build a democratic society, and strengthen national statehood. Naturally, the union must be capable of preserving the identity of its members and protecting their national interests. In no case will Ukraine become a member of any union or association that does not meet these conditions. In this respect Chancellor Kohl's idea that a future pan-European federation must be based on two pillars – Germany in the West and Russia in the East – seems very dangerous because it anticipates the domination of some states by others. As history shows, unions based on such domination are unstable and disastrous for all their members in the long run. The impetus for a pan-European union must be principles that reconcile ideas of nation statehood and interdependence between nations. There is no point in contrasting these ideas. Nation states and their interdependence are realities we must reckon with.

Notes

The notes were added by the editors with the research assistance of Motria Onyschuk.

1 Vladimir I. Lenin, *CPSU on the Struggle with Nationalism* (Kiev 1976), 11, 15.
2 The Bolsehviks were routed by the Germans and Austrians, and the Central Rada returned to power. The Germans, however, lost patience with the Central Rada's inability to keep its part of the 'Peace of Bread,' namely, the delivery of foodstuffs to the Central Powers, and disbanded the Central Rada in April 1918. These events led to the establishment of the Hetmanate, a conservative Ukrainian government whose ouster, after less than eight months in power, would usher in a period of total chaos. Orest Subtelny, *Ukraine: A History* (Toronto: University of Toronto Press 1988), 353-4.
3 On Lenin's theory of federalism, see also Viktor Knapp, 'Central and Eastern European Federations: Communist Theory and Practice,' Chapter 19 in this volume, 321-2.
4 In Vladimir I. Lenin, *Questions of National Policy and Proletarian Nationalism*

(Moscow: Progress Publishers no date), 188.

5 *Soviet Treaty Series*, ed., Leonard Shapiro, vol. 1 (1917-1928) (Washington: Georgetown University Press 1950), 199.

6 *USSR: Sixty Years of the Union 1922-1982* (Moscow: Progress Publishers 1982), 162-4.

7 See Knapp, Chapter 19, 'Central and Eastern European Federations,' 321-2.

8 For the texts of the successive Soviet Constitutions, see Aryeh L. Unger, *Constitutional Development in the USSR: A Guide to the Soviet Constitutions* (London: Methuen 1981).

9 On these features as definitive of Central and Eastern European federations, see Knapp, Chapter 19, 'Central and Eastern European Federations,' 322-4.

10 'Accord on Commonwealth of Independent States,' *New York Times*, 10 December 1991, A9.

11 *Current Digest of the Soviet Press* 43, No. 51 (1991):4.

12 Ibid.

13 For the text of the treaty, see Europe agence internationale d'information pour la presse, Europe Documents No. 1759/60 (7 February 1992).

Part Five:
Conclusion

21

Multinationalism and the Federal Idea: A Synopsis
John Meisel

One of the most revealing metaphors of our times is the simultaneous growth in popularity of *USA Today* on the one hand, and the free, neighbourhood newspaper on the other. The growing universalism exemplified by *USA Today* is paradoxically accompanied by the increasing particularism illustrated by the neighbourhood newspapers available at every street corner. These throwaways do not just describe what is going on in the local grocery store; they also broadcast the loss of kittens and ear-rings. The simultaneous popularity of a global newspaper and of a neighbourhood weekly is instructive. This example shows that as individuals enter McLuhan's global village they also yearn for the intimacy of the parish pump. The phenomena of Maastricht and Copenhagen encapsulate the current coexistence of (and resulting tension between) universalizing and particularizing trends. And of course both federalism and the nation state are compelled to adjust to this reality.

In what follows, I focus on three main topics. First, I will identify some of the key characteristics of federalism in the context of the nation state. Second, I will specify some conditions under which federalism seems to function best. I shall conclude with some guidelines for the future.

Relevant Characteristics of Federalism
Let us consider the salient characteristics of federalism highlighted by the chapters in this volume. Nine points can be briefly summarized. First it is clear, but all too often forgotten, that federalism is no panacea – 'Federalism is not enough,' as Alan Cairns points out.[1] Federalism is basically a technique and its effectiveness depends on the external and internal conditions of the countries in which it is adopted. But while it is, in itself, merely a technique, it frequently creates loyalties and states of mind which affect the way in which it is used.

Second, while some assume that there is a link between democracy and federalism, federalism is not necessarily democratic – it can serve autocracy or any other kind of system.

Third, federalism reflects the sociopolitical, economic, and cultural characteristics of its context. Consequently, since political, economic, and other sorts of power are distributed unevenly in federal, as in all, states, federalism tends to serve the dominant groups in a society, sometimes at the expense of neglected groups. There is a chasm between the political class – bureaucrats, politicians, eurocrats – on the one hand and, on the other, the people who make up what is fuzzily called the general public and who care little about constitutional arrangements or political structures generally. This is one of the explanations for the eloquent arguments that Canada's Aboriginal Peoples have not benefited from Canadian federalism as others have, or that women have not benefited as others have. This compels us to consider what other groups or individuals are systematically neglected, without the knowledge of mainstream society.

The fourth characteristic is that federalism often suffers from what may, for lack of a better term, be called a 'territorial fixation.' There is a slow and sometimes inadequate response to the fact that only some interests in federal states are territorially based. Others arise within non-territorial groupings and require the attention of 'functional authorities' – complementary mechanisms which make up for the territorial impediments or limitations of federalism.

Fifth, 'federalism up or out' is linked to 'federalism in.' The move towards supracountry formations is related to local regionalisms which are also developing, and which also spill over national boundaries.

Sixth, federalism is needed most when ethnicity and tribalism are seething. But these conditions – the virulent boiling up of ethnic interests and tribalism – make the adoption of federal forms of government particularly difficult. Primarily because of technological innovation, but for other reasons as well, social, economic, political – and, therefore, historical – change now occurs at a very much faster pace than before. Similarly, developments in one place quickly affect those in another. Under these circumstances, the political institutions required to cope with new circumstances do not have time to take root. The psychic states of mind among the population essential for the development of a federal infrastructure are thus absent, and even if federal solutions are tried, they may fail under these conditions.

Mounting evidence documents the existence of my seventh characteristic of federalism. Certain federalisms may lead not just to unifying communities, but also to their unravelling. Self-determination often has a domino effect. When one group breaks away from another; it may then itself become subject to divisive forces and may engender other new challenges to the old order. Czechoslovakia, which has split into two republics, is a good case in point. Now there are the Czech and Moravian lands and Slovakia, but there is a possibility that Moravia will eventually want to spin-off from the Czech lands and a likelihood that the Hungarians in Slovakia will also decide that they somehow want to opt out. This may be an unending process, with no logical stopping place. This process may well test the limits of democracy, not to mention economic and administrative efficiency.

The eighth point raises a question about one of the characteristics of federal states. Is the size of the units involved related to the dominant mentality espoused by the population? Are attitudes towards tolerance and human rights related to the territorial base? It has been suggested that a larger unit is likely to be more tolerant than smaller ones. That assumption clearly needs to be tested. People who are carving up old and launching new polities ought to be aware of this aspect of governance.

The last characteristic is that federalism flourishes in many parts of the world but, as we have seen, it is also in decline in others. One of the things one needs to look at is the pathology of federalism. When and under what conditions does federalism disappear?

Conditions Conducive to Effective Federalism

Under what conditions does federalism work best? First, it seems essential for the success of a federation that the federal regime be accepted by the population – in other words, that there be a voluntary process of acquiring federalism rather than its being thrust on the population from the top or by outside forces. Federal institutions must be sustained by a federal culture. There has to be what David Easton calls 'support.'[2] This support may not be present at first but must emerge if the federal framework is to survive.

Second, federalism works best when it is flexible – when it is capable of responding to changing conditions. There is no such thing as a rigid, timeless federalism. It has been a hallmark of successful federal states that they have managed to embrace new political, regional, or ethnic pressures.

Third, there has to be present in the successful federal state an appropriate social, psychological, and emotional infrastructure. Effective federalism requires that it be held together by a social glue. One author uses the metaphor of cement. I am leery about that, since concrete lacks the needed flexibility. But whatever the imagery, there has to be an appropriate societal base for the political and institutional structures of federalism.

Fourth, federalism in almost all circumstances will function best if it is asymmetrical. Not all partners need always be guided by identical rules and conditions. While many people may be unaware of the somewhat lopsided reality – Canada is a good example of that – many successful federations embrace special arrangements to suit the unique requirements of some members.

Fifth, federalism, it is obvious, will function best when the incentives for its existence are strong and clearly perceived. It must be associated with clear economic or other benefits and compare favourably with the available or plausible alternatives, whether a unitary state or outright independence.

Finally, federalism functions best when there is time to develop the federal institutions. It is highly desirable that the citizens of a federal state acquire the sense that their well-being is linked to the existence of federal arrangements. This state of what we might term 'federalism dependence' takes a long time to emerge and to take root. Because of the 'shortening of time' so characteristic of the modern age, it is increasingly difficult for the conditions necessary for the birth and entrenchment of a federal mentality to emerge and prevail for a sustained period. Rosenbaum argues that we are in a era of exceptional turbulence; extremely rapid change raises obstacles to the evolution of the preconditions necessary for a smoothly functioning federal system.[3] This means that the new order, which many people dream of in heterogeneous countries where constitutional experiments are under way, may never materialize. Yugoslavia and Czechoslovakia provide the two European polar extremes of what may happen under these circumstances. Africa and Asia offer depressing evidence that throughout the world the Yugoslav model is the more common one.

On Cross-National and Cross-Discipline Studies

Finally, this volume has looked at federalism from many vantage points. Unusually in this age of scholarly specialization and national parochialism, it has brought together representatives from several disciplines and from diverse parts of the world. It, therefore, provides an opportunity to meditate on the strengths and weaknesses of cross-disciplinary and cross-national research. Most of us agree that in the rapidly changing world such boundary-crossing is essential, but it is not easy.

First is the problem that bedevils much of human discourse: the meaning of the words we use. The terms 'federalism' and 'democracy' convey different things at different times to different people. Although we know that to equate Swiss federalism with German federalism and with developments in the European Union is unrealistic, we have unwittingly tended to lump too much under the federalism rubric. There are as many federalisms as there are communities adopting them, each with its own idiosyncrasies. Federalism, therefore, needs to be used with greater finesse than we have done.

Second, while federalism is a critical factor – both in terms of its institutional structure and its social and cultural underpinnings – its importance should not be exaggerated. Students of federalism – like specialists on other phenomena – always run the risk of developing what Richard Simeon calls the 'vested interest in the independent variable.'[4] We all wear our own blinkers, and create our own somewhat isolated, and, hence, partial view of the world. One result is that we exaggerate the importance of the things we are interested in. Students of federalism must ensure, therefore, that they explore the interactions between federalism and other institutional and social characteristics.

In addition, we need to link federalism to such phenomena as the environment, hunger, food, health, and the population explosion in the world (with its implications for immigration and emigration, which of course are very relevant to federalism). Each can, and often does, directly affect federal arrangements and may also be affected by them; yet the nature of the relationships is for the most part unexplored.

Third, important changes are taking place in almost all parts of the world in the degree of trust prevailing between political leaders and the mass; there is an almost universal lack of confidence in political leadership and in political institutions. The underpinnings of Arend Lijphart's 'consociationalism' are disappearing.[5] To what extent is federalism either a cause of or a solution to this disaffection? What is its relation to such crucial contemporary developments as the rise of Islamic fundamentalism or the growth of tribalism and ethnic consciousness? What is the impact of the information revolution and the information society?

These contextual circumstances are critical for the future of federalism, and our models must take them into account. We also need to establish criteria for identifying successful federalism, moderately successful federalism, and failed federalism, and to be more systematic in identifying the benefits and liabilities of federalism.

Finally, I shall offer a modest guideline for the future directed at architects, builders, and maintainers of federal arrangements wherever federalism may seem to be a desirable option. What I am going to say is possibly trite, maudlin, and precious, but nevertheless profoundly true. What the doers must remember most is the human quality, the needs of the individuals who are affected by federal arrangements. It is easily forgotten that while symbolic politics are very important, people are more often moved by bread and butter issues. By that I do not mean just economic well-being, but local issues that are germane to their lives. With very few exceptions, ordinary personal and family concerns count for much more than public causes and public policies. Furthermore, individual ethics are normally superior to state ethics.

Václav Havel says it best:

There is no simple set of instructions on how to proceed. A moral and intellectual state cannot be established through a constitution, or through law, or through directives, but only through complex, long-term, and never-ending work involving education and self-education. What is needed is lively and responsible consideration of every political step, every decision; a constant stress on moral deliberation and moral judgement; continued self-examination and self-analysis; an endless rethinking of our priorities. It is not, in short, something we can simply declare or introduce. It is a way of going about things, and it demands the courage to breathe moral and spiritual motivation into everything, to seek the human dimension in all things. Science, technology, expertise, and so-called professionalism are not enough. Something more is necessary. For the sake of simplicity, it might be called spirit. Or feeling. Or conscience.[6]

Notes

1 Alan Cairns, 'Constitutional Government and the Two Faces of Ethnicity: Federalism Is Not Enough,' Chapter 2 in this volume.
2 David Easton, *A Systems Analysis of Political Life* (New York: John Wiley 1965), 153-243.
3 James Rosenau, *Turbulence in World Politics: A Theory of Change and Continuity* (Princeton, NJ: Princeton University Press 1990).
4 Richard Simeon, personal communication.
5 Arend Lipjhart, *Democracies: Patterns of Majoritarian and Consensus Government in Twenty-one Countries* (New Haven: Yale University Press 1984), passim.
6 Václav Havel, *Summer Meditations on Politics, Morality and Civility in a Time of Transition* (London: Faber 1992), 20.

Contributors

Samuel H. Beer is Eaton Professor Emeritus of the Science of Government at Harvard University. He received his Ph.D. from Harvard University and has taught at the Department of Government since 1938.

Raymond Breton is a Professor Emeritus with the Department of Sociology at the University of Toronto. He obtained his B.A. from the University of Manitoba, his M.A. from the University of Chicago, and his Ph.D. from Johns Hopkins University.

Alan C. Cairns is a Professor of Political Science at the University of British Columbia. He received his B.A. and M.A. from the University of Toronto and his D.Phil. from Oxford.

Paul L.A.H. Chartrand is the Head of the Department of Native Studies at the University of Manitoba and a Commissioner on the Royal Commission on Aboriginal Peoples. He obtained his education from the University of Winnipeg, the Queensland Institute of Technology in Australia, and the University of Saskatchewan.

Robert Howse is an Assistant Professor at the University of Toronto Faculty of Law. He was educated at the University of Toronto and Harvard Law School.

Thomas O. Hueglin is a Professor of Political Science at Wilfrid Laurier University. He received his doctoral and post-doctoral degrees from St. Gall University, Switzerland, and Konstanz University in Germany.

Bakhtior Islamov is Head of the International Economic Development

Department, Tashkent State Economic University in Uzbekistan. He has a Ph.D. in international economics.

Jane Jenson is a Professor of Political Science at the University of Montreal. She obtained her B.A. at McGill University and her Ph.D. at the University of Rochester.

Guy Kirsch is the Professor for Public Finance at the University of Fribourg in Switzerland. He has also served as the Assistant to the Secretary General of CECAL in Paris.

Viktor Knapp is a Professor at Charles University in Prague, Director of the Institute of State and Law, and Vice-President of the Czech Academy of Sciences.

Karen Knop is an Assistant Professor in the Faculty of Law at the University of Toronto. She has studied at Columbia University, Moscow State University, and Dalhousie University.

Mihailo Markovic is a member of the Serbian Academy of Sciences and a member of the International Philosophical Institute in Paris. He received his Ph.D. from the University of London and has taught philosophy and political science at the University of Belgrade and the University of Pennsylvania.

John Meisel is the Sir Edward Peacock Professor of Political Science at Queen's University. He earned his B.A. and M.A. from the University of Toronto and his Ph.D. from the University of London.

Kenneth Norrie is a Professor of Economics at the University of Alberta. He obtained his B.A. for the University of Saskatchewan and his Ph.D. from Yale University.

Sylvia Ostry is Chair, Centre for International Studies, University of Toronto, and Chancellor, University of Waterloo. She has a Ph.D. in economics from McGill and Cambridge Universities.

Tommaso Padoa-Schioppa is an Italian economist and Deputy Director General of the Bank of Italy. He graduated from Bocconi University and the Massachusetts Institute of Technology. He is Chairman of the Basel Committee on Banking Supervision.

Jacques Pelkmans is Senior Research Fellow at the Centre for European Policy Studies (CEPS) in Brussels, Director of EUROSCOPE, and Professor of European Economic Integration at Maastricht University. He studied at Tilburg, where he also obtained his Ph.D., and at Johns Hopkins University.

Alice M. Rivlin is an economist. At the time her chapter was written, she was a Senior Fellow at the Brookings Institution in Washington, D.C. From January 1993, she served as Deputy Director of the Office of Management and Budget of the United States government. She graduated from Bryn Mawr College and received her Ph.D. in Economics from Radcliffe College of Harvard University.

Richard Simeon is a Professor of Political Science at the University of Toronto and a Vice-Chair of the Ontario Law Reform Commission. He received his B.A. from the University of British Columbia and his M.A. and Ph.D. from Yale.

Katherine Swinton is a Professor in the Faculty of Law at the University of Toronto, cross-appointed to the Department of Political Science. She obtained her B.A. at the University of Alberta, her LL.B. at Osgoode Hall Law School, and her LL.M. at Yale.

Vsevolod I. Vasiliev is a Professor and Scientist in Chief at the Institute of Legislation and Comparative Law under the Russian Federation Government. He received his Ph.D. at the USSR Academy of Sciences Institute of State and Law.

Volodymyr Vassylenko is a Professor of International Law at Kiev University. He is Chief Advisor to the Ukrainian Parliament and Vice-Chairman of the Constitutional Commission drafting the new Constitution of Ukraine. He was a member of the Grand Council of the Popular Democratic Peoples' Movement of Ukraine (Rukh) and has been nominated as Ukraine's ambassador to the Benelux countries.

Index

of Rights, 252; and constitution, 110, 111, 294-5; and federalism, 259; and minority rights, 19-20, 35, 113, 295, 298-309; and Quebec, 20, 35, 255, 298-9, 301-2, 305

Charters, and protection of minority rights, 32-3

Citizenship: in Baltic states, 89-91; in Canada, 101, 103-14; and collectivity, 53; in Commonwealth of Independent States (CIS), 89, 91-4; dual, in former USSR, 88-9; input in decision-making, 50-2; issues in Russia (former RSFSR), 87-97, 95-6; and representation, 99-101; rights, 101-2; and social programs, 52-3

Collective identity. *See* Identity, collective

Common market: and Canadian constitution, 303; and Commonwealth of Independent States (CIS), 193-4; definition, 138

'Common taxes,' 199

Commonwealth of Independent States (CIS): citizenship issues, 89, 91-4; economic interdependence, 183, 192-4; formation, 333; purpose, 336; sovereignty, 193; taxes, 193

Communist party: role of, in Central and Eastern European federations, 322-3, 324; suppression of ethnic nationalisms in Eastern Europe, 22

Compact theory of federalism, 226, 228, 234-5, 237

Competition policy, in European Union, 173, 174

Confederalism, 78, 79, 144

Constitution: Canada, 18-19, 104, 110, 111, 112, 127, 210-11, 227, 238, 255, 265, 294-309; change, and nationalism, 18-19; and ethnic diversity, 33-4; and federalism, 24, 33, 34, 35-6; Russia, 96-7; United States, 227

Courts. *See* Judicial system

Croatia, 80, 81-2, 320

Currency: in European Union, 167, 176; and market integration, 139

Czechoslovakia (former): as 'analytic' federation, 318, 319, 321, 322; democracy, tradition of, 326; ethnic conflicts, 23, 325; federalism, 23, 211, 244, 317, 325, 342-3; governance, 325; as member of Visegrad Three, 336; political tradition, 76, 319, 320-1, 329; role of Czech nation, 323; and socialist federalism, 6

Decentralization: and advocacy groups, 277; and bureaucratic duplication, 283-4; in Canada, and federalism, 235-6, 253; comparison with federalism, 9, 78-80, 281-2; and delegation of power, 285; and democracy, 273-80; and equalization payments, 282-3; problems of, 282-5; in United States, 197-200, 266-8

Declaration of the Rights of Man and the Citizen, 102

Declaration on the Human Rights of Individuals who are not Nationals of the Country in which they Live, 93

Democracy: and advocacy groups, 274-5; and centralization, 280-1; in Czechoslovakia (former), tradition of, 326; and decentralization, 273-80; and Eastern Europe, 75-6; and European Union, 167; and federalism, 6, 7, 8, 34-5, 84-6, 261-3, 277-8, 341-2; and majority tyranny, 20, 275-6; and Federal Republic of Germany, 205

Drahomanov, Mykhailo, 329

Eastern Europe. *See* Europe, Eastern

EC. *See* European Union

Economic association, and the nation state, 151

Economic organization, and collective identity, 42

Economic theory, and federalism, 155-6

Economic union: definition, 139-40; and federalism, 144-6; and globalization, 146-50; governance issues, 140-4; principles, 137-40; vertical integration, 141-4

EEC. *See* European Union

EMU Treaty, 163

England. *See* Great Britain

English Constitution, 234

Environment: activists, as advocacy group, 276; federal initiatives, 281; policy, of European Union, 175

Equalization payments: in Canada, 262; and decentralization, 282-3; in European Union, 170-1, 178

Estonia, 90, 91, 332

'Ethnic cleansing,' 7

Ethnic conflicts: emergence with change in governance, 20-1; and failure of federalism in Eastern Europe, 244-6; and federalism, 318-19, 342; xenophobia, in European Union, 68-9. *See also* names of countries and regions

Ethnic diversity: in Canada, 19, 225, 258, 319; in Central and Eastern European federations, 321-2; in Czechoslovakia (former), 325; and federalism, 7, 26-8, 31-2, 34-5, 225, 318, 319; and regionalism, 224; in Russia (former RSFSR), 97; in Union of Soviet Socialist Republics (former), 325; in Yugoslavia (former), 325

Ethnicity: and European Union, 242-4; and nationalism, 83-4, 225, 239-40

EU. *See* European Union

Europe. *See* Europe, Central; Europe, Eastern; Europe, Southern; Europe, Western; European Union

and Freedoms); in Commonwealth of Independent States (CIS), 92-4; and federalism, 219-20; international declarations, 90, 93, 96; in Russia (former RSFSR), 96-7; in United States, 252
Hungary, 76, 282, 317, 336

Identity: collective, 41-4; and economic association, 151; in European Union, 47; Pan-Canadian, 16, 103, 107-14
Immigration: effect on ethnic demography, 19, 28-32; and federalism, 30-1; illegal, 29. *See also* names of specific countries and regions
Independence movements (Europe), 71. *See also* Quebec
Indian Act (Canada), 17, 127
Indians (Canada). *See* Aboriginals (Canada)
Institutional design, 10
International Covenant on Civil and Political Rights, 90
International Covenants on Human Rights, 93
Inuit (Canada). *See* Aboriginals (Canada)
'Isolationist' political culture, 46-7

Judicial system (Canada): and definition of Aboriginal rights, 122, 123-5; and federalism, 253; and interpretation of Canadian constitution, 294-309; role of, 8, 10

Kant, Immanuel, 154
Kazakhstan, 92, 185, 188, 189, 190, 191
Kirghizstan, 185, 190, 191, 192

Labour force: in European Union, 174, 213; mobility, 149-50, 174; in Switzerland, 208-9
Labour market: and European Union, 167; and subsidiarity, 171
Language: and federalism in Canada, 253, 299, 300-1; and nation, 62; official, 49-50, 325-6; variation, in European Union, 69-70
Latvia, 89-90, 91, 332
Lenin, V.I., 321, 330, 331
Lithuania, 90, 91, 332
Lobbyists. *See* Advocacy groups
Local governments: and democracy, 277-8; and federalism, 135, 235, 236; and globalization, 148-50
Luxembourg, 63, 65

Maastricht Treaty (European Union): and economy of European Union, 175-7, 336; and federalism, 156, 164, 166; and fiscal policy, 161; and governance, 214; and harmonization of technical requirements, 175; and regionalism, 163, 180; resistance to, 242; and social charter, 220

Macdonald, John A., 227, 232, 233
Macedonia, 80, 82
Madison, James, 228, 229, 230, 231
Majority tyranny, 20, 275-6
Market: economy, transition to, in Eastern and Central Europe, 324; free, and federalism, 168; integration, 137-40; internal, of European Union, 173
Markets and Hierarchies, 140
Meech Lake Accord (Canada), 210-11, 238-9, 255, 259, 262-3, 301, 305
Métis (Canada). *See* Aboriginals (Canada)
Mexico, 282
Mill, John Stuart, 275, 285
Minorities. *See* Ethnic diversity
Modernization: and ethnicity, 240; and globalization, 265
Moldova, 92, 191, 245
Monarchism, and Canadian federalism, 232, 233-4
Monetary policy, of European Union, 161-2, 175-6
Montenegro, 80, 81

Nagorno-Karabakh, 92, 245
Nation, definition, 61-2
Nation state: definition, 60, 62-4; and economic association, 151; and European Union, 25-6; and federalism, 7, 203; and globalization, 135-6; origins of identity, 41. *See also* Nation; Nationalism; State
National theory of federalism, 226, 229-32
Nationalism: constantly in flux, 17; and ethnicity, 225, 239-40; and federalism, 34-5; multiple, 118. *See also* Identity; names of specific countries and regions; Nation; Nation state
Native Canadians. *See* Aboriginals (Canada)
Net Material Product (NMP), 188-9

'Pan-Canadian' identity, 16, 103, 107-14
Participation bribes, 145-6
Poland, 76, 317, 336
Politicians, in Switzerland, 207-8, 209
Portugal, 163

Quebec (Canada): and Canada-United States Free Trade Agreement, 41; and Charter of Rights and Freedoms, 20, 35, 255, 298-9, 301-2, 305; conflict with Aboriginal nationalism, 16, 17, 18, 19, 126-7, 211, 259-60; and federalism, 5, 31, 48, 224, 253-60; identity, 48, 109-10; independence movement, 34, 48, 211, 236, 237-9, 240-2, 253-60; and modernization, 240; nationalism, 16, 17, 18, 19, 22-3, 26; and subsidiarity, 266

Race, and federalism in US, 235, 236, 253, 261